GIRLS, TEXTS, CULTURES

Studies in Childhood and Family in Canada Series

A broad-ranging series that publishes scholarship from various disciplines, approaches and perspectives relevant to the concepts and relations of childhood and family in Canada. Our interests also include, but are not limited to, interdisciplinary approaches and theoretical investigations of gender, race, sexuality, geography, language and culture within these categories of experience, historical and contemporary.

Series Editor:
Cynthia Comacchio
History Department
Wilfrid Laurier University

Send proposals to:
Lisa Quinn, Acquisitions Editor
Wilfrid Laurier University Press
75 University Avenue West
Waterloo, ON N2L 3C5
Canada
Phone: 519-884-0710 ext. 2843
Fax: 519-725-1399
Email: quinn@press.wlu.ca

GIRLS, TEXTS, CULTURES

Clare Bradford and
Mavis Reimer, editors

WILFRID LAURIER
UNIVERSITY PRESS

Wilfrid Laurier University Press acknowledges the
financial support of the Government of Canada through
the Canada Book Fund for our publishing activities.

Library and Archives Canada Cataloguing in Publication

Girls, texts, cultures / Clare Bradford and Mavis Reimer, editors.

(Studies in childhood and family in Canada)
Includes bibliographical references and index.
Issued in print and electronic formats.
ISBN 978-1-77112-020-3 (pbk.).—ISBN 978-1-77112-022-7 (epub).—
ISBN 978-1-77112-021-0 (pdf)

1. Girls—Congresses. 2. Girls in literature—Congresses. 3. Girls in popular
culture—Congresses. 4. Politics in literature—Congresses. 5. Popular culture in
literature—Congresses. I. Bradford, Clare, editor II. Reimer, Mavis, 1954–, editor
III. Girls, Texts, Cultures (Symposium) (2010 : University of Winnipeg)
IV. Series: Studies in childhood and family in Canada

HQ798.G73 2015   305.23082   C2014-908367-X
                                   C2014-908368-8

Cover design by David Drummond.
Text design by Janette Thompson.

© 2015 Wilfrid Laurier University Press
Waterloo, Ontario, Canada
www.wlupress.wlu.ca

This book is printed on FSC® certified paper and is certified Ecologo.
It contains post-consumer fibre, is processed chlorine free,
and is manufactured using biogas energy.

Printed in Canada

Every reasonable effort has been made to acquire permission for copyright material
used in this text, and to acknowledge all such indebtedness accurately. Any errors and
omissions called to the publisher's attention will be corrected in future printings.

MIX
Paper from
responsible sources
FSC® C004071

CONTENTS

LIST OF FIGURES

ACKNOWLEDGEMENTS

This book is the result of the "Girls, Texts, Cultures" symposium hosted by the Centre for Research in Young People's Texts and Cultures at the University of Winnipeg in October 2010. The symposium was funded by the Trudeau Foundation through Clare Bradford's Visiting Trudeau Fellowship and by the Social Sciences and Humanities Research Council of Canada through its Aid to Workshops program. Additional funding and support came from the Centre for Research in Young People's Texts and Cultures and the Office of the Vice-President (Research) at the University of Winnipeg.

We would like to thank Nicole Necsefor, who provided assistance at the symposium and in research for the introduction; Kirstian Lezubski, who copy-edited the first draft of the manuscript; and Larissa Wodtke, who managed the collection of the image files and prepared the manuscript for submission.

Girls, Texts, Cultures

Cross-disciplinary Dialogues

Clare Bradford and Mavis Reimer

The chapters in this book traverse disciplinary fields, sampling a wide range of approaches and theoretical perspectives. Most of these essays were workshopped at the "Girls, Texts, Cultures" symposium at the University of Winnipeg in 2010. This symposium was designed to generate and sustain dialogues between two groups of scholars: those focusing on texts for and about girls, and those who investigate contemporary girlhoods. Scholars from girls' studies and children's literature rarely participate in the same conferences and have, for the most part, conducted their research along two quite distinct lines. Yet these two fields have much in common: both developed from larger disciplinary formations; both have experienced marginalization in comparison with established disciplinary fields; and in both cases this marginalization relates to wider cultural and scholarly assumptions about girls and children. As Mary Celeste Kearney remarks in her essay "Coalescing: The Development of Girls' Studies" (2009), the historical marginalization of girls relates to their lack of visibility and presence in Western societies until the late twentieth century: the field of girls' studies gained ground in the academy only in the 1990s, after male domination in academic institutions had eroded and when feminist scholars turned to research on girls' experiences and practices. Children's literature, similarly, is a relatively new scholarly field, emerging during the

1970s and drawing upon the disciplinary areas of literature, cultural studies, and education. Its status is frequently downgraded in the academy, due to the assumption that children's literature is the "immature simple sister to mainstream literature" (Stephens and McGillis 367), lacking in complexity and unworthy of a place in scholarly hierarchies.

In the academy, girl-related research is carried out across the disciplines of sociology, psychology, education, literary studies, history, media studies, and communication studies. Kearney observes that this research is increasingly interdisciplinary in its approach (20), reflecting the emergence of such fields as disability studies, cultural studies, and postcolonial studies, where girl-related research is carried out. Nevertheless, there remains a divide between studies focusing on girls and their cultures, and studies of texts for and about girls, a division that the historical formation of the fields helps to explain.

The development of girls' studies as an international and multidisciplinary field of inquiry occurred at the intersection of cultural studies and feminist studies. It first became visible as a distinct field of study during the 1970s at the Centre for Contemporary Cultural Studies (CCCS) at the University of Birmingham (UK). The history of cultural studies, according to Ziauddin Sardar and Borin van Loon, "has provided it with certain distinguishable characteristics" that can be identified in terms of what cultural studies "aims to do": these include the aim to examine power relationships in cultural practices; to analyze the social and political contexts within which culture manifests itself; to attend to the differences between local and so-called universal forms of knowledge; and "to be both an intellectual and a pragmatic enterprise," with the commitment "to social reconstruction by critical political involvement" (9). At Birmingham, where cultural studies first coalesced as a scholarly practice, early researchers focused their work on the analysis of contemporary popular, working-class culture and its fragmentation into subcultures; the articulation of the struggles and negotiations over the meaning of cultural texts and products by different cultural groups; and the development of participant-observer methods for the study of groups and ethnographic methods for the study of audiences. These aims and commitments, lines of inquiry, and development of methods were an important foundation for girls' studies, but its emergence as a separate set of questions was precipitated by a gap in the field of cultural studies.

In 1975, Angela McRobbie and Jenny Garber, then graduate students newly arrived at Birmingham, were invited to write a critique of the subcultural theory of the ongoing research at CCCS. Their essay "Girls and Subculture" appeared that year in *Resistance through Rituals: Youth Subcultures in Post-War Britain*, a collection of essays edited by Stuart Hall and Tony Jefferson that continues to be cited in youth studies. McRobbie later described the piece as "a kind of running commentary on the absence of girls in the work of subcultures which was being published in the Centre and elsewhere at the time" (xvii). In their essay, McRobbie and Garber observed that the apparent marginality of girls to "spectacular" male sub-cultures (often focused on street life) might suggest that researchers needed to ask different questions about girls: "If subcultural options are not readily available to girls, what are the different but complementary ways in which girls organise their cultural life?" (3). Among their speculations were that girls' cultures might be organized around commercial texts (such as maga-zines for girls); that "the extremely tight-knit friendship groups formed by girls" might be read as resistance to moving into teenage sexual life (14); and that such groups also allowed girls "to gain private, inaccessible space" outside the scrutiny of both adults and boys (14). The various strands of questions proposed by McRobbie and Garber in this early essay—about the lived experiences of girls, about "bedroom culture," and about the role of popular and commercial texts in girls' cultures—contributed to shap-ing the emergent field of study. Several essays in this collection, including those by Dawn H. Currie, Pamela Knights, Elizabeth Bullen, and Shauna Pomerantz and Rebecca Raby, continue to take up these concerns.

The suggestion by McRobbie and Garber that studying girls requires not only that new groups of subjects be brought into view but also that new ques-tions be formulated was confirmed by contemporaneous work being done in the United States on the psychology of women and girls. Jean Baker Miller proposed in *Toward a New Psychology of Women* (1976) that psychologists needed to move away from a deficiency model of women in order to under-stand their particular strengths. In *The Reproduction of Mothering* (1978), Nancy Chodorow analyzed mothering as a socially constructed rather than "natural" practice. Perhaps most importantly, through the Harvard Project on Women's Psychology and Girls' Development, Carol Gilligan and her students and collaborators produced a series of groundbreaking studies, beginning with Gilligan's *In a Different Voice: Psychological Theory and Women's Development* in 1982, in which she demonstrated that women typically reach moral decisions through a consideration of relationships rather than rules, working within an ethics of care rather than an ethics of justice.

The new feminist work of these decades had a significant impact on cultural studies, Simon During observes in his overview of the field, in that it shifted scholarly attention from a focus on "communities positioned against large power blocs [such as the state] and bound together as classes or subcultures" to an affirmation of "'other' ways of life on their own terms," specifically to the ways in which ethnic and women's groups maintained and elaborated "autonomous values, identities, and ethics" (13). But a focus on women as groups does not necessarily extend to an interest in girls as groups with autonomous values, identities, and ethics. As Catherine Driscoll has noted about feminist revisions of Freud and the narratives of psychology in general, while many such revisions rework the story of the "difficulty of the transition from girl to woman," most of these accounts are interested in "resignifying Woman or the maternal" rather than in resignifying girlhood (122). Girls are an important ground for the debates about womanhood in feminism, she concludes, "but less on their own terms than as necessary precursors to women/feminists" (131).

In short, both cultural studies and feminist studies contributed necessary but not sufficient theories and methods for girls' studies. These studies continue to settle and to shift, responding to new practices of girlhood (for example, the girl power phenomenon in popular culture in the 1990s), adapting theories in the light of new technologies and modes of textual production (such as the online fanfiction communities in which girls are often dominant participants), and taking up new inquiries in the face of social events and anxieties (as seen, for example, in current educational debates about failing boys or mean girls). One attempt to articulate an overarching set of principles for research in the field is Claudia Mitchell and Jacqueline Reid-Walsh's statement about "Girl-Method" in their encyclopedia *Girl Culture*. Girl-Method, they propose, involves working with girls in participatory research and advocating for girls; thinking about girls in scholarly analysis; taking into account who researchers are and what their relationship to girlhood is; and addressing the cultural contexts of girls in intersectional terms, such as in terms of race and class as well as of age and gender (17). Several essays in this collection exemplify these principles, including Mitchell's own essay, and those by Kabita Chakraborty, Sandrina de Finney and Johanne Saraceno, and Stephanie Fisher, Jennifer Jenson, and Suzanne de Castell.

The emergence of girls' studies from cultural studies and feminist studies has meant that the field is less a discipline in itself than a set of questions about the cultural functions of girls and girlhoods that are taken up by scholars trained in a variety of disciplines. To this point, however, literary scholars working with girls' books and women writers have not generally seen themselves or been recognized by other scholars as involved in girls' studies. Yet literary scholars have been central to the formation of both academic cultural studies and feminist studies. The Birmingham Centre was founded by Richard Hoggart, whose 1957 book *The Uses of Literacy* used the principles of literary criticism to study the popular songs of working-men's clubs of 1950s Britain, thereby giving cultural studies its "first identifiable, intellectual shape" (Sardar and van Loon 27). Another early and influential scholar in the field was Raymond Williams, who was trained as a literary critic and historian. In 1958, he articulated the concept of culture as "ordinary" that continues to be central to cultural studies: culture, he said, is "a whole way of life" as expressed by a human society (11). Immediately following this assertion, he added that the term "culture" simultaneously carries a second meaning, that of "arts and learning—the special processes of discovery and creative effort," and that the "conjunction" of the two meanings is significant (11). As Fred Inglis explains, Williams took it as his intellectual and political project to "grasp the multiple connections between imagination and power," "reach[ing] for the purposes and modes of expression to which politics and letters . . . *each puts the other*" (53). Literary scholarship was a major strand of work among second-wave feminists in the American academy in the 1970s and 1980s, with such important critics as Kate Millett, Adrienne Rich, Elaine Showalter, Sandra Gilbert, and Susan Gubar working on several related fronts, including projects to retrieve women writers from the silences of literary history, to analyze the "sexual politics" (Millett) that systematically excluded the work of women from the canon, and to explore paradigms for reading that allowed for a revaluation and "re-visioning" (to use Rich's neologism) of texts by women. Like the feminist psychologists of the period, these literary scholars focused on woman-centred approaches that emphasized the differences of women from men, an approach that came to be known as "cultural feminism" (Kearney 12).

It was in the context of these movements within literary historical scholarship that critics in children's literature turned their attention to writing by women for young people generally and for girls specifically. One of the key contributors to this discussion was the American scholar Mitzi Myers. Standard histories of children's literature in the late 1970s, when Myers first began publishing in the field, were structured on the opposition of didactic texts and entertaining texts. Such histories regarded the turn from instruction to delight as the principal feature of literature for young people in the mid-nineteenth century, often attributing this turn to the publication of Lewis Carroll's *Alice's Adventures in Wonderland* in 1865. Myers pointed out that this narrative not only privileged a canon of male-authored texts that began with the Romantic poets, but also erased the earlier history of children's literature authored by a group of eighteenth-century women who were particularly concerned with the education of girls, among them Mary Wollstonecraft and Maria Edgeworth. That erasure, Myers demonstrated again and again in her work, derived from the fact that scholars uncritically accepted the Romantic poets' denigration of the "'monstrous regiment'" of women who had preceded them ("Impeccable Governesses" 31) and regarded the Romantics' new valuation of the child of nature and of fantasy as a "transhistorical, universal body of truth about childhood" rather than a "culturally conditioned ideology, a tissue of assumptions, preferences, and perspectives" ("Little Girls" 135). Myers understood the purpose of her own scholarship to be to demonstrate how historical children's literature "reflects its period's concerns," "how it comments on its social and intellectual milieu, how it tries to answer its era's questions about childhood and especially girlhood, how it functions as a cultural critique of contemporary educational practice and gender definition" ("Socializing" 52). No doubt in part because her work coincided with the early recognition in the American academy that "children's literature was a legitimate field of scholarly study" (Adams and Ruwe 237), Myers helped to establish historical children's literature—and, in particular, historical girls' books—as an important site of ideological and, more generally, cultural critique. In this collection, the essays by Michelle Smith, Kristine Moruzi, Reid-Walsh, and Knights sustain the approach taken by Myers in their examinations of historical texts.

The flood of feminist theories and models that emerged during the 1970s and 1980s informed readings of texts in the light of the gendered, political, economic, and cultural contexts of their production, circulation, and consumption, prompting critics of children's literature not only to reconsider the previous valuations of girls' books but also to look again at the very constitution of their field of study. In 1982, the *Children's Literature Association Quarterly* produced a special section (edited by Anita Moss) in which writers reviewed eight recently published books of feminist literary theory and criticism, in order to suggest ways in which these methods might illuminate texts written by women for children. While it was a widely acknowledged fact that women were dominant in the field of children's literature as writers, teachers, librarians, and critics—indeed, it was generally assumed that this was one of the reasons for the low status of the field in the academy—the *Quarterly* special section, as Perry Nodelman observed in a later issue of the journal, gestured toward the "intriguing" possibility "that children's literature as a whole" takes up many of the characteristic themes and structures of women's writing for girls (32). Since the 1980s, feminist critics of children's literature have paid much attention to the ways in which a wide range of texts produced for or appropriated by young people—award-winning literary fiction as well as popular texts— reproduce or challenge dominant societal views of gender, sexuality, power, and subjectivity, as Kerry Mallan's essay does in this collection. One particular focus of feminist studies of children's literature has been fairy tales and the ways in which these traditional narratives and variations on them have moved across formats and platforms from picture books and novels to films and video games.

As this account suggests, feminist scholars of children's literature have been more interested in past locations, practices, and texts of girlhood than have scholars from the disciplines of sociology, education, or media studies, who typically focus on contemporary practices. But understanding how formations of girlhood have functioned in other times, with what interests they have been aligned, how they have secured, negotiated, or contested dominant values, and which of these structures of feeling have entered the present, can allow researchers to ask better questions about girls' cultures in contemporary contexts. On the other hand, scholars from sociology, education, and media studies often ground their studies in participatory research with girls or in ethnographic studies of audiences. For literary scholars, such empirical work provides useful evidence of the ways in which actual readers do and do not take up the positions and the values apparently offered to them by texts, and can prompt more nuanced understandings of the ways in which the desires of readers and the event of reading interact in the creation of meaning. Indeed, the chapters in this book demonstrate that any simple division (between sociological, educational, and media/communication studies on the one side, and historical and literary studies on the other) is insupportable. Not only do the scholars whose work is represented in this collection deploy wide-ranging theories and approaches, but also they have in common a repertoire of knowledge, theoretical perspectives, and research questions which transcends disciplinary differences. This elasticity means that the essays talk to each other in multiple ways.

Girls, Texts, Cultures

To glance through the biographical notes on the authors of this collection is to appreciate the fluidity of disciplinary formations in the twenty-first century, and the extent to which individual scholars and fields of study engage with cultural change, international politics, and technological innovations. Contemporary girl-related research often situates itself at the intersections between disciplines; thus, Fisher, Jenson, and de Castell work between pedagogical and new media research, responding to the global production and circulation of digital games and the intersections of gender and gaming; Moruzi and Smith locate their research on formulations of girlhood between postcolonial and gender studies; Bullen combines sociological studies of globalization and literary analysis to investigate the influence of consumer capitalism on texts for girls. Mitchell's work moves among girls' studies, teacher education, and participatory visual methodologies, while Pomerantz and Raby's research takes up sociological and cultural studies paradigms to investigate girls' identity formation.

The authors' biographies demonstrate that girl-related research is often aligned with activism and policy development: de Finney and Saraceno, Mitchell, and Chakraborty engage with the lived experience of girls who grapple with poverty, racialization, or cultural marginalization; Currie designs pedagogical material for students working in African settings. Authors whose research addresses texts for and about girls are strikingly alert to the gender politics that shape textual ideologies, as Reid-Walsh is, and to new (queer) modes of subjectivity that unsettle gender binaries, as Mallan is. Scholars working in girl-related research have almost always carried out their initial training in disciplines or fields other than girls' studies. So, too, the authors of this book have commenced their scholarly lives in fields including education, sociology, literary studies, librarianship, health, and social work. Their girl-related work exemplifies the new and emerging fields of research that have transformed older disciplines.

The title of the book signals its disciplinary and conceptual breadth. Rather than using the term "girlhood," which can imply a unitary state of being a girl, we chose "girls" to emphasize the diversity of girls' locations and the ways in which familial, cultural, and national discourses shape subjectivities. The authors represented in the collection resist the idea that girlhood is merely a preliminary or transitional phase antecedent to womanhood. Rather, they focus squarely on girls, girl cultures, and texts by, for, and about girls, foregrounding the historical and cultural specificities that shape girls' experiences and inform discourses of girlhood. Many of the authors explore the materiality of girls' lives through participatory research and audience studies; others consider how girls are represented and situated by texts of many kinds. The real girls positioned as audiences, citizens, and participants are often beyond the reach of researchers. But girls are vividly present within texts because texts for and about girls are always purposeful and always imply readers. Narrative texts, for instance, position audiences to prefer one character over another, to desire certain narrative outcomes, or to accede to the normalized values of the fictional world.

Texts and textuality are crucially implicated in the socialization of girls and their identity formation. The chapters in this book adopt an expansive view of texts and their genres, forms, styles, and functions. The flap books and paper doll books produced in the eighteenth and nineteenth centuries and examined by Reid-Walsh, just as much as the video games discussed by Fisher, Jenson, and de Castell, constitute what Fisher and her collaborators describe as "important cultural texts." Such texts do not merely mirror or reflect reality, but they advocate ways of being in the world. They do this through the manifold strategies whereby they construct subject positions for their audiences. This is not to say that girl audiences of fiction, games, digital media, and regulatory documents are powerless to resist the pull of textual positioning. For instance, Chakraborty points out that young Muslim women in the slums of Kolkata "pick and choose" the aspects of Bollywood culture that provide them with useful information as they embark on romantic encounters. Currie reminds readers that girls' studies is itself a "textual practice" produced and sustained through language, and that scholarly texts "bring some girlhoods (and therefore girls) into view, while rendering others unknown." She does not call for a kind of tokenistic sampling of girls of different ethnicities, cultures, ages, and classes, but emphasizes the importance of self-reflexivity to inform scholars about the assumptions evident in their selection of girl-related topics, girl populations, and above all research strategies.

The plural "cultures" in the book's title alerts readers both to the diversity of cultural contexts in which girls are located, and also to the fact that girls are active in producing texts and engaging with others to create cultural forms. The girls we encounter in Fisher, Jenson, and de Castell's study of young game players, for instance, develop their own "community of praxis" in contradistinction to the normative (masculine) culture of gameplay. In her chapter, Mitchell points to the ethical and conceptual questions that arise when researchers work with girls in community-based participatory projects. If girls' identity formation is imbricated with their relations with institutions and dominant cultures, it is also shaped by the practices and relationships that produce girls' cultures.

The four chapters listed under the heading "Contemporary Girlhoods and Subjectivities" concern themselves with theories of subjectivity as they relate to girls, with subject positions offered to girl audiences across a range of texts, and with represented female subjectivities. Currie's chapter outlines her past and ongoing research, reflecting on how frames of analysis have shifted since the 1980s. The concept of "Subject-ivity" initially enabled Currie to connect the Subject of sociology with poststructuralist approaches to subjectivity. Currie's subsequent investigations into girl audiences and texts have led her to reflect on how researchers locate themselves in relation to notions of girlhood; that is, how researchers' own subjectivities shape their scholarly practices. Mallan's "On Secrets, Lies, and Fiction" considers the strategies of survival proposed by contemporary texts for girls; these strategies include dissimulation, secrets, and concealment. The texts Mallan has selected—Jacqueline Wilson's *Secrets*, Mariko and Jillian Tamaki's *Skim*, and Marjane Satrapi's *Persepolis*—construct female subjectivities forged in settings where girls must guard their privacy. Mallan analyzes how these texts position reading subjects as observers and as players in textual games of illusion. Bullen's "Disgusting Subjects" takes up questions of consumerism, taste, and class to consider the discourses of desire and disgust that inform depictions of girls as sexual subjects in Cecily von Ziegesar's *Nothing Can Keep Us Together*, the eighth novel in the Gossip Girl series, and Julie Burchill's novel *Sweet*. Desiring subjects feature, too, in Knights's "Still Centre Stage?," an examination of ballet fiction and the female bodies it places at centre stage. Ballet novels, as Knights demonstrates, track the contradictions that have always surrounded performances of female subjectivity.

The chapters brought together in the section "The Politics of Girlhood" address national, institutional, and cultural politics and their impact on girls and formulations of girlhood. These chapters embrace Canadian, African, Indian, Australian, American, and British contexts and texts. Moruzi's discussion of girls' fiction published during and immediately after the 1914–18 World War identifies a transnational girlhood that both transcends discourses of nationhood and relies upon the circulation of texts and discourses across national boundaries. De Finney and Saraceno address the experience of Indigenous girls living in three communities on Vancouver Island, British Columbia. Young people in Indigenous communities make up a far higher proportion of the population than is the case in non-Indigenous communities, yet little attention is paid to the knowledge and experience of Indigenous girls when decisions are made about policy and resources. This chapter identifies the discourses that shape conceptualizations of Indigenous girls in the three communities, and foregrounds the girls' experience, their struggles to articulate Indigenous identities, and the political and bureaucratic processes that inhibit their self-determination. Mitchell and Chakraborty, too, address the politics of identity formation among marginalized girls. Mitchell discusses case studies she conducted among girls in Canada, South Africa, Ethiopia, and Rwanda. Much of Mitchell's chapter focuses on what happens when the girls are encouraged to interpret the visual images they themselves have produced, and the issues that arise from this style of participation. The lives of the young Muslim women who feature in Chakraborty's chapter are regulated by the local and particular practices, both social and religious, of the *bustees* (slum communities) of Kolkata. They are simultaneously engrossed by the global products constituted by Bollywood films, whose narratives typically involve heterosexual romance. Chakraborty offers an analysis of how these young women negotiate the interplay between global media and local practices.

Two of the chapters in the section "Settling and Unsettling Girlhoods," those by Reid-Walsh and by Smith, focus on early texts for girls, and the versions of girlhood they advocate; the other two, Fisher, Jenson, and de Castell's "Dynamic (Con)Texts: Close Readings of Girls' Video Gameplay" and Pomerantz and Raby's "Reading Smart Girls," focus on video games and popular culture. All these essays probe the extent to which textual forms unsettle dominant discourses or afford the potential for subversion on the part of their audiences. The flap books and paper doll books analyzed by Reid-Walsh propose highly conservative versions of conventional femininity; yet, as Reid-Walsh demonstrates, these interactive texts are susceptible to resistant and even parodic manipulation on the part of young readers. This potential for unsettling is not dissimilar to the behaviours of the girl video game players profiled in Fisher, Jenson, and de Castell's chapter. Through their gameplay and their production of alternative narratives, these girls formed "gaming identities" that destabilized the male/female gamer binary, which has been promulgated by gaming companies and accepted as a given in much gaming research. Smith's "Wild Australian Girls" considers how depictions of Australian heroines in British texts between 1885 and 1926 construct a version of colonial femininity that critiques the British class system and asserts the virtues of imperial identity.

Pomerantz and Raby examine how the "post-nerd smart girl," attractive, intelligent, and sexually desirable, is portrayed in *Gilmore Girls*, *High School Musical*, and *Veronica Mars*. Analyzing the figures of Rory, Gabriella, and Veronica, Pomerantz and Raby consider the extent to which these "smart supergirl" figures are inflected by post-feminist and neo-liberal discourses, comparing them with the figures of Juno MacGuff from the 2007 film *Juno* and Rachel Berry from *Glee*.

The twelve chapters in this collection, then, cover a wide gamut of texts, theoretical and methodological approaches, and disciplinary fields. In contemporary Western societies, girls and girlhoods function to some degree as markers of cultural reproduction and change. As girls have become more publicly visible they have often become the locus of moral panics, many of which centre upon their bodies and behaviours, and which are exemplified by debates over topics such as the sexualization of young girls, obesity, eating disorders, and consumerism. These flurries of concern are often characterized by generalized and homogenizing depictions of girls, and they tend to state or to imply comparisons with masculine adolescence. Moreover, they treat girlhood as a preliminary or transitional phase through which girls pass en route to womanhood. The scholars whose work is represented in this collection locate girls in relation to the historical and cultural specificities that shape their experience and inform discourses on girlhoods. They offer compelling accounts of the diversity of girls' experience and the complex significances of texts by, for, and about girls. This collection reaches out to readers across disciplinary fields in the social sciences and humanities, and brings into focus the common concerns that unite research on girls and girlhoods.

Works Cited

Adams, Gillian, and Donelle Ruwe. "The Scholarly Legacy of Mitzi Myers." *Culturing the Child 1690–1914: Essays in Memory of Mitzi Myers*. Ed. Donelle Ruwe. Lanham: Scarecrow P, 2005. 227–40. Print.

Driscoll, Catherine. *Girls: Feminine Adolescence in Popular Cultures and Cultural Theory*. New York: Columbia UP, 2002. Print.

During, Simon. "Introduction." *The Cultural Studies Reader*. Ed. Simon During. 2nd ed. London: Routledge, 1999. 1–28. Print.

Inglis, Fred. *Cultural Studies*. Oxford: Blackwell, 1993. Print.

Kearney, Mary Celeste. "Coalescing: The Development of Girls' Studies." *NWSA Journal* 21.1 (Spring 2009): 1–28. Print.

ronco el humanist

McRobbie, Angela. Introduction. *Feminism and Youth Culture: From* Jackie *to* Just Seventeen. Cambridge: Unwin Hyman, 1991. ix–xix. Print.

McRobbie, Angela, and Jenny Garber. "Girls and Subcultures." *Working Papers in Cultural Studies* 7/8 (1975): 209–22. Rpt. in *Feminism and Youth Culture: From* Jackie *to* Just Seventeen. Cambridge: Unwin Hyman, 1991. 1–15. Print.

Millett, Kate. *Sexual Politics.* New York: Ballatine, 1970. Print.

Mitchell, Claudia A., and Jacqueline Reid-Walsh. "How to Study Girl Culture." *Girl Culture: An Encyclopedia.* Vol. 1. Ed. Claudia A. Mitchell and Jacqueline Reid-Walsh. Westport: Greenwood P, 2008. 17–24. Print.

Myers, Mitzi. "Impeccable Governesses, Rational Dames, and Moral Mothers: Mary Wollstonecraft and the Female Tradition in Georgian Children's Books." *Children's Literature* 14 (1986): 31–59. Print.

———. "Little Girls Lost: Rewriting Romantic Childhood, Righting Gender and Genre." *Teaching Children's Literature: Issues, Pedagogy, Resources.* Ed. Glenn Edward Sadler. Options for Teaching. New York: MLA, 1992. 131–42. Print.

———. "Socializing Rosamond: Educational Ideology and Fictional Form." *Children's Literature Association Quarterly* 14.2 (1989): 52–58. Print.

Nodelman, Perry. "Children's Literature as Women's Writing." *Children's Literature Association Quarterly* 13.1 (Spring 1988): 31–34. Print.

Rich, Adrienne. "When We Dead Awaken: Writing as Re-Vision." 1971. *On Lies, Secrets, and Silence: Selected Prose 1966–1978.* New York: Norton, 1979. 33–49. Print.

Sardar, Ziauddin, and Borin van Loon. *Introducing Cultural Studies.* Ed. Richard Appignanesi. Thriplow: Icon Books, 1997. Print.

Stephens, John, and Roderick McGillis. "Critical Approaches to Children's Literature." *The Oxford Encyclopedia of Children's Literature.* Ed. Jack Zipes. New York: Oxford UP, 2006. 364–67. Print.

Williams, Raymond. "Culture Is Ordinary." *Convictions.* Ed. Norman McKenzie. London: MacGibbon and Kee, 1958. Rpt. in *The Raymond Williams Reader.* Ed. John Higgins. Oxford: Blackwell, 2001. 10–24. Print.

Contemporary Girlhoods
and Subjectivities

CHAPTER 1

From Girlhood, Girls, to Girls' Studies

The Power of the Text

Dawn H. Currie

Some of the chapters in this collection explore representations of girlhood in texts produced for girl readers. Treating texts as representation helps us see how gendered identities such as adolescent femininity are cultural constructions. While sociologists have contributed to this body of work by treating texts as cultural artifacts, they are interested in the role these constructions play in the social lives of readers. In my own work, I have explored this role in terms of girls' agency—everyday practices that render readers socially identifiable as girls (see Currie, *Girl Talk*; Currie, Kelly, and Pomerantz). This work arises from my interest in commercially produced texts as legitimating, and hence sustaining, some identities, while rendering others unthinkable. It is not that these texts determine human agency, but rather that they have the potential to make certain things, like girlhood, happen. The operative word here is "potential"; precisely how texts work in this way is a matter of ongoing debate. The purpose of this chapter is to revisit these debates, in order to explore texts as a vehicle of social power.

This review is framed through interrogation of my own past and ongoing research. Individual research practices, of course, are shaped by the more general state of knowledge claims, the kinds of unsolved puzzles these claims invite, and the conventions that endow one's research with the authority of knowledge.[1] This chapter is part of ongoing personal reflection on how our frames of analysis are an ontological commitment (see Mason); they shape what we see, and hence what we come to know as researchers. The need for this kind of interrogation was expressed at the conference that inspired this chapter, where a consensus emerged that reflexivity is necessary if girls' studies—itself a textual practice—is to remain committed to the feminist goal of enlarging *all* girls' potentials. The conference led me to ask how academic texts themselves bring some girlhoods (and therefore girls) into view, while rendering others unknown.

Terms of Reference

At the onset, let me state that my work is informed by my position as a materialist feminist; like Rosemary Hennessy, I define "material feminism" as an approach that historicizes social identities such as gender in order to investigate their relationship to totalities such as capitalism, patriarchy, globalization (27). Such a commitment has historically given primacy to the social rather than the cultural dimensions of everyday life through the study of institutions (such as the family and school settings); institutionalized roles (such as those of mothers, daughters, and pupils); and the way these institutions and roles operate to reconstitute the social world in specific ways, according to specific social interests. Beginning in the 1980s, materialist feminists began to question how the symbolic order does not simply reflect these totalities in ways that conventional Marxists imply, but rather works to re/constitute them (see Barrett); feminist theorizing required an analysis of identities as cultural expressions of how individuals are embedded in such institutions. The notion of intersectionality was introduced as a way to signal that our gendered identities are constituted through a complex of cultural markers specific to time and place (see Lorde; hooks; Wing). In recent decades, the monolithic "girlhood" of early scholarship has been challenged by recognition of the varying, unstable, and changeable ways that young females "do girlhood" as an enduring and socially significant identity (see, for example, Bettie; Durham, "Girls, Media"; Durham, "Constructing"; Durham, *The Lolita Effect*).

The specific trend that my work follows is one that investigates meaning-making as formative of social life. It grants agency to girls as producers of the cultural category of girlhood, through which claims about what it means to be a girl can be made. While girls' claims to girlhood take expression through embodied practice, academic claims come in the form of scholarly texts. In this chapter I show how such texts legitimate girlhood as a social identity; in the conclusion I explore limitations in thinking about texts primarily as identity practices.

Before I begin, it is important to keep in mind that, in this chapter, "text" refers to concrete representations that can be read socially because they invoke a shared system of meaning-making. These representations can be written or visual, but embodiment is also read socially as "text." Despite criticisms expressed in this chapter, I maintain that the study of texts will remain important in the study of girls' lives as texts now expand to embrace the Internet used by so many youth. As I describe below, beginning in the 1990s, textual analysis has been largely displaced by interest in discourse analysis in sociology. "Discourse" refers to constellations of spoken state-ments as well as to textual representations that construct objects and ways of thinking about those objects, operating to bring these objects into existence (for example, femininity and masculinity). In my work, discourses operate as knowledge that supports specific gender practices and the reception of these practices socially while rendering alternatives unthinkable. As Michel Foucault observes, rather than representing something that already exists, discourse constructs something that does not exist—socially speaking— prior to the discourses that bring it into existence. The "something" in my work is adolescent femininity.

Girls as Consumers of Girlhood: Girl Talk

My interest in the cultural construction of youthful femininities was sparked in the 1980s when, as a relatively new (but not young) profes-sor, I taught sociology and women's studies. From classroom discussions, I became interested in the relevance and status of feminism for young women who seemed to me to be ambivalently positioned between an acceptance of second-wave criticisms of conventional standards of hetero-femininity and the pleasures they derived from bodily embracing these standards. What was the source of these young women's ambivalence toward femininity, and how did it relate to their ambivalence toward feminism? Like many soci-ologists of that time, and as an adherent to political economy, I looked first to commercial texts[2] for women and girls for answers. While not an advocate of the socialization theory that was the dominant sociological approach throughout the 1980s, I tended to (and still do) see commercial interests as major players in normalizing societal expectations about what it means to be a woman and, by extension, to be a girl. Fashion and beauty texts for young readers seemed like a logical place to begin an exploration of girlhood as a cultural construction. As documented in my earlier work, scientific study of the content of these magazines confirms what a casual perusal would suggest: these magazines idealize beauty standards based on whiteness and a prepubescent, virginal body. While women's magazines perpetuate the domestication of women (Winship "A Woman's World"; Winship, *Inside Women's Magazines*; Ferguson; Keller; Fox), teenage magazines coach girls in the beautification of their female bodies in order to secure their stake in this domestication. At the time of my research, these claims were based on content analysis showing, for example, that ads in teen magazines equate adolescent femininity with "beauty, innocence, and softness" (Currie, *Girl Talk* 122). The irony is that, at the same time that this femininity is presented as natural and authentic, readers are instructed that its accomplishment requires physical and psychological interventions and ongoing discipline (see also Bordo, "Anorexia"; Bordo, "Reading the Slender Body"; Wolf). In short, these magazines advocate what I have come to call "prescribed authenticity." At the same time, I never accepted magazine representations as determining the construction of social reality. Drawing on semiotician Roland Barthes's work in his *Mythologies*, I saw them as offering readers mythologies of consumption that naturalize and thus depoliticize consumption of the commodified femininity promoted by these texts. Mythologies smooth over the contradictory process of transforming a natural female body into a cultural expression of authentic Selfhood based on an appropriately gendered identity (see Currie, "Going Green").

More important than findings based on content analysis, my research distinguishes between girlhood as a textual construction and girls as embodied readers (see also Driscoll; Harris). I theorize girls' investments in dominant representations of femininity through the notion of "Subject-ivity," as a construct that connects the Subject of sociology to poststructuralist analyses of subjectivity. Subject-ivity evokes an embodied Self that operates through a practical mode of consciousness arising through attachments to cultural representations that offer "subject positions through which we come to understand who and what we are" (Adams 15–16). Subject-ivity thus blurs longstanding boundaries in sociology between the social and the cultural, and hence between the social sciences and humanities. At the time, I found this blurring to be productive: Subject-ivity analytically connects textual constructions of girlhood and the thoughts and behaviours of embodied girls. As I go on to argue, however, I now believe that current analytical conundrums in the study of girls, texts, and culture can be traced to this blurring.

In work I published at that time, I argued that commercial texts work to orchestrate readers' sense of what is appropriate, what is sayable, and what makes sense in specific places and times, while rendering some things (like feminism) unthinkable and unsayable. Texts can have this regulatory capacity because they are fixed cultural artifacts, replicable in character and easily commodified (Smith). If analysis focuses on the content of ideological representations, power is typically characterized as lying in the text itself (a position I reject later in this chapter; see also Nelson 180–89; Barthel; Peirce). In contrast, I was interested in the way that magazines operate as a social rather than merely textual phenomenon, leading me to ask how girls (as the intended readers of teenage magazines) rather than adult research-ers[3] make meaning from these texts. Unlike magazine representations of girlhood, actual readers are not all white, not all skinny and pretty with flawless skin. In this way, the inclusion of embodied girls in text-oriented research opens girls' studies to a broader range of girlhoods than can be found within commercial texts; it therefore invites the researcher to explore how intersectionality as a theoretical construct operates at the empirical level. As a case in point, my audience study, *Girl Talk: Adolescent Magazines and Their Readers*, recruited ninety-one girls aged thirteen to seventeen from mixed ethnic and class backgrounds in an attempt to replace analyses that assumed white femininity as a cultural ideal with analyses of lived femininity intersected by race, class, and age; given the taboo surround-ing research on adolescent sexuality, my study remained trapped within a framework of hetero-normative femininity.

Importantly, this approach concedes power to readers of the text. As it turned out, however, understanding how various girls read magazines proved to be more challenging than I initially had imagined. One strat-egy of data generation was to hold focus-group discussions where study participants responded to advertisements from their favourite magazines, for example, *Seventeen*, *YM*, and *Sassy*. Unlike content analysis, where the researcher limits her meaning-making to what is found on the page (pur-portedly by suspending her personal biases), in everyday reading personal values and beliefs cannot be ignored. Overlooked in many claims based on the study of texts alone, lived experience is a resource that enables the researcher to treat readers as knowledgeable decoders of commercial texts produced for their consumption. Consider the comments of the teenaged girls in my study on the following ads.[4] Looking at a Liz Claiborne fra-grance ad that depicted a man painting the toenails of a recumbent woman, Alyssa (16, Chinese Canadian from a working-class family) remarked, "I would think, 'why is he painting her toenails—how would he know how to do it?'" With regard to an ad depicting a woman standing beside a car in the desert, Alyssa said, "I don't understand why she would be wearing something like that when it's all cloudy and stuff." Chelsea (15, Euro-Canadian from a middle-class family) said, "I wonder how they got the car in the middle of nowhere."

In these readings, girls reasoned in ways that enabled them to question these ads as meaningful. So, it is interesting to see how they read representations of adolescent femininity. When given an ad that showed a Caboodles makeup kit being used at an all-girls pyjama party, girls responded, "Oh, this is neat! Like being with friends and having fun. A typical 'girls' night.' This is a good one because all girls have been there" (Heather, 15, working-class family from Fiji). And: "This appeals to me because I can relate to this. In this picture, like I can relate to sitting around with your friends and everything. It looks like sort of an average—just getting ready to go out. . . . I can relate to the picture" (Kristen, 15, Euro-Canadian from a working-class family). And another: "It kind of shows people doing real things. I would do that" (Amanda, 13, middle-class family from Guyana). At the same time, by drawing on lived experience, other girls dismissed the same ad: "These are commercials we laugh at! . . . From a teenage point of view, from *my* teenage point of view, from where *I* am—this kind of thing doesn't happen. We will do this. These kinds of things happen. But we all don't look like this" (Jamie, 17, Euro-Canadian from a middle-class family). And: "It seems a bit fake to me! . . . So much like TV—that's what they do on TV. But it's kind of fake to me" (Elizabeth, 15, Jewish from a middle-class family).

These readings are, I think, a good illustration of reader agency. They might lead us to challenge the worry generated by many girl advocates about the negative influence of commercial media on young readers. In this light, the next excerpts are interesting, based on ads employing traditional icons of adult femininity: a diamond engagement ring, a bride, and a woman holding a newborn. These representations took reading beyond the realm of participants' lived experiences. Despite the fact that girls in my study came from a range of backgrounds, virtually all participants read these images through dominant understandings of gender. With regard to the diamond ring: "I like this one . . . he's really in love with her and it kind of shows" (Roshni, 17, Indo-Canadian from a working-class family). Looking at the ad for Beautiful Perfume, in which the illustration included a woman in a white wedding gown, Lindsey (16, Euro-Canadian from a working-class family) responded, "I like that—it says what it means. They're advertising for Beautiful and she's in a wedding dress and you always think about a bride as beautiful." An ad for Eternity Perfume, depicting a woman holding an infant, prompted this comment: "Yeah. Like this is one of my favourite ones. . . . The picture's just—I don't know. I just think it's kind of cute and I think it really looks like a mom and daughter. . . . It's kind of a loving picture" (Rachel, 14, Euro-Canadian from a middle-class family). While previous commentators suggested that contradictory or overly ambiguous meanings can invite girls to question messages (for example, see Mayne), in these ads readers drew upon ideologies of romantic love and motherhood to arrive at unambiguous meaning. It is interesting that the picture of a woman holding an infant was not interpreted by participants as a mother and *child*, but rather as a mother and *daughter*. In some cases, participants stated that there was no need to discuss these ads because they "said what they mean." In other words, heterosexual romance and motherhood were a "natural" reading because these readings "felt" right (Currie, *Girl Talk* 128–39; see Hall).

Reflecting my Marxist orientation, I described these textual images as ideological, arguing that "it is not simply that ideology provides a mistaken or distorted representation of reality. . . . Ideology becomes everyday practice because of its ability to dominate the discursive space through which we make sense of the social world and our place in it." At the same time, "ideology does not rule out agency": the girls in my study were not "cultural dupes" (Currie, *Girl Talk* 63–68). Like adult researchers, the young readers in my study did not uncritically embrace textual constructions as necessarily plausible reflections of reality. Most girls freely discussed the ways that magazine models do not represent actual girls. They criticized their beauty as artificially constructed, through makeup and airbrushing of photos, for example. At the same time, these readers could grant textual constructions ontological status. This practice was evident in what I call "comparative reading," a practice that led me to conclude that these readers do not have the power to subvert patriarchy or capitalism through alternative readings of fashion magazines (Currie, "Decoding" 474).[5]

Comparative reading considers magazine representations as a point of reference: while readers showed very little interest in illustrated fashion pages (which they dismissed as unrealistic), many identified advice columns as favourite reading. This preference was not based on their interest in what adult advice experts have to say. The girls in my study preferred to read the questions rather than the answers given in advice columns (see Currie,

"Dear Abby"). They read questions submitted by other (purported) readers in order to verify whether their own experiences were shared with other girls. One consequence could be a contradiction between what the reader knows about magazines and what she feels is right. Knowing is based on what she has learned about commercial media from parents, teachers, and media critics, while feeling comes from reading as a girl: while concerned adults may tell girls to ignore beauty standards in order to "be themselves," the importance of beautification is confirmed by girls' everyday lives, especially at school. One possible outcome could be that the reader internalizes this disjuncture: rather than asking what is wrong with the text, she might ask what is wrong with herself. This disjuncture gives magazines the power to simultaneously "do" and "undo" the Subject.

"Doing" refers to moments during interviews when a participant spoke confidently as a girl, from a coherent sense of Self. In these moments, girlhood has been accomplished in ways that accord with the counsel to readers of fashion and beauty magazines. In contrast, "undoing" refers to moments when self-doubt and uncertainty leaked unexpectedly into interviews. I did not see this undoing as a result of girls' immaturity or lack of experience; rather, it reflects contradictions in prescribed authenticity.

Girls as Cultural Producers of Girlhood: "Girl Power"

In summary, throughout this early work based on girls' reading of fashion magazines, I tended to locate power *within* the text, operating *as* text. By the time *Girl Talk* was published in 1999, however, the notion of girls as casualties of commercialized girlhood was being displaced by the popular celebration of girl power. Promoting a post-feminist ethos in both academic and commercial culture, as Anita Harris notes, girl power signifies young women as the independent and successful inheritors of a new world order (17). Generally attributed to the success of second-wave feminism, "girl power" is defined in the *Oxford English Dictionary* as "a self-reliant attitude among girls and young women manifested in ambition, assertiveness, and individualism." Harris argues that "[n]owhere is girl power more evident . . . than in popular culture, particularly in the promotion of certain pop stars, comic book heroes, TV and film characters, and advertising icons" (17). This culture helps construct a popularized belief in the existence of a "generation of young women as a unique category of girls who are self-assured, living lives lightly inflected but by no means driven by feminism, influenced by the philosophy of DIY [do-it-yourself], and assuming they can have (or at least buy) it all" (17). Within this celebratory context, girls' studies emerged as a distinct field of inquiry at the turn of the millennium. This context encouraged me and Deirdre Kelly to ask how girls "do" girlhood in the context of (seemingly) feminist messages of empowerment: messages that girls and women can enjoy sexualized hyper-femininity as a celebration of womanhood and still escape a male-defined destiny for women. Within this context, 'Girl Power': Girls Re-inventing Girlhood explores girl power in the lives of girls aged twelve to sixteen. As the subtitle suggests, we refer to our study as an exploration of how *girls* re-invent girlhood through their everyday gender practices. How much control do individual girls exercise over who they are and who they might become? Which girls are likely to inherit the future? What happens to the others? How does feminism figure into girl culture on the ground?

Challenging girlhood as a monolithic category, our study purposefully recruited girls from a range of class and ethnic backgrounds (69 in total). Our interview protocol was loosely structured, inviting participants to describe their social life at school. While the girls we recruited enacted a range of girlhoods, it was common to encounter the kinds of contradictory meaning-making documented in my study of magazine ads (Currie, *Girl Talk*). An obvious example comes from an interview with two enthusiastic twelve-year-old friends, GG and Vikki (both Euro-Canadian), who were interviewed together. They described themselves to Shauna:

> *GG:* With the guys, you just have to show that you are tough and not the little sissy that they think you are. A lot of guys, like they think you are like this little innocent girl. They're wrapped around you, like "I will protect you." All macho man. . . . But that's not what we're all about. I mean, we can defend ourselves!

> *Vikki:* You have to be like one of those outgoing controlling people who like, knows what to do in every situation.

> *GG:* Or everyone is going to treat you like some sissy who needs to be defended all the time, which is not so true. Girls can defend themselves. ('*Girl Power*' 69)

This excerpt interested us because the speakers draw upon the popularized rhetoric of girl power. This discourse allowed GG and Vikki to construct two mutually exclusive identities for girls: the "little innocent girl" who needs male protection versus the girl who can "defend herself" and who can control any situation. At first GG ridiculed the innocent girl by describing her as "little" and by calling her a "sissy." GG and Vikki rejected this identity category in order to align themselves instead with "girls who can defend themselves." It is interesting to listen to the continuation of this exchange:

Shauna: And we're talking not physical, we're talking—

GG: Oh no. Even verbally or mentally or emotionally. Like we can defend ourselves in all of those categories. We don't need some macho man to stand up for us. I mean, it's so cool when a guy does, but . . . I like it when a guy—I think it's so cool when a guy is like "Don't mess with my girl" sort of thing. . . . You know that the guy cares for you, obviously. Right? And when he stands up to one of his buddies and says, "Hey. Don't mess with my girl," like that's pretty good. Like he is actually going against one of his really good friends for you and that's gotta mean a lot. (*'Girl Power'* 69)

Neither GG nor Vikki saw this subsequent talk as contradicting their claims to be girls "in control" who "can defend themselves." In order to understand the basis of her reasoning, Shauna asked GG whether or not it has ever happened to her, that a guy "stood up" for her. At this point GG confessed, "No. Only in the movies."

What are we to make of such reasoning? At first glance it may be tempting to decide that these young participants are attempting to please Shauna, whom they have identified as a powerful woman, giving her at first a response that she might expect before revealing their true feelings. However appealing, such an interpretation is problematic: it expects to find and looks for authentic identities for participants. It also locates contradiction within the individual speaker. On the contrary, contradictory reasoning was not limited to GG and Vikki; we also heard it in other interviews. For us, it signalled the way in which girls have available to them a range of competing discourses about what it means to be a girl. We thus set as our task an understanding of how participants constructed and sustained coherent and stable identities at school (and throughout and across interviews).

It was not uncommon for girls to slide over or simply dismiss self-contradiction. Such dismissal occurs above when GG invokes the discourse of romantic love. The way this discourse wins out is both theoretically and politically important. The spectre of a boy protecting "his" girl does not simply undermine GG's construction of herself as a girl who can "defend herself"; it engages GG in a discourse that offers cultural support for male violence, so this mundane example is not innocuous. In GG's talk, the discourse of romantic love helps reconstitute the world of male entitlement to girls' and women's sexuality, an issue that, although not named by most girls in our study, accounted for stories about difficulties they experienced at school (for a fuller account, see Currie, Kelly, and Pomerantz). Because the discourse of romantic love trumps their discourse of girl power, we refer to heterosexual romance as an example of a "trump discourse."

A trump discourse is the discourse that overrides competing discourses that introduce contradiction in meaning-making. It is analytically significant because it imparts context-specific coherence to a speaker's statements, no matter how inconsistent or contradictory her statements may seem to an (adult) listener. Because it operates as common sense to the speaker, a trump discourse is more often than not latent in girls' talk; that is, although necessary for meaning-making, it remains unspoken. Identifying trump discourses thus helped us to see how power works *through* (but not *as*) texts, in the form of discourse. More importantly, trump discourses (which we can see are sustained by commercial texts) helped us to distinguish between agency and power.

In our work, "agency" refers to what girls said and did, while "power" is what made some things sayable and doable, other things not. This distinction led us to challenge the claim made by clinical psychologist Mary Pipher and those who follow her work that patriarchal culture silences girls. On the contrary, we could see how it positions girls to speak in specific ways. To be sure, not all girls took up subject positions offered by dominant discourses of girlhood, such as that of girl power. Given our interest in feminism, we deliberately sought out girls who defied the mandate of traditional femininity. As a result, in 'Girl Power' we give prominence to Skater Girls who consciously rejected hyper-femininity and Cyber Girls who "played" with gender online. While I do not have the space to discuss these other girlhoods, we were less successful in identifying discourses that trumped those supporting conventional girlhood. I suspect this failure has to do with the fact that adult researchers seldom become competent members of the communities of practice that constitute youth cultures. What I can consider in the remainder of this chapter are the implications of our analysis for girls' studies scholarship. Thinking about girlhood as a textually mediated discourse, how do our own texts operate as a venue of power? As raised at the conference for which this paper was written, which girlhoods (and girls) have been rendered visible through academic study of texts and culture? Which girls remain unknown, or even unknowable in our research? Stated another way, how do our frames of analysis operate as ontological commitments, shaping what we see and come to know? What trump discourse(s) operate through our own work, shaping how we think about, and hence come to know, girlhood?

In Search of Girlhood: Inauspicious Beginnings

While it is (perhaps) obvious why adult feminists ask, "What does it mean to be a woman?" it is not so obvious why we (continue to) ask, "What does it mean to be a *girl*?" Upon reflection, it seems to me that explorations of girlhood—at least initially—were primarily a way for adult feminists to understand ourselves. Here I speak as a senior feminist (60+ years of age). For younger colleagues, it may be difficult to appreciate the extent to which the lives of mothers of second-wave feminists acted as negative role models.[6] My own stay-at-home mother's life, for example, was a great source of unspoken dissatisfaction for her. During the heyday of second-wave feminism, the study of media texts reassured us that we would not inevitably become our mothers. We were able to show (scientifically, we claimed) that womanhood is a socio-cultural and not biological construct. We were rescued by the emergence of gender, something that we could show to be constructed in commercial venues such as women's magazines and television. The central role of textual analysis in girls' studies today can be traced to this interest.

In the early days, critiques of femininity led us to view commercial texts for women—women's magazines, romance novels, televised soap operas—as ideological in the sense that they conceal the underlying relations of their production and the interests embedded in these relations. From this perspective, a focus on texts worked to sustain a victim ideology characteristic of second-wave feminists' analysis of womanhood and, by later extension, girlhood. Feminist writers like Simone de Beauvoir, Betty Friedan, and Germaine Greer, who enjoyed large popular readerships in the industrialized worlds, warned women off commercialized fantasies of marriage and motherhood. Anglo second-wave researchers in North America, in particular, were influenced by the work of Betty Friedan. Her "problem with no name" inspired what was then called "sex role" research rooted in socialization theory. Much of this research begins from the assumption that the lived reality of women's subordination is fostered through commercial representations of adult femininity, rather than assuming that representations reflect what already exists, as claimed by marketing proponents (see Walker). For feminists, girlhood became the turning point when things went wrong (see Beauvoir, ch. 13): girlhood was the developmental stage at which adult women had learned compliance to subordinate gender roles.

In effect, based primarily on educated white women's aspirations, much scholarship that laid the groundwork for the emergence of girls' studies viewed girlhood as a way to understand the status of adult women. It is interesting that writers continue to preface their monographs with recollections or comparisons to their own girlhood (see, for example, Friedman 1; McDonough 13; White 11; Driscoll 1). The trump discourse underlying these points of reference comes from developmental psychology, which supports the seemingly self-evident notion, influential today, that as humans we proceed through a number of developmental stages on our way to adulthood. Movement through each stage is premised on resolving the existential crisis of figuring out the answers to questions like "Who am I?" and "Where do I fit in?" While answers to these existential questions are undoubtedly influenced in many ways, many feminist researchers and public commentators since the 1970s have seen commercial media as promoting scripts of acceptable hetero-normative femininity.

Such a view has encouraged the portrayal of young readers as immature consumers of ideologically loaded messages. During the 1980s, the few embodied girls who were featured in academic research tended to be "girls in trouble." While agency could be claimed for adult feminist women who somehow escaped gender socialization, girls were characterized through a focus on problems that girls face as documented by clinical psychologists: hatred of the female body, disordered eating, self-harm, and low self-esteem. These problems—especially low self-esteem—were seen to prevent girls from claiming the legacy of second-wave activism. Although granted agency, girls have thus been identified as the source of their problems. Whether the focus was psychological problems of especially white middle-class, over-achieving girls[7] or working-class girls in conflict with authorities (see Alder and Worrall), girls' thinking and girls' decisions have been characterized as needing intervention. Informing this work, but not always visible, are teleological assumptions about adolescent development (see Reimer and peters).

Important here is the way in which linear theories of human development reconstitute normalcy along very specific lines. One result is the academic reification of adolescent difference—whether racialized, pregnant, queered, Aboriginal, or otherwise outside mainstream adult expectations and hopes for young girls. By reification, I refer to the way in which identity as the object of analysis has come to overshadow the study of processes that work to structure difference in ways that marginalize and oppress specific girls. As noted above, pluralization of girlhood comes for the most part through notions of intersectionality, so that most empirical researchers are careful to inform their readers that they work with ethnically and racially diverse participants, from a range of economic households. Alternatively, if the focus is girls who have been marginalized by academic texts (working-class girls, girls of colour, bisexual or lesbian girls),[8] studies are based on a homogeneous group of participants in order to highlight difference.

To be sure, the advances of opening up girlhood to diverse identities have been many (see, for example, Weir and Faulkner; Schaeffer-Grabiel; Durham, "Girls, Media"; Durham, "Constructing"; Durham, *The Lolita Effect*). Despite these gains, as feminist scholar Valerie Hey argues, analyses are too easily sectional rather than intersectional, which can contribute to individualized rather than social analysis (18). In some ways, I think this problem is unavoidable in the qualitative methods suited for the study of lived culture. We deal with small numbers of participants, recruited either to ensure diversity or to represent a specific type of girlhood. In both cases, the numbers of participants are empirically too small[9] to arrive at much more than suggestions about the way that race and class (which have received the most research attention) work to shape girls' lives and futures. Yet I argue that the problem is not empirical as much as conceptual; that is, the problem will not go away with more of the same.

While it may seem counterintuitive, I think that gains will be made by moving away from treating girlhood as an identity. It is true that the concept of identity helped us to challenge the tendency to think about youth through biomedical categories. It also has served us well in thinking about how girls re-constitute girlhood as a situated social practice by enabling us to theorize girls' agency. And yet, we need to ask how these analyses mirror, rather than challenge, constructions of neo-liberal subjects. In short, reading agency off identity practices brings the danger of encouraging us to look for what we used to treat as social structures of race/class/gender *within* girls (see Walkerdine). This approach can contribute to the everyday persuasive language of individualized psychology that has displaced feminist political talk about exploitation, subordination, and gender inequality. This is where the blurring of the social and the cultural does not bring the analytical advances I had hoped.

To my mind, the intuitive appeal of documenting various youth identities reflects the fact that we work in a consumer culture that normalizes the self-regulating Subject. There are alternative ways for sociologists to think about girlhood—as a role, as a social relation, as a social location, as a cultural category, and so on. For a while, I would like to know where some of these approaches could lead us in terms of understanding how power works through texts. My personal preference is to think about girlhood as a textually mediated social relation. Such an approach directs researchers to different kinds of texts. I have in mind, for example, school policies that regulate especially girls' dress; education curriculum, especially life sciences and sexuality education; medical texts, especially those that classify youth as "special needs" as a practice that creates hierarchies among young learners; legal texts, especially those that shape the relationship between youth as minors and adults; texts that govern the everyday lives of racially marked youth, such as the Indian and Immigration Acts; and—as suggested here—academic texts that support much of this regulation through acts of omission as much as acts of commission. Despite the fact that these texts actively construct and normalize categories of girlhood, I seldom hear them discussed at academic conferences on girls, texts, and culture. And yet our academic texts account for the increased surveillance of girls by an array of adults: parents, educators, psychologists, marketers, medical practitioners, police, and academics. Viewing girlhoods as textually mediated social relations might enable us to see not only how power is exercised, but also how it helps to re/constitute social hierarchies among youth as well as between youth and adults.

Finally, we need to question our own investments in recounting girlhood. Girls' studies itself is productive of a growing volume of texts about girlhood and girls. As Marnina Gonick remarks about her own work, "[S]ince I am interested in analyzing identity as an effect of discursive practices, this book is part of the story it is trying to tell" (16). In other words, academic research plays a role in re/constituting what it claims to have discovered: girlhood. The problem cannot be sidestepped by turning the burden of authorship over to girls, as in the case of voice research or research that invites girls to author(ize) research texts. As Hey reminds us, "In building new feminist futures we might need to be alert as to how our investment in things past regulates a misconception of the present" (24).

Notes

1   Of course, by reading my own work "backwards," I am engaged in a rewriting; the result is theoretical coherence that may not be so readily apparent in original entries. For other accounts of the emergence of feminist cultural studies through a focus on "feminine identities," see Hollows; Thornham.

2   Unlike many other commentators, I differentiate commercial from popular culture. While commercial culture takes a commodified form (produced for exchange value), popular culture is culture produced by people for its use value. Although the latter typically draws on commercial culture (in part, because of its ubiquity), in doing so it "transforms" commercial culture (for example, through parody; see Fiske 20–21).

3   By the 1990s, feminist condemnation of women's magazines (along with pornography) was challenged by scholars viewing them as venues of women-centred pleasure. Janice Winship, for example, argued that because women now read fashion and beauty magazines within the context of "women's liberation," they recognized textual constructions as fantasy ("The Impossibility"). These kinds of arguments began to redeem both commercial magazines and the pleasures that female readers take from representations of hetero-sexualized femininity marketed by these magazines.

4   As for the girls cited later in this paper, each participant chose a pseudonym.

5   Following Janice Radway's *Reading the Romance*, feminist commentators began to celebrate the ways in which women's magazines can not only offer "escape" from the mundane aspects of everyday gender relations, but challenge everyday gender relations.

6   This may be true especially for Anglo, white, hetero-identified feminists with educated mothers.

7   In other words, girls who most closely approximated idealized girlhood.

8   Still missing is academic interest in girls with disabilities.

9   At the same time, the issue is not about numbers; more participants of the same kind will not make any findings more valid or representative.

Works Cited

Adams, Mary Louise. *The Trouble with Normal: Postwar Youth and the Making of Heterosexuality*. Toronto: U of Toronto P, 1999. Print.

Alder, Christine, and Anne Worrall, eds. *Girls' Violence: Myths and Realities*. Albany: State U of New York P, 2004. Print.

Barrett, Michele. "Words and Things: Materialism and Method in Contemporary Analysis." *Destabilizing Theory: Contemporary Feminist Debates.* Ed. Michele Barrett and A. Phillips. Stanford: Stanford UP, 1992. 201–19. Print.

Barthel, Diane. *Putting on Appearances: Gender and Advertising.* Philadelphia: Temple UP, 1988. Print.

Barthes, Roland. *Mythologies.* Trans. Annette Lavers. New York: Hill and Wang, 1972. Print.

Beauvoir, Simone de. *The Second Sex.* Trans. H. M. Parshley. New York: Bantam, 1961. Print.

Bettie, Julie. *Women Without Class: Girls, Race, and Identity.* Berkeley: U of California P, 2003. Print.

Bordo, Susan. "Anorexia Nervosa: Psychopathology as the Crystallization of Culture." *Feminism and Foucault: Reflections on Resistance.* Ed. Irene Diamond and Lee Quinby. Boston: Northeastern UP, 1990. 87–117. Print.

———. "Reading the Slender Body." *Body/Politics: Women and the Discourses of Science.* Ed. Mary Jacobus, Evelyn Fox Keller, and Sally Shuttleworth. New York: Routledge, 1990. 83–112. Print.

Currie, Dawn H. "Dear Abby: Advice Pages as a Site for the Operation of Power." *Feminist Theory* 2.3 (December 2001): 259–81. Print.

———. "Decoding Femininity: Advertisements and Their Teenage Readers." *Gender and Society* 11.4 (1997): 454–78. Print.

———. *Girl Talk: Adolescent Magazines and Their Readers.* Toronto: U of Toronto P, 1999. Print.

———. "Going Green: Mythologies of Consumption in Adolescent Magazines." *Youth and Society* 26.1 (1994): 92–117. Print.

Currie, Dawn H., Deirdre M. Kelly, and Shauna Pomerantz. *'Girl Power': Girls Re-inventing Girlhood.* New York: Peter Lang, 2009. Print.

Driscoll, Catherine. *Girls: Feminine Adolescence in Popular Culture.* New York: Columbia UP, 2002. Print.

Durham, Meenakshi Gigi. "Constructing the 'New Ethnicities': Media, Sexuality, and Diaspora Identity in the Lives of South Asian Immigrant Girls." *Critical Studies in Media Communication* 21.2 (2004): 140–61. Print.

———. "Girls, Media and the Negotiation of Sexuality: A Study of Race, Class and Gender in Adolescent Peer Groups." *Journalism and Mass Communication Quarterly* 76 (1999): 193–216. Print.

———. *The Lolita Effect: The Media Sexualization of Young Girls and What We Can Do about It.* Woodstock: Overlook P, 2008. Print.

Ferguson, Marjorie. *Forever Feminine: Women's Magazines and the Cult of Femininity.* London: Heinemann, 1983. Print.

Fiske, John. *Understanding Popular Culture.* London: Unwin Hyman, 1989. Print.

Foucault, Michel. *Power/Knowledge: Selected Interviews and Other Writing, 1971–1977.* Ed. Colin Gordon. New York: Pantheon, 1980. Print.

Fox, Bonnie J. "Selling the Mechanized Household: 70 Years of Ads in *Ladies Home Journal.*" *Gender and Society* 4.1 (1990): 25–40. Print.

Friedman, Sandra Susan. *When Girls Feel Fat: Helping Girls through Adolescence.* Toronto: HarperCollins, 1997. Print.

"Girl Power." *The Oxford English Dictionary.* N.d. Web. 15 Sept. 2012.

Gonick, Marnina. *Between Femininities: Ambivalence, Identity and the Education of Girls.* Albany: State U of New York P, 2003. Print.

Hall, Stuart. "Culture, Media and the 'Ideological Effect.'" *Mass Communication and Society.* Ed. James Curran, Michael Gurevitch, and Janet Woollacott. London: Edward Arnold, 1977. 315–48. Print.

Harris, Anita. *Future Girl: Young Women in the Twenty-First Century.* New York: Routledge, 2004. Print.

Hennessy, Rosemary. *Profit and Pleasure: Sexual Identities in Late Capitalism.* New York: Routledge, 2000. Print.

Hey, Valerie. "The Girl in the Mirror: The Psychic Economy of Class in the Discourse of Girlhood Studies." *Girlhood Studies: An Interdisciplinary Journal* 2.2 (2009): 10–32. Print.

Hollows, Joanne. *Feminism, Femininity and Popular Culture.* Manchester: Manchester UP, 2000. Print.

hooks, bell. *Feminist Theory: From Margins to Center.* Boston: South End, 1984. Print.

Keller, Kathryn. "Nurture and Work in the Middle Class—Imagery from Women's Magazines." *International Journal of Politics, Culture and Society* 5 (1992): 577–600. Print.

Lorde, Audre. "Age, Race, Class, and Sex: Women Redefining Difference." *Sister/Outsider: Essays and Other Speeches.* Berkeley: Crossing P, 1984. Print.

Mason, Jennifer. *Qualitative Researching.* London: Sage, 2002. Print.

Mayne, Judith. "The Female Audience and the Feminist Critic." *Women and Film.* Ed. Janet Todd. New York: Holmes and Meier, 1988. 22–40. Print.

McDonough, Yona Zeldis, ed. *The Barbie Chronicles: A Living Doll Turns Forty.* New York: Simon and Schuster, 1999. Print.

Nelson, Adie. *Gender in Canada.* 3rd ed. Toronto: Pearson Prentice Hall, 2006. Print.

Peirce, Kate. "A Feminist Theoretical Perspective on the Socialization of Teenage Girls Through *Seventeen* Magazine." *Sex Roles* 23.9–10 (1990): 491–501. Print.

Pipher, Mary. *Reviving Ophelia: Saving the Selves of Adolescent Girls.* New York: Putnam, 1994. Print.

Radway, Janice. *Reading the Romance: Women, Patriarchy, and Popular Literature.* Chappell: U of North Carolina P, 1984. Print.

Reimer, Mavis, and charlie peters. "Theorizing Young People." *Jeunnesse: Young People, Texts, Cultures* 3.2 (2011): 88–140. Print.

Schaeffer-Grabiel, Felicity. "Mixed Race and Third Wave Feminism." *Feminist Waves, Feminist Generations: Life Stories from the Academy.* Ed. Hokulani K. Aikau, Karla A. Erickson, and Jennifer L. Pierce. Minneapolis: U of Minnesota P, 2007. 211–31. Print.

Smith, Dorothy E. "Femininity as Discourse." *Texts, Facts, and Femininity: Exploring the Relations of Ruling.* London: Routledge, 1990. 159–208. Print.

Thornham, Sue. *Feminist Theory and Cultural Studies: Stories of Unsettled Relations.* London: Arnold, 2000. Print.

Walker, Nancy A. *Women's Magazines 1940–1960: Gender Roles and the Popular Press.* Boston: Bedford/St. Martin's, 1998. Print.

Walkerdine, Valerie. "Reclassifying Upward Mobility: Femininity and the Neo-liberal Subject." *Gender and Education* 15.3 (2003): 237–48. Print.

Weir, Sara, and Constance Faulkner. *Voices of a New Generation: A Feminist Anthology.* Boston: Pearson, 2004. Print.

White, Emily. *Fast Girls: Teenage Tribes and the Myth of the Slut.* New York: Scribner, 2002. Print.

Wing, Adrien Katherine. *Critical Race Feminism: A Reader.* New York: New York UP, 1997. Print.

Winship, Janice. "The Impossibility of *Best*: Enterprise meets Domesticity in the Practical Women's Magazines of the 1980s." *Cultural Studies* 5.2 (1991): 131–56. Print.

———. *Inside Women's Magazines.* London: Pandora, 1987. Print.

———. "A Women's World: 'Woman'—an Ideology of Femininity." *Women Take Issue: Aspects of Women's Subordination.* Ed. Centre for Contemporary Cultural Studies. London: Hutchinson, 1978. 133–54. Print.

Wolf, Naomi. *The Beauty Myth: How Images of Beauty Are Used Against Women.* Toronto: Vintage, 1991. Print.

CHAPTER 2

On Secrets, Lies, and Fiction

Girls Learning the Art of Survival

Kerry Mallan

My attention to the "art of survival" in this chapter does not include the important things girls need to know in order to be happy, popular, well-balanced individuals who will survive adolescence. Nor am I interested in examining survival in terms of outliving others, or passing on ancient knowledge and beliefs. My perspective of survival here serves a different purpose. In this chapter I am interested in how literature for young people depicts survival as a complex activity that negotiates silence, subjugation, and subjectivity. I am also interested in how secrets and femininity are theoretically linked with truth and concealment. As a way of framing my discussion of the texts, I want to briefly consider these intersections.

The "art of survival" in my title approximates Friedrich Nietzsche's phrase "art of simulation," which he felt expressed how human existence relies on necessary fictions as a way of preserving oneself against others (*The Portable Nietzsche* 44). Nietzsche lists the many forms such simulation takes: "deception, flattery, lying and cheating, talking behind the back, posing, living in borrowed splendor, being masked, the disguise of convention, acting a role before others and before oneself" (43). Further, he argues that such simulations are "so much the rule and the law" that the "urge for truth" is incomprehensible (43). Nietzsche was radical in his proposition that truth is itself an invention: "A mobile army of metaphors . . . truths are illusions about which one has forgotten that this is what they are" (46–47). Although Michel Foucault was influenced by Nietzsche's ideas about truth, he was not concerned with the problem of truth, but with the problem of the truth-teller and of truth-telling. For Foucault, truth-telling revolved around four questions: Who is able to tell the truth? About what? With what consequences? With what relation to power? He asks, "[W]hat is the importance for the individual and for the society of telling the truth, of knowing the truth, of having people who tell the truth, as well as knowing how to recognize them?" (170). In the fiction discussed in this chapter, these questions have significance for characters who are faced with situations in which they have to choose between telling the truth, telling lies, or keeping secrets as a survival strategy. Consequently, these texts show how, when faced with death or trauma, one may quickly learn that to lie may afford the means of surviving, even if the consequences may, ironically, make life unlivable.

Much fiction for young people is concerned with the articulation of truth, truth-telling and the truth-teller, and the consequences that arise when lies are told or concealed, secrets hidden or revealed. The violence or marginalization that is characteristically directed against the figure of the liar also finds its counterpart in assaults upon the truth-teller, who may similarly be subjected to acts of violence or psychological maltreatment for telling the truth or aspects of the truth. Given that the truth-teller is often subjected to the same kinds of violence as the liar, Nietzsche's point that human existence depends on necessary fictions, or the art of simulation, can be understood as a strategy of survival, one that is frequently deployed in fiction. A key feature of the art of simulation is concealment. Concealment of the truth or simply not telling (or showing) the truth may be tied to the experience of fear, mourning, anxiety, or forbidden love. When characters are presented as first-person narrators, readers are generally positioned to accept their words and viewpoints as "truth" unless the narrative shows them to be unreliable. As a character's account of another character or an incident can be understood only within the context of the story, and is not validated by an actual person or event, there is no possibility of verifying such an account by resorting to facts. When an author claims to be writing a true account of a life, readers generally accept a degree of creative reconstruction in dialogue and descriptions. When the author is found to be a fraud, however, readers and critics can be unforgiving of the lies perpetrated under the guise of truth.

In *Beyond Good and Evil*, Nietzsche proposes the idea of truth as a woman: "Supposing that Truth is a woman—what then?" (ix). He subsequently writes of the relation between woman and truth: "But she does not *want* truth: what does woman care for truth? From the very first, nothing is more foreign, more repugnant, or more hostile to woman than truth—her great art is falsehood, her chief concern is appearance and beauty" (101). There are a number of ways of looking at this statement. One is that truth, like woman, prefers appearance, beauty, and illusion to "truth." Colloquially we speak of "dressing up the truth" or the need to "uncover the truth of the matter." These suggest that the elusive nature of truth (and woman) demands that it conceal itself, and, more than that, that it beautify its appearance as part of this concealment. Another view is that, if the nature of truth is concealment and beautification, it might be more significant to consider the ways that truth presents itself than to consider what lies beneath its adornment. In other words, do we gain better insight or knowledge not by removing the adornment, but by considering what the use of that adornment reveals about the character of what lies beneath it?

Nietzsche's reference to "a woman" suggests that it is a particular kind of woman that is the metaphor for truth, and the appearance of this particular woman named truth is established in terms of revelation and unveiling. Bringing a feminist and psychoanalytic perspective to Nietzsche's image of truth as a veiled woman, Mary Ann Doane notes his shifting position with respect to truth and femininity: "Nietzsche both reinscribes and criticizes philosophy's tropological system linking the woman, truth, and the veil" (56). Doane points out that Nietzsche uses the image of the veil to argue that the structure of truth is one of surface and depth. Furthermore, Nietzsche's truth is modesty itself, as it refuses to be unveiled. Writing about film noir, Doane considers the veiled woman as serving a different purpose from the one that Nietzsche proposes: "the veil functions to visualize (and hence stabilize) the instability, the precariousness of sexuality" (46). According to Doane, the figure of the *femme fatale*, with her mysterious but powerful sexuality, harbours a threat to masculinity which is transformed into a secret that "must be aggressively revealed, unmasked, discovered," and in this way the secret and its uncovering are compatible with "the epistemological drive of narrative" (1). However, she suggests that epistemological certitude is not always guaranteed; there is a "precariousness of vision" because appearances can be deceiving, and are "most apt to deceive when they involve a woman" (46). The veil takes on additional meaning when it is located within cultural discourses, where the "precariousness of vision" is perhaps exacerbated, a point that I address later.

In the following discussion, I take up the key elements identified by Nietzsche and Doane: truth, femininity, fiction, and concealment. The question of literature (and fiction) as truth or lie has occupied many writers and theorists, including Jacques Derrida and Frank Kermode. Derrida's view on literature and secrecy is that literature withholds as much as it reveals, always leaving readers to ask questions of characters, events, motivations, and meaning—What happened after . . . ? Why did . . . ? How is . . . ? Who said . . . ? Thus, readers come to literature with a sense of its secret "that is at the same time kept and exposed, jealously sealed and opened like a purloined letter" (131). Kermode contends that readers' interests in the secrets found between the covers of a work of fiction remain at the level of message and closure, and they remain uninterested in (or unaware of) the text's secrets. As he suggests, "[t]he capacity of narrative to submit to the desires of this or that mind without giving up secret potential may be crudely represented as a dialogue between story and interpretation" ("Secrets" 86). One of the ways in which texts work to keep their secrets is by diverting readers' attention through unreliable narration, ellipsis, foregrounding and backgrounding, and so on. These devices are important for us to consider when thinking about the extent to which the treatment of survival in literature is contingent on secrets and lies. At a wider level, the issue of whether or not fiction itself is a lie or contains a "truth" speaks to the relations between imagination, representation, and truth.

My interest here in fiction's relationship to truth, lies, and secrecy is not so much a matter of how closely fiction resembles or mirrors the world (its mimetic quality), or what we can learn from fiction (its epistemological value). Rather, the concern is both literary and philosophical: a literary concern that takes into account how texts that thematize secrecy work to withhold and to disclose their secrets as part of the process of narrating and sequencing, and a philosophical concern that considers whether survival is contingent upon secrets and other forms of concealment such as lies, deception, and half-truths. The texts selected for examination are *Secrets* (2002), *Skim* (2008), and *Persepolis: The Story of a Childhood* (2003). These texts draw attention to the ways in which the lies and secrets of the female protagonists are part of the intricate mechanism of survival, and demonstrate the ways in which fiction relies upon concealment and revelation as forms of truth-telling.

Girls Learning to Survive: Veiling and Unveiling Secrets

A recent publishing trend of self-help guides offers young girls advice on how to survive the teenage years. These texts are typical of the betwixt and between state of girlhood in the new millennium in that they attempt to construct a subjectivity for girls that is a dynamic state of becoming, constituted by a set of agencies and experiences, and limited by external social conditions. The addressees of these texts are generally white, middle-class girls, and the ideological imperative of the lessons to be learnt reinforces a neo-liberal subject who is constantly caught up in the dilemma of lack and potential. These dilemmas are often resolved through narratives where the subject finds the path of least resistance, a survival path that affords at least transitory routes for achieving a temporary illusion of individuality, popularity, confidence, and a respectable "cool" rating on the social barometer. These self-help guides sit alongside other popular fictions targeted at a female readership. Collectively, these books serve a pedagogical function, instructing young girls in the art of survival as well as in the art of being a good (girl) guide who is able to steer other girls confidently through the turbulent waters of adolescence. A common recommendation in these texts is for girls to keep a diary (see, for example, Carnegie; Collins and Rideout; DeVillers; Ford).

Diary writing has traditionally been associated with women, and keeping a journal or a diary continues to be recommended to girls as part of a self-improvement regime. In this view, diaries and journals often become confessional sites for pouring out one's emotions, cataloguing one's failings, castigating oneself over choices made, and recording resolutions for a renewed selfhood. Critics have observed that this form of female narration positions the diarist as a passive subject, a mere witness to events. For example, Alison Case suggests that the genre deprives the narrator of "the interpretative advantage of hindsight with which to shape a narrative" (177). This privileging of hindsight, and presumably rationalism, underestimates the value of intuition and spontaneity. In fictional diaries, by contrast, spontaneity appears to be privileged, but such spontaneity is, of course, only a pretense, a cover to disguise the process of drafting and editing that the writing and publishing of a book requires. While the forward momentum of a daily or regular diary entry impels the writer to record the *presentness* of emotions and events, this does not prevent the diarist from reflecting on actions, or from engaging in truth-telling or deception. As readers of diaries, we are positioned to accept the "truths" presented to us from the point of view of the diarist, since there is no corroborating or contradictory viewpoint. Even in fictional diaries readers may willingly suspend their disbelief. The following discussion examines this issue of a diarist's relationship to the truth in the novel *Secrets* by Jacqueline Wilson.

Secrets is narrated in alternating diary entries written by the two main characters, Treasure and India. The diary mode in *Secrets* offers a literary foil to bring together the stories of two girls living in very different, and very difficult, family circumstances; diary writing is the common element they share. The diary entries are polished and extended texts, and there is no attempt to mimic the diary writing of adolescent girls. The cover of *Secrets*, which depicts the two diaries and two small keys dangling from the title, further connotes the message of secrecy. The preface by author Jacqueline Wilson underscores her role as author and the text's status as fiction: "I'm the author. I have power over the plot! So of course I made the girls meet and get to know each other properly. They tell their stories in alternate chapters . . . " (n. pag.). Wilson adopts the mask of author to both seduce the reader and offer a truth; she is the playful doppelgänger of Nietzsche's gendered truth. Assuming the guise of woman as truth, Wilson allows readers a glimpse of what lies beneath the mask, while at the same time she undermines the text's mimetic value.

Wilson's statement firmly locates this text as a narrative, a story with a plot. This disclosure of the narrative's secret is at odds with its purpose to deceive, which the cover image of diaries and the subsequent diary entries attempt. Treasure's diary is a notebook, which she tells us on the first page is the "Official Terry Torture Manual." Terry is her stepfather who makes her life a misery, and from the outset readers are positioned to see Terry as aggressive and violent. (For example, when he discovers Treasure's notebook, he rips out the pages and strikes Treasure with his belt: the buckle causes a long and deep cut on her forehead and the force of the attack breaks her glasses.) Whereas Treasure does not address her diary in her entries, India begins each entry with "Dear Kitty," borrowing from Anne Frank, who created an imaginary friend to whom she confided her thoughts and situation. India's infatuation with Anne Frank runs deeper as the story progresses. While Jacqueline Wilson distances herself from the characters she has created, she nevertheless lifts the mask again to reveal that "I was obsessed by Anne Frank like India, reading her very moving diary again and again. I had a photo of Anne by my bedside for years" (n. pag.). We can read this piece of truth-telling as imposing a kind of self-perpetuation: like Jacqueline Wilson and Anne Frank (and India), the implied girl readers may themselves become famous writers or diarists.

The self-perpetuating author-as-diarist notion continues through to the endpapers, where readers are invited to "[j]oin the FREE online Jacqueline Wilson fan club," with further exhortation to "[r]ead Jacqueline's monthly diary," among other promotional and social networking activities. This invitation to explore the epitext takes readers from the bounded text to a site of diverse "textual cultures" (Whitlock 16) that are materially and ideologically based processes surrounding the production, transmission, promotion, and reception of books written by Wilson. These accounts, which reveal personal aspects of Wilson's childhood and the invitation to become part of a Jacqueline Wilson fan club, attempt to produce an identification between the text's female writer and its presumably female readership, and offer the possibility of an expanded subjectivity for young readers. Wilson's performance as author from peritext to epitext can be likened to a dance of veils: as each one is lifted, readers glimpse something of what lies beneath. But instead of revealing the real truth, there remain appearance, illusions, and adornment. Gillian Whitlock argues that in textual critique there is a need for further layers to be lifted and removed:

> Peel away the layers of peritext: the covers, introductions, acknowledgments, dedications, blurbs. Add to this your ongoing immersion in epitexts: reviews and criticism across various mass media, the carefully synchronized marketing and trade of . . . narratives; the movements of the celebrity circuit; the book prizes and the calendar of literary festivals. (14)

In "peeling away," we are not necessarily attempting to uncover final truths that we suspect lie beneath the surface, but opening up the path to new ways of evaluation from different perspectives.

As a work of fiction, *Secrets* could be seen as not making claims to literal truth, except possibly in its references to Anne Frank and her life as recorded in her diary. The inclusion of Anne Frank as a subject of interest for the characters can be traced back to Jacqueline Wilson's girlhood fascination with her, which she mentions in the peritext. But even the authenticity of Frank's text as having been written by a teenage girl has been the subject of legal deliberations and ongoing public debate. Apart from these truth-claims, secrets and secrecy are both theme and form in this text. Treasure and India have secrets which they reveal to the reader, and which place the reader in the position of confidante. The first secret revealed by Treasure is that her stepfather, Terry, cut her forehead with his belt buckle in an act of physical aggression. Treasure recounts that this fact or truth is covered up by her mother, who fears the repercussions if doctors or social workers hear of it. This incident recalls Foucault's questions: Who is able to tell the truth? About what? With what consequences? With what relation to power? Later, Treasure's grandmother, her beloved "Nan," reluctantly becomes part of the secret and also decides not to reveal the truth to the authorities, and so confirms her daughter's fears about the consequences of truth-telling. Meanwhile, Treasure and India forge a friendship and, when Treasure flees the safety of her Nan's home to avoid being taken back by her mother and Terry, India decides to hide Treasure in the attic of her family home. India is bound by this secret because to disclose the whereabouts of Treasure could result in her being returned to an abusive environment. When India hides Treasure in her attic, the two girls simulate to some extent Anne Frank's life of hiding in a secret annex.

This "simulation," to use Nietzsche's term, necessitates secrecy, deception, and lying. As readers we become knowers of the secret, which is not only part of the plot, but also an intrinsic feature of the fiction; the fiction gradually converts a state of unknowing (which we experience at the beginning of any fiction) to a state of knowing or thinking about the secret. This is what Frank Kermode terms the literary "genesis of secrecy" that aims at converting "unknowing" itself into a secret form of knowledge. Kermode's point is given expression when, at the conclusion of the preface, Wilson invites readers to regard the fictional world as truth by asking: "Do you think Treasure and India will stay best friends forever? I do hope so" (n. pag.). The direct address to the reader is what Kermode would regard as a veiled "invitation to interpretation," rather than an appeal "to a consensus" ("Secrets" 93). Wilson's comment foreshadows the uncertainty that the girls express at the end of their own diaries, wondering if their friendship will continue forever.

Ultimately, this text seems to be concerned with the secrecy of secrets and their effects. In refusing to break her friend's confidence and reveal where Treasure is hidden, India is caught up in a moral dilemma: if she reveals her friend's whereabouts, Treasure could be returned to an abusive home, but if India doesn't reveal the secret hiding place, Treasure's escalating asthma could threaten her life. Both girls conclude that hiding is a necessary step to ensure Treasure's survival. Hiding serves a double purpose: in hiding Treasure in the attic, India conceals Treasure's location, as well as the truth behind her reason to hide. Metaphorically, the girls embody "truth" in that the nature of truth is to conceal itself. To recall Nietzsche, "her great art is falsehood." The girls literally learn the art of survival: India takes on a caretaker's role, skilfully creating a comfortable space for Treasure, tending to her needs, and deceiving her parents and the au pair by lies, cunning, and creativity. Treasure, too, learns a different art of survival by finding ways to entertain herself and learning how to be quiet and brave. The secret is tested, however, when media coverage of her disappearance mounts and Treasure's mother and Terry appear tearfully on television news. The situation escalates further when Treasure's asthma becomes a risk to her physical survival, leaving India with the dilemma of whether to reveal or not to reveal the location of her friend. Paradoxically, but necessarily, survival, which first depended on secrecy and concealment, now requires unveiling and openness.

Not all secrets require unveiling or revelation. The inviolability of a secret is taken up in *Skim*. The diary by fourteen-year-old Kim, who is known as "Skim," is presented in the form of a graphic novel, with the seasons of autumn and winter marking the temporal course of the story. Two secrets are central to this text, and both concern gay sexuality. One is the secret tryst that Skim has with her drama and English teacher, Ms. Archer. The other is about the secret gay sexuality of the school volleyball player John Reddear, who commits suicide. While the first secret is confined to Skim and Ms. Archer, the second is revealed and spreads through the school after John's death. Before his death, John apparently had to cover the truth of his sexuality and his love for another boy by dating Katie Matthews, the popular girl at school, and performing his role in the heterosexual couple. As John's secret about his sexuality is revealed by gossip and hearsay, the reader can either accept this as a truth or remain ambivalent. No ambivalence is possible with the other secret the text reveals, as the reader is witness to the secret relationship between Skim and her teacher, and the intimate kiss they share. The illustrated moment of the taboo kiss is captured without words, yet it reveals a truth that requires a veiling in order for it to continue to be a secret in the fictional world of the characters. John's secret—if there was one—remains shrouded in mystery and speculation, since the truth is outside the phenomenality of the text.

The diary is the means by which Skim writes and illustrates her life at that time. The dating of the diary as 1993, and its correlation to the year when the author, Mariko Tamaki, was seventeen years old, may work to convince readers that this is a true story. Readers might, perhaps, even assume that "Skim" is a fictional version of the author: there is a physical likeness between the two and, according to Erin Kobayashi in the zine *Broken Pencil*, the story contains other personal similarities to Mariko's high school life. How these influences inform the narrative and take on the status of truth or fiction is part of the text's secret.

Skim, too, is interested in secrets and secrecy—she enjoys Wicca, tarot cards, astrology, and philosophy, a diverse set of interests that embody esoteric ideas. She maintains an altar with its quasi-sacred objects and mystery ingredients. The form of the book merges first-person female narration and incidental drawings with a third-person illustration and comic-strip frame sequence. The overt third-person omniscient illustrator reveals the intimacies of Skim's life and secrets to us as readers, but the perspective is necessarily partial and biased because of its focus on tracking Skim. While Skim conceals the secret of her relationship with Ms. Archer from others, we have no knowledge as to whether this act of privacy is reciprocated by Ms. Archer. Ms. Archer leaves the school and we are positioned to know only as little as Skim does about her motivations for doing so. We might presume to know that the illicitness of their relationship is the motivation, but we do not know if other people were responsible for her decision to leave.

Skim's secret and her successful attempts at keeping aspects of her life private contribute to a subjectivity that is only partially known by both readers and herself. She does not feel the need to reveal to others her secret desires and heartbreak and suffers in silence—drifting through the days at school, spending endless hours lying on the couch, preoccupied with thoughts of Ms. Archer, despite her attempts to erase her from her mind: "I am trying not to be obsessive. It is not good to only think about one ~~person~~ thing" (76). A teacher interprets her withdrawal as depression and suggests she is in need of counselling.

Doane, in her discussion of cinematic close-ups and the veil, comments that "the face, more than any other bodily part, is *for* the other" (47). In *Skim*, eyes become important, as the "most *readable* space of the body" (Doane 47). Initially, Ms. Archer tells Skim that she has "the eyes of a fortune teller" (13); subsequently, Skim notes that Ms. Archer "says she can't stop looking at my eyes" and tells her that they "are very serious" (31). When Halloween arrives, Ms. Archer dresses as a fortune teller, providing a symbolic connection between herself and Skim (with her fortune-teller eyes), which precedes the taboo kiss. After the kiss, the seduction stops, and Ms. Archer begins to distance herself from Skim, averting her gaze in class: "She didn't really look at me" (70). When Skim hears that Ms. Archer is leaving the school, she hides her eyes and her sorrow behind her tarot cards—an image captured in a series of three frames from middle-distance, to close-up, to extreme close-up. The close-up functions in a similar way to the camera in Doane's cinematic reading, as Skim is the female subject upon whom the reader gazes. Unlike the translucent veil that the *femme fatale* uses to lure the male, the cards serve as a mask, an opaque surface that resists any attempt to probe the depth that hides behind it. The mask thereby ensures that the truth is not revealed.

While Ms. Archer no longer looks at Skim, it seems to Skim that everyone else does. She feels the intrusiveness of their gaze. Like the traditional philosophers whom Nietzsche suggests seek to unveil "truth" in order to expose an essence, the students seek to discover the reality behind Skim's sorrowful appearance. Skim argues with her friend Lisa, who tells her to "get out into the REAL WORLD every once in a while" (112). Secrecy becomes a burden weighing her down and isolating her from the social world. The philosopher Sissela Bok notes that "[s]ecrecy guards . . . not merely isolated secrets about the self but access to the underlying experience *of* secrecy" (21). Skim closes to others any access to the secrecy that envelops her. When Lisa reflects on her own transformation since falling in love, she tells Skim that being in love changes you, adding, "No one can put it into words" (141). Lisa's comment resonates with Skim, who is unable to speak of her love for Ms. Archer not just because it is taboo, but also because it is too complex to put into words. In this way, the diary with its images and minimal text breaks the silence by sharing the burden of her secret love. Her diary, like all diaries, is a public-private object; it is public in its sense of an audience, which is conveyed by Skim's opening address, "Dear Diary," but this address also suggests a private communication in that the diary itself is the patient listener or receptor of her secrets, and as readers we also serve this function.

In *Skim* subjectivity is predicated on the harbouring or disclosing of secrets. John's subjectivity is fractured and erased through his suicide and the gossip that it generates about his sexuality and double life. Skim harbours her own secrets and finds silence the best way to cope with the shifting emotions that come with the blossoming and disappearance of love. Skim can be seen as Nietzsche's free spirit who "[is] not exactly the most communicative [of] spirits" (*Beyond Good and Evil* 60), but who grapples with the idea of what it can free itself from and where it will then be driven. Whether Skim wants to free herself from the desire that binds her to Ms. Archer remains part of her secret and silent misery.

This story is not so much a winter of discontent as a story of star-crossed lovers. Shakespearean references occur in the text in several ways. The students are studying *Romeo and Juliet* with Ms. Archer, and a metaphorical bleakness reminiscent of *Richard III*'s winter of discontent resonates in the black-and-white illustrations of a dark and cold autumn and winter, mirroring the turmoil and misery that engulf the lives of the characters. The subtle play of Shakespearean signifiers creates the effect of a *mise en abyme*, where the play *Romeo and Juliet* is simultaneously studied, lived, and queered by Skim and her teacher, and by John and Katie. Skim is no Juliet, however, and survives her winter by discovering a new friendship with Katie, moving on from her friendship with Lisa, and remaining content to keep her secret.

Unlike John, who could not live his life with the boy he loved, Skim learns the art of survival through her silence, gradually moving toward social interaction and a renewed subjectivity. This course of silence and withdrawal is not one that is recommended in self-help guides written for teenage girls. *Skim* illustrates how the confessional and celebratory approach is not necessarily the best way to cope with loss or depression: a group of girls form the "Girls Celebrate Life Club" as a way of helping Katie to overcome her depression following John's suicide and as a way to commemorate John's life. They even have a movie night at which the feature film is *Dead Poets Society*. The members of the Girls Celebrate Life Club, with their determined goodwill crusade, resemble Nietzsche's "idealists," "who are enthusiastic about the good, true, and beautiful, and let all kinds of motley, coarse, and good-natured desirabilities swim about promiscuously in their pond" (*Beyond Good and Evil* 53). The club and the film are interventions that carry a survivalist ethic, which ironically works against its own rationale by perpetuating an at-risk subjectivity, especially for Katie, who breaks both arms, ostensibly by falling off a roof. Skim and Katie are resistant to the intended cathartic activities of the club. By putting pressure on the two girls to participate in the club, the organizers fail to see how desire and femininity can be understood without recourse to phallogocentrism. They assume that Katie is heartbroken and they construct her as a victim, someone who lacks agency. The folly of trying to construct the female subject within a binary frame is subtly played out in the text in various ways across the public-private domains. For example, the school dance with its party atmosphere and mixed-couple imperative holds no interest for Skim or Katie, who prefer each other's quiet company. The traversing of the public-private space also points to the paradox of secrets and subjectivity: both require and do not require public revelation. Just as there is never a point of fixed subjectivity, there is never a point of total revelation. As Bok says, "at the very moment of disclosure . . . yet further secrets remain to be unveiled" (36). Survival is a continual process of veiling and unveiling, even if the unveiling is confined to a diary.

Another kind of veiling and unveiling occurs in *Persepolis* by Marjane Satrapi. Unlike *Skim*, which is fiction, *Persepolis* is described in the cover blurb as a memoir, a term echoed by Gillian Whitlock when she describes it as a "graphic memoir" (188). *Persepolis* begins in 1979, during what would come to be known as the Islamic Revolution. By 1980 it had become obligatory for girls to wear the veil, and the first chapter references this fact: entitled "The Veil," it is accompanied by an icon of an eye, which implies that this is a text of witness (Chute). The narrative that provides the temporal sequence to the text is written in the reflective voice of Satrapi, whereas the first-person address that is embedded within the text is the voice of the young Satrapi, known as "Marji." The narrator explains how the significance of the veil eluded her and other children: "we didn't really like to wear the veil, especially since we didn't understand why we had to" (3). The accompanying illustration shows children mocking, playing, and complaining about the veil. This scene carries a generational significance, as the children's behaviour indicates that they have no knowledge of the cultural significance of the veil. Even with adults there are tensions and differences of ideological viewpoints, with the Iranian women represented in the text seeing the veil as an object of either oppression or religious observance. Satrapi's family members belong to the former group and are educated and liberal in their attitudes, opposing the Shah and his totalitarian regime. Her parents often take part in dangerous demonstrations. The matter of female survival is an unbroken thread in the family. Satrapi's grandfather, who was a prince of Persia, lost everything to the father of the shah and was imprisoned for becoming a communist. During his imprisonment, Satrapi's grandmother had to learn literally the "art" of survival by taking in sewing as a means to support her family.

After the shah is forced into exile and the Islamic regime assumes power, the ideological divide between fundamentalist and modernist Islam is made clear by the clothing worn by women and men. The illustrations capture the contrast with paired images of fundamentalist and modern subjects (75). Under the new regime, the telling of lies becomes a survival strategy for the more liberal citizens. Marji's mother tells her, "If anyone ever asks you what you do during the day, say you pray, you understand?" (75). Marji finds that learning to lie comes quickly and that a fine line separates lying and exaggeration, as children compete to be the most devoted. When one of her friends piously claims, "I pray five times a day," Marji replies, "Me? Ten or eleven times . . . sometimes twelve" (75). Marji learns that in order to survive and not be killed, one must find ways to avoid total subjugation: lying becomes a survival strategy.

This returns us to Foucault's questions about who is able to tell the truth, about what, with what consequences, and with what relation to power. Since protesting on the streets means encountering violent attacks, activists need to find other ways to protest. In public, Marji, her mother, and her grandmother cover their heads with scarves, and the older women wear modest black dresses. Later, Marji openly flaunts her revolutionary spirit, creating her own Western-styled aesthetics by publicly wearing a new denim jacket with a Michael Jackson sticker, jeans, and a new pair of Nikes. She also trades in the black market to pay for two music tapes by Western pop stars. These visible signs of rebellion and freedom, however, almost result in her being taken to HQ when two women, "guardians of the revolution," attempt to arrest her for being improperly veiled. Marji narrowly avoids being arrested by telling a pack of lies: "Ma'am, my mother's dead. My stepmother is really cruel and if I don't go home right away, she'll kill me. . . . She'll burn me with the clothes iron! **She'll make my father put me in an orphanage**" (134; emphasis in original). Marji's lies for survival illustrate how the binary of truth and falsehood is far from uncomplicated, especially when individual freedom is at stake. It also illustrates Nietzsche's point that survival is contingent upon lies. Marji's contradictory self-representations as a revolutionary activist and a victim of abuse demonstrate the relations between fiction, truth, and lies.

Her memoir as a whole, however, offers a rendition of truth that transcends this singular event, and readers have to take her truth-telling at face value. While the graphic form of the memoir with its comic-strip format may work against a sense of truth-telling, it is the "authority" derived from the mode of memoir that secures a reader's acceptance of this account. The term "memoir" is specifically mentioned in the peritext only in the cover blurb on the endpapers. The front cover of the book gives the title *Persepolis: The Story of a Childhood*. The use of the term "story" connotes a fictionalized account or poetic licence where exaggerations or extensions of the truth are permitted. The illustrated format also gives an additional power to the storytelling. Hilary Chute sees the graphic narrative form enabling "dialectical conversations," whereby "Satrapi's older, recollective voice" and her "younger, directly experiencing voice" and the "visual voice" of the pictorial space constitute "many narrative levels" (97). As the storyteller, Satrapi takes on a responsibility for the perpetuation of the history of this period of her homeland, and for *the* story of a childhood. The choice of the definite article suggests that this is an authorized account of a childhood and thereby lends a quality of truthfulness to the story. Further, the truth-telling is supported by the temporal and cultural context from which the story emerges. As a storyteller-memoirist-artist, however, Satrapi is in control of how she wishes to tell her story, including its "truths" and "fictions." Ultimately, her memoir offers a perspective that does not demand acceptance by readers as bedrock truth, but offers itself as a possible truth.

Silence, Subjugation, and Subjectivity

The texts discussed in this chapter provide interesting examples of the ways secrets contribute to female subjectivity and relations with others. Knowing a secret can be difficult because there is always a temptation to share it with someone else. In telling someone a secret, our purpose may be to confide in another, to share the burden of the secret, or to gossip. When we choose not to tell, we carry the secret silently within ourselves. Each of the main characters in the texts I've discussed achieves a relational subjectivity by sharing or disclosing aspects of herself with others; what the protagonists choose to share is contingent on what they understand to be necessary for survival. In the fictional diaries that form *Secrets*, the need to be acknowledged by others is a strong feature of the friendship that develops between Treasure and India. The girls share their diaries with one another, further demonstrating their desire to disclose secrets and develop trust. The secret circle that develops between the two girls and Anne Frank's diarist persona becomes an important feature of their friendship and a testament of the trust they share. Outside this circle, lies circulate as a way of disguising the truth and as a means of self-preservation.

In contrast to India and Treasure, Skim does not actively seek the acknowledgement of others, apart from Ms. Archer. She prefers a solitary selfhood that she carefully regulates. In her friendship with Lisa, Skim withholds her thoughts, and the diary becomes the means for voicing these silences. She does not feel compelled to confess or expose the truth about her feelings toward Ms. Archer. Indeed, their secret protects her, unlike the revealed secret about Katie's boyfriend. The tragedy of Reddear's suicide comes unbidden into Katie's life and, despite the affirmation that the girls' circle in *Secrets* appears to offer, the Girls Celebrate Life Club only adds to her emotional burden. Rather than tell lies as a way of escaping life's hard times, Skim and Katie find that silence and retreat are paths for survival. Their growing friendship returns a sense of fun to their lives, but secrets remain and relationships change. The penultimate images show Skim walking alone along the empty street and toward the park that was her secret meeting place with Ms. Archer. The final image is of a paper-folding numbers-colours game, which is commonly known as "the fortune teller," and as such carries a special significance in this text. Blue is the colour shown; from the opening page readers know that this is not Skim's favourite colour. But while blue could be read as a sign that she continues to be depressed, it could also signify that nothing stays the same. There is no truth in either proposition—this is fiction's secret.

Satrapi in *Persepolis* explores the truth in terms of her desire to know her family's history and its relationship to the current political regime. But, within the story of childhood she tells, she becomes adept at telling lies in order to achieve a certain status among her social group and to escape an interrogation by the Guardians of the Revolution. The rhetoric of truth is not elevated above the rhetoric of lies, as both are part of her storytelling repertoire and serve as a means of survival. Thus, Marji learns that there is value in untruth for personal survival. Furthermore, the comic-strip format of *Persepolis* juxtaposes a graphic tradition of fantasy or untruth with a memoir that carries a tradition of truth-telling. Photographs are often part of the truth-telling that memoirs or autobiographies attempt; the black-and-white images of Satrapi's graphic novel demonstrate that truth-telling need not rely on conventional styles of illustration. Whether drawn or photographic, the image conveys its own silences and ellipses and is complicit in the narrative movements of the revelation and disclosure of secrets.

All three texts ultimately support Nietzsche's proposition that life and truth are at odds, that life requires untruths, secrets, and other simulations. The girls in these stories are not tropes for truth. Rather, they illustrate Nietzsche's point that there is no simple or straightforward truth, or, by extension, simple or straightforward path to survival. The art of survival that the girls manage comes through their deft negotiation of the conditions that contribute to their silence, subjugation, and inchoate subjectivity.

Works Cited

Bok, Sisella. *Secrets: On the Ethics of Concealment and Revelation.* New York: Vintage Books, 1989. Print.

Carnegie, Donna Dale. *How to Win Friends and Influence People for Teen Girls.* New York: Fireside, 2005. Print.

Case, Alison. "Authenticity, Convention, and *Bridget Jones's Diary.*" *Narrative* 9.2 (May 2001): 176–81. Print.

Chute, Hilary. "The Texture of Retracing in Marjane Satrapi's *Persepolis*." *WSQ: Women's Studies Quarterly* 36.1–2 (2008): 92–110. Print.

Collins, Yvonne, and Sandy Rideout. *Totally Me: The Teenage Girl's Survival Guide*. Avon: Adams Media, 2004. Print.

Derrida, Jacques. *The Gift of Death; and, Literature in Secret*. Trans. David Wills. Chicago: U of Chicago P, 2008. Print.

DeVillers, Julia. *GirlWise: How to Be Confident, Capable, Cool, and in Control*. New York: Three Rivers P, 2002. Print.

Doane, Mary Ann. *Femmes Fatales: Feminism, Film Theory, Psychoanalysis*. New York: Routledge, 1991. Print.

Ford, Amanda. *Be True to Yourself: A Daily Guide for Teenage Girls*. Berkeley: Conari P, 2000. Print.

Foucault, Michel. *Fearless Speech*. Ed. Joseph Pearson. Los Angeles: Semiotext(e), 2001. Print.

Kermode, Frank. *The Genesis of Secrecy: On the Interpretation of Narrative*. Cambridge: Harvard UP, 1979. Print.

———. "Secrets and Narrative Sequence." *Critical Inquiry* 7.1 (1980): 83–101. Print.

Kobayashi, Erin. "Mariko Tamaki Shows Some Skim." *Broken Pencil*. April 2008. Web. 16 March 2011.

Nietzsche, Friedrich. *Beyond Good and Evil: Prelude to a Philosophy of the Future*. *Basic Writings of Nietzsche*. Trans. Helen Zimmern. Ed. William Kauffman. New York: Dover, 1997. Print.

——— *The Portable Nietzsche*. Trans. and ed. Walter Kaufmann. New York: Viking P, 1954. Print.

Satrapi, Marjane. *Persepolis: The Story of a Childhood*. New York: Pantheon, 2003. Print.

Tamaki, Mariko, and Jillian Tamaki. *Skim*. London: Walker Books, 2008. Print.

Whitlock, Gillian. *Soft Weapons: Autobiography in Transit*. Chicago: U of Chicago P, 2007. Print.

Wilson, Jacqueline. *Secrets*. London: Corgi Yearling, 2002. Print.

CHAPTER 3

Disgusting Subjects

Consumer–Class Distinction and the Affective Regulation of Girl Desire

Elizabeth Bullen

In a special issue marking the fifteen-year anniversary of the publication of Michelle Fine's 1988 essay "Sexuality, Schooling, and Adolescent Females: The Missing Discourse of Desire," Anita Harris contends that "the emergence of a genuine discourse of young women's sexual desire has both already occurred and is not unproblematic" (39). Referring to sex education in the 1980s, Fine argued that not only was desire an absence, but also what girls were taught about their sexuality was framed in terms of violence, victimization, and morality. In the new millennium, girl sexual desire is now a conspicuous presence in media, press, policy, and popular culture texts. This turnabout points to the fact that discourse, which in a Foucauldian sense refers to a system of representation or signification, "provide[s] a language for talking about . . . a particular topic at a particular historical moment" (Hall 44). It also constructs knowledge about, and attitudes toward, a given topic. It organizes what can be said and not said, which in turn influences "how ideas are put into practice and used to regulate the conduct of others" (44). According to Harris, the discourse of desire, which is public in the sense of its open circulation, is just as regulatory as discourses of violence, victimization, and morality (39).

The public discourse of desire, which disarticulates sex from romance and reproduction and re-articulates it with consumerism, has been mobilized in the service of neo-liberal capitalism or the "new economy" (McRobbie, "Good Girls"; Walkerdine, Lucey, and Melody; Harris). Young women have been offered a "new sexual contract" (McRobbie, *The Aftermath*): they are ostensibly permitted sexual pleasures that were traditionally deferred until marriage. These apparently more liberal attitudes to female sexuality, however, are contingent on young women taking up roles as producer and consumer citizens. In an inversion of what second-wave feminist Betty Friedan called the "feminine mystique," the current generation of girls and young women "must not procreate," and certainly not "while enjoying casual and recreational sex" (85). This discursive shift has produced greater state intervention into the regulation and discipline of girls' bodies and fertility in the interests of delaying motherhood (Harris; McRobbie, *The Aftermath*). It has also (re)invoked the public emergence of a parallel discourse of disgust.

The subject of the discourse of disgust is not the sexually active young working woman, but the sexually excessive adolescent girl, often from a working- or underclass background, with the teenage mother figuring as the epitome of the failed sexual citizen. The preoccupation with the sexuality of the economically marginalized is hardly a novel state of affairs; working-class women and girls were historically vilified for their sexual excesses, perceived or real, and Beverly Skeggs offers a useful overview of the nineteenth-century origins of this stereotype in her longitudinal study of working-class female respectability, *Formations of Class and Gender: Becoming Respectable*. The stigma attached to working- and underclass girls' sexuality and reproduction has not changed, although the ideological drivers have. What has changed is that female sexual respectability no longer depends on the construction of the opposition between a chaste middle-class subject and her sexually active, less privileged counterpart. Public discourses of desire undo the strict separation of middle-class femininity from sexuality and its denial of female desire. The affirmation of female pleasure, desire, and sexual/sexualized subjectivity in popular-culture texts, in particular those informed by a post-feminist sensibility (Gill), has destabilized the boundaries that once separated respectable and abject femininities. Taking the ubiquitous HBO television series *Sex and the City* as an exemplar, Skeggs explains why:

The expansion of explicit and excessive hetero-sexuality from one class of bodies to another generates an uncertainty about the good/bad moral value that can be known: the historical location of the immoral with the white and black working-class women as the site of sexual agency and contagion, is now in the contemporary extended into the category of the professional white middle-class urban women. The boundaries of the lascivious, dangerous and contagious are therefore no longer absolutely clear. ("The Making of Class and Gender" 969)

Public discourses of desire have also extended the site of sexual agency into girlhood. Popular-culture texts, including adolescent fiction for girls, promote a "postfeminist sexual rationality" (Bullen, Toffoletti, and Parsons 503) through the partial separation of sex and romance (albeit a separation never complete, even in *Sex and the City*) that arguably prepares girls to take up their roles as producer and consumer citizens. Certainly it introduces them to a contemporary sexual sensibility that positions them to understand themselves as desiring subjects and career women, if not now, then in the future. However, as increasingly younger girls become sexually active pragmatists, this, too, has generated moral uncertainties and anxieties about the boundaries between the "desiring" and "disgusting" girl sexual subject.

This chapter is concerned with how these boundaries are being redrawn through the simultaneous circulation of discourses of desire and disgust, and how they manifest in two novels for girls, Cecily von Zeigesar's *Nothing Can Keep Us Together* (2005), the eighth novel in the Gossip Girl series, and Julie Burchill's *Sweet* (2007), the sequel to *Sugar Rush* (2004). The protagonists of these young adult novels exist at the poles of privilege and disadvantage in their respective communities, making class central to this inquiry. The comparative analysis I undertake, however, focuses on the role of consumer-class aesthetics and the taste distinctions (Bourdieu) that inform the discourses of desire and disgust in these novels. The commodity, I will argue, functions as an ideoaffective mechanism that classifies which girls count as successful sexual citizens and which ones do not. In this regard, it is equally important to ask what it is that protects the privileged girl when she expresses her sexuality as it is to ask what it is that makes the less privileged girl vulnerable. I begin, therefore, with a discussion of the role of the commodity and consumption in the broader sexualization of culture, the role of a high-class commodity and lifestyle aesthetic in "dignifying" middle-class female sexuality, and its influence on the representation of girl desire in *Nothing Can Keep Us Together*.

Sex in the Commodity

In an essay attending to the sexualization of culture in late modernity, Feona Attwood discusses the way in which class informs texts "which appear to 'speak sex' from a woman's point of view; in advertising, in magazines and lifestyle journalism and in a range of fictional texts" (84). Contextualizing her argument with reference to the contemporary political, economic, and socio-cultural transformations that also produced a post-feminist sexual sensibility, Attwood claims in regard to *Sex and the City* that

> late modern hedonistic sexuality can be associated with the rise of a new petite bourgeoisie whose members are typically located in occupations concerned with presentation and representation such as marketing, advertising, fashion and the media. For this group, a view of sex as "fun," and a corresponding concern with sex as aesthetic rather than ethic, has functioned as a means of defining itself as sophisticated. (84–85)

By virtue of their occupations as cultural intermediaries of style, members of this petite bourgeoisie establish their sophistication in relation to a glamorized world of production. They also do so through their consumption of glamorous commodities. Frequent reference to couture fashion labels and chic lifestyle products is not insignificant here, given that the address of these texts to women "as sexual subjects and consumers [is typically] achieved through claims to aesthetic value and 'class'" in relation to consumer goods (86). Indeed, Attwood asserts that the "'classiness' of female sexual activity is extremely important [in] establishing its legitimacy" (85).

The same holds for the way the Gossip Girl series addresses girls as post-feminist subjects. As Kim Toffoletti notes, "The attributes associated with the post-feminist girl are often realised through consumption, both material and sexual," and they are manifest in "the Gossip Girl storylines, which frequently link sex and consumer goods" (72). Of course, like the schoolgirls who read them, the characters in Gossip Girl cannot belong to the occupational groups of the post-feminist petite bourgeoisie. Their capacity to consume luxury goods, and the novels' capacity to establish the high-class aesthetic that legitimates the representation of girl desire, is entirely reliant on the protagonists' class location.

The narrator, Gossip Girl, only hints at the extent of the wealth of her protagonists in the eponymous title novel:

Welcome to New York's Upper East Side where my friends and I live and go to work and play and sleep—sometimes with each other. We all live in huge apartments with our own bedrooms and bathrooms and phone lines. We have unlimited access to money and booze and whatever else we want, and our parents are rarely home, so we have tons of privacy. We're smart, we've inherited classic good looks, we wear fantastic clothes, and we know how to party. Our shit still stinks, but you can't smell it because the bathroom is sprayed hourly by the maid with a refreshing scent made exclusively for us by French perfumers.

It's a luxe life, but someone's got to live it. (von Ziegesar, *Gossip Girl* 3)

Over the course of this and the ensuing twelve novels, some of them ghostwritten, the "luxe life" enjoyed by Blair Waldorf and Serena van der Woodsen, the main characters, is established through references to high-end department stores and boutiques like Barneys and Henri Bendel; landmark New York City hotels such as the Pierre and the Plaza; holidays in the Caribbean, Sun Valley, and St. Barts; country houses in the Hamptons; and the Ivy League universities the characters aspire to, and eventually do, attend. More persuasive, however, is the relentless stream of luxury brands and designer fashion labels. In a sample of six chick lit novels, including books one and ten of Gossip Girl, Naomi Johnson identified nearly six hundred brand names (55). In *Nothing Can Keep Us Together*, they include Manolo Blahnik, Hermès, Givenchy, Tiffany, Louis Vuitton, Balenciaga, and Ferragamo. Much like perfume, the product placement of high-end brands cloaks the sexual and other exploits of the characters in an aura of glamour and good taste (see Bullen).

The importance of taste in constructing the consumer aesthetic in *Nothing Can Keep Us Together* is made explicit when Blair looks for a high school graduation outfit at a Williamsburg bridal and formal wear boutique. It occurs to her that if she buys her dress from an "off the map" store like "Isn't She Lovely," there will be no danger of another graduate wearing the same outfit. "The problem," however, is that "with no designer label to show their merit, she wasn't sure if the dresses were ugly in a cool way or just plain ugly" (40). Suddenly, she is furious at herself for even contemplating buying anything from this store, which she thinks would be more aptly named "Isn't She Ugly." More significantly, she wonders, "Who was she kidding pretending to not need a graduation dress made to order by

Oscar de la Renta or Chanel?" Hitching her "nude pink Fendi purse up on her shoulder" and sliding her "tortoiseshell Parsol [*sic*] sunglasses up on her nose," Blair sniffs, "When had her life become so base?" (41).

Designer brands are critical in constructing a sexual aesthetic that separates itself from base sexualities. This is implicit in the way Blair plans her sexual encounters in the Gossip Girl novels—even if she is repeatedly thwarted in her attempts to have sex. In *Nothing Can Keep Us Together*, her former boyfriend Nate is going out with her erstwhile best friend Serena, so Blair sets her sights on Lord Marcus Beaton-Rhodes. Her plan is to have sex with him on her graduation night in her suite at the Yale Club. In anticipation, she has filled it "with Diptyque candles in the scent of sandalwood, bergamot, and lime, and underneath her suit she [is] wearing her favorite new cream-colored embroidered cotton Cosabella camisole-and-thong set" (180). When Blair slips upstairs from the after-party to find Marcus, she considers "stripping down to only her Bvlgari pearls right there in the hallway" (212), but reconsiders at the prospect of encountering a Yale professor who might end up being her future teacher. As these examples suggest, prestige brands, in this case Yale, Diptyque, Cosabella, and Bvlgari, establish a sexual as well as a consumer aesthetic.

In relation to advertising, Wolfgang Fritz Haug argues that, when "sexual enjoyment becomes the commodity's most popular attire . . . what is being thrust upon the public is a whole complex of sexual perception, appearance, and experience" (56). Of course, in *Nothing Can Keep Us Together*, it is specifically high-class commodities and commodified environments that shape the way readers are positioned to perceive sexuality. The chapter entitled "Guess Who's Bonking in Bergdorf's" shows how: Nate has accompanied Serena to choose a dress at Bergdorf Goodman, "one of the oldest and most beautiful luxury department stores in Manhattan" (89). The couple take the "sleek ivory-colored elevator" to the third floor, where Serena is "immediately drawn to a rack of exquisitely made white Oscar de la Renta suits—swishy pleated knee-length skirts and fitted jackets with cool white leather belts decorated with adorable little white leather bows" (89–90).

Fuelled by Viagra, Nate follows Serena into the dressing room where she is undressing and yanks her camisole from her body. She is not about to "miss this opportunity," having not had sex with him since Blair discovered them together in an episode in the closing stages of the previous novel, *Nobody Does It Better* (2005). Reminding her of when they were in the tub together in tenth grade, their third time, Nate grabs "the other pristine white satin Oscar suits off their hooks and scatter[s] them at their feet," asking her to "[p]retend all these white dresses are the bubbles" (91). Conventional sexual mores might well condemn sex in a public place, not to mention lascivious sex between a couple keen to prove the reason they are together is not "just some random, horny hookup between two beautiful, self-centered people who couldn't control themselves" (11). The narrative forestalls moral judgment about the sex act and the protagonists in two ways, however: first, through the aesthetics of this scene and, second, through the reaction of the sales assistant who discovers the couple. I consider the second of these narrative strategies later in this chapter.

Debra Curtis's research on sex and capitalism suggests that desire cannot be understood independently of the "social fields, such as the market" (100) in which it is constituted. In this episode, which links sex and shopping, girl desire is constructed through a commodity aesthetic, which, to recall Blair's assessment of the dresses at Isn't She Lovely, assumes "merit" through the Oscar de la Renta and Bergdorf brands and lends the sex encounter a "chic signification" (Attwood 86). It is notable, however, that the descriptors of the department store, the gowns, and even Serena's polo shirt and underwear—"sleek," "pristine," "ivory," not to mention the redundant repetition of "white" in the textual examples quoted above—juxtapose the imagery of purity with the protagonists' lust. To the extent that the scene is erotic, its sensuality resides in the texture of the "crisp" satin suits, Serena's "flimsy" camisole, and the "heavy" velvet curtain of the dressing room (90). What is clear is that the scene is constructed entirely through the play of the commodity and commodified surfaces, including "the confusion of tanned, writhing limbs and white satin on the floor of the dressing room" as witnessed by the sales assistant (91–92). The high-class commodity aesthetic is used to transcend the sensual pleasures the couple gives into, a "transcendence of the body" that Stephanie Lawler argues has historically informed middle-class concepts of beauty and superior taste (439).

According to Haug, when "commodities borrow their aesthetic language from human courtship . . . the relationship is reversed and people borrow their aesthetic expression from the world of the commodity" (19). One might say that they borrow their values as well. This reversal is evident in *Nothing Can Keep Us Together*, not least because its discourse of desire foregrounds the aesthetic and monetary value of the commodities and thereby backgrounds sexual ethics or values. The emphasis on the commodity also speaks to the mind–body split, which Stephanie Lawler locates in Kantian and middle-class aesthetics. This split is based on the assumption that "[u]nlike the facile pleasures of the flesh which *anyone* might enjoy, appreciation of beauty is held to demand a transcendence of the body that only *some* . . . can attain," a distinction that is "mapped on to broader classed relations" (Lawler 439; emphasis in original). In a cultural context where the enjoyment of sensual pleasures is ostensibly available to anyone, "good taste" becomes all the more important, especially since bourgeois sexuality "derive[s] quite precisely from the rejection of the low class characteristics expressed most coherently in the production of a 'white trash' figure of the 'slut' elsewhere in the culture" (Attwood 85).

One such figure is Ave Maria Sweet, also known as Sugar, and the main protagonist of Burchill's novel *Sweet*. Like Serena, Sugar also has sex in a public place (more than once, in fact). Unlike Serena, however, she is a chav—the British equivalent to "white trash." Although the pairing of a British novel with a product of the American cultural economy clearly raises issues about national differences, Burchill's novel shares a common if diametrically opposed preoccupation with the role of taste in commodity and sexual aesthetics. Like *Nothing Can Keep Us Together*, *Sweet* reflects broader cultural judgments about styles of conspicuous consumption that stand in place of judgments about sexual mores and morality. Indeed, it shows how class taste distinctions act to elide the similarities in girl desire across social classes in order to redraw the boundaries of the lascivious, dangerous, and contagious.

Class and the Girl as Cheap Goods

In contrast to Serena and Blair, who have all they need and more to successfully enter into the post-feminist sexual contract, Sugar already qualifies as a failed sexual citizen. At seventeen, she is a comic caricature of the single teen mother: she has left school early, served time in prison and kicked the heroin habit acquired there, and is unemployed when the novel commences. The only job she can get is as domestic cleaner, spraying perfume in other people's bathrooms. She lives with her mother and siblings in a council flat and, unlike the gossip girls, she does not "have tons of privacy" (von Ziegesar, *Gossip Girl* 3), probably one of the reasons for her public sexual escapades. The current object of her desire, Asif, much like Nate, has been less than sexually forthcoming. A Christian Pakistani immigrant, Asif is more interested in increasing his cultural capital than his erotic capital. It thus transpires that the couple has sex at the Booth Museum of Natural History.

On face value, there is negligible difference in the sexual behaviour of Sugar and Serena. In spite of the deep economic gulf that separates these characters, the representation of girl sexual desire in both novels points to the way the boundaries that once differentiated respectable and disreputable girl desire have blurred. It was once the visible sexuality of the "slut" that offended "the bodily and sexual proprieties intrinsic to upholding class distinctions: good manners, privacy, the absence of vulgarity, the suppression of bodily instincts into polite behavior" (Kipnis 174). Given that both Serena and Sugar transgress these proprieties, what differentiates them is the commodity aesthetic that distinguishes the desire of bourgeois Serena and white trash Sugar.

As I have explained, when Serena and Nate have sex in Bergdorf's, the sexual aesthetic is constructed through the play of commodity surfaces. Burchill's narrative, by contrast, juxtaposes sexual bodies with the body stripped bare: not of clothing—Sugar keeps hers on—but of flesh. Leaning against a glass case holding a human skeleton, she pulls up her skirt and Asif against her, "and away we went—celebrating life against a boxful of death" (*Sweet* 129). This image strips away surface; it metaphorically exposes desire as a drive that the Gossip Girl series covers with fashionable clothes. Significantly, this instance of public sex takes place in a museum, not an exclusive department store. It is a space belonging to the public commons, a place that "doesn't cost anything," and with unconscious irony Sugar observes, "Surely that means it's worthless?" (127). She may lack the cultural capital to appreciate the value of museums, but this observation is acute; in contemporary consumer culture, lifestyle experiences, including sexual experiences, are more highly valued when they are associated with the consumption of luxury commodities and commodified geographies. The difference between Serena and Sugar, then, is asserted through the aesthetic distinction between chic, high-class sexuality and the underclass sexuality associated with white trash or the chav.

The chav has also become central to an emerging public discourse in the United Kingdom that "recapitulates the discursive creation of the underclass, while simultaneously reconfiguring it within the space of commodity consumption" (Hayward and Yar 16). Chav is one of a number of derogatory slang terms for the British working poor and unemployed, including regional variants such as Pikey and Shazza.[1] The chav girl, or chavette, is strongly stereotyped by her sexuality through both her promiscuity and early motherhood, and is thus labelled by a further range of derogatory names that invoke abject femininities, including "pramface" and "pricktease."

According to Imogen Tyler, however, "one of the things that distinguishes the figure of the chav from previous accounts of the underclass" and, by extension, underclass girl sexuality, "is the emphasis on the excessive consumption of consumer goods and branded goods" (21). Arguing that the chav is "bodied forth" in the media and press, Tyler (inaccurately) quotes journalist Gina Davidson's description:

> And we will know them by their dress . . . and trail of fag ends, sparkling white trainers, baggy tracksuit trousers, branded sports top, gold-hooped earrings, "sovvy" rings and the ubiquitous Burberry baseball cap. Throw them together, along with a pack of Regal, and you have the uniform of what is being described as the UK's new underclass—the chav. Call them what you will, identifying them is easy. They are . . . the slack-jawed girls with enough gold or gold-plated jewellery to put H Samuel out of business. They are the dole-scroungers, petty criminals, football hooligans and teenage pram-pushers. (Tyler 21, quoting Davidson 14)

As this description suggests, the male dress code is more easily stereotyped than it is for girls. However, a survey of *urbandictionary.com* indicates that, in addition to ostentatious gold jewellery (often multiple hoop earrings in each ear), chav girls can be identified by their poorly applied makeup, puffa jackets, tracksuits, hair pulled back in a scrunchie, a propensity for pink, and a pram—for daywear at least.

A number of these stereotypes are mobilized when Sugar dresses to go to the job centre to find work. Deliberately toning down the "glamour" for the occasion, she

> settle[s] for pale pink pedal pushers, a shocking-pink bomber jacket and puce wedges. Only two earrings—two in each ear, that is—two shades of eyeshadow and one coat of Marvelash. And for the rest I went "au naturel," as they say—nude lipgloss rather than lipstick, cheek stain rather than blusher and crimped hair instead of proper straightened. (Burchill, *Sweet* 7)

There are no designer labels to show the merit or otherwise of her ensemble, but Sugar's idea of "au naturel" suggests a disjunction between her perception and the reality. This disjunction calls her taste into question, even for implied readers unfamiliar with the chav discourse. For those familiar with it, or its regional and national equivalents, Sugar's clothes label *her*. She is classified by the taste aesthetic of the commodities through which she constructs and commodifies her identity, branding her as chav.

The fashion worn by the characters in Gossip Girl must be at once recognizable and unique—a point implicit in Blair's reasoning when she briefly entertains the idea of buying her graduation outfit from Isn't She Lovely and her horror at finding Serena in the same suit at the ceremony and a twelve-year-old wearing it at the after-party. In *Nothing Can Keep Us Together*, fashion taste distinctions are the basis of class affiliation and exclusion, but they are also paradoxically individualist. Chav style bespeaks the converse: it is an affiliation based on conformity. It is how Sugar recognizes her "people," which she registers with joy in an episode at Stanwick Airport. Her people, a group of girls on their way to a hens' party in Ibiza, are "wearing identical gear—cropped baby-pink Ts with FALLEN ANGEL scrawled across their tits in sparkling silver scrawl, tiny denim hot pants and cowboy boots" (107).

Of course, the girls do not look identical in their matching outfits, being of all shapes and sizes. Sugar surmises that the young woman she refers to as Barbie Girl conceived the outfit, given it "showcase[s] her wares so wantonly" (108), but makes every other girl look like "a hippo in a condom" (107). In spite of this observation, Sugar is not particularly critical of Barbie or her girlfriends, having "once worn a skirt out to Creation that was so short some sarky student said to me, 'That's a nice belt—why don't you get some more material like it and make a skirt as well!'" (108). Here, the novel evokes a vulgar chav sexuality made visible through fashion, blurring the boundary between the visual availability of the exposed body and sexual availability, the fashion commodity and sexual self-commodification. The narrative suggests, however, that a longer skirt would not make any difference to how girls like Sugar are viewed. This is made clear in an episode that links the creation of fashion with procreation, and the class cloth from which Sugar is cut with the contemporary social fabric, making explicit what is implicit in the sexual allusions in Sugar's commentary on the girls at Stanwick.

Sugar's trip to the job centre is successful, and she takes a job as a house cleaner for a gay couple. The position includes doubling as a pattern model, but this is initially out of the question, partly because Sugar has a size-16 bust and size-10 hips, but mostly because the fashion designers, Agnewe and Bagshawe, recognize her as a chav. They treat her with open contempt and disgust until she reveals her distress over the loss of her lesbian lover, Kim, a relationship explored in *Sugar Rush*, and with whom she is reunited at the end of *Sweet*. Revealing the logic that conflates the discursive construction of underclass girlhood with sexual reproduction, Agnewe admits they "misjudged" Sugar. Until this revelation, they regard her as "a typical chavette. An under-educated, over-made-up breeder, to be blunt. Just one of those . . . drones that's pregnant at fifteen, a grandma by thirty and quite frankly fit only for cat meat by forty—"He shuddered, then brightened up. "But you're not—you're a baby dyke! You're one of us!" (25–26)

The fact that Agnewe could well be describing her mother is not lost on Sugar, even if the significance of her sexual preference in terms of reproduction is. Regardless, she is thrilled to find that the designers want her to be the muse and model for a new fashion collection. While they fit her with toiles, cheap fabric used to test the pattern, Sugar fantasizes about the collection and a glamorous future. There turns out to be a vast difference, however, between what she imagines and the actual finished products.

When Sugar is shown photos of the finished garments on a mobile phone, she discovers that her princess dress is labelled "WHITE-TRASH TINKERBELL" and made out of black plastic rubbish bags; her micro-mini skating skirt with attached knickers is called "PRAM-FACED PRICKTEASE." A dress called "LATE AGAIN!" has pregnancy tests hanging from the hem, and other designs are called "PIKEY-PRINCESS" and "CHIPSHOP CHIC." "MUM'S ABORTION"—the designers have subsidized Sugar's mother's abortion—is a pair of culottes: "bright yellow, with gurgling babies printed all over them. And a trickle of blood running down from the crotch" (65). Each piece in the Council Couture Collection is deeply associated with the abject female body. The materials used to construct and to trim the garments and the names used to identify them allude to bodily wastes like menstrual fluids and the byproducts of abortion, failed contraception, and pregnancy. The novel here makes material the symbolic meaning of the currently fashionable epithets used to denigrate British working- and underclass girls.

Considered together, *Sweet* and *Nothing Can Keep Us Together* point to the centrality of consumer-class taste distinctions in the textual production of a chic female sexuality that is legitimate, and a chav cheap sexuality that is illegitimate. Von Ziegesar's Gossip Girl novel supports Attwood's contention that a "progressive" female sexuality is strongly linked to statements about high-class taste and aesthetics (86). Burchill's novel suggests that a regressive attitude to female desire is linked to similar statements, whereby cheap goods and a vulgar aesthetic cheapen girl desire to produce the "slut." These narratives, and cultural texts like them, clearly contribute to contemporary public discourses of desire and disgust. But what is it that gives them social force? In the final section of this chapter, I discuss the role of affect in organizing the pulses and poles of attraction and repulsion, desire and disgust, the glamorous and grotesque, invoked by the consumer-taste distinctions encoded in the textual representation of commodities in these novels. I speculate on how affect might also inform the social consensus requisite for the discourses of desire and disgust to find a purchase in the public consciousness—and in texts that address girls as sexual subjects.

The Ideoaffective Effects of Desire and Disgust

Contending that the aesthetics of objects, bodies, and spaces are the "hallmark of allure," Nigel Thrift argues that "affluence brings with it the construction of the quality of glamour as a key imaginary in producing allure" and that it is constituted in and by "the commercial sphere" (14). Glamour, he continues, "blurs the boundary between person and thing in order to produce greater captivation" (10). It "demands envy, but also identification" (15). Referring to celebrities—Gossip Girl's blog owes much to the celebrity gossip column, and includes "sightings" of the characters—he makes the case that "[t]hey exist in the realm of mediated imagination, as stimuli promoting further exploration, stirring up inchoate urges, desires and identifications that we can't help but scratch" (19). Their appeal is affective, rather than cognitive or rational.

The vulgar and grotesque also blur the boundary between the person and thing, but produce dis-identification and the affect of disgust rather than glamour and envy. Following Marilyn Adler Papayanis, Skeggs argues that "attempts to control the visibility of feminine sexuality often turns bodies of desire in to bodies of disgust using the language of outrage" ("The Making of Class and Gender" 968). In this sense, the disgusting also exists in an imaginary mediated by the symbolic and, in the contemporary, in a mediatized imaginary (see Tyler for a survey of media and entertainment iterations of the chav in the UK). Disgust, however, is also now constituted in the commercial sphere. Clothes, shoes, hairstyles, jewellery, and more—what Graham Harman calls a "whole geography of objects" (138)—are an integral part of the "lively fabrications" (Thrift 19) that produce the allure of the aesthetics and the sex lives of celebrities and gossip girls. As the Council Couture Collection in Burchill's novel suggests, a further set of "lively fabrications" is used to construct vulgarity.

In their study of vulgarity in the Victorian period, Susan David Bernstein and Elsie Michie explain how this term, "[o]nce employed to define language use and class position," came to refer to "style, taste, and comportment, a form of behavior whose definition shifted with fluctuating social boundaries and with the changing and unspoken rules of its obverse, refinement" (3). They note a shift in the way that notions of vulgar taste became "less a matter of *what* one said or did than *how* one did it and in what context. This switch in emphasis meant that it was associated less with the possession of specific objects, such as garish furnishings and ostentatious dress, than with the way one thought about those objects" (170; emphasis in original). In light of the aestheticization of everyday life in late modernity, it appears that consumer objects are once again integrated into discourses of desire and disgust, where they form the context for both taste distinctions and moral discrimination.

The social power of both discourses requires social consensus about what is desirable and disgusting. In regard to this consensus, the extant literature on negative affects is more forthcoming. In *The Anatomy of Disgust*, William Miller states that disgust, contempt, and shame are mechanisms that "rank us and order us in hierarchies; these emotions provide the basis for honoring and respecting as well as for dishonoring and disrespecting" (202). In her study of affect in literature, *Ugly Feelings*, Sianne Ngai notes Derrida's notion of the disgusting as the "absolute 'other' of the system of taste" (334). The social power of disgust, she argues, derives from the fact that "it seeks to include or draw others into its exclusion of its object, enabling a strange kind of sociability" (336). This sociability is evident in the public discourses of disgust, but there is also a strange kind of sociability entailed in the system of good taste.

If allure produces identification and desire as Thrift suggests, it too demands consensus about what is desirable, what is tasteful, what is aesthetically pleasing. The Gossip Girl novels draw on the discourses of high fashion in magazines, advertising, and the media to establish an aesthetic consensus, which is taken for granted in *Nothing Can Keep Us Together*, and achieved in spite of the unappealing characters. Compared with the funny, resilient, ribald, and endearing character of Sugar, Blair is a pompous, self-absorbed snob, and it is arguable that the narrator, Gossip Girl, is also such a snob. Although her observations are often wryly ironic, she rarely disagrees with Blair's contempt for failures of style, and often makes judgments of her own. For instance, the reader is positioned to concur with the narrator's sarcastic description of Kati Farkas's and Isabel Coates's matching graduation dresses and her snide remarks about Joan, the Bergdorf sales matron. It is Joan who discovers Serena and Nate having sex in the fitting room, an incident that explicitly links consumer-class taste distinctions with judgments about entitled girl sexuality.

The narrative uses focalization techniques to convey the sales assistant's reaction to the scene she witnesses:

> That sort of vulgar behavior was completely unladylike and therefore completely un-Bergdorf's, but there wasn't much she could do. Serena van der Woodsen had opened a Bergdorf's charge account when she was seven and had been a loyal customer ever since. And of course it was nice to see that she was so comfortable in the store. (von Ziegesar, *Nothing* 93)

Generational differences clearly influence Joan's initial response. Just as clearly, Serena's wealth lends her a kind of impunity within the commodity environment. The girl occupies a higher place in the class hierarchy than the sales assistant, even though Joan wears a Chanel suit. In fact, the Chanel suit suggests that she is interpolated into a high-class aesthetic, and it is this that leads her to rationalize her disgust and excuse Serena's behaviour. Although the text raises the issue of sexual vulgarity, the reader is not invited to subscribe to the sales assistant's point of view, especially since her suit does "nothing for her lumpy hips and piano legs" (90). Configured as a generational and class interloper in the world of the gossip girls, Joan's failure to realize that her suit is unflattering calls into question her aesthetic judgment and, thus, her opinion of Serena's behaviour as vulgar.

In John Ruskin's estimation, vulgarity pertains to a lack of awareness of the impression created on others, not least of all the impression "vulgar" individuals create upon those who determine or subscribe to dominant notions of good taste. Although hardly vulgar, Joan is not aware of the impression she creates. She also lacks the power to determine what constitutes sophistication and vulgarity according to the new sexual contract. This power is assumed by Gossip Girl, the narrator and the arbiter of good taste and sexual mores in the novel. The dynamic is different in Burchill's novel; unlike Joan, Sugar is acutely aware of her class location, but she displays a similar, even exaggerated, lack of awareness of the impression she creates on others. *Sweet* is a first-person narrative, and like Gossip Girl, Sugar assumes agreement with her point of view. In contrast to *Nothing Can Keep Us Together*, however, it is the implied reader who is empowered to determine good taste and vulgarity because she is positioned to disagree with the protagonist's taste. This positioning is achieved through multiple comic disjunctions between the way the protagonist and the implied reader perceive the same object—for example, an "au naturel" look that involves full makeup and hair crimping and Sugar's belief that Pizza Express is where one has "a proper meal out. . . . No more Domino's for us, now I was a model" (Burchill, *Sweet* 31–32). It is also apparent in the way Sugar sees herself and how she believes she is seen—"jealous mingers called me a slut cos I was so pretty" (214)—and in the language and imagery she uses to describe her clothes and body.

Blair might wear a tasteful Cosabella camisole or a La Perla demicup bra in anticipation of sex. Dressing for a party, Sugar chooses a pair of underpants with "laces at the back and bows at the side," with the aim of looking like a "raunchy slut" (170). Pulling up her dress and surveying herself in the mirror, she describes herself as "the prettiest gift-wrapped present the world has ever seen" (170). She is quite oblivious to this narrative allusion to her sexual self-commodification, and when she decides "I better leave now or I'll get myself pregnant" (170), she makes precisely the link between sex and reproduction that the public discourse of desire refuses. Sugar is also unconscious of the tastelessness of the simile she uses when she likens her trademark walk to "four stoned puppies fighting in slo-mo in a partitioned sack—two in front, two behind!" (7). "Serena's boobs [are] hard looking, like the small Empire apples" (von Ziegesar, *Nothing* 89) grown on Nate's family's country estate in Maine; the simile Sugar uses to describe her breasts and buttocks alludes to the drowning of unwanted litters. The former image connotes literal and metaphorical cultivation; the latter evokes unrestrained fertility and expendable lives. Through her likeable protagonist and arguably at her expense, Burchill reveals an unruly girl body and animal desires unrestrained by the high-class commodity aesthetic that makes them acceptable in *Nothing Can Keep Us Together*.

Sugar's vulgarity, consumer and sexual, may or may not produce disgust in a reader, but I would argue that it does promote affective dis-identification. Ngai argues that affective responses to narrative discourses cannot be reduced to the representation of feeling in the text, such as those experienced by the characters. They are also influenced by narrative tone, that is, the text's "affective bearing, orientation, or 'set toward' its audience and world" (Ngai 43). As such, readers are influenced by an apperception of the relation between the discourses in the text and larger ideological economies. From this point of view, the way in which *Sweet* and *Nothing Can Keep Us Together* position the implied reader to regard their protagonists' sexualities is calibrated by the resonances and dissonances with the public discourses of desire and disgust.

To the extent that the implied girl reader is interpolated into the discourse of desire and accepts the narrative values about sexuality in Gossip Girl, she is positioned—although not compelled—as the subject of discourses of "chic" or "classy" sexuality and the post-feminist sense of entitlement to sexual citizenship that Attwood and Toffoletti identify in texts for women and girls. The reader who brings an awareness of the "emergent" and "residual" discourses (Williams) about underclass girls and women discussed at the beginning of this chapter to their reading of *Sweet* need not subscribe to them to be aware that Sugar's performance of her sexuality is at odds with the aesthetic and consumer values encoded in the new sexual contract. The novel's comic caricature of shameless girl sexual vulgarity, its protagonist's failure to understand the impression she creates, positions the knowing reader as superior, with Sugar as her inferior. Yet in invoking public discourses of disgust for the purpose of othering Sugar, Burchill's narrative simultaneously uses it as an aesthetic of subversion. By reproducing the consumer-class taste distinctions that code and control underclass girl sexuality, *Sweet* also evokes a further affective response: shame. In so doing, the novel shifts the focus from the protagonist as other to the implied reader as "self" to reveal the "shameful" basis upon which a sense of class and moral superiority depends.

This shift in reader subject positioning occurs when Sugar sees the photographs of the Council Couture Collection. She discovers that her Princess dress is not "the way it had been described to [her]." PRAM-FACE PRICKTEASE was to have been made "in lush red velvet—with matching muff! But now it was in a horrible check—even worse than Burberry!—and as for the muff . . . well, you can guess what that was made to resemble" (Burchill, *Sweet* 65). On one level, the disjunction between the imagined and actual garments alludes to chavs' reputed misrecognition of the vulgar as stylish and the slutty as sophisticated. However, Sugar had never envisioned them according to a chav aesthetic, and she does not regard the clothes in the collection as stylish. She can see perfectly well that the collection for which she was the muse is ugly. Sugar now understands the impression she creates on others, realizing that "where I saw a princess, the rest of the world just saw a pikey. And always would, because of everything about me, from my blood to my postcode" (66). There is no comic irony in this narrative moment, which arguably produces a moment of aesthetic concurrence between protagonist and implied reader, and of affective identification that subverts the subject position of superiority the narrative has hitherto invited the implied reader to occupy.

Although the repartee between Sugar, Agnewe, and Bagshawe during the creation of the collection may retrospectively indicate otherwise, Burchill's narrative does not overtly foreshadow the designers' duplicity. As such, it is discovered simultaneously by protagonist and implied reader, with the first-person narrative providing direct access to the hurt and betrayal Sugar feels. She had come to believe that the fashion designers were her friends and she trusted them. Aware that the toiles used to produce the outline of the garment were never an indication of the final product, the unfinished garments seem "to sum up for some dumb freaking reason every dumb freaking thing I'd hoped for, and I suddenly saw how I'd been SO fooled by these bastards into believing I could be something I wasn't, when all I'd ever be was a chav" (66). Weeping with humiliation ("Yeah, I know—I never cried" [66]) she reflects, "I'd been so much stronger before I knew what irony was. Maybe you're just better off not knowing certain things" (67).

To the extent that the predominant narrative technique in *Sweet* is comic irony, Sugar has discovered what the knowing reader already knows, producing a moment of concurrence and identification between the implied reader and protagonist. It exposes the manner in which negative affects like disgust "*block* sympathetic identification" in order to mobilize morality—and in the contemporary, commodity aesthetics—as an ideology of exclusion (Ngai 340; italics in original). According to Bourdieu, "[t]aste classifies, and it classifies the classifier" (6). Sugar's taste classifies her as vulgar, but this episode in *Sweet* classifies the basis upon which she is judged by others as shameful.

Texts, Culture, and the Ideoaffective Regulation of Desire and Disgust

In a chapter called "The Affective Fallacy," written in 1946, literary critics W. K. Wimsatt and Monroe Beardsley argue that criticism informed by an emotional response to the text lacks rigour and objectivity. The problem is that emotion "has a well known capacity to fortify opinion, to inflame cognition, and to grow upon itself in surprising proportions to grains of reason" (26). In fact, emotion's capacity to do so is precisely why affect is so pertinent to the aesthetics at work in the representations of girl desire in *Sweet* and *Nothing Can Keep Us Together*. If Lawrence Grossberg is correct, affect also underpins the ideological and disciplinary power of the public discourses of desire and disgust. For while some theorize affect to be a visceral, preconscious, and pre-personal response (see, for instance, Massumi), it nevertheless has social force. Grossberg argues that affect is the missing term in an adequate understanding of ideology, for it offers the possibility of a "psychology of belief" which would explain how and why ideologies are sometimes, and only sometimes, effective, and always to varying degrees. It is the affective investment in particular ideological sites (which may be libidinal or nonlibidinal) that explains the power of the articulation which bonds particular representations and realities. It is the affective investment which enables ideological relations to be internalized and, consequently, naturalized. (82–83)

With regard to girl sexuality, the bonding of class, commodity aesthetics, and sexuality creates the affects of desire and disgust to re-naturalize hierarchies of sexual entitlement and disenfranchisement within the commercial sphere. It is the affective aspect of the commodity aesthetic that is pivotal in the class coding of girl desire and in differentiating disgusting bodies from desirable bodies.

The increased media visibility of the sexually excessive lower-class girl functions to regulate girl sexuality by offending the new forms of consumerism that uphold class distinctions. Consumer goods and lifestyle aesthetics, I have argued, distinguish successful and failed sexual citizens, and thereby underpin the affective economies and moral geographies that regulate which girls can do what. Girl sexual respectability is less a matter of avoiding sex than image management, less a matter of strict moral positions (for example, purity discourses in some parts of the United States) than an affective positioning based on consumption patterns that are used to determine the object of disgust and desire. Commodities, then, are not simply class-coded, but morally loaded and regulatory in their effect. They are critical to the power of contemporary discourses of desire and disgust.

Note

1   According to Hayward and Yar, "most lexicographers agree that 'chav' owes its origins to the Romany dialect word for small child ('chavo' or 'chavi')." However,

> several popular and wholly inaccurate acronymic etymologies of the word "chav" (and increasingly "chavette") have since taken hold within the public imagination, including, "[C]ouncil [h]oused [a]nd [v]iolent," "[C]ouncil [h]ouse [v]ermin" . . . fabrications [that] serve to firmly realign the word "chav" with stereotypical notions of lower-class, disaffected urban youth. (16)

Works Cited

Attwood, Feona. "Sexed up: Theorizing the Sexualization of Culture." *Sexualities* 9.1 (2006): 77–94. Print.

Bernstein, Susan David, and Elsie Browning Michie. *Victorian Vulgarity: Taste in Verbal and Visual Culture.* Farnham: Ashgate, 2009. Print.

Bourdieu, Pierre. *Distinction: A Social Critique of the Judgement of Taste.* Trans. Richard Nice. Cambridge: Harvard UP, 2002. Print.

Bullen, Elizabeth. "Inside Story: Product Placement and Adolescent Consumer Identity in Young Adult Fiction." *Media, Culture and Society* 31.3 (2009): 497–507. Print.

Bullen, Elizabeth, Kim Toffoletti, and Elizabeth Parsons. "Doing What Your Big Sister Does: Sex, Postfeminism and the YA Chick Lit Series." *Gender and Education* 23.4 (2011): 1–15. Print.

Burchill, Julie. *Sugar Rush.* London: Young Picador, 2004. Print.

———. *Sweet.* London: Young Picador, 2007. Print.

Curtis, Debra. "Commodities and Sexual Subjectivities: A Look at Capitalism and Its Desires." *Cultural Anthropology* 19.1 (2004): 95–121. Print.

Davidson, Gina. "Sites to Check Out if You Chav What It Takes." *Edinburgh Evening News* 4 Feb. 2004: 14. Print.

Fine, Michelle. "Sexuality, Schooling, and Adolescent Females: The Missing Discourse of Desire." *Harvard Educational Review* 58.1 (1988): 29–51. Print.

Gill, Rosalind. "Postfeminist Media Culture: Elements of a Sensibility." *European Journal of Cultural Studies* 10.2 (2007): 147–66. Print.

Grossberg, Lawrence. *We Gotta Get Out of This Place: Popular Conservatism and Postmodern Culture.* New York: Routledge, 1992. Print.

Hall, Stuart. *Representation: Cultural Representations and Signifying Practices.* London: Sage Publications and Open U, 1997. Print.

Harman, Graham. *Guerilla Metaphysics: Phenomenology and the Carpentry of Things.* Chicago: Open Court, 2005. Print.

Harris, Anita. "VII. Discourses of Desire as Governmentality: Young Women, Sexuality and the Significance of Safe Spaces." *Feminism & Psychology* 15.1 (2005): 39–43. Print.

Haug, Wolfgang Fritz. *Critique of Commodity Aesthetics: Appearance, Sexuality and Advertising in Capitalist Society.* Trans. Robert Bock. Minneapolis: U of Minnesota P, 1986. Print.

Hayward, Keith, and Majid Yar. "The 'Chav' Phenomenon: Consumption, Media and the Construction of a New Underclass." *Crime, Media, Culture* 2.1 (April 2006): 9–28. Print.

Johnson, Naomi. "Consuming Desires: Consumption, Romance, and Sexuality in Best-selling Teen Romance Novels." *Women's Studies in Communication* 33.1 (2010): 54–73. Print.

Kipnis, Laura. *Bound and Gagged: Pornography and the Politics of Fantasy in America*. New York: Grove, 1996. Print.

Lawler, Stephanie. "Disgusted Subjects: The Making of Middle-class Identities." *Sociological Review* 53.2 (Aug. 2005): 429–46. Print.

Massumi, Brian. *Parables for the Virtual: Movement, Affect, Sensation*. Durham: Duke UP, 2002. Print.

McRobbie, Angela. *The Aftermath of Feminism: Gender, Culture and Social Change*. London: Sage, 2009. Print.

———. "Good Girls, Bad Girls: Female Success and the New Meritocracy." *British Cultural Studies: Geography, Nationality, and Identity*. Ed. David Morley and Kevin Robins. Oxford: Oxford UP, 2001. 361–72. Print.

Miller, William. *The Anatomy of Disgust*. Cambridge: Harvard UP, 1997. Print.

Ngai, Sianne. *Ugly Feelings*. Cambridge: Harvard UP, 2005. Print.

Papayanis, Marilyn Adler. "Sex and the Revanchist City: Zoning Out Pornography in New York." *Environment and Planning D: Society and Space* 18.3 (2000): 341–53. Print.

Ruskin, John. "Of Vulgarity." *The Complete Works of John Ruskin*. Vol. 6. New York: Thomas Y. Crowell & Co., 1990. 261–76. Print.

Skeggs, Beverley. *Formations of Class and Gender: Becoming Respectable*. London: Sage, 1977. Print.

———. "The Making of Class and Gender Through Visualizing Moral Subject Formation." *Sociology* 39.5 (2005): 965–82. Print.

Thrift, Nigel. "The Material Practices of Glamour." *Journal of Cultural Economy* 1.1 (2008): 9–23. Print.

Toffoletti, Kim. "Gossip Girls in a Transmedia World: The Sexual and Technological Anxieties of Integral Reality." *Papers: Explorations in Children's Literature* 18.2 (2008): 71–77. Print.

Tyler, Imogen. "'Chav, Mum, Chav, Scum': Class Disgust in Contemporary Britain." *Feminist Media Studies* 8.1 (2008): 17–34. Print.

von Ziegesar, Cecily. *Gossip Girl: A Novel*. New York: Little, Brown and Company, 2002. Print.

———. *Nobody Does It Better*. New York: Little, Brown and Company, 2005. Print.

———. *Nothing Can Keep Us Together*. New York: Little, Brown and Company, 2005. Print.

Walkerdine, Valerie, Helen Lucey, and June Melody. *Growing Up Girl: Psychosocial Explorations of Class and Gender.* Basingstoke: Palgrave, 2001. Print.

Williams, Raymond. *Marxism and Literature.* London: Oxford UP, 1977. Print.

Wimsatt, W. K., and Monroe Beardsley. "The Affective Fallacy." *The Verbal Icon: Studies in the Meaning of Poetry.* W. K. Wimsatt. Lexington: U of Kentucky P, 1954. 21–40. Print.

CHAPTER 4

Still Centre Stage?

Reframing Girls' Culture in
New Generation Fictions of Performance

Pamela Knights

"Isn't the classical dancing ballet slipper the
ultimate heel? The heel which makes dancers closer
than any other women to the sky, closer to heaven."
—Christian Louboutin[1]

Photographs of Christian Louboutin's designer ballet slippers—pink, bejewelled, and with eight-inch stiletto heels—were widely published at the end of June 2011. The image of luxury and vertiginous aspiration seems a fitting climax for a year when ballet as commodity soared to a fashion peak.[2] Like the year's other high-profile ballet-related product, director Darren Aronofsky's award-winning film *Black Swan* (2010), Louboutin's heels give visible form to an extreme form of gender-inflected longing. Film and slippers dramatize the contradictions played out over, and within, the female body: in forcing one's feet into impossibly beautiful shoes, and in the telos of achieving and performing impossibly perfect forms of femininity, both products present a story of extreme feminine desire. For Peter Bradshaw, such a story could not be further removed from girls' literature: "This is not based on anything by Noel Streatfeild." It is possible, however, to view these artifacts as part of a continuum within the long tradition of the ballet genre, as written in fictions for children by Streatfeild and her numerous successors, and which are being played out again and for ever-younger readers in a fresh generation of texts today.

My focus in this chapter is on a selection of ballet novels—fictional narratives featuring, and targeted at, young girls (from pre-readers up) who hope to rise heavenwards in ballet shoes, to excel in the tradition of Western classical dance. Although this might seem a narrow sphere, it nevertheless offers one mode of entry into a broader topic. In an insightful survey, Juliette Peers makes clear the extent to which ballet, mediated and commodified through multiple agencies, has infused and shaped young girls' spaces, tastes, activities, ambitions, and desires.[3] As Peers points out, ballet texts (books, alongside film and opera) represent a major force in that process (80). My own interests lie in the detailed history of these narratives, especially in fiction, and in the significance of the repetitions and reconfigurations that emerge as the ballet genre evolves. While I make occasional reference to non-fiction, stage, film, and electronic media associated with these narratives, to keep discussion within the limits of a single chapter, I generally confine my attention here to print publications from England and the United States.[4] Narratives from these two locations have been influential in establishing the tradition from the 1930s on and are still vigorous in disseminating the ballet novel today. Within a broader literary taxonomy, these narratives form part of a sub-category of the *Künstlerroman*, related to artist and performance stories, particularly acting and music, but also sports, such as skating or gymnastics.[5] Exceptionally long-historied and resilient, such stories constitute the most distinctive group of narratives of artistic aspiration; as a persistent and significant presence within Western girls' cultures, they have developed into a genre in their own right, and warrant close attention.[6] In this chapter, I indicate some of the configurations typical of this genre and suggest some continuing threads in recent years.[7] My main inquiry is into the forms of agency—in both individual and wider, public terms—that these fictions have seemed to hold out to readers at different historical moments, and, in particular, into the kind of energies being presented to girls today.

Through all its reincarnations, over some eighty years, the genre of the ballet story has built in what Jessica Ringrose and Valerie Walkerdine sum up as a key question for researchers in girlhood: "How *are* assertiveness and femininity to be reconciled and navigated?" (8). In their 2008 study, the authors focus on anxieties over perceived shifts since the 1980s across a binary axis: from worries about girls' vulnerability, self-effacement, and passivity—a pathology of over-feminization—to troubled debates, in the twenty-first century, over girls' success, aggression, meanness, willpower, and drive—qualities traditionally marked as masculine. Where and how does the ballet novel play out in such discussions? To be a dancer "closer than any other women to the sky, closer to heaven" entangles two incompatible forms of desire: a competitive, even ruthless, individualism, and a longing for a distilled self-erasure, to be the vessel for others' dreams. The teleology of the ballet plot, from first steps to prima ballerina, embeds both. Read in one light, the text privileges the single-minded drive of the heroine: to take centre stage, *en pointe*, all eyes on her solo. At the same time, this plot—centred on the girl's body, as expression and display, as perfect artwork and as artifact—foregrounds a hyper-refined model of femininity as ethereal, beautiful, silent, and sublime. With such co-existing extremes, ballet fictions offer girlhood studies a fascinating set of navigational coordinates. Taking as an underlying frame of reference Etienne Balibar and Pierre Macherey's suggestion that literary formations seek "the imaginary solution of ideological contradictions" (285), I suggest that we see in the dialectic of ballet narrative strategies a continuing negotiation between these constantly shifting binaries. Ballet narratives, I argue, are a significant symbolic holding space for managing the conflicts.[8]

Assertiveness and femininity: playing between and across these elements, ballet books have tended to polarize critics. In 1976, Patricia Craig and Mary Cadogan influentially dismissed these narratives as too slight to merit discussion—as impoverished formula fiction, feeding girls' narcissistic dreams of facile success (300). Such criticisms have also been aired from early on in self-referential scenes in which girls devour ballet books (and now DVDs) within ballet texts themselves. Often simultaneously, such scenes self-reflexively propose their own advanced textual realism by disparaging as simplistic the "imaginary solution[s]" of putative earlier fictions. In 1957, for example, in Jean Estoril's *Ballet for Drina*, a character complains: "They're always about little girls who want be ballerinas and who manage it with no effort at all" (24).[9] Undeterred, Drina, the addressee here, becomes rapt with the vision—"*Prima ballerina assoluta!* Of all the titles in the world that seemed to her most satisfying" (183)—and, albeit with token delays, she rises through the eleven books of her series to achieve beauty, the *assoluta* title, and marriage to a Manhattan businessman, all by age eighteen. Echoing the complaint fifty years later is Beatrice Masini's twelve-year-old Italian Zoe. She, too, has "quite a large collection of books about dance" (2),[10] including the *Billy Elliot* book and film, a deluxe edition of Andersen's *The Red Shoes*, *Angelina Ballerina*, and some "rather silly stories about girls who had their minds set on just one thing: becoming a prima ballerina—the best ballerina of all. This was something the Ballet Academy discouraged," for at the school and, by implication, in the series itself, "it was more important to concentrate on being the best ballerina you could be" (2).

Other readers outside the texts have been more positive. Angela McRobbie's 1991 groundbreaking feminist reading, *Feminism and Youth Culture*, reframed the genre as powerfully girl-centred: for her, in a cultural climate still stirred by second-wave feminism, these narratives presented readers with strong images of ambition and professional achievement. Others, like Nancy Huse and Marissa K. Lingen, have agreed. Fan sites, tributes in reader reviews on Amazon, and affectionate adult memoirs are all witness to the way even the oldest series still command fierce reader attachment—often from "adult girls"—as a centre for shared female experience. New writers, too, have cited them as influences. Famously mega-assertive-girl Julie Burchill (whom Elizabeth Bullen discusses in her chapter in this volume) names Lorna Hill's Sadler's Wells series, one of the founding UK series of the 1950s to 1960s, in her top ten reads for teens: "If only I hadn't grown to be 5'10 and a size 16, I would have now become the world's greatest prima ballerina. These books were my pubescent crack cocaine" ("Julie Burchill's Top 10").[11] UK former children's laureate Jacqueline Wilson also claims the inspiration of ballet stories, from *Ballet Shoes*, Noel Streatfeild's classic of 1936, to those in the *Girl* comics of the 1950s and 1960s. Wilson, herself named in February 2010 as the most borrowed author from UK libraries over the past decade (Adams), pays tribute to Streatfeild, in particular, for teaching her to write. She recalls how she loved *Ballet Shoes*, and learned from it the "realistic little details of girl life" (Wilson 227).

For positively marked assertiveness, *Ballet Shoes*, a bestseller published at the height of 1930s "Balletomania,"[12] set the benchmark early. Its force might be epitomized in a single image (see fig. 4.1), capturing a key transitional moment, a passage into maturity. The image is of the working licence for the main character of *Ballet Shoes*, Pauline Fossil, which authorizes her, at the age of twelve, to work in a theatre. Presented as a double-page illustration in the text, it has a quasi-materiality in that it forces the reader to break the narrative flow in order to turn the book sideways: in doing so, these pages, for that moment, become the licence—putting authority,

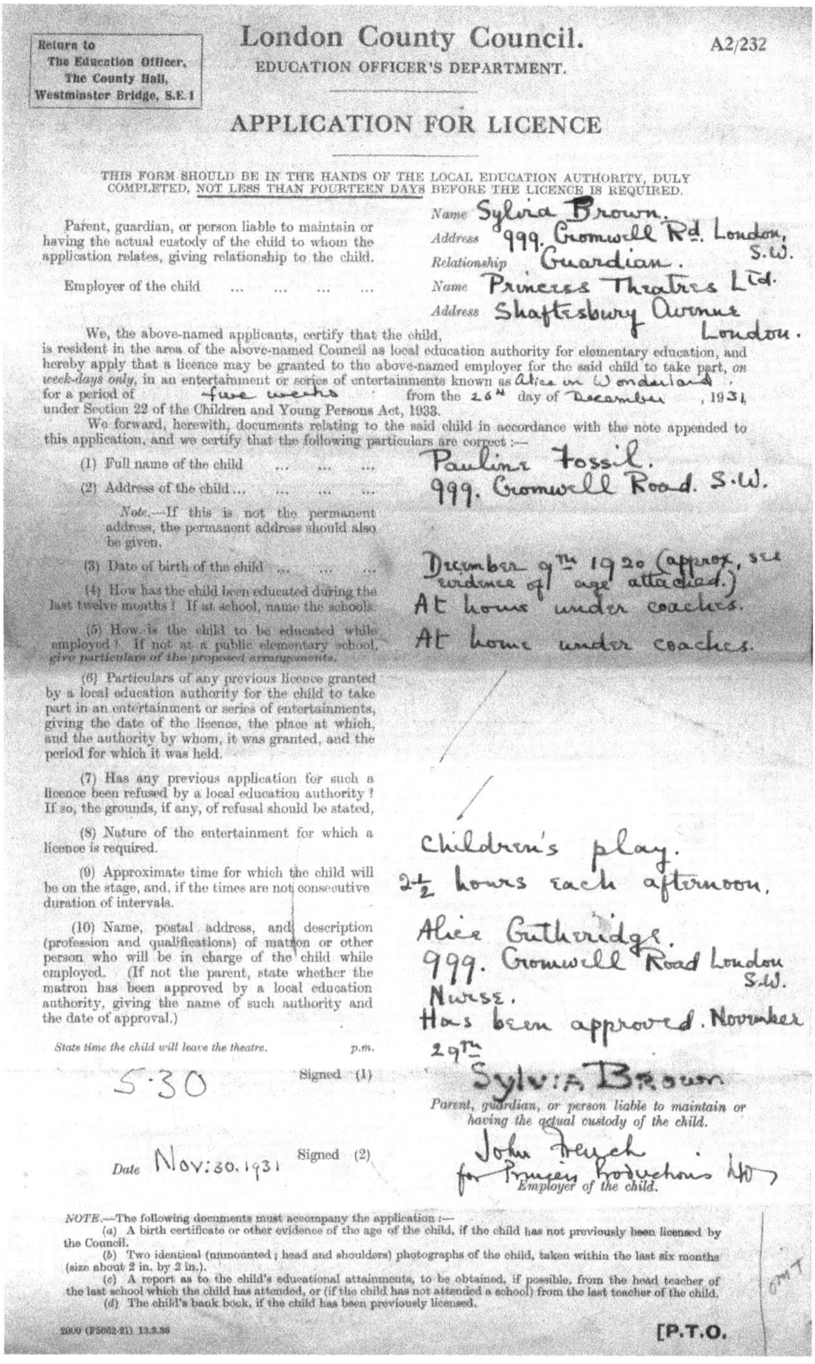

Return to
The Education Officer,
The County Hall,
Westminster Bridge, S.E.1

London County Council.

A2/232

EDUCATION OFFICER'S DEPARTMENT.

APPLICATION FOR LICENCE

THIS FORM SHOULD BE IN THE HANDS OF THE LOCAL EDUCATION AUTHORITY, DULY COMPLETED, NOT LESS THAN FOURTEEN DAYS BEFORE THE LICENCE IS REQUIRED.

Parent, guardian, or person liable to maintain or having the actual custody of the child to whom the application relates, giving relationship to the child.
Name Sylvia Brown.
Address 999. Cromwell Rd. London, S.W.
Relationship Guardian.

Employer of the child ... ...
Name Princess Theatres Ltd.
Address Shaftesbury Avenue London.

We, the above-named applicants, certify that the child, is resident in the area of the above-named Council as local education authority for elementary education, and hereby apply that a licence may be granted to the above-named employer for the said child to take part, on *week-days only*, in an entertainment or series of entertainments known as Alice in Wonderland for a period of five weeks from the 26th day of December, 1931, under Section 22 of the Children and Young Persons Act, 1933.

We forward, herewith, documents relating to the said child in accordance with the note appended to this application, and we certify that the following particulars are correct:—

(1) Full name of the child ... ... Pauline Fossil.

(2) Address of the child ... ... 999. Cromwell Road. S.W.

Note.—If this is not the permanent address, the permanent address should also be given.

(3) Date of birth of the child ... ... December 9th 1920 (approx, see evidence of age attached.)

(4) How has the child been educated during the last twelve months? If at school, name the schools. At home under coaches.

(5) How is the child to be educated while employed? If not at a public elementary school, *give particulars of the proposed arrangements.* At home under coaches.

(6) Particulars of any previous licence granted by a local education authority for the child to take part in an entertainment or series of entertainments, giving the date of the licence, the place at which, and the authority by whom, it was granted, and the period for which it was held. /

(7) Has any previous application for such a licence been refused by a local education authority? If so, the grounds, if any, of refusal should be stated. /

(8) Nature of the entertainment for which a licence is required. Children's play.

(9) Approximate time for which the child will be on the stage, and, if the times are not consecutive duration of intervals. 2½ hours each afternoon.

(10) Name, postal address, and description (profession and qualifications) of matron or other person who will be in charge of the child while employed. (If not the parent, state whether the matron has been approved by a local education authority, giving the name of such authority and the date of approval.) Alice Guthridge. 999. Cromwell Road London S.W. Nurse. Has been approved. November 29th

State time the child will leave the theatre. 5·30 *p.m.*

Signed (1) Sylvia Brown
Parent, guardian, or person liable to maintain or having the actual custody of the child.

Date Nov: 30. 1931

Signed (2) John French for Princess Productions Ltd
Employer of the child.

NOTE.—The following documents must accompany the application:—
(*a*) A birth certificate or other evidence of the age of the child, if the child has not previously been licensed by the Council.
(*b*) Two identical (unmounted; head and shoulders) photographs of the child, taken within the last six months (size about 2 in. by 2 in.).
(*c*) A report as to the child's educational attainments, to be obtained, if possible, from the head teacher of the last school which the child has attended, or (if the child has not attended a school) from the last teacher of the child.
(*d*) The child's bank book, if the child has been previously licensed.

2000 (F5662-21) 13.3.36

[P.T.O.

FIGURE 4.1 • Manuscript illustration from the Ruth Gervis papers at Seven Stories: The Centre for Children's Books Archives in Newcastle-upon-Tyne (RG/01/04a "Ballet Shoes" n.d. [c. 1936].). Reproduced by permission of Seven Stories.

as it were, right into the reader's hands. The image frames Pauline not as a powerless minor or as a conflicted, inward-turned adolescent, but as a responsible wage-earning citizen, an apprentice professional artist. The image also has a tangible provenance: it is a facsimile of an actual document that inserts Pauline's fictional details into an official permit of the 1930s, and which has survived and is held now in the Seven Stories archive in Newcastle among the original illustrations for *Ballet Shoes*, drawn by Ruth Gervis, Streatfeild's sister. The document is reproduced exactly in the fictional text, with only a tiny correction—tweaking "1931" to "1932," to make Pauline twelve at the date of signing. The blurring of material and textual artifacts suggests not only professional care on the author's part, but also an intensely imagined backstory as a piece of method acting. Such an authorial performance produces a kind of claim to accuracy and an air of reality that inducts both characters and readers into the materiality of the stage, the years of work ahead, the progress of the girls as, penny by penny, skill by skill, they take themselves from dependent orphans to economically and artistically self-supporting subjects.

The ethics of sisterly regard, foregrounded throughout *Ballet Shoes*, serve to deflect self-interested individualism into a more acceptable value system, in an imaginary solution that dissolves contradiction into loyalty to family. While the narrative represents talent as a gift, the text (and its sequels) at the same time emphasizes that supremacy results from discipline. The Fossil sisters are interested in technique, and unlike most of the children at the Academy, "did not really" believe "that holding your thumbs brought luck" (123). Streatfeild presents in dancer Posy her most steely construction of egotistical ambition, one that comes close to destabilizing family unity; but even Posy recognizes the force of work. The sisters, as a group, learn self-reliance, concentration, and control; and the rewards are immeasurable.[13] As Nancy Huse comments, for large numbers of Streatfeild's readers, the tedium of practice was the stamp of authenticity (45).

The Fossil sisters' story channels individual dreams, talents, and discipline into serious roles on an international stage. While Petrova Fossil flies closer to heaven in a different sphere as a pilot, as actor and as dancer, Pauline and Posy (also glimpsed in later books) rise in ways that also distill a hyper-feminine identity into authority and command. *Ballet Shoes* itself remains prominent: it is frequently reprinted, translated, and recorded,[14] and was accorded the prime schedule time for BBC UK television family viewing at Christmas 2007.[15] Streatfeild's model of toughness and tenacity seems surprisingly absent, however, when we ask what narrative paradigms readers might be encountering in ballet fictions today. The semiotics of many modern bookshops consign ballet to a space worlds away from Pauline's licence and, on the surface, at least, present no hint of any contemporary agitation about "mean girl" pathologies (whether admired or anathematized). Over the last decade, stores have become less likely to shelve ballet stories in rows of miscellaneous, alphabetized, general fiction, or, for non-fiction titles, somewhere between "classic stories" and career manuals. With intensifying strategies of brand consciousness, they often conspicuously assign a specialist area to titles with predominantly pink and lilac packaging, grouping ballet stories with stories about fairies and princesses (sometimes, between the covers, all three). There, ballet inhabits a single section, inside a soft pink line. Fine-tuned targeting of different age groups aims to draw girls into the ballet dream from their early years. In 2009, for example, Egmont Publishers—with the mission statement, "[w]e bring stories to life"—offered to readers ages three and up Julie Clough and Sheryl Bone's *Pretty and Pink: Colouring Time* ("with four fun crayons"). With a choice of blue, green, pink, or (another) pink crayons embedded in a plastic case in the cover, the text invites a girl to use her "favourite crayons" to colour fairies, mermaids, and ballerinas: "This ballerina loves wearing pink!" the reader is told, and is to be coloured "Carefully" (in other words, between the lines). More liberally, Fiona Watt's *How to Draw Princesses and Ballerinas* (2005), suggests: "Mix some watery pink paint and brush it all over the ballerina" (24).[16]

The narrative models of these texts, though purportedly interactive, reinforce monologic versions of girls' creative possibilities. No alternative options are voiced; all routes lead to "Pretty and Pink." More developed literary fictions for this age group, however, exhibit more anxieties over girlhood. These worries appear as "signs of . . . contradictions," in Balibar and Macherey's terms, "which appear as unevenly resolved conflicts in the text" (283). We might look, for example, at the exploits of Ballet Kitty in the picture books of Bernette Ford, an inspirational editor and activist for interracial publications. The first of these, *Ballet Kitty* (2007), a basic narrative of ballet slippers lost and found, introduces "little ballerinas everywhere" (as its blurb proclaims) to its ditzy heroine, Kitty. Readers encounter her caught in between pink candy stripes on the cover and the framing endpapers, reminiscent of a twenty-first-century Milly-Molly-Mandy (1928),[17] or a wallpaper rosebud pattern, or a small ballerina trapped at a giant barre. In the early stages of the narrative, pictures and words infuse Kitty with some energy. In contrast with the stiffly frozen ballerina who features on Kitty's musical box, she is drawn, visually and verbally, in kinaesthesic terms, leaping free on a clear white space: "Kitty jumped out of bed and did a little pirouette," "leaped across her room," "kicked off her trainers" (n. pag.).[18] But such moments never quite destabilize the quintessential pinkness that, stated declaratively by an unseen narrative voice at the story's opening, constructs and composes Kitty for the reader:

> Kitty woke up happy!
> Her ears were pink. Her nose was pink.
> Even her little toes were pink.
> Kitty loved ballet and she loved pink.

The page concludes, in the text's single simile: "And today she was feeling *as pretty as a ballerina*—from her head to her toes!" (n. pag.; emphasis added).

Reinforcing this, Kitty is drawn in outline, as if with a charcoal-grey wax crayon, and washed in with the soft pink that characterizes the world of the illustrations. Visual semiotics of comfort underpin the assertions of feminine security, with notes of both an infantile and a more markedly sophisticated girly register picked up in more vibrant shades of pink. In the vignette above the paragraph, Kitty, nestling on an elegantly tasselled cushion, peeks out of a cozy pastel cover; below, she stretches in a modish Chinese-style pyjama suit; in the whole-page facing plate, she nuzzles a pale pink sash, next to a teenage vanity case (complete with mirror and hairbrush). But dressing to perform as a ballerina, Kitty falls at the first hurdle: "'MUMMY!' wailed Kitty. 'I can't find my ballet slippers'" (n. pag.). The text gives her direct speech for the first time, only in this distressed dependency. Her slippers lost, her identity collapses: "Now Kitty was grumpy. Her ears were pale. Her nose was pale. She did not feel happy! She did not feel pretty!" (n. pag.). On the final pages, in a consoling solution, both Kitty's slippers and the colour pink return. The slippers were under the table: "Just where she had left them the night before!" (n. pag.). The narrative presents some alternative signs of creative autonomy: that Kitty recomposes herself through friendship, play, and a picnic, and through her own artistry and imagination (the pictures show her paintbrushes and closed book, possibly a journal). But the slippers present a more passive model of feminine happiness: that these are the reward for being a good kitty, and put the pink back in her cheeks.

For the next tier of readers there is a range of new series, some, in the tradition of Streatfeild, by single authors, and others mass-produced by teams of writers. Examples of the former include, for five- to eight-year olds, Ann Bryant's Ballerina Dreams (from 2004),[19] and for ages seven to ten, Alexandra Moss's Royal Ballet School Diaries (from 2005). It is in the mass-produced series that craft and individuality—of characters and of author, as projected by Streatfeild's licence—seem particularly absent. A notable example, marketed for five years and upwards, is the multitudinous, and still growing, Rainbow Magic sequence, by the corporate "Daisy Meadows."[20] As Karen Pakula summarizes its launch, between 2003 and 2006, the series of "42 slim, sparkly fantasies, amount[ed] to sales of more than 1.5 million in Australia and more than 6 million in Britain." When the question of their authorship was raised in 2006, the children's book editor of the *Sydney Morning Herald*, Meg Sorensen, deplored the pseudonym as a cheat to young girls: "There's something holy about a book. . . . I think authors should be honest with us" (qtd. in Pakula). The imprimatur of a genuine superstar ballerina, Darcey Bussell, gives a glow of authenticity to another bestselling series: The Magic Ballerina books, launched by HarperCollins in October 2008, the year following Bussell's retirement from the Royal Ballet. Announcing the series, *The Bookseller* cites Ann-Janine Murtagh, HarperCollins's children's literature specialist who oversaw the deal, in terms that again fuse discourses of commodity and aesthetics. The publisher declares ambitions "to build ballet star Darcey Bussell as a long-term brand in children's fiction . . . 'across different media and long-term,'" and asserts the value of the series: "The world of ballet is wondrous, and Darcey has such integrity and has danced all the major roles" (Murtagh qtd. in Richardson). Interviews and publicity credit Bussell with the concept, but again background the authorship by others; the books employ a range of writers, Ann Bryant among them; they are illustrated now by Dynamo Ltd., a design consortium,[21] and have been vigorously marketed by HIT Entertainment, with special display carousels, boxed sets, and a plethora of associated artifacts. Inviting readers to "[j]oin the Magical Dance Academy," the Magic Ballerina website offers an array of cross-media hooks: readers' clubs, newsletters, downloads, games, and opportunities to "dress" the characters in tutus online ("Fun and Games"). While all these fictions explicitly model and acknowledge girls' creativity, hard work, and free choice, how far they covertly impose limits is open to question. I return to this group of fictions later in the chapter.

With my two sets of examples—*Ballet Shoes*, and the pink-wrapped titles, some seventy years apart—I have represented the extremes of narrative forces that perhaps cannot be so easily differentiated. Passive pink perfection and agentic power are not simple alternatives: the Fossils, Kitty, and girls in ballet stories in between generally want both. Although, as with Kitty's distress, the cost might be washed over, these fictions have always tapped into debates that have now become urgent. As Balibar and Macherey emphasize, the "implacable ideological contradictions" (284) inscribed within literary texts act out material and historical conditions. Here, in ballet fictions, they emanate from the kind of pressures on girls that Ringrose and Walkerdine highlight as "the drive for perfection, for supergirlhood," with the managing "of impossible contradiction" and anxieties "over not being good enough," and the consequence that "most girls are likely to experience anything less than perfection as failure—their failure, their pathology" (10). Angela McRobbie also reflects on this pathology as passing into female self-definition as a form of "illegible rage" (*The Aftermath* 97). Drawing on Judith Butler and Shelley Budgeon, among a range of cultural analysts, McRobbie suggests that actual self-punishing illnesses (along a broad spectrum of intensity) have now become "normal, part and parcel of being a woman" (97). In relation to the life of a dancer, with the physical and emotional strains, and constant self-criticism, glimpsed even in the most anodyne fictions, this remark holds particular force.

Ballet fiction leads its readers, implied and actual, into and through questions about self-definition: about how a girl might become Superkitty, Supergirl, or *Prima Ballerina Assoluta*—the cleverest, hardest-working, most ruthlessly focused and, at the same time, the most fragile, graceful, and beautiful. As Balibar and Macherey argue of literary works in general, these texts make such contradictions visible in their own conjunction of "disparate and diffuse" (284) elements: the repressed anxieties of their culture (or even symptoms of McRobbie's "illegible rage") can be read in the gaps, the awkwardnesses, the sutures of plot. So, in these narratives, even the most self-effacing ambition emerges conspicuously at the points of fracture: the auditions, the exams, the casting decisions, the promotions. Many splinter off unacceptably aggressive female desire into the mean girl, figured as rival; but it is through the central characters, with whom empathy is invited, that these series stake their appeal. It is through these characters, and through the model of self-identification they hold out to their readers, that these texts conduct the movement toward smoothing over contradictions and managing resolutions. Such efforts are the prime movers of literary productions, as the story works itself toward its "imaginary reconciliation of irreconcilable terms": in the process, "it finds a language of compromise which presents the conciliation as 'natural' and so both necessary and inevitable" (Balibar and Macherey 285).

In this light, one continuing and significant strategy to legitimize girls' ambition is to naturalize it as part of a female lineage, demonstrating bonds between generations of girls and women. In Ann Bryant's *Rose's Big Decision*, part of the Ballerina Dreams series, Rose steps down from gymnastic triumph to pursue ballet, following her grandmother's road not taken. Female friendship is another connection; Bryant's series structures each novel as a first-person narrative by one of a group of three friends who are linked by a shared passion for their ballet class. Each girl relates her own story of a period of significant choice or crisis. In so doing, she also steps into the same special shoes, and follows in the footsteps of the many girls who came before her in themes of dancing legacies, talents or roles passed on from mothers to daughters, lessons from teachers to pupils, or inspiration from older to younger dancers, be they friends or sisters. In Streatfeild's *Ballet Shoes*, the sisters are awed by older pupils' names on schedules, and, gazing into rehearsal, cannot wait to become them: "They would peep through the glass on the doors of the rooms where the rehearsals were taking place, and stare at the children who were already twelve and old enough to earn money" (57).

The promise here is realized—and ritualized—in *Ballet Shoes* when Pauline's licence itself materializes five chapters later. In Jan Ormerod's picture book *Ballet Sisters: The Duckling and the Swan* (2007), it is enough for the little sister simply to hear a class as she waits outside the door: represented, for the first time in the book, in an exuberantly tripled image on a single page, "[s]he quacks, waddles, and flaps" (31). In these stories, most ducklings become swans. Their talents are shared with their target audience by scenes in the class, demonstration exercises spelled out in the main narrative, or paratexts that encourage readers to learn and to try, sometimes, as in Joan Elizabeth Goodman's *Ballet Bunnies* (2008), with cautionary warnings: "Turn-out positions have been modified for young bunnies to avoid injury" (n. pag.). The talents are passed on in signifiers of gifts between characters; shoes are particular favourites, but there are many other variants, such as the scarlet stockings, which inaugurate Charlotte Kandel's ongoing fantastic quest series of that title. At times, these gifts (along with pendants, charms, tiny tutus, or, as in the latest Magic Ballerina set, stickers) are also offered to readers.[22] While for publishers, stickers encourage reader adhesion, within the narrative sphere these stand as tokens, above all, for the renewal of the girls' story: the retelling of ballet narratives (of actual and fictitious dancers) and of the narratives of the most famous ballets perpetuates the line. Where novels are located in a special dance school (often linked with a company), especially in a series, they have something in common with the school story, tracing characters' development and engaging read-ers' investment in their success. Series invite readers to join their friends in this special circle, literalizing the gesture with "taster" extracts and "party invitations" at the back of the book, and get-to-know-you pages online.[23]

The cult of celebrity adds its force to these narrative channels, infusing and modelling energy. The repeated references to real-life ballet icons, from Margot Fonteyn to Darcey Bussell, inspire and legitimize girls' ambition within and beyond the text. In intertextual moves, girls who read ballet books themselves often imagine, or even grow up to see, their images fea-tured on posters, signs, and programs, or in biographies and film. Even at lesser heights of fame, the narrative climax often sees the girl, poised, triumphant, and celebrated, commanding the stage and the audience (whether at playschool show or Gala Theatre): an image repeated in endless iterations, over the decades.

Such lineages, as represented in these endings, seem to code assertive-ness in a way that dissolves unacceptable elements, figuring it as female destiny—the epitome, in short, of what seems "'natural' and so both neces-sary and inevitable" (Balibar and Macherey 284). Compounding this inevitability further, in one persistent strand of signification this destiny is embodied. As Jacqueline Wilson writes:

> *I* wanted to be a ballet dancer too. . . . I had read enough books about girls longing to be dancers to realize that I had ballet dancer's *feet*. My second toe is longer than my big toe, which means I could go up on my points more easily, and I have very high arches. I was sure this was a genuine sign that I could be a Belle of the Ballet. (225–26; emphasis in original)[24]

For Wilson, as for numerous girls within the narratives, the signs were in place, a central part of the overdetermined semiotic system of these texts. Reading her feet, Wilson (like Dorothy in Oz) sees the path ahead as beyond choice in a story already written on her body and inscribed within the very structures of desire. Similarly, in Beatrice Masini's fourth Ballet Academy book, *On Your Toes*, twelve-year-old Zoe reflects on her first pair of satin shoes: "They were real ballerina's shoes, the sort that you start dreaming about even before you realise you want a pair of your very own" (10). Even a picture book for very young readers can charge slippers with eroticized allure. Susan Hampshire, for example, opens Rosie's story with her joy at the gift from her mother for her first ballet lesson of "a pair of pale pink ballet shoes. They were the prettiest shoes that Rosie had ever seen" (n. pag.). In the illustration, Rosie falls back on a cushion, one arm flung behind her neck, a bright-coloured toy parrot at her side; she gazes, seemingly ecstatic, at the slipper—a pinkly shell-like female image—in her other hand, its empty pink box open on her lap over her crotch.[25]

In pre-1970s texts, before second-wave feminism brought questions of gender construction into the arena of public debate, this association of artistic aspiration and feminine essentialism might not seem so surprising. More problematic are the doubts raised by modern novels. Do they as often intensify as interrogate the links? In some ways, Masini's and other current preteen narratives take the opportunity to make contradictions more explicit, and to create narrative spaces where normative regulatory binaries can be opened to debate and acknowledged as sites of conflict. Alexandra Moss's *Boys or Ballet?* in the Royal Ballet School Diaries series offers a succinct summary in the title and cover image, with a photograph of a young girl and her boy partner locked in a formal pas de deux, but gazing ambiguously into each other's eyes. A background frame of pink slippers and an unfurling pink rosebud underline the conflicting poles of the dilemma. In other ways, the alignment reaffirms a sense of "naturalness," of exclusively female destinies: the girl's body is shaped for a vocation. In the vision of the ballet shoes a girl wants before she knows she wants them, such ambition is imprinted in the very unconscious, part of the bedrock of subjectivity. In narrative texts from instruction manuals to novels, the emphasis is that the pointe shoes will arrive, when girls are "ready," at around twelve, the age of puberty. At such a time, as Masini's Zoe reflects, "It felt as though all of the girls were going through a major change together" (10).

Whether or not biology is destiny, throughout the genre a further plot strand typifies the journey as adventure, a form of female heroic quest into the hazardous public arena of the dance. The ballet narrative typically opens with the young dancer at a liminal point (her first steps, early lessons, or first encounter with ballet), moving into a trajectory of discovery, dedication, growth, and control, as she works to conquer that dangerous space. The entrance is often figured as a literal cultural threshold—the door to the school, or theatre—or as a gateway to another world (see also Knights, "Dangerous Thresholds"). Always slightly estranged, it may be framed in the proscenium of a historic stage, described in the text, visualized in picture books, or glimpsed through the screens of modern technology (see fig. 4.2). Such scenes have a generic continuity: in Drina's epiphany in Estoril's 1957 narrative, it is the television itself that enhances the novelty; in Kemp and Ogilvie's 2010 reprise of the topos, a commonplace scene is itself defamiliarized by a pink-washed screen and the presence of the ballet-struck dog. In all such moments, again, the texts seem strangely ambiguous, offering mixed, contradictory signals, both celebrating and critiquing the space into which the narrative is encouraging girls: to enter a High Culture world, with its own rituals, moves, artifice, and language. The genre typically builds language lessons into scenes of class (usually through technical terms for movements, with their French pronunciation), and increasingly often includes a glossary to help instruct new readers.[26] Occasionally, a girl's first flickers of bewilderment intensify into questions that move into the foreground. Erika Tamar's young adult novel *Alphabet City Ballet* (1996), for example, uses the central character to explore more fully the problems of trying to keep faith with her diverse family cultures while entering the dance. With her Puerto Rican/Haitian background, Marisol feels estranged from dance talk: "'You understand all that?' she asks a classmate: 'Is French like Creole?'" (86).

Graceful, white-clad figures were dancing (on the television screen).

FIGURE 4.2 • Illustration from *Ballet for Drina*, by Jean Estoril, illustrated by Eve Guthrie and M. P. Steedman Davies. Copyright © 1957.

Once inside this culture, the girl becomes the instrument of a long tradition that is embodied in her arms, legs, hands, and every move, and reinforced in the repeated scenes of class, step sequences, and reiterated exercises. As Marisol realizes, "[i]t's only a curtsey . . . but there was a very particular way to do it. There was a very particular way to do everything in ballet" (88). Some seem to offer reassurance. For young readers of the picture book *The Ballet Class* (2003), Adèle Geras and Shelagh McNicholas construct the school as a special, but not a sacred, space. Here, at the start of her own series, Tutu Tilly goes to class in a community hall, enclosed and fenced, but part of the neighbourhood visible beyond its threshold, blurring the High Art boundary line. Even this, however, contains unsettling visual notes, in odd juxtapositions of old and new, sharp lines and safe curves, brick and concrete, giving an impression of forced hybridity, of a studio grafted on to a more domestic structure, or to an institution: a place of security, but also perhaps of limit.

Many of these celebratory texts seem similarly anxious. Rosie, for example, who glows over her slippers in her own colourful space (at home, on the sofa, with cushion and bright toy parrot) at the start of Hampshire's *Rosie's First Ballet Lesson*, is viewed in the frontispiece as a potential ballerina. Her stance, possibly positioned in a mirror (as if the reader were also gazing in as an invisible bystander) seems cramped, rendered in monochrome, bisected. She may be wary and on guard, or even defiant, but her hands seem tense, her body trapped. As spectators, readers enter the class not through Rosie's eyes, but by looking down at the children with their heads appearing compressed by the barre, caged, glassed in. Hampshire's late-twentieth-century text seems to foreground such unease, initially projecting an air of fear, only to dispel apprehension in the denouement. The troubling notes return, however, more problematically, in a recent, prestigious series.[27] James Mayhew's Ella Bella Ballerina picture books play up the sense of aura. Ella Bella joyfully enters Madame Rosa's class in an imposing metropolitan theatre at the starting point of her first book, *Ella Bella Ballerina and* The Sleeping Beauty (2007), and of the others so far in this series. The weight of tradition seems built into these walls, along with the signifiers of pre-twenty-first-century values. There are allusions to books and fairy tales (a rose in Ella Bella's city street in *The Sleeping Beauty*, a dropped slipper in *Cinderella*) and, in a more contemporary note, a decorous advertisement for deluxe swan feather quilts in Ella Bella's third book, *Ella Bella Ballerina and* Swan Lake. Style reinforces heritage: Mayhew, as author/illustrator, says that he tried deliberately to create a nostalgic older look.[28] Ella Bella is brave and undaunted, but as a tiny figure in pink wellingtons, seems diminished and vulnerable, undermined as a hero, in an ambiguous balance that seems peculiarly disturbing. In these texts, as often elsewhere, images of the stage space—itself the space of performance—are terrifying, blank, vertiginous, full of aura and menace. In *Ella Bella Ballerina and* The Sleeping Beauty, which sets the pattern, Ella Bella stays behind on an empty stage, positioned in the light, but surrounded by the looming vastness of a shadowy, silent, tiered auditorium. Such images compel questions: Whose eyes will be looking? What does the girl face in the dark? What does she have to do, or become? Is she to be her own self-fashioning agent, or is she here to serve as another's instrument?

Here, and in the other texts I've discussed more generally, the central character carries the freight of such contradictions; and, again, the sites of ambiguity are the girl's body and her powers of speech. Projected through those unseen eyes in the looming dark spaces of the stage that repeatedly face the girl in the fiction and the reader in her bedroom, the figure of the ballerina is both the very summit of aspiration and an impossible desire: to be both subject and object, to be viewed as a perfect practitioner in a traditional art, and to acquire a language of the body that promises self-realization. The image of the classical dancer herself exemplifies an aesthetic of essence, an illusion of immateriality, inseparable from the dance itself. Such a figure, presented in story and often in illustration, evokes the ideal of "the work" as flawless in "its totality, self-sufficiency and perfection," an ideal that is challenged by materialist accounts (Balibar and Macherey 283). The highest and purest form of dance, worshipped by most of the girl characters until at least the 1990s, is to be white and spiritual: the sylph in ballet blanc, the swan, Pavlova, in her white tutu. Earlier series often posit the silence of this figure as a form of female power: typified above all by the sylph in the all-female woodland glade, this power is a withdrawal from the everyday, masculine sphere. This is the image, above all, that first enraptures the girl character in many a novel. (It is the scene, for instance, that drifts, in fig. 4.2, out of Drina's spellbinding television.) In the mid-twentieth century, Lorna Hill's Sadler's Wells series, among others, endorses at some level the oft-quoted mantra of 1930s male dance critics (the "balletomanes") that the dancer is most perfect and most naturally feminine when seemingly weightless, disembodied even, and voiceless—an exquisite spectacle produced for the male appreciator.[29] This aspirational trope is extraordinarily persistent. Even in 1995, toward the end of Davida Wills Hurwin's young adult novel *A Time for Dancing* (and in its 2002 film adaptation), Jules, dying of cancer in her teens, evaporates from the shared narration, but becomes for her friend the purest of all dancers in death: the last words of the novel represent her as weightless, out of the body, like "a seagull. Dancing. And free" (257).

From Hill's series onward, however, there are also motifs of obstacles and resistance that give signs of the contradictions: girls who cannot or do not conform, who will insist on speaking, or whose bodies do not fit. These motifs have intensified from the late 1980s to today by the attention of realist texts to eating disorders, or to the restrictions of classical movements, and injuries from the strain. Although at the forefront of many adult dancing narratives, such as director Robert Altman's film *The Company* (2003) or Aronofsky's *Black Swan*, in girls' fictions the more violent moments of "illegible rage," to borrow McRobbie's term again, are often kept at a remove from the central narrative. It is the friend or the rival who destroys herself, not, as in many adult narratives, the main character. Tamar's Marisol repudiates even the extreme romanticized pathologies of *Red Shoes*,[30] returning a friend's gush, "[s]o she died gloriously, for her art," with "[i]t would be better if she danced gloriously and stayed healthy" (104). In a counter-register to silence, the contemporary inclusion of slangy dancers, vigorous high-fives, and repeated cheers at moments of triumph seem to represent even the fairies of the Rainbow Magic series as free at last from decorum and restraint.

But freedom and self-expression are never simple, and, even where challenged overtly, the feminine silence trope still troubles the genre as the ghost of an ideal. At best, the narratives hold the question out to readers, as in Masini's *On Your Toes*, which opens with Zoe meditating over the gift of "a shoe-shaped book" from her grandmother: "The general pinkness, the little bow to tie the book closed and the laced-up ribbons beneath the title. . . . It was called *The Ballerina's Handbook* and you could immediately see that it was meant for very young girls" (1). Navigating her own ambitions, Zoe sets out to write her own manual, at first copying the handbook's style, but then seeking her distance. Her first entry directly picks up earlier proclamations, immediately to renounce them:

> *A ballerina does not speak. She has no need to speak. No, that's not true. They have a different vocabulary made up of gestures that express emotions and sensations. The difficult thing is feeling those emotions deeply enough, but if you manage to really feel them, you find that your body follows your mind, and does what it's supposed to, and then you can express anything you want. Well, most of the time, anyway.* (4; italics in original)

The qualifiers and hesitancies here are telling. Zoe draws the reader into complex questions of subjectivity: whether identity is performative ("feeling those emotions deeply enough") or essential ("to really feel them"), free or determined ("your body follows your mind and does what it's supposed to . . ."). These, in turn, lead to larger questions about whose or what cultural plots the little dancer serves, whose language the girl speaks, and what it is that she expresses. Three chapters later, the novel presents Zoe and reader with a tableau: the class practise arabesques, at which Zoe's rival, Laila, excels. Zoe sees Laila as "a loose-limbed doll, like a Barbie," subject to undignified manipulation:

> It looked as though a huge, invisible hand was moving Laila's legs from one position to another (if she listened carefully, Zoe imagined she might hear the sound of plastic on plastic, *click, click, click*) and holding her in those impossible postures. Her torso and her leg formed a wide, tilted, perfect V. There was no uncertainty to Laila's movements. She was an arabesque machine. (33; italics in original)

This extended figurative passage presents readers with a knot of central questions. This motif, the puppet dancer, is a feature of many actual ballets (most famously *Petrouchka*) and is often staged within the fictional narratives. It is also one of the repeated images for the flawed (that is, non-feminine) dancer: the manipulative rival, the girl without a heart, who is sometimes redeemed by friendship or failure, sometimes left as a tragic or monitory figure. The predominantly realist mode of Masini's and earlier cognate texts works to present the central character, in contrast, as the empathic antitype: a girl, ambitious, but with her own centre, flesh, and feelings, a truly "feminine" spirit, where movement comes from within. As modelled in Zoe's journals, she is a sentient being, not a technically perfect plastic automaton. In a variant image presented in Ann Bryant's series, Rose's grandmother approves her newfound "Ballerina Dreams" by saying that Rose is like a Russian doll: "You had so much inside you, and now you're starting to find it all!" (314). In Siena Cherson Siegel's *To Dance: A Ballerina's Graphic Novel* (2006), an interwoven Russian doll motif similarly marks Siena's passage into the arcane and expressive secrets of Balanchine's School of American Ballet.[31] In a simple narrative formation, the reader can look forward to "the fiction of a forthcoming conciliation," an imaginary solution that restores art and artifice to the "natural" (Balibar and Macherey 285). Such a resolution presents a moment where the girl will look inside herself to dance from her heart—a movement articulated and frequently encouraged of the characters in the Ballerina Dreams series and many of today's fictions.[32] But contradictions cannot be so easily dispelled: Zoe's sense of "a huge, invisible hand" directing the girl, especially in her most skilled and expressive moves, haunts the entire genre. Individuals cannot just be read autonomously; questions of individual agency are also fused with wider public plots.

I have suggested that, as acolyte dancer and practitioner, a sylph in the making, the girl acts out a long tradition. In spite of the symbols of female lineage, the culture she transmits has its roots in Western European aristocratic and court heritage. With music and choreography by famous male maestros and composers, ballet is also an imperial high masculinist art, deeply bound up with the forms of supreme whiteness, which are held up for display in the airy female sylph. Many of the charismatic teachers in novels up to the 1990s are white Russians in exile after the Revolution, still carrying the Cold War memories of star performances for the Czar. Masini's Zoe, a twenty-first-century girl, is under the sway of Madame Olenska, who has family in St. Petersburg. In a similar vein, images of British Imperial rule and its imminent fading fill English novels from the 1930s through to the late 1960s. Even in the London household in *Ballet Shoes*, Empire forms a background frieze, with casual references to Kuala Lumpur, rubber planting, and slumps; and a family friend offers reassurance about an audition with reminiscences of his fears before successfully facing and suppressing a "native" strike (Streatfeild 72, 95).[33] In the Cold War 1950s and 1960s, in Lorna Hill, Streatfeild and others, young dancers play key roles. The rhetoric of aesthetic sublimity, in other words, often occludes sharply honed political ideologies, where the girl in her tutu is an agent in uniform, the dance her weaponry and language. Earlier generations of fictions often conspicuously urged public mission, subsuming unacceptable personal assertiveness into higher national purpose. English novels in the years leading up to and following World War II represent girl performers like Posy and Pauline Fossil as potentially powerful global ambassadors for Britain after the end of Empire. Their reward, all too often, is to dance before the King or Queen at the climax of the text.[34] Ambition is reframed as selflessness, suffused, as often in that period, with an even more compelling sense of spiritual vocation: the girl performs to speak transcendently. In a 1950 UK series novel, Elfrida Vipont's *The Lark on the Wing*, an older male artist explains this, particularly clearly, to the heroine, an aspiring singer: "[I]f you're an artist, you can't just express your own feelings and your own experiences. You're interpreting something much bigger than yourself, something universal, and you mustn't narrow it down" (204).

At less exalted levels, these narratives also draw rhetorical energy and deploy particularly persuasive forms of unifying reconciliation from representations of dancers as families, crossing boundaries of generations, regions, and nations, and speaking in one tongue. As English dance critic and famous self-styled balletomane Arnold L. Haskell expressed in 1943, company members are "citizens of their miniature Commonwealth" (*National Ballet* 64). In *The Beaver Book of Ballet* (1979), an information book for young readers, Robina Beckles Willson suggests both a lineage of auto-generation, where dancers give birth to dancers, and, again, a worldwide family: "[D]ancers have often created their own ballets, as choreographers. They have created the next generation as teachers. It is a closely knit chain. Dancers are like an extraordinary family, which is now winged and can fly from one part of the world to another" (31). In one of Willson's earlier works, *A Time to Dance*, a novel for younger teens published in the early 1960s, her heroine muses after a display of limbo dancing that "dancing is almost an international language," and readers are told of a cultural mission to India where seventeen nationalities converse successfully in balletic mime (109–10). In these mid-century novels, however, the "unevenly resolved conflicts" (Balibar and Macherey 283) of the England of the period now seem all too plain. Ethnicities and nations remain distinct, represented like Willson's dancers from Trinidad as exotically other; few or no exceptions to the approved North European face are permitted visibility in the exclusive sylvan glade.

But the political power of dancers' speech and the responsibilities it entails remain in force, reconfigured for readers according to different socio-historical circumstances. In the United States it manifests itself, for example, in 1937, when Elizabeth Borton's Pollyanna (in the ballet-centred *Pollyanna's Door to Happiness*) is involved with Zionists and Russians; and again, as young performers traverse the fractured and threatened spaces of the late-twentieth-century United States. In Tamar's *Alphabet City Ballet*, or in Laurence Yep's *Ribbons*, young adult novels published in Clinton's mid-term, journeys beginning in Puerto Rico and the Lower East Side or in rural China forge new American identities. The emphasis in these texts on diaspora, family memory, and memorabilia reaffirms ethnicity and origins in the face of the globalizing erasures of late capitalism, but, at the same time, in the "imaginary solution" of the narrative, allows readers and heroines a place at the cultural centre. In their struggles and revisions of the language of ballet, these heroines honour their grandmother's bound feet, but dance in the Lincoln Plaza. In Gloria Whelan's young adult novel *The Turning* (2006), the heroine, a Russian teenager at the time of *perestroika*, chooses not to defect to the West, but to help at home: "[Y]ou will be doing your country a great service. We have come to the moment when Russia's fate will be decided" (160). Playing a key part at the supreme moment of crisis, she saves Russia for democracy—celebrated by pizzas for all—and for globalized capitalism. The final page draws explicit comparison with her dreams of beauty and fame as a ballerina; the reality of "hours of exercises, aching limbs, tortured toes"; and the blossoming of her country: "Why shouldn't it be the same for Russia?" (309).

In all these fictions, girls' ambition fuels powerful purposes—albeit of ideologically worrying kinds. What has become of such energies in the contemporary ballet corner? Let me return to recent fictions, and, first, to the Magic Ballerina website, and to the pleasures and powers it offers. On the introductory page, the reader/spectator is invited in "the Journey to Enchantia Game" to be the unseen hand that clicks to makes a little dancer leap into the air—as in Masini's image of Leila, "*click, click, click.*" Apart from the gratification and pace of clicking to music before the dancer, on her ever-rising plinth, runs beyond permitted limits, the reader perhaps receives the ghost of a promise: that if she herself clicks enough in hours of practice, she, too, will become a Leila, or even a Darcey Bussell, whose genuinely hard-earned super-stardom animates the series. Beyond this, however, we might wonder about the forces that animate this fictional dancer, and about where her efforts take her.

In many ways, in the more individual revisions of the genre, the girl seems forgotten, left bouncing and smiling on her plinth. With reinvigorated interest in boys' struggles and achievements, especially since the success of *Billy Elliot* (as film, then book and musical),[35] many fictions take the spotlight off girls to reassign ambition and desire to male characters. In the sequel to *Ballet Kitty*, *Ballet Kitty: Ballet Class* (2008), with blue stripes now on the cover, Kitty and her friend are joined by a boy named Ginger Tom, who despises ballet shoes but leaps into the narrative centre stage. The girls are pink, skilful, conscientious, and compliant, and represented as a unit; Ginger Tom is clumsy but individual and charismatic. It is he who earns his teacher's pride, and who is celebrated in the largest illustrations. Surrounded by female admirers, his creativity legitimated, it is Tom who now steps, rightfully, into the shoes. Kimberly Brubaker Bradley's *Ballerino Nate* (published in America in 2006) interrogates some forms of normativity ("Nate hated shoes. He hated pink. He hated dresses" [n. pag.]), but casts girls as the negative, conservative force. The ballet needs young dancers, but it is young dogs, boys, and men who are at the centre of the action. Girls' bodies, represented in pink tights and shiny pink shoes, focalized through Nate as "big scary girls doing exercises" (n. pag.), are now the monstrous stuff of nightmares. Nate is the transgressive energy, the questing young dancer positioned to command the reader's approval. The traditional intimidating stage space appears again, but here is conquered and appropriated for male self-affirmation. Nate meets a male dancer, a "Ballerino," and is affirmed with an offer of new territory for endeavour, new terminology, and an aspirational identity.

Anna Kemp and Sara Ogilvie's picture book, *Dogs Don't Do Ballet* (published in the UK in 2010) tells a similar story, again reinforcing the right to difference, but on the part of the boy dancer. The little girl narrates, but only to acclaim her male dog's triumph. Again, in the visual text, women and girls represent the regulatory structures of the conventional, while the dog is the trespasser in class and in the visit to the ballet. In a recurrent joke, the dog stalks the girl in an intertextual play with Satoshi Kitamura's *Lily Takes a Walk*, but here the reader's anticipation and pleasure are channelled into the dog's adventure. When the pink ballerina stumbles, it is the dog's leap onto the stage that forms the climax, and the girl's role to celebrate. "'Hooray!' I shout. 'That's my dog!'" (n. pag.). In this text, there is some comic scrambling of gender codes; the cross-dressing dog is less resistant than Nate to feminine semiotics. He appropriates the tutu and the female role, and, glowing pink with happiness, might even be read as a subversive heroine, a fat little girl. But it is he, not the girl narrator, who steals the show and the headlines. In the final vignette, the girl's gesture is opaque. Surrounded by the roses thrown to the hero, she embraces the pug, her eyes shut—possibly in pride, as her dialogue suggests, but perhaps in submission. The inner cover is blank, except for the newspaper story: "Sugar Pug Fairy Takes Ballet By Storm" (n. pag.); the girl's voice is silent.

With ambition (and fictional energies) rerouted into plots of masculine drives and desires—stories where super pug becomes Sugar Pug—it may be hard to see what is left for girls. While there are still missions, narratives of girls as cultural and political agents, as might be expected, such agendas have faded somewhat, at least from the foreground of the texts. In some ways, this has significantly re-energized the genre: characters and readers are actors in a widening world that is less exclusive and more multicultural—thus breaking down nationalist frames. Many texts now present quietly diversified groups: in schools, classes, and sometimes in animal or toy communities in texts for younger readers. Mayhew's elegant Madame Rosa, who welcomes Ella Bella Ballerina into the grand portals of the dance, is perhaps South Asian; in the second book, a small boy has appeared, though at the margins of the class; in *Ella Bella Ballerina and* Swan Lake (2010), an East Asian girl has joined the circle. In Bussell's series, one small black sylph looks out of illustrations in book 19 of the Magic Ballerina series, *Jade and the Enchanted Wood*, published in the same year. That such details coexist with traditional forms complicates any straightforward model of change. The genre still often valorizes a regal, imperial space: for instance, Lesley Rees's *Ballerina Belle* (UK, 2001) presents the eponymous main character in her own proscenium-shaped board book, and in the final climactic 29-page opening she performs for the King and Queen. In Katharine Holabird and Helen Craig's Angelina Ballerina series, the mouse Angelina is an ever-enthusiastic guest at the Royal Palace of Mouseland. In an extensive series of books, along with the spin-off TV series, DVDs, and related accessory products, she enacts stories that fuse details of domesticity with a panoply of fantastic regal, aristocratic, and medieval signifiers;[36] and, in the first of her own specially choreographed live ballets, *Angelina's Star Performance* (2007)—a notable accolade for a fictional ballet heroine—prepares her own production of *The Sleeping Beauty* for a royal performance.[37]

But this space is also often democratized and open to all. *I Want to Be Angelina Ballerina* offers all girls a chance to "find lots of surprises that will turn you into a fairy princess and make you the star of your very own show" (back cover). As the characters enact their story, the book includes the reader, who can search the text for book pockets concealing a tutu, a wand, wings, and other kit. In a further self-reflexive turn, the mice read one of the enclosed ballet books and present their own readers with the gift: to transform themselves into a dancer—a magical resolution that operates through sparkle rather than drudgery. In Ford's *Ballet Kitty*, before her final retreat into dependency, pink Ballet Kitty and her friend, grey Pussycat, "set up a stage. They pranced and preened and pretended to be princesses all morning" (n. pag.). In Mandy Ross's picture book *Ballerina Becky*, Becky's space of imagination, presented in a thought bubble like a spotlight, transforms with a page turn into free movement, in an arabesque, unframed, across the page division: "She danced like a true fairy princess, flittering and fluttering across the stage without even a single wobble" (n. pag.). In the final spread, in an actual spotlight, imagination becomes truth: Becky is "[t]he best fairy princess ever!" (n. pag.).[38]

In the realist mode, particularly in the United States throughout the 1990s, and now increasingly in the UK, visual and textual images present politics, if at all, through family and relationships. In Bryant's Ballerina Dreams series (2004–2005), British Asian Jasmine's arguments with her father are a pervasive strand throughout the series, in a collision of forms of ambition in a second-generation immigrant household. But public embassy remains vigorous, displaced but dominant, in the new fantastic variants of the genre. The Rainbow Magic series, for example, recalls Willson's simile: dancers as "an extraordinary family, which is now winged and can fly from one part of the world to another" (31). As represented in Rainbow Magic's fairy ambassadors, dancers are literally winged, and the gulf between ordinary and ballet worlds now develops a magic boundary. Girls still take on huge national causes, with resonances of fears of the war on terror, climate change, or, in coded terms, sexual exploitation. Judith Butler has characterized contemporary post-feminist identities in terms of melancholia and rage, conditions McRobbie persuasively applies to many pathologies of modern girlhood.

In counter, however, to the pervasive images of solipsistic, self-absorbed, feminine ennui—as in the fashion shoots McRobbie analyzes (*Aftermath* 98–122)—new ballet series fictions emphasize the ethics of outer-directed co-operation and of citizenship. Each character dances her solo but works as part of a network or line of very diverse friends. So, in 2007, in books 50 through 56 of the Rainbow Magic series, the Dance fairies unite in pan-dance alliance (from ballet to salsa) to save the ribbons of dance from Jack Frost's goblin cohorts, imposter performers that are grotesquely marked as the dangerous other. In Bussell's Magic Ballerina books, the ballet world of Enchantia reels again from threats to the very spirit of dance by the devious King Rat or Wicked Witch. (The series website is revealing: in the Ballerina Quiz, where readers identify their parallel character, any expression of preferring isolation produces a resemblance to King Rat.)[39] As in 1950s ballet fictions, the small hometown and the cozy nation-state are under threat. The familiar map in the endpapers of each of these series offers a mix of reassurance and menace (Jack Frost's castle looms northeast of Wetherbury Village in *Rainbow Magic*; King Rat's castle, to the southeast of the village in Magic Ballerina's Enchantia; see also Meadows, *Bethany*; Bussell, *Delphie and the Magic Spell*). The domestic centre is threatened in each story, only to be defended, as in Magic Ballerina, by the sequence of prepubescent heroines wearing little but leotards and the inherited magic shoes. Royalty is ever present, calling on the dancers to save the show—the rituals, courtships, nuptials, christenings, feasts, and pageants—that keep traditional hierarchies in place. So, for example, in Meadows's *Kate the Royal Wedding Fairy* (published opportunistically on 11 April 2011, in time for the ceremony in London of Catherine "Kate" Middleton and Prince William), the goblins again pirate the dance. The human girls assist the fairies to unmask and defeat "the Goblinovski Festival Ballet" to retrieve "The True Love Crown," essential to the stability of palace, state, and royal connubiality: "'Thank you for letting us help,' said Kirsty. 'A royal fairy wedding is the best celebration in the world!'" (69).

What these plots also keep in place is story, the Western cultural narratives and fairy tales that are grounded in the fabric of the ballet itself. Entrance to the ballet, they suggest, is a portal to the spellbinding power of tradition. Ballerina Becky dances for Story Town. In Magic Ballerina, girls are whirled away to Enchantia, after the reverie of a hypnotically repeated prelude, identical in each text: in this land where the ballet characters live, their power comes from replicating the steps of the apposite dance. To enlist untutored readers, the most recent incarnations of the series also print a synopsis of the ballet at the end of the book. Similarly, Ella Bella finds herself swept into saving the ballet stories, helping characters find their way, to enact and renew the plots. The series title format, "James Mayhew Presents," figures the book cover almost as a programme for a show of masterpiece theatre; the small figure of Ella Bella, in her signature pink tutu, will take centre stage in recreating the stories of the ballet before a very young audience. Outside the texts, Mayhew involves himself in a public project of dissemination, educating readers in this artistic heritage and publicizing his work. Here, we almost see the "unseen hand" manipulating the girl, as Mayhew blogs: "Wistfully I wondered as I drew the last figure of Ella Bella whether it would really be the final time I let my nib follow the curve of her little cheek. But no; Orchard books are already considering her future" ("*Swan Lake*").[40]

All these fictions, then, might seem to invest girls and ballet with fresh agency, though perhaps with troubling implications: that these fictions now serve, primarily, to keep alive a set of elite cultural narratives whose time may be up. Interviewed when launching her own new "concept" series, new celebrity UK writer Arlene Phillips recalls her moment of inspiration: when in a bookshop looking for gifts to buy for young children, she had been shocked to discover that "everything I could buy was about ballet." She quotes her own riposte—"*No!* There need to be books about jazz, Bollywood, hip-hop, Latin, ballroom!'"—and describes her own vision of a series that would feature "an ordinary little girl who has magic adventures with a real, feelgood ending" (Phillips).[41] Although valorizing other modes of dance, the first set of Phillips's series mirrors the magic quest structure of rival series; and, with its "rescue" of alternative cultural dance traditions by its UK-based heroines, to some degree reinforces conservative, colonialist narratives of cultural supremacy.[42]

We might ask, further, what kind of power this new generation of narratives approves. The magic of the dancer emerges here, not from her willpower and work, but from being thoroughly feminine. Every magic ballerina learns from visits to Enchantia to regulate her character flaws and smooth over contradictoriness: to learn to dance as part of an ensemble, to be gentle, kind, and caring. With the most recent, Jade, a street dancer, this entails self-erasure. In Bussell's first Jade adventure, *Jade and the Enchanted Wood*, Jade meets the sylphs themselves. On hearing about "their magical white light . . . [that] makes the Enchanted Wood so special for the rest of us" (38), she suspects that "[s]he clearly wasn't the right person to be the owner of these magic shoes" (39). But, drawn as if by a magnet to the glade itself, like Estoril's Drina in 1957, she is awestruck, feeling "a wave of pure wonder": "It was the most beautiful dance Jade had ever seen. A lump came into her throat. So *this* was the magic of ballet" (64–65).

Nevertheless, after many adjustments, she remains out of line. Her third book opens in class, where Jade, though "dancing with all her heart," knows that she is failing to express the music: "Her feet had too much bounce in them, her wrists had too much flick in them and her arms had too much stretch in them" (Bussell, *Jade and the Silver Flute* 11). In apologizing to her teacher, she accepts her mission: to save the Silver Flute to which the First Fairy of Enchantia dances. As Jade learns from her mentor, the White Cat, "[t]he dance makes sure that baby birds hatch out from their eggs" (28). If the First Fairy does not dance before sunset and the fledglings do not hatch, Jade is warned, "there won't be any new birdsong and so eventually the music in Enchantia would die out" (28). This seems the quintessence of a "solution" represented as natural, positing an end to female contrariness and contradiction—a revelation that sublimates girls' individual story into a larger, eternal plot of renewal. In this astonishing reassertion of a deeply passive female destiny, brought to fertility by a magic pipe, we seem a very long way from Pauline Fossil's licence and the spheres where Streatfeild's sisters fly.

Nevertheless, the genre can still throw out surprises. Cheryl Willis Hudson's picture book, *My Friend Maya Loves to Dance* (2010), for example, places power back in the domain of Maya, the young African American girl who dances "strong and free" (n. pag.). The more muted colours of Maya's ballet scenes coexist in Eric Velasquez's illustrations with the vibrant dynamism of many alternative dance traditions. The book celebrates the creative effort and collaboration of two girls, narrated by a girl who uses a wheelchair and who holds a sketchbook, which is revealed self-reflexively, in the final plate, as a dedication to Maya. In an interview for Black History Month in 2010, Velasquez himself tacitly acknowledges the problem of representation:

> I always wanted to do a book about a ballerina, however I never took into account how technical a project it would be. Inspired by the work of Edgar Degas, I figured I'd hire a model and photograph her in a variety of poses. . . . Once I read the manuscript six times, I realized that Cheryl was telling her story in a very personal and heart-felt way. It demanded attention. (Velasquez)

In contrast to Mayhew, he rejects the authority of tradition, abandoning the idea of using pastels—"[s]uddenly I wanted the images to be far from those of Degas"—and turning to real girl dancers: "Cheryl and I went to a ballet school in an African American community, in New Jersey. We hired the dancers, and had the staff pose them. Every pose in the book is the real thing, as well as the model for Maya; she is a real ballet student" (Velasquez). His solution is a compromise, and problems remain: as illustrator, he, too, is the powerful unseen hand who creates the characters and story; the girl, as model and muse, is still the object of his shaping eye and of the words of the adult author.

But, in its play with narration, the text conceals its own backstage conflicts and presents its readers positively with two kinds of accomplishment. Readers see Maya's triumph in performance, but also, during the course of her story, learn of the other girl's equally joyous achievement. After a sequence of images of Maya's varied dances, the seventh main page opening (halfway through the book) shows a spectator. The young wheelchair user, holding her closed sketchbook, watches from the sides (and across the page divide) as Maya "has a ball" (n. pag.) in the bright space of the mall. Taken in isolation, the image of this girl might leave a wistful impression, an image of immobility, passivity, and exclusion, especially as Maya's exuberant physical movements and ballet ambitions again become the focus in the remaining seven full-page openings. But the final page returns to the second girl. Here, in a front-facing double portrait, she shares the bow with Maya, smiling broadly and holding up for the reader the book she has written and illustrated. Showing a sketch of Maya as ballerina and the dedication to her friend, the plate reveals her hitherto hidden role as the story's first-person, diegetic narrator and illustrator. In the book's close, then, accorded an image of full agency, both girls are depicted as artists. They make their own generous imaginary and imaginative resolution: "Dancing is magic/For her and for me" (n. pag.). With such a note of renewal, of culturally and physically diverse girls making their own way, with their own energies, there is, perhaps, yet a future for ballet novels and for ballet readers.

Notes

1   Qtd. in Burkitt, with accompanying photograph.
2   This has been a rapid ascent: as Juliette Peers writes, "[b]allet appears to have slipped behind opera to some degree in the public imagination in Britain, Europe, and Australia in the early twenty-first century" (83).
3   Peers draws most of her examples from Europe and North America, but also mentions the extension of such influences into Asia: "from communist Shanghai to capitalist Singapore, as well as in Japan" (83).
4   For a fascinating parallel study, focused on English girls' comics of the 1950s, see Gibson.
5   For salient parallels with many of the fictional narrative elements identified in this essay, see Joan Ryan's study of girls' training for the higher levels of competitive gymnastics and figure skating. These fictions also intersect with tropes of dance biography and autobiography, with those of major figures crossing international boundaries, even at times of intensified division, such as the Cold War.
6   Still missing is the further ethnographical dimension—the kind of empirical field work among diverse readers and authors that would demand detailed cross-generational and cross-national investigation. As a literary scholar, in this chapter I am concentrating on the textual end of the spectrum.
7   For a fuller account of the earlier generation of fictions mentioned throughout this chapter, see Knights, "The World at Her Feet." A larger corpus of texts, representing a wider range of and more nationally, geographically, and culturally diverse performance traditions, is the subject of my work in progress, part of which is to be published as *Reading Ballet and Performance Narratives for Children: Critical Moves.*
8   For a more extended argument about the grounding of literary production in its cultural conditions, see also Macherey.

9   Jean Estoril was one of the pseudonyms of the prolific Mabel Esther Allan, who also wrote under her own name. Her Drina series was published in ten books, from 1957 to 1965, with a further volume, to complete a new edition of the series in 1991.

10 Masini's series, originally published by Edizioni EL in Italian *Scarpette rosa* ("pink shoes"; www.edizioniel.com) is published in English, in translation by Laura Watkinson, as Ballet Academy.

11 Lorna Hill published fourteen novels in this series, beginning with *A Dream of Sadler's Wells* (1950).

12 The phenomenon received its fullest expression in the book of that name, published in 1934 by dance authority and critic Arnold L. Haskell.

13 Success, as Malcolm Gladwell has more recently emphasized, emerges from "hours of hard practice. Ten thousand hours is the magic number of greatness" (41). Gladwell suggests that this model may be generalized across many fields of practice and performance, from music to money-making. Streatfeild's narrative anticipates Gladwell's stress on the labour and material conditions occluded in the discourse of "magic."

14 For a recent example, see *Ballettschuhe* (2009), a four-CD audiobook for a German audience.

15 Among the many stars of *Ballet Shoes* (directed by Sandra Goldbacher), Emma Watson, already famous from the *Harry Potter* films, took the role of Pauline.

16 For similar activities, using stickers, see also Pratt; and, for some scope, to shape each scene of the story, with magnets, Apsley.

17 Milly-Molly-Mandy's pink-and-white candy-striped dress features in the author's original illustrations, and the motif is echoed on many covers in reprints. See, for example, the much reprinted *Milly-Molly-Mandy Stories* (the first book in the series, 1928) in the Penguin-Puffin edition, 1972. Joyce Lankester Brisley's series of stories was first published on the children's page of the *Christian Science Monitor* in 1925, and the stories are still known for their charm and sweetness.

18 For an account of kinaesthesic effects in picture books, see Happonen.

19 Moss's series was introduced in 2005; Bryant's in 2004. For more, see also Bryant's website.

20 For details of the books and their categories, and for associated games, reader newsletters, and other marketing, see the website *Rainbow Magic*.

21 Dynamo Ltd.'s website, *Dynamo Design*, offers customized templates: see, for example, the Rainbow Magic and Tiara Club sections.

22 For the part such tokens play in the novels' constructions of cultural memory, see Knights, "The World at Her Feet" (26).

23   See, for example, the invitations in the end pages of the Magic Ballerina books, and the "Join the Magical Dance Academy" area of the website.

24   "Belle of the Ballet," written by George Beardmore and drawn by Stanley Houghton, was a regular strip in the UK comic *Girl* (1951–64), and its associated annuals, and offered readers narratives of ballet, humour, and adventure. Gibson's detailed analysis makes clear the central significance of this strip in the history of ballet narratives for girls.

25   Opening of main narrative (n. pag.). For a fascinating discussion about the place of red shoes, more prevalent in women's narratives, see Calvert.

26   See, for example, Moss 138–42; Bryant, *Rose's Big Decision* 321–24. See also the final page opening of Goodman's *Ballet Bunnies* and the "Darcey's Magical Masterclass" pages at the end of each Magic Ballerina book.

27   Janet Evans, for instance, has emphasized the beauty of these picture books as fine art. In a prefatory note to *Ella Bella Ballerina and* The Sleeping Beauty, Mayhew acknowledges the support of Anglia Ruskin University, UK, for a research grant for the series (n. pag.).

28   Mayhew describes the "retro" influences on his construction of Ella Bella in a sequence of postings on his blog; see "Creating Ella Bella."

29   For an overview of this strand of ballet writing, see Sayers; for an influential critical exposition of its roots in the aesthetics of fin-de-siècle poetics and the Symbolist movement, see Kermode.

30   Powell and Pressburger's 1948 film, *The Red Shoes*, is considered a classic of cinematic art; the role of the heroine, Vicky, who, torn between love and dance, takes her own life, was played in a celebrated performance by the ballerina Moira Shearer.

31   This recurring motif is one of a diverse and often contradictory range of visual and verbal elements that prompt close reading of this complex and sophisticated narrative, which is listed on the back cover as for eight-to fourteen-year-olds. See Knights, "Dangerous Thresholds."

32   Delphie, for example, is promised a return to Enchantia (the magical land of ballet): "Sugar's words [the Sugar Plum Fairy] suddenly seemed to echo in her head: *Dance with your heart and you will return*" (Bussell, *Delphie and the Birthday Show* 90; italics in original).

33   For more on the contexts of the imperialist themes of ballet stories, see Knights, "The World at Her Feet"; and for a detailed reading of *Ballet Shoes* in terms of such themes, see Stoneley, "Ballet Imperial."

34   For more on this master patriotic narrative in Streatfeild, Hill, and Estoril, see Knights, "The World at Her Feet."

35 For an overview of the Billy Elliot branding, see the website *Billy Elliot: The Musical.*

36 For an early example, see *Angelina and the Princess* (1984), or, two decades later, *Angelina at the Palace* (2005). Conceived as a human girl, in illustration Angelina turned into a mouse. For the extent of the relatively recent development of the Angelina Ballerina brand by the group that also manages Rainbow Magic, see "Angelina Ballerina" at the HIT Entertainment website. For an examination of the broader phenomenon of medievalism in girls' literature, see Bradford.

37 For details of Larson and Beaumont's production, see Martland. A successful tour, including performances in Australia, followed the London opening. A second ballet, *Angelina Ballerina's Big Audition*, followed in 2009; see Branton.

38 My own copy includes a gift bookplate inscribed from her playgroup for a young girl starting school, and suggests that the adult leader, at least, read the narrative as positive and enabling.

39 See the game entitled "Which Character from Enchantia Are You?" at the "Fun and Games" section of the Magic Ballerina website.

40 James Mayhew's blog and the public responses to his posts give Ella Bella a high profile, and demonstrate the impact of his creation worldwide: see, for instance, the account of his sell-out ballet concerts (Mayhew, "Stories from the Ballet").

41 Phillips (founder of the Pineapple Dance Studios, and, in 2009, aged 66) was deposed as judge of the popular television contest *Strictly Come Dancing*, and was also at the centre of another controversy about feminine images, in this case, the relegation of older women in the media. The BBC received over two thousand complaints, and a question was raised in Parliament. For a summary, see Holmwood.

42 For a vigorous expression of the view that Phillips's books exemplify a stale reprise of a limited genre and insult girl readers, see McClements; and for a fuller discussion of ballet novels as apologia for colonialist agendas, see Knights, "The World at Her Feet."

Works Cited

Adams, Stephen. "Jacqueline Wilson Is Most Popular Library Book Author of Noughties." *Telegraph* 12 Feb. 2010. Web. 12 Sept. 2011.

"Angelina Ballerina." *HIT Entertainment.* N.d. Web. 25 Nov. 2011.

Apsley, Brenda. *Magnetic Ballet*. Illus. Jo-Anne Shilliam. N.p.: Anness-Lorenz, 2009. Print.

Balibar, Etienne, and Pierre Macherey. "On Literature as an Ideological Form." *Marxist Literary Theory*. Ed. Terry Eagleton and Drew Milne. Oxford: Blackwell, 1996. 276–95. Print.

Ballet Shoes. Dir. Sandra Goldbacher. Granada for BBC, 2007. DVD.

Ballettschuhe [*Ballet Shoes*]. Narr. Sascha Icks. Trans. Irmela Bender. Hamburg: Hörbuch, 2009. CD.

Beardmore, George. "Belle of the Ballet: Come to the Fair." Drawn by Stanley Houghton. *Girl Annual Number Nine: 1961*. London: Longacre, [1960]. 31+. Print.

Billy Elliot: The Musical. N.d. Web. 16 Nov. 2011.

Black Swan. Dir. Darren Aronofsky. Perf. Natalie Portman and Mila Kunis. Phoenix Pictures Studio, 2010. DVD.

Borton, Elizabeth. *Pollyanna's Door to Happiness*. 1937. London: Harrap, 1939. Print.

Bradford, Clare. "Archaic Signifiers: Contemporary Medievalisms in Texts for and about Girls." Girls, Texts, Cultures Symposium. University of Winnipeg, Winnipeg. 17 Oct. 2010. Presentation.

Bradley, Kimberly Brubaker. *Ballerino Nate*. Illus. R. W. Alley. New York: Penguin-Dial, 2006. Print.

Bradshaw, Peter. "*Black Swan*—Review." *Guardian* 20 Jan. 2011. Web. 22 Jan. 2011.

Branton, Rachel. *Angelina Ballerina's Big Audition*. 23 Feb. 2009. Web. 24 Nov. 2011.

Brisley, Joyce Lankester. Milly-Molly-Mandy Ser. 1928. London: Penguin-Puffin, 1972. Print.

Bryant, Ann. *Ann Bryant—Home*. N.d. Web. 22 June 2010.

———. *Rose's Big Decision*. Ballerina Dreams Ser. London: Usborne, 2006. Print.

Budgeon, Shelley. *Choosing a Self: Young Women and the Individualisation of Identity*. Westport: Praeger, 2003. Print.

Burkitt, Laura. "Louboutin Ballet Pointes." *Pagesdigital*. 29 June 2011. Web. 3 July 2011.

Bussell, Darcey. *Delphie and the Birthday Show*. Magic Ballerina Ser. London: HarperCollins Children's Books, 2008. Print.

———. *Delphie and the Magic Spell*. With Linda Chapman and Katie May. Magic Ballerina Ser. London: HarperCollins Children's, 2008. Print.

———. *Jade and the Enchanted Wood*. With Ann Bryant and Dynamo Ltd. Magic Ballerina Ser. London: HarperCollins Children's, 2010. Print.

———. *Jade and the Silver Flute*. Magic Ballerina Ser. London: HarperCollins Children's, 2010. Print.

Butler, Judith. *The Psychic Life of Power*. Standford: Standford UP, 1997. Print.

Calvert, Melanie. "The Red Shoes: Obsessive and Contagious Narratives." Diss. Deakin U, 2001. Print.

Clough, Julie. *Pretty and Pink: Colouring Time*. Illus. Sheryl Bone. London: Egmont, 2009. Print.

The Company. Dir. Robert Altman. Perf. Neve Campbell and Malcolm McDowell with the Chicago Joffrey Ballet. Sony Pictures Classics, 2003. DVD.

Craig, Patricia, and Mary Cadogan. *You're a Brick, Angela! The Girls' Story 1839–1985*. 1976. London: Gollancz, 1986. Print.

Dynamo Design. Dynamo Ltd., n.d. Web. 16 Nov. 2011.

Estoril, Jean [Mabel Esther Allan]. *Ballet for Drina*. London: Hodder, 1957. Print.

Evans, Janet. "Reading the Visual: Creative and Aesthetic Responses to Picturebooks and Fine Art." The Child's Plaything: Literature, Creativity and Childhood Conference. University of Exeter, Devon. 5 Nov. 2010. Presentation.

Ford, Bernette. *Ballet Kitty*. Illus. Sam Williams. London: Boxer Books, 2007. Print.

———. *Ballet Kitty: Ballet Class*. Illus. Sam Williams. London: Boxer Books, 2008. Print.

"Fun and Games." *Magic Ballerina*. N.d. Web. 12 Sept. 2010.

Geras, Adèle. *The Ballet Class*. Illus. Shelagh McNicholas. London: Orchard, 2004. Print.

Gibson, Mel. "Nobody, Somebody, Everybody: Ballet, Girlhood, Class, Femininity and Comics in 1950s Britain." *Girlhood Studies* 1.2 (Winter 2008): 108–28. Print.

Gladwell, Malcolm. *Outliers: The Story of Success*. London: Penguin, 2008. Print.

Goodman, Joan Elizabeth. *Ballet Bunnies*. Tarrytown: Marshall Cavendish Children, 2008. Print.

Hampshire, Susan. *Rosie's First Ballet Lesson*. Illus. Maria Teresa Meloni. London: Egmont-Mammoth, 1997. Print.

Happonen, Sirke. "Choreography of Characters: Movement and Posture in Illustrated Texts for Children." *Literacy* 35.3 (Nov. 2001): 99–105. *ERIC*. Web. 13 June 2011.

Haskell, Arnold L. *Balletomania: The Story of an Obsession*. London: Gollancz, 1934. Print.

———. *The National Ballet: A History and Manifesto*. London: Black, 1943. Print.

Hill, Lorna. *A Dream of Sadler's Wells*. Sadler's Wells Ser. London: Evans, 1950. Print.

Holabird, Katharine. *Angelina and the Princess*. Illus. Helen Craig. 1984. London: Penguin-Puffin, 2001. Print.

———. *Angelina at the Palace*. Illus. Helen Craig. London: Penguin-Puffin, 2005. Print.

———. *I Want to Be Angelina Ballerina*. London: Penguin-Puffin, 2004. Print.

Holmwood, Leigh. "Strictly Ageism?" *Guardian* 17 July 2009. Web. 29 Sept. 2011.

Hudson, Cheryl Willis. *My Friend Maya Loves to Dance*. Illus. Eric Velasquez. New York: Abrams, 2010. Print.

Hurwin, Davida Wills. *A Time for Dancing*. New York: Little, 1995. Print.

Huse, Nancy. *Noel Streatfeild*. New York: Twayne, 1994. Print.

"Join the Magical Dance Academy." *Magic Ballerina*. N.d. Web. 12 Sept. 2010.

"The Journey to Enchantia Game." *Magic Ballerina*. N.d. Web. 12 Sept. 2010.

"Julie Burchill's Top 10 Books for Teens." *Guardian* 1 Dec. 2004. Web. 20 Aug. 2010.

Kandel, Charlotte. *Scarlet Stockings: The Enchanted Riddle*. New York: Penguin-Dutton, 2007. Print.

Kemp, Anna. *Dogs Don't Do Ballet*. Illus. Sara Ogilvie. London: Simon and Schuster, 2010. Print.

Kermode, Frank. *Romantic Image*. London: Routledge, 1957. Print.

Kitamura, Satoshi. *Lily Takes a Walk*. London: Sunburst, 1998. Print.

Knights, Pamela. "Dangerous Thresholds? First Steps in the Ballet Narrative." Fear and Safety in Children's Literature. 21st IRSCL Congress, Queensland University of Technology, Brisbane. 7 July 2011. Presentation.

———. *Reading Ballet and Performance Narratives for Children: Critical Moves*. New Critical Approaches to Children's Literature Ser. Basingstoke: Palgrave-Macmillan (forthcoming).

———. "The World at Her Feet: Cultural Embassy in the Post-War English Ballet Novel." *Papers: Explorations into Children's Literature* 10.2 (2000): 22–34. Print.

Larson, Paul, and Laura Beaumont. *Angelina's Star Performance*. Chor. Antony Dowson. Music Sergei Tchaikovsky. HIT Entertainment and English National Ballet. New Wimbledon Theatre, London. 6–9 Sept. 2007. Performance.

Lingen, Marissa K. "Ballet Stories." *The Oxford Encyclopedia of Children's Literature*. Ed. Jack Zipes. Vol. 1. Oxford: Oxford UP, 2006. 117. Print.

Macherey, Pierre. *A Theory of Literary Production*. Trans. Geoffrey Wall. London: Routledge, 1978. Print.

Martland, Lisa. "Review of *Angelina's Star Performance*." *Stage* 11 Sept. 2007. Web. 24 Nov. 2011.

Masini, Beatrice. *On Your Toes*. Trans. Laura Watkinson. Ballet Academy Ser. London: Piccadilly Press, 2010. Trans. of *Sulle Punte!* Trieste, Italy: Edizioni EL, 2005. Print.

Mayhew, James. "Creating Ella Bella." *James Mayhew Presents Ella Bella Ballerina*. Blogspot.com. 5 parts. 15 Aug.–2 Dec. 2009. Web. 15 Sept. 2010.

———. *Ella Bella Ballerina and* Cinderella. London: Orchard Books, 2009. Print.

———. *Ella Bella Ballerina and* The Sleeping Beauty. 2007. London: Orchard Books, 2008. Print.

———. *Ella Bella Ballerina and* Swan Lake. London: Orchard Books, 2010. Print.

———. "Stories from the Ballet: The Concert!" *James Mayhew Presents Ella Bella Ballerina*. Blogspot.com. 8 Nov. 2010. Web. 15 Sept. 2010.

———. "*Swan Lake:* Allego ma non troppo." *James Mayhew Presents Ella Bella Ballerina*. Blogspot.com. 26. Jan. 2010. Web. 15 Sept. 2010.

McClements, Melissa. "Girls' Fiction Needs to Learn Some New Routines." *Guardian* 6 Oct. 2010. Web. 10 Oct. 2010.

McRobbie, Angela. *The Aftermath of Feminism: Gender, Culture and Social Change*. London: Sage, 2009. Print.

———. *Feminism and Youth Culture: From "Jackie" to "Just Seventeen."* Basingstoke: Macmillan, 1991. Print.

Meadows, Daisy [Narinder Dhami]. *Bethany the Ballet Fairy*. Rainbow Magic Ser. London: Orchard. 2009. Print.

Meadows, Daisy [Rachel Elliot]. *Kate the Royal Wedding Fairy*. London: Orchard, 2011. Print.

Moss, Alexandra. *Boys or Ballet?* The Royal Ballet School Diaries Ser. New York: Penguin: Grosset and Dunlap, 2006. Print.

Ormerod, Jan. *Ballet Sisters: The Duckling and the Swan*. New York: Cartwheel-Scholastic, 2007. Print.

Pakula, Karen. "Mystery of the Missing Author." *Sydney Morning Herald* 2 Oct. 2006. Web. 17 Nov. 2011.

Peers, Juliette. "Ballet and Girl Culture." *An Encyclopedia of Girl Culture*. Ed. Claudia A. Mitchell and Jacqueline Reid-Walsh. Vol. 1. Westport: Greenwood, 2008. 73–84. Print.

Phillips, Arlene. "Arlene Phillips: Why I'm Still Haunted by Strictly." Interview by Laura Barton. *Guardian* 4 Oct. 2010. Web. 5 Oct. 2010.

Pratt, Leonie. *Ballerinas*. Illus. Stella Baggott and Vici Leyhane. Sticker Dolly Dressing Ser. London: Usborne, 2006. Print.

Rainbow Magic. N.d. Web. 16 Nov. 2011.

The Red Shoes. Dir. Michael Powell and Emeric Pressburger. Perf. Moira Shearer, Marius Goring, and Anton Walbrook. Rank, 1948. Film.

Rees, Lesley. *Ballerina Belle*. Illus. Jo Brown. Bright Sparks Ser. Royal Leamington Spa: Complete Works, 2001. Print.

Richardson, Anna. "Bussell Dances with HarperCollins." *Bookseller* 23 March 2008. Web. 10 Aug. 2010.

Ringrose, Jessica, and Valerie Walkerdine. "What Does It Mean to Be a Girl in the Twenty-First Century? Exploring Some Dilemmas of Femininity and Girlhood in the Contemporary West." *An Encyclopedia of Girl Culture*. Ed. Claudia A. Mitchell and Jacqueline Reid-Walsh. Vol. 1. Westport: Greenwood, 2008. 6–16. Print.

Ross, Mandy. *Ballerina Becky*. Illus. Emma Dodd. Little Workmates Ser. London: Ladybird Books, 2004. Print.

Ryan, Joan. *Little Girls in Pretty Boxes: The Making and Breaking of Elite Gymnasts and Figure Skaters*. London: Women's Press, 1996. Print.

Sayers, Lesley-Anne. "'She Might Pirouette on a Daisy and It Would Not Bend': Images of Femininity and Dance Appreciation." *Dance, Gender and Culture*. Ed. Helen Thomas. London: Macmillan, 1993. 165–83. Print.

Siegel, Siena Cherson. *To Dance: A Ballerina's Graphic Novel*. Art by Mark Siegel. New York: Aladdin-Schuster, 2006. Print.

Stoneley, Peter. "Ballet Imperial." *Yearbook of English Studies* 32 (2002): 140–50. Print.

Streatfeild, Noel. *Ballet Shoes*. 1936. Harmondsworth: Puffin, [1949]. Print.

Tamar, Erika. *Alphabet City Ballet*. New York: HarperCollins, 1996. Print.

A Time for Dancing. Dir. Peter Gilbert. Perf. Larisa Oleynik and Shiri Appleby. East of Doheny. 2002. DVD.

Velasquez, Eric. "Eric Valasquez." *The Brown Bookshelf*. Blogspot.com. 16 Feb. 2010. Web. 16 Nov. 2011.

Vipont, Elfrida. *The Lark on the Wing*. Oxford: Oxford UP, 1950. Print.

Watt, Fiona. *How to Draw Princesses and Ballerinas*. Designed and illus. Antonia Miller, Jan McCafferty, Non Figg, Katie Lovell, and Stella Baggot. Photo. Howard Allman. Usborne Activities Ser. London: Usborne, 2005. Print.

Whelan, Gloria. *The Turning*. New York: HarperCollins, 2006. Print.

Willson, Robina Beckles. *The Beaver Book of Ballet*. Illus. Shirley Soar. London: Hamlyn, 1979. Print.

———. *A Time to Dance*. London: Collins, 1963. Print.

Wilson, Jacqueline. *Jacky Daydream: The Story of Her Childhood*. Illus. Nick Sharratt. London: Random House-Corgi, 2008. Print.

Yep, Laurence. *Ribbons*. New York: Putnam-PaperStar, 1997. Print.

II

The Politics of Girlhood

CHAPTER 5

Warrior Girl and the Searching Tribe

*Indigenous Girls' Everyday Negotiations
of Racialization under Neocolonialism*

Sandrina de Finney and Johanne Saraceno

Rianna, a fifteen-year-old First Nation community organizer and youth leader, is sitting in a circle with a group of other Indigenous girls, discussing common representations of Indigenous girlhood that they encounter in their daily lives. Her voice rises animatedly as she describes a list of problematic stereotypes:

> Let's see . . . there's the drunk, the ho, like all Native girls are on the street, you know? There's the dirty Indian, broke. Then there's the whole Indian woman in a blanket thing, with the braids, like 200 years ago. The whole Pocahontas thing. That's what we have to choose from.

Her friend, sixteen-year-old Seeka, a Coast Salish girl who lives on reserve, jumps in: "No wonder . . . Native girls disappear and stuff and it never makes it to the news." How do articulate, confident Indigenous girls like Rianna and Seeka come to see the roles available to them as embedded in such damaging colonial stereotypes? A ubiquitous image of Indigenous girls as "exploitable and often dispensable" (Downe 3) is an outcome of the ongoing historical racialization of Indigenous women and girls in Canada.

As Rianna and Seeka explain, this damaging narrative casts Indigenous girls as voiceless, broken objects of colonial imagination, obscuring their complex experiences, knowledges, and strengths. The girls' description of pervasive misrepresentations echoes Pamela Downe's assertion that little is known about the daily lives of Indigenous girls in Canada, including

> how or to what extent they experience the vulnerability to various forms of violence, how they cope with cultural dislocation and uprootedness, and where the sources of strength and pleasure lie. In fact, Aboriginal girls remain among the most invisible and silenced in Canadian society, erased from even the most exemplary postcolonial work in the area of Indigenous rights and identity construction. (2)

In this chapter we examine how such erasures occur by looking at the historical construction of Indigenous girlhood across deeply racialized, gendered, and sexualized colonial state practices, policies, and discourses. We focus on understanding how state and popular discourses of Aboriginality and Anglo-nationalism take hold in the lives of Indigenous girls who live under dominant whiteness in relatively small Canadian cities and towns. We are concerned about the lack of nuanced representations of Indigenous girls in contemporary girlhood studies, popular culture, Canadian research and policy related to Aboriginal people, and girls' everyday spheres such as home, community and peer groups, public spaces, neighbourhoods, schools, and social services.

Such an analysis is becoming increasingly important given that Indigenous youth are the fastest-growing youth population in Canada; nearly half of the total Aboriginal[1] population is under the age of twenty-five, while this ratio is only one-third for the dominant population (Urquijo and Milan 11). This rapid growth, combined with the increasing urbanization of Indigenous families, highlights the importance of a policy focus on Aboriginal youth. From 2001 to 2006, the Aboriginal female population grew 20 percent, "more than triple the 6% growth of Canada's overall female population" (Urquijo and Milan 11). Yet Indigenous girls are largely ignored in policy debates and current research about Indigenous youth, despite their potential to richly inform such debates. To date, the intersecting effects of gendering, sexualization, and racialization have not been substantially examined in studies of Aboriginal youth, which tend to subsume girls under the boy-centred youth category (de Finney, "We Just Don't Know Each Other"; Jiwani, Steenbergen, and Mitchell).

Futhermore, a research and policy focus on Indigenous youth living either on reserve or in large Canadian cities such as Vancouver, Winnipeg, and Toronto ignores not only the constitutive effects of gender, but also the realities of Indigenous girls who live off reserve in smaller, less diverse centres (de Finney, "Under the Shadow of Empire"; de Finney, "We Just Don't Know Each Other"; Downe; Fleming and Kowalski; Lee and de Finney; Ruttan, LaBoucane-Benson, and Munro). These knowledge gaps result in inappropriate or insufficient policy and service responses to meet the needs of diverse Indigenous girls (Lee and de Finney) and constrain possibilities for more complex representations of Indigenous girlhood.

To address these gaps, we propose a conceptual cross-pollination of postcolonial and feminist Indigenous theories with girlhood studies to elaborate a reshaped girlhood framework that conveys the complex and often contradictory ways that Indigenous girls from diverse backgrounds negotiate intersecting formations of nationality, age, gender, race, class, and sexuality under neocolonialism. To this end, we take up Anita Harris's call to both make girls a focus of feminist theorizations and to make racialized girls more visible in girlhood studies. Indigenous girls remain largely absent in feminist debates about colonialism, which tend to focus on adult women (Hernandez and Rehman), and in girlhood studies, which tend to focus on girls from mainstream backgrounds (de Finney, Loiselle, and Dean; Ward and Benjamin).

We also draw on postcolonial feminist theorists, for example, Inderpal Grewal and Caren Kaplan, Trinh T. Minh-ha, and Chandra Talpade Mohanty, who have expanded on Foucault's concept of governmentality and on material feminism to track the ways in which state discourses and relations operate as technologies of subject formation in the lives of women and girls. We are interested in how colonial material-discursive formations shape Indigenous girls' bodies, spirits, and affects, and their cultural political and economic realities. Particularly helpful in this analysis is the notion of "scattered hegemonies" elaborated by Grewal and Kaplan, who contend that racialized women enact and live across diffused, mobile forms of domination, including multiple patriarchies, nationalisms, and intersecting formations of race, gender, sexuality, and class.

Our analysis is further informed by Indigenous theorizations of territoriality, self-determination, and Canadian and North American neocolonialism—debates that are often overlooked in postcolonial and migration studies (St. Denis). While domestic and transnational migrations have produced new sites of identification and subject formation for

Indigenous people, powerful neocolonial state discourses, policies, and practices safeguard the hegemony of a white Anglo-Franco nation. Indigenous gender theorists Marie Battiste and Helen Semeganis, Bonita Lawrence and Enakshi Dua, Andrea Smith, and Verna St. Denis argue for a sharpened focus on the repetitive circulation of colonial policies and practices, particularly given their effects on Indigenous women.

Finally, we engage in a delicate balancing act of highlighting various examples of Indigenous girls' survivance while making sense of important structural gaps and challenges. We draw on Eve Tuck's research framework that is "intent on convoking loss and oppression, but also wisdom, hope, and survivance" ("Breaking Up" 639). According to Anishinaabe scholar Gerald Vizenor, survivance storytelling constitutes an "active repudiation of dominance, tragedy, and victimry" (*Fugitive Poses* 15). Vizenor's emphasis on survivance is distinct from survival: it is "moving beyond our basic survival in the face of overwhelming cultural genocide to create spaces of synthesis and renewal" (*Manifest Manners* 53). Our efforts to honour strategies and practices that sustain hope, spirit, and vitality in the face of deeply entrenched structural inequities underpins every aspect of our research and work with girls.

Conceptualizing Indigeneity under Neocolonialism

As "a settler society with a history of genocide and colonization" (S. Razack 89), the Canadian state has maintained its colonial authority through policies that have included forced sterilizations and scientific experimentations; deliberate infection with lethal diseases such as smallpox; forcible removal of entire Indigenous communities from their homelands to allow European immigrants to access desired territories; preventing Indigenous people from voting, studying, travelling, meeting in groups, practising their culture, and participating in business; and the incarceration of thousands of children in residential schools, where they were subjected to physical, spiritual, sexual, emotional, and cultural abuses (Battiste and Semeganis; Lawrence; Smith). Despite the fact that Indigenous nations continue to sustain their own sovereignty and diverse political, land-based, cultural, and linguistic traditions, after two hundred years of colonization, Indigenous societies have been decimated to the extent that First Peoples currently represent less than 6 percent of Canada's total population.

Colonial policies are deeply embedded in current conditions and ideologies that shape the lives of Indigenous people (Schutte; Sinclair). Even today, Aboriginal people in Canada are governed by the 1876 *Indian Act*, which "rests on the principle that the Aborigines are to be kept in a condition of tutelage and treated as wards or children of the state" (1876 Annual Report of the Department of the Interior qtd. in Indian and Northern Affairs Canada 172). Thus, in countries that remain actively colonial, like Canada and the United States, the idea that colonialism occurred in the past is inaccurate. Ongoing colonial processes sustain a system of chronic poverty, social exclusion, and political and cultural disenfranchisement, with particularly dire effects on Indigenous women and girls. We use the term "neocolonialism" to theorize this active coloniality and to focus attention on Canadian society as dominated by normative social values and practices that have systematically, over many generations, positioned Indigenous cultural and social norms as inferior (Lawrence). Our analysis disturbs the positioning of Britain as Canada's founding nation and the associated Anglo-nationalism that is a predominant social discourse in western Canada.

Using data gleaned from three participatory community-based studies, we examine how state policies and discourses (for example, the *Indian Act*) reinforce an image of Indigenous girls as inadequate and problematic, and illustrate how Indigenous girls take up, reconfigure, and contest colonial constructions of Indigenous girlhood such as "Indian princess," "dirty squaw," "drunken Indian," and "vanished race." Documenting girls' everyday negotiations of these discursive and material effects might open up urgently needed alternative conceptualizations of Indigenous girlhood that more adequately reflect girls' complex realities and multiple strategies of survivance, engagement, and resistance. Although our focus is on girls living in communities on Canada's west coast, our analysis builds on the work done by others across Canada who have called for a disruption of monolithic, objectifying representations of Indigenous girls and women.

Methodology

The analysis presented here is rooted in three participatory community-based studies conducted with and by more than fifty Indigenous girls, aged eleven to eighteen, over five years. The girls self-identified in some way as Native, Aboriginal, or Indigenous. Their diverse backgrounds included on and off reserve, status and nonstatus, First Nations, Métis, Inuit, and mixed. They came from and/or lived in both urban and rural areas. Family backgrounds included everything from dual- and single-parent households, to blended and extended families, to girls living in foster care and those who were adopted into Indigenous or non-Indigenous homes.

The studies were held in three communities on Vancouver Island, British Columbia: the capital city of Victoria (pop. 330,000), the town of Duncan (pop. 40,000), and the mill town of Port Alberni (pop. 18,000). The district of Greater Victoria occupies the territories of several Coast and Straits Salish First Nations, including the Lekwungen and WSÁNEĆ nations; Duncan was settled on the territories of the Cowichan Tribes, and Port Alberni lies on the territories of the Nuu-chah-nulth Nations. Each of these nations maintains their distinct political, social, and cultural structures and traditions, as well as distinct histories of settlement through the founding and development of Victoria, Duncan, and Port Alberni. Following hundreds of years of colonial appropriation and migration, almost 85 percent of the population in all three locations now identifies as white, with a majority claiming British (English, Scottish, and Irish) heritage. Only a small percentage of the communities' populations consist of visible minorities, and only 4 percent in Victoria, 10 percent in Duncan, and 13 percent in Port Alberni are Indigenous, including Indigenous people who migrated to the region from other communities (Statistics Canada, "Table 1"). Our emphasis on smaller, less diverse centres represents an important addition to the prevalence of Aboriginal research in larger, more diverse Canadian cities and in specific Indigenous communities such as reserves or bands.

The first study, involving girls from Victoria and Duncan, focused on the intersection of gender, sexuality, race, and class in shaping relations among racialized minority and Indigenous girls[2] (de Finney, "Under the Shadow of Empire"; de Finney, "We Just Don't Know Each Other"; Lee and de Finney). The second, based in Victoria, explored the needs of urban Indigenous young people who have been adopted or live in foster care[3] (de Finney, *The NONG SILA*). The Port Alberni study, by Johanne Saraceno, engaged Indigenous girls in exploring their experiences of gendered and sexual exploitation.

In each study, Indigenous girls engaged in making their complex realities more visible through the use of critical, participatory, action-centred methodological approaches. Acting as researcher-participants, girls co-designed and implemented various research projects using engaged, expressive methods (for example, photography, theatre, focus groups, peer interviews, journals, cultural camps) to document and share their experiences in a variety of contexts. We want to acknowledge that, in participatory research, not everyone can or wants to participate in similar ways in all aspects of collective analysis and dissemination. While we have taken on the task of writing about the findings in publications such as this book, many of the girls and other research partners have presented the research in avenues of their choosing, including conferences, videos, blogs, workshops, zines, and other publications.

The quotations presented here are drawn from various individual and group conversations and the girls' writing and art. We have indicated each speaker's age and her background as she describes it. Some girls asked that their real names be used; we use pseudonyms where girls requested them. To protect confidentiality, any references to specific communities have been deleted. We have chosen to use terms that the girls used to iden-tify themselves and others, including Indian, Native, mixed race, not white, Aboriginal, Métis, status/nonstatus, on/off reserve, and First Nations, among many others. While we recognize that all these terms are loaded and constitutive, using them to initiate critical conversations with girls about their uses and impacts is an important goal of our work.

The three studies presented here were distinct in their focus, but each interrogated the everyday realities of Indigenous girls living in small Canadian cities and towns whose populations tend to be overwhelmingly white. It is important to note that our work focuses on three specific and very distinct communities on Vancouver Island in western Canada. Each location has unique Indigenous histories, colonial and settlement patterns, internal community dynamics, and socio-cultural, economic, and political realities. There are also important regional differences related to Indigenous nationhood and colonial settlement that are unique to Canada's west coast. These contextual distinctions shape the nuanced experiences that girls shared with us; we certainly do not claim that they are easily generaliz-able to other girls, to other small centres, and to diverse Indigenous com-munities across Canada. At the same time, many of the issues and themes identified by the girls speak to shared histories and structural gaps affecting First Peoples generally, and girls more specifically, across Canada. In this regard, we seek to balance the push and pull of attending to contextual specificities while highlighting common threads and concerns.

Neocolonial Geographies

It is important to theorize the ways the specific colonial histories and geog-raphies of our three research sites shape the construction of Indigenous girl-hood. As we have stressed, smaller Canadian towns and cities face unique challenges and histories in this regard. Place and landscape, Narda Razack reminds us, "are not inert but actively participate in the identity formation of the individual" (88). Victoria, Duncan, and Port Alberni represent salient aspects of Canada's colonial geographies wherein Aboriginal peoples have been spatially contained in marginalized areas of towns and cities through the "theft of Native lands and the forceful segregation of Natives away from mainstream society" (Crichlow 91). As our research shows, the girls in our studies experience colonial geographies at every level of their interactions. The colonization of the physical, socio-cultural, economic, and political landscapes of these communities reinforces the problematic construction of Indigenous people as relics of the past, as peripheral to contemporary city life, and as inferior to the dominant population (Dei; Said). In many of the studies' focus groups, girls talked about encountering tangible markers and effects of colonialism across space and place. For example, during a photo-voice exercise in which we asked girls to walk around downtown Victoria taking pictures of representations of Indigenous people, Rianna, quoted at the beginning of the chapter, photographed statues and monuments. She observed: "Those statues of the [queen] and explorers everywhere, they're basically celebrating that they stole our land and killed our ancestors. It's so messed up to me."

In spaces where the public art and architecture mark Indigenous peoples as vestiges of European empires, the historic production of dominant whiteness is ubiquitous. Sherene Razack links colonial appropriation to a mindset that "not only enabled white settlers to secure the land but to come to know themselves as entitled to it" (129). This sense of entitlement is evident in the caption eleven-year-old Sienna wrote to describe her photo of a monument in downtown Victoria that celebrates British Columbia's "founding fathers": "I took this picture because they say they 'found us' and I find [this] a bit weird. . . . We were here before they ever came and we had our own territories and we knew what was going on." Sienna aptly articulates how, in Canada, the rich histories of Indigenous communities are constructed as inconsequential to a nation imagined as Anglo-Franco in origin. In a focus group discussion, a group of girls from Duncan and Victoria described how European place names erase Indigenous geographies:

> Our town has, like, names of explorers on things that are our traditional territory. Like, our mountain where we come from, it's named for an explorer that basically treated us like animals. (Candace, 17, First Nation living on reserve)

Or, like even when it's a Native name, like they change it to make it more English-sounding . . . like they're never saying, "this is actually a Native river that we took without paying for it," but guess what, now it's called like England River or whatever, "isn't that great, let's celebrate ourselves." (Seeka, 16, First Nation living on reserve)

Candace's and Seeka's comments struck a chord with the other girls, who described how, through the process of colonial spatial claiming, Indigenous traditional scientific knowledge related to animal migration, cultivation, medicinal plant use, and so on, is also negated:

When they settled . . . here, the whites who came early, they used what we knew about nature, how to use animals and all that, fishing, the tree bark, how we used . . . our berry patches and everything. (Seeka)

Yeah, it saved their life. (T.J., 14, Métis and Irish)

Okay, but they will never admit that. It's more like, "oh those Natives are dumb, they don't know anything." (Seeka)

These reflections both highlight and disrupt colonial discourses of first contact. The girls explained that their counter-narratives had been passed down through generations of stories about resistance to colonial appropriation:

I learned about how we were from my grandpa and like how the British made up stories about us so they could take the land. (Seeka)

My mom explained this to me growing up, like all the women kept the language alive and they even went to jail for it. (T.J.)

Alongside these stories of intergenerational survivance, shared with and by many of the girls, were stories of multiple forms of racialization. One means of establishing the inferiority of subordinated peoples is "the construction of psychological knowledges that portray the colonized as inferior" (Lesko 465). The girls shared many examples of how such negative psychological constructions manifest in local contexts through racial slurs and stereotypes. In response to our question "What's the biggest stereotype people have about Native people?" the girls listed the following: "welfare hos," "lazy. Drunk. Doesn't want to work," "living off the government," "Dirty chugs." The girls' frequent descriptions of racist terms resonate with Kim Anderson's claim that "Native girls begin to hear racial slurs from a young age, often before they even understand the terms themselves" (105).

The girls often acknowledged that colonialism had a cumulative "wearing us down" and "breaking us up" effect on their communities. Indeed, one of the most profound impacts of colonization, according to the Native Women's Association of Canada, has been "a denial of our traditional economic structures, loss of our land base, and traditional governing structures. This has resulted in a condition of poverty for many Aboriginal peoples and Aboriginal women . . . have been disproportionally affected" (5). Indigenous women, compared to all other groups of women in Canada, experience higher rates of incarceration; involvement in the child welfare system; mental illness; residence in substandard housing; unequal access to employment, health, and social services; stigmatization; and everyday experiences of discrimination, racism, sexism, and violence (Aleem; Blackstock and Trocmé; Downe; Fast and Collin-Vézina). These indicators are rooted in a history of chronic gendered poverty and social and economic exclusion: not only are Indigenous women twice as likely to be poor as non-Indigenous women in Canada, they are also significantly poorer than Indigenous men (Statistics Canada, "Women in Canada"; Wilson and Macdonald), and their location at the margins of the economy increases their vulnerability to violence and exploitation (Sethi; Sikka). These alarming statistics are too often taken as normal and irreversible, rather than as indicators of a deeply broken social system.

Certainly, many of the girls spoke passionately about the importance of talking honestly and openly about the racism and violence facing Indigenous women and girls in Canadian society. They also linked gendered violence to the impact of racial segregation in their communities. The ongoing appropriation of Indigenous territories and knowledge, which disrupted the possibility for traditional economic modes of sustenance for many communities (Blackstock and Trocmé), limited people's, particularly women's, independence and self-determination, and, simultaneously, shaped the colonial image of Indigenous people as poor, lazy, and dangerous. The examples shared by the girls illustrate how place and space become racialized through legal and social constructs that "naturalize these spatial relations of dominance . . . highlighting white respectability and Aboriginal criminality" (S. Razack 128). T.J.'s and Candace's comments illustrate this point:

They think once you cross over the bridge, that's like the dangerous part of town. We're all drunk and we're gonna attack you or something. (T.J.)

My white friends told me their parents told them not to come here, they would get robbed or something. (Candace)

These reductive binaries of racialized criminality—safe/white and dangerous/other—underlie the dominant stereotypes of Indigenous youth as dangerous and untrustworthy that Indigenous girls take up and are subjected to. What is particularly problematic about these constructions is that research, policies, and services too often take this othered status as natural and normal. As we discuss later, programs that target "at-risk" Aboriginal youth are often offered in marginalized, highly racialized neighbourhoods where the notion of "high risk" becomes entangled with unquestioned racialized assumptions about the needs and circumstances of Aboriginal youth. In contrast, when girls attend mainstream social or recreational programs designed for youth or specifically for girls, they are typically a minority surrounded by non-Indigenous peers. Indigenous issues are rarely discussed beyond the superficial "cultural celebrations" that further tokenize and alienate the girls, as expressed by seventeen-year-old Hannah: "They'll make us cut out paper totems but won't talk about racism."

Following on Hanna's comment, many girls underscored the importance of spaces for Indigenous survivance and advocacy, or what they called "all-Native and "Native-only" programs:

I go to an all-Native drop-in group. It's open to all Natives. As long as you're Native you can go and do cultural activities. . . . I can feel proud of being First Nations there. (Seeka)

I learn so much about my culture. We do dances and field trips, Elders come and teach us. (Lynn, 13, Métis, adopted into a white home)

It connects me to role models, like this one counsellor is Native and she's always there for us. They helped me with job search and homework. It, like, it keeps me close to my ancestry, it's a place to learn who you are. (Bonnie, 15, unknown Indigenous background, lives in a white foster home)

The girls identified multiple benefits of community activities and programming, including mentoring, connections, supports, advocacy, and belonging.

They also stressed that living in smaller towns posed barriers: for instance, in one girl's smaller community, there was an annual outdoor cultural camp, but no centre or Longhouse for year-round cultural events, and the school and recreation centres were all located a long drive away and often locked after hours.

In addition to these limitations, some girls also talked about outsiders' perceptions of "Native-only" programs, describing a sense of stigmatization because the services are often provided in what they termed "the bad part" of town or are seen to target "high-risk" and "problem" families:

> Plus I feel like our Native centre, people look at it, like, down. They think, that's where all the troubled Indian kids go [so] I don't want to go there. (Tara, 13, First Nation, off reserve)

> This one kid was all, "they go pray all weird in there, they're all dancing around with their feathers." (Seeka)

Tara's and Seeka's comments reflect colonial images of Indigenous people as "high risk" or "mysterious savages." Here again, any possibility for a richer, more layered understanding of the vibrancy and richness of Indigenous communities is muted. While the purpose of many Indigenous-specific programs is to support cultural, political, and economic resilience, the girls' descriptions stress that little understanding exists outside their communities that Indigenous people have lobbied for specialized cultural services as a critical and urgently needed self-determination strategy. A majority of the girls described their engagement in diverse cultural, recreational, and community activities and programming that contribute to invaluable leadership, skill building, cultural and language teaching, community capacity building, volunteering, and intergenerational mentoring, among many other benefits. Some of their family members hold positions of leadership in community programs and activities, and these events provide opportunities for significant engagement in community life. Yet many of the girls observed that their engagement in Indigenous-specific programs and spaces, rather than fostering in their non-Native peers a sense of understanding of their communities' diverse cultural traditions and political self-determination, often contributed to panic, judgment, and further backlash:

> They're all . . . against us having our own club for Natives. They say it's reverse racism. (Krista, 15, Inuk, Métis, and Scottish)

Yeah, they're like, "why do you get your own program?" They do think we're getting something for free. (Bonnie)

Like Krista and Bonnie, several girls emphasized that, even when they tried to trouble dominant whiteness, it was often reinstated as entitled and neutral, while Indigenous advocacy was recast as threatening and inappropriate. During one conversation, when asked, "What do you think they are scared of?" seventeen-year-old Hannah, who lives on reserve, replied, "Of being challenged, of losing their power."

Hannah's, Ella's, and Bonnie's comments were echoed by many of the girls across their discussions. What jumps out in these examples is the depth of analysis, courage, and persistence the girls demonstrate in continuously challenging problematic assumptions. Despite facing both implicit and explicit backlash, girls shared myriad examples of spirited survivance, including questioning; standing proudly; speaking back; challenging; celebrating their backgrounds, families, and communities; troubling assumptions and stereotypes; using humour; reaching out; and calling attention to the many facets of their realities.

In addition to these tangible everyday moments of advocacy, the girls shared many other nuanced examples of resistance and survivance. Many talked about the inspiration they drew from childhood memories, dreams, stories, teachings, connection to land, and knowledge of their family background and ancestry. They told stories about finding a positive sense of comfort, pride, and safety in their Indigenous communities, territories, and cultural traditions. In response to experiences of racism, many said they anchored themselves even more solidly in a strong Indigenous identity:

This is our land, this is native land. . . . I don't care what anybody thinks, I will always speak up for my community. (Willow)

I would identify as a strong warrior Indian woman. I know I am 100 percent Cowichan. (Hannah)

It is important to celebrate the fact that so many of the girls spoke in great detail about the sense of pride and belonging they gain from their Indigenous backgrounds and from their engagement in Indigenous communities, cultural events, and practices. These stories maintain spaces of possibility and change by and with girls that contribute to decolonization efforts across diverse Indigenous communities.

At the same time, just as many girls reported that a celebrated, identifiable, or rooted sense of Indigenous identity or community belonging was not readily accessible to them. Many shared that they "struggled a lot" with their Native backgrounds, always "trying to find out where I come from" or "trying to make [my reserve] feel like home when it's not." Many said that they coped with racism by "going along with it," "checking out," "avoiding it," and trying to fit into dominant whiteness by making themselves "as white as possible." These experiences have to be seen as active acts of survivance by girls to preserve dignity and safety in the midst of very difficult and unequal circumstances. But, as fifteen-year-old Liney stressed as she recounted one such story while choking back tears, it is also "so unfair" that "we Indians are even put in these situations," and it "totally wears you down."

Liney's story accentuates the need to honour, in her words, the "good, the bad, and the ugly" of "what girls do." In response to everyday instances of active coloniality, girls deploy a full spectrum of manoeuvres and negotiations. It is this very complexity that emphasizes how a singular focus on either gaps or strengths is limited and can even lead to blame, shame, and further silencing of complex situations. The girls may be resistant and defiant in one context and feel immobilized or silenced in another. Some girls described how, in one day, they may engage in both covert and overt efforts to speak back and make Indigenous issues more visible, while also feeling a tremendous burden of isolation, anger, and silencing. This dynamic speaks to the paradoxical positioning of Indigenous girls that sustains both the hyper-visibility of their racialized bodies—scrutinized, gendered, sexualized, pathologized—and their invisibility as diverse and complex subjects. Take, for instance, Rianna's observation at the beginning of the chapter that the only roles available to Indigenous girls are those of the dirty, drunken squaw or the noble Indian princess seduced by a white colonial soldier. These colonial images are reproduced in popular culture, emphasizing that Indigenous girls face multiple erasures across contexts. As Shandra Spears articulates, "I grew up within an ideology that said I did not exist, because Native people did not exist, except as mascots or objects of desire. Through this process of symbolic annihilation, I ceased to exist as a Native person within my own mind" (83).

The media are a dominant force in the definition, objectification, and oppression of girls (Coy; Katz). Popular culture supports "hegemonic femininities articulated through preferences which are race, class, ability, and sexuality-based" (Jiwani, Steenbergen, and Mitchell xiii). Many girls noted that the absence of Indigenous women in the media leaves them with few role models with whom they can identify; they do not see their realities reflected in the dominant narratives to which they are exposed in their daily lives (Hernandez and Rehman; Jiwani, Steenbergen and Mitchell). As Hannah, Ella, and Sonia express, they are usually positioned against normalized white, heterosexual femininity that marginalizes them as others:

> You hardly see Natives on TV . . . people wouldn't watch it if . . . like they think white girls are more hotter and attractive and stuff like that. (Ella, 15, First Nation, off reserve)

> Yeah, they're always in the music videos and you never see Aboriginals. (Sonia, 14)

> I do think Native women are beautiful but the media is contradicting that. It's white and skinny versus dark and curvy. It puts pressure on Native girls. (Hannah, 17)

Whether or not Indigenous girls can fully articulate the inner workings of these hegemonies of race, gender, sexuality, and class, their effects take hold as lived social exclusion, with concrete impacts on Indigenous girls' lives and their sense of being and (un)belonging in the towns and cities in which they live. In this sense, (neo)colonialism is at once fluid and adaptive, yet insidious and resilient; its ideologies and material practices are reproduced through the dominant formations of political systems, the media, social policy and services, educational institutions, and urban geographies, all of which underpin girls' everyday encounters with the colonial imaginary.

As we emphasized in our discussion of methodology, the perspectives represented here are drawn from community projects in three communities on Vancouver Island, on Canada's west coast. It is important to pay attention to the differences among different locations and regions in understanding how these dynamics operate. At the same time, we acknowledge that there are threads that reflect experiences common across history and geography. While the state does not operate as a coherent entity, the reproduction of colonial relations over centuries can work to resolidify these stratifications rather than rendering them more syncretic and permeable. As fourteen-year-old Annielee, a First Nation girl who lives on reserve, so aptly observed, "Well, I guess things have changed a lot, and at the same time, they really haven't changed at all."

How Native Are You? Colonial Management of Indigeneity

Although tremendous diversity exists within and among the hundreds of Indigenous nations that live in Canada, it can be said that gender and community roles were typically conceptualized differently from the rigid Euro-Western dichotomy that positions male as superior to female (Anderson). Colonialism "introduced gender itself as a colonial concept and mode of organization of relations of production, property relations, of cosmologies and ways of knowing" (Lugones 187). Andrea Smith argues that the imposition of a gender hierarchy was a deliberate outcome of the residential school system: "For the most part, schools prepared Native boys for manual labor or farming and Native girls for domestic work . . . the primary role of this education for Indian girls was to inculcate patriarchal norms into Native communities so that women would lose their place of leadership in Native communities" (37).

Furthermore, assimilative colonial policies have for centuries carefully managed who could be enrolled as members of First Nations and Métis and Inuit communities, with particularly harmful effects on women.[4] The *Indian Act* has reproduced this paternalistic gender framework and stripped Indigenous women of the dignity and power they traditionally held in their communities by restricting who could be considered "Indian" and positioning women in roles of dependency on men:

> The historical disenfranchisement of First Nations women has been discussed at length by many authors and is due to the regressive membership regime in the *Indian Act*. Until 1985, a First Nations woman who married a non-First Nations man lost her membership and identity (status) as an "Indian" whereas if a First Nations man married a non-First Nations woman, his partner gained First Nations membership and status. (Sayers and MacDonald 11)

Although Bill C-31 reversed this disenfranchising policy to some extent with the 1985 reinstatement of status to women and their children, the policy maintains significant restrictions and negative impacts. For example, many women who were disenfranchised from their communities and the grandchildren of women who had lost their status are still not included (11). Furthermore, political and social tensions erupted as a result of Bill C-31 because many women were suddenly reinstated as members of resource-strapped bands, leaving them open to acrimony and exclusion and unable to find housing or employment on their reserves. Although Bill C-31 targeted First Nations women, similar policies also affected Métis, Inuit, and other mixed-race Indigenous women and children, resulting in their alienation from their communities and cultures and their migration to cities (Lawrence) like Port Alberni, Duncan, and Victoria.

Knowledge related to assessing and compartmentalizing "who belongs," "who is registered," and "who has status" is ingrained in many Indigenous children from a young age. The girls' recirculation of this knowledge in their everyday negotiations with their peers, families, and community members gives credence to Jo-ann Episkenew's assertion that "Canada's policies have affected us so profoundly that many Indigenous peoples have adopted a policy number (Bill C-31) as an identity marker! Only in Indigenous Canada would people instantly know the meaning and significance of that label" (21). In session after session of our different studies, the girls emphasized how intimately aware they are of politics of recognition and membership, which they constantly code, circulate, and question to identify themselves and one another. In the following discussion among a diverse group of First Nations, Métis, and mixed-race girls, the question "How would you describe your background?" elicited a complex positioning process:

I am half Swampy Cree; my grandparents were [name of family and birth place]. I am also a quarter Tsimshian, and a quarter Irish and French. (Willow, 14)

I'm a full-status Indian. (Annielee, 14)

I'm a member of the Métis Nation. My family is Red River Métis. We're scrip. (Lisa, 15)

We're Bill C-31. My mom married my dad and my dad is white, so we're not fully registered. (Krista, 13)

I know it's weird; some people don't believe me because I'm blond. But actually I have status. We're more, like I consider us to be real First Nations because we're like, that's how we identify. Some of my family, on my mom's side, they're Métis. They're more mixed, like they're dark, too, but they're mixed. But they have like a whole different culture, too. (Leanne, 14)

Many girls reported that, when coming from other Indigenous people, the question "Where are you from?" is never neutral, but rather is a not-so-subtle code for finding out, in Annielee's words, "how Indian you are." On the one hand, the question requests that girls articulate their location among traditional family and community structures, in genealogies that are rooted in relations of belonging and power within and among communities that predate colonial systems. Yet the question is also meant to elicit a response that (re)establishes a hierarchy of legitimacy and authenticity based on colonial policy categorizations within and across the three groups—First Nations, Métis, and Inuit—who are considered Aboriginal in Canada but are in themselves incredibly diverse and complex and have different histories of colonization and relations with the Canadian government and with one another. These negotiations might be based on factors ranging from where the families are registered and what sort of Aboriginal status they hold, to how they look physically, how they identify culturally and linguistically, how they were raised, whom they are related to and whether they have mixed heritage, where their ancestral lands were located, whether they were placed in foster care or adopted out, whether they left or stayed in the community, and myriad other compounding factors.

A full exploration of the nuances of identity politics within and across Indigenous communities is beyond the scope of this chapter, but the girls' assertions about who "doesn't know," who does or doesn't "look Native," who is "registered," "real," "mixed," and "full" allow a glimpse into the complex knowledge of colonial policy categories they negotiate, highlighting the many possible trajectories for imposing and accessing different Indigenous subject positions under Anglo-nationalism and under Indigenous community laws and traditions. Thus it is critical not to overgeneralize and reproduce one-dimensional depictions of complex Indigenous identities and experiences, but rather to pay attention to the complexities and contradictions that girls negotiate in their everyday lives.

Given these complexities, as we saw earlier, it is understandable that many girls anchor themselves in a deeply rooted anticolonial "Indian warrior" identity that provides a sense of congruence, pride, and belonging. Such an identity is also vital to Indigenous sovereignty, cultural resurgence, and decolonization. Yet it is important to underscore the fact that a more identifiable, rooted Indigenous identity is not available to all Indigenous girls in similar ways. Indigenous identity is a site of tremendous struggle and tension on multiple levels. In contrast to the warrior girl stands an image of "the searching tribe," an experience of "not knowing" or living "in-between" with which many girls identified:

> My mom says we're the searching tribe. . . . We're not really seen as real, like we don't really fit in one or the other. I guess I know I'm Native but I don't really know what kind. My mom, she doesn't really go home and we lived in town all my life. She . . . kinda doesn't talk a lot about it. I look Native but I just don't really know about it. (Larissa, 13)

> Yeah, like an apple—red outside, white inside. (Ashley, 16)

> Oh, I'm like a reverse apple, I'm white on the outside and red inside. (Lisa, 14)

The sense of ambiguity and the gaps in knowledge and access these girls describe must be understood as more than the natural and inevitable outcome of a growing cultural hybridity and mobility in a Canadian multicultural mosaic. Girls who do have access to a documented, legitimized Indigenous identity report that they are sometimes blamed and further marginalized by both settler and Indigenous communities for being "whitewashed" when in fact their marginalization and assimilation are direct and deliberate outcomes of carefully orchestrated policies of the *Indian Act*. Compounding the exclusion of generations of Indigenous women from status rights and membership and belonging in their communities is the history of residential schools, child apprehension, and external adoptions that has been so damaging to the fabric of Indigenous communities and which has seen many thousands of Indigenous children removed from their families and communities. Downe calls for an examination of how this gendered history established "a pattern of dislocation, uprootedness and abuse that continues to characterize the lives of Aboriginal girls"; this, she contends, is very much a lived history kept alive through the ongoing "traumatic disconnection" of thousands of Aboriginal girls from their communities (2). This ongoing history brings to light the urgent need for theorizing and activism related to how gendering and sexualization shape the racialization of Indigenous girls and women under a colonial state. One such recent example involves how Indigenous communities, and women in particular, have rallied together to bring attention to the ongoing disappearances and murders of Indigenous girls and women. The issue of missing and murdered Indigenous women in British Columbia and across Canada continues to be addressed inadequately by federal, provincial, and local authorities, as evidenced by a recent announcement by the United Nations Committee on the Elimination of Discrimination against Women (CEDAW) that the situation has reached epidemic proportions and that they will undertake an investigation of generations of missing Indigenous women in Canada (Kornacki).

Downe argues that tracing these generational links is critical to advocating for justice and to understanding contemporary Indigenous girlhoods, since "the abuses experienced by Aboriginal girls over the past 130 years are not isolated occurrences; they are connected through a pervasive colonial ideology that sees these young women as exploitable and often dispensable" (2–3). Indigenous girls are seen as less deserving of public empathy, of government resources, and of comprehensive social, economic, and political interventions. What is missing in this representation is the multiple stories of strength, advocacy, pride, joy, hope, and humour that permeate Indigenous girls' lives. And, of course, despite their personal knowledge of the complex dynamics of their lives, Indigenous girls are too often excluded from research, policy, and programming debates that affect them (de Finney, "Under the Shadow of Empire"). It is to these negotiations of visibility/invisibility and inclusion/exclusion that we turn our attention in our conclusion.

Survivance under Neocolonialism

As incredibly diverse as they are, Indigenous girls who live in less diverse Canadian cities also share common experiences of living under a colonial state. Their negotiations within, across, outside, and against such categories as Native/non-Native, mixed race, Métis, First Nations, on/off reserve, status/non-status, Aboriginal, and Indigenous reveal how intersecting relations of ruling operate in their lives to produce a plethora of complex negotiations and sites of resilience and survivance. Our discussion highlights how Indigenous girls constantly reconstitute and unsettle their (im)mobility across multiple borders of inclusion and exclusion through their strategic reading and coding of such markers as birthplace, family and ancestral background, registry membership, skin colour, class location, cultural knowledge, and level of assimilation into mainstream Canadian society. An important focus of this discussion involved centring girls' resourcefulness, creativity, and tenacity. We also emphasized their complicated struggles with the historical reproduction of mobile, overlapping colonial hegemonies of gender, race, class, and sexuality that shape their representation as "dispensable." These stories are also worth highlighting, as their prevalence and significance in the girls' accounts is a reflection of deep-seated colonial effects, rather than evidence that girls (and our representations of them) lack strength and spirit. The stories shared here emphasize how girls actively ignore, resist, stand proudly, seek solidarity, build community, dream and laugh, and articulate alternative, decolonizing accounts—but also how easily their voices are dismissed, silenced, and trivialized. As they navigate through the asymmetries of "scattered hegemonies," they must cope with being repositories of anxieties about their legitimacy and purity. They are expected to represent their nations while they struggle to establish their belonging to these same nations. From their multifaceted subject positions, they are loyal to overlapping kinships, homelands, and cultural teachings, all of which are negotiated through competing expectations about their classed, gendered, sexualized, and racialized locations (de Finney, "We Just Don't Know Each Other").

Our collective efforts to document a range of stories have been inspired by the work of diverse Indigenous women scholars (Anderson; Anderson and Lawrence; Battiste and Semeganis; Gross; Smith; Tuck, "Breaking Up"; Tuck, "Suspending Damage"; Tuhiwai Smith) who have taken up the notion of survivance and decolonization in some way to foreground the importance of collecting and sharing stories in the spirit of "documenting not only the painful elements of social realities but also the wisdom and hope" (Tuck, "Suspending Damage" 416). We emphasize again the creative and multiple ways that Indigenous women and girls have for hundreds of years contested colonial hegemonies and mobilized culturally, socially, spiritually, and politically as activists, teachers, healers, leaders, and advocates. Indigenous women and girls have pushed for legislative and policy change, initiated grassroots organizing and international advocacy, created community-based services and alternative economies, and acted as political, spiritual, and cultural leaders. As we saw, many of the girls we work with are aware of this tremendous ongoing legacy of strength and resilience, and many have participated in individual and collective resistances of all kinds.

Growing calls for supporting girls' collective survivance and resurgence resonate with existing literature to indicate that a more nuanced understanding of the complexity and diversity of Indigenous girlhoods is urgently needed (de Finney, "Under the Shadow of Empire"). To ignore deep-seated historical inequities and to collapse complex dynamics into depoliticized, singular accounts limits Indigenous girls' engagement and visibility on multiple levels, and curtails the potential for building solidarity and engaging in decolonizing efforts. Without decolonizing solidarity, Indigenous girls may lack opportunities to come to know, as Annielee expressed, that "we are . . . awesome, Native women, we're awesome! And anybody that doesn't see that, it's their problem."

Notes

1   Under the Canadian constitution, the term "Aboriginal" designates First Nations (both on and off reserve), Métis, and Inuit peoples. The concept of aboriginality is deeply contested, both for its conflation of hundreds of distinct First Peoples and because their constitution as objects of colonial control has evolved over centuries through concerted settlement and assimilative policies that reproduce their political, economic, and socio-cultural exclusion. In this paper we use the term "Indigenous" to make visible the impact of European colonialism on over 85 percent of the world's Indigenous communities (Jiwani, Steenbergen, and Mitchell) and to foreground Indigenous peoples' shared struggle with colonialism and efforts to pursue political solidarity across the world. Where we use "Aboriginal," it is to reflect the specific use in the context of Canadian policy and legislation.

2   This study was part of a much larger Social Sciences and Humanities Research Council (SSHRC) study under the direction of Dr. Jo-Anne Lee at the Department of Women's Studies, University of Victoria.

3   This study was funded by the Victoria Foundation (Adoption and Permanency Trust Fund) and the B.C. Ministry of Children and Family Development.

4   A full discussion of these policies and practices exceeds the scope of this chapter, but families were denied status based on factors such as family names/family origin, blood quantum, and rights that are traced through fathers rather than mothers. Families were also left out of registry lists for reasons such as being away hunting when the Indian agent came to register members; giving up status rights in order to be able to vote, own property, or study; or being deliberately excluded due to their political views.

Works Cited

Aleem, Rebecca. "International Human Rights Law and Aboriginal Girls in Canada: Never the Twain Shall Meet?" *Justice for Girls International.* 2009. Web. 18 May 2012.

Anderson, Kim. *A Recognition of Being: Reconstructing Native Womanhood.* Toronto: Sumach Press, 2000. Print.

Anderson, Kim, and Bonita Lawrence, eds. *Strong Women Stories: Native Vision and Community Survival.* Toronto: Sumach Press, 2003. Print.

Battiste, Marie, and Helen Semeganis. "First Thoughts on First Nations Citizenship: Issues in Education." *Citizenship in Transformation in Canada.* Ed. Yvonne M. Hébert. Toronto: U of Toronto P, 2002. 93–111. Print.

Blackstock, Cindy, and Nico Trocmé. "Community-based Child Welfare for Aboriginal Children: Supporting Resilience Through Structural Change." *Pathways to Resilience: A Handbook of Theory, Methods, and Interventions.* Ed. Michael Ungar. Thousand Oaks: Sage, 2004. 1–28. Print.

Coy, Maddy. "Milkshakes, Lady Lumps, and Growing Up to Want Boobies: How the Sexualisation of Popular Culture Limits Girls' Horizons." *Child Abuse Review* 18.6 (2009): 372–83. Wiley Online Library. Web. 18 May 2012.

Crichlow, Wesley. "Western Colonization as Disease: Native Adoption and Cultural Genocide." *Canadian Social Work* 5.1 (2003): 88–107. Print.

de Finney, Sandrina. *The NONG SILA Urban Adoptions Project: A Community-based Model for Urban Aboriginal Adoptions.* Victoria: Surrounded by Cedar Child and Family Services Society, 2008. Print.

———. "Under the Shadow of Empire: Indigenous Girls' Presencing as Decolonizing Force." *Girlhood Studies* 6.2 (2014): 8–26. Print.

———. "'We Just Don't Know Each Other': Racialised Girls Negotiate Mediated Multiculturalism in a Less Diverse Canadian City." *Journal of Intercultural Studies* 31.5 (2010): 471–87. Print.

de Finney, Sandrina, Elicia Loiselle, and Mackenzie Dean. "Bottom of the Food Chain: The Minoritization of Girls in Child and Youth Care." *Critical Perspectives in Child and Youth Care: Working the Borders of Pedagogy, Practice and Policy.* Ed. Alan Pence and Jennifer White. Vancouver: UBC P, 2011. 92–121. Print.

Dei, George J. Sefa. "Rethinking the Role of Indigenous Knowledges in the Academy." *International Journal of Inclusive Education* 4.2 (2000): 111–32. Print.

Downe, Pamela. "Aboriginal Girls in Canada: Living Histories of Dislocation, Exploitation and Strength." *Girlhood: Redefining the Limits.* Ed. Candis Steenbergen, Yasmin Jiwani, and Claudia Mitchell. Montreal: Black Rose Books, 2006. 1–14. Print.

Episkenew, Jo-ann. *Taking Back Our Spirits: Indigenous Literature, Public Policy, and Healing.* Winnipeg: U of Manitoba P, 2009. Print.

Fast, Elizabeth, and Delphine Collin-Vézina. "Historical Trauma, Race-Based Trauma and Resilience of Indigenous Peoples: A Literature Review." *First Peoples Child and Family Review* 5.1 (2010): 126–36. Print.

Fleming, Tara, and Kent Kowalski. "Body-Related Experiences of Two Young Rural Aboriginal Women." *Journal of Aboriginal Health* 4.2 (December 2009): 44–51. Print.

Grewal, Inderpal, and Caren Kaplan, eds. *Scattered Hegemonies: Postmodernity and Transnational Feminist Practices.* Minneapolis: U of Minnesota P, 1994. Print.

Gross, Emma R. "Native American Family Continuity as Resistance: The Indian Child Welfare Act as Legitimation for an Effective Social Work Practice." *Journal of Social Work* 3.1 (2003): 31–44. Print.

Harris, Anita, ed. *All About the Girl: Culture, Power and Identity.* New York: Routledge, 2004. Print.

Hernandez, Daisy, and Bushra Rehman, eds. *Colonize This! Young Women of Color on Today's Feminism.* New York: Seal Press, 2002. Print.

Indian and Northern Affairs Canada. *Treaty Research Report.* Ottawa: Department of Indian and Northern Affairs Canada. 15 Sept. 2010. Web. 17 May 2012.

Jiwani, Yasmin, Candis Steenbergen, and Claudia Mitchell, eds. *Girlhood: Redefining the Limits.* Montreal: Black Rose Books, 2006. Print.

Katz, Jackson. *The Macho Paradox: Why Some Men Hurt Women and How All Men Can Help.* Naperville: Sourcebooks, 2006. Print.

Kornacki, Chris. "UN Committee to Investigate Missing and Murdered Aboriginal Women." *Wawatay News Online.* 6 Jan. 2012. Web. 17 May 2012.

Lawrence, Bonita. *"Real" Indians and Others: Mixed-Blood Urban Native Peoples and Indigenous Nationhood.* Vancouver: UBC P, 2004. Print.

Lawrence, Bonita, and Enakshi Dua. "Decolonising Anti-Racism." *Social Justice* 32.4 (2005): 120–43. Print.

Lee, Jo-Anne, and Sandrina de Finney. "Using Popular Theatre for Engaging Racialized Minority Girls in Exploring Questions of Identity and Belonging." *Child and Youth Services* 26.2 (2005): 95–118. Taylor & Francis Online. Web. 17 May 2012.

Lesko, Nancy. "Past, Present, and Future Conceptions of Adolescence." *Educational Theory* 46.4 (1996): 453–73. Print.

Lugones, Marìa. "Heterosexualism and the Colonial/Modern Gender System." *Hypatia* 22.1 (2007): 186–209. Print.

Minh-ha, Trinh T. "Not You/Like You: Postcolonial Women and the Interlocking Questions of Identity and Difference." *Dangerous Liaisons: Gender, Nation and Postcolonial Perspectives.* Ed. Ella Shohat and Anne McClintock. Minneapolis: U of Minnesota P, 1997. 415–19. Print.

Mohanty, Chandra Talpade. *Feminism without Borders: Decolonizing Theory, Practicing Solidarity.* Durham: Duke UP, 2003. Print.

Native Women's Association of Canada. *Aboriginal Women and Health Care in Canada*. Ottawa: Commission on the Future of Health Care in Canada, 2002. Print.

Razack, Narda. "Bodies on the Move: Spatialized Locations, Identities, and Nationality in International Work." *Social Justice* 32.4 (2005): 87–104. Print.

Razack, Sherene. *Race, Space, and the Law: Unmapping a White Settler Society*. Toronto: Between the Lines, 2002. Print.

Ruttan, Lia, Patti LaBoucane-Benson, and Brenda Munro. "'Home and Native Land': Aboriginal Young Women and Homelessness in the City." *First Peoples Child and Family Review* 5.1 (2010): 67–77. Print.

Said, Edward. *Orientalism*. New York: Vintage Books, 1979. Print.

Saraceno, Johanne. *Indigenous Girls and Sexual Exploitation in a Rural BC Town: A Photovoice Study*. Victoria: U of Victoria, 2010. Print.

Sayers, Judith, and Kelly MacDonald. "A Strong and Meaningful Role for First Nations Women in Governance." *First Nations Women, Government, and the Indian Act*. Judith F. Sayers, Kelly A. MacDonald, Jo-anne Fiske, Melonie Newell, Evelyn George, and Wendy Cornet. Ottawa: Status of Women Canada, 2001. 1–54. Web. 17 May 2012.

Schutte, Ofelia. "Postcolonial Feminisms: Genealogies and Recent Directions." *The Blackwell Guide to Feminist Philosophy*. Ed. Linda Martín Alcoff and Eva Feder Kittay. Malden: Blackwell, 2007. 165–76. Print.

Sethi, Anupriya. "Domestic Sex Trafficking of Aboriginal Girls in Canada: Issues and Implications." *First Peoples Child and Family Review* 3.3 (2007): 57–71. Print.

Sikka, Anette. *Trafficking of Aboriginal Women and Girls in Canada*. Aboriginal Policy Research Series. Ottawa: Institute on Governance, 2009. Print.

Sinclair, Raven. "Identity Lost and Found: Lessons from the Sixties Scoop." *First Peoples Child and Family Review* 3.1 (2007): 65–82. Print.

Smith, Andrea. *Conquest: Sexual Violence and American Indian Genocide*. Cambridge: South End Press, 2005. Print.

Spears, Shandra. "Strong Spirit, Fractured Identity: An Ojibway Adoptee's Journey to Wholeness." *Strong Women Stories: Native Vision and Community Survival*. Ed. Kim Anderson and Bonita Lawrence. Toronto: Sumach P, 2003. 81–94. Print.

Statistics Canada. *Table 1: Size and Growth of the Population by Aboriginal Identity, Canada, 1996 and 2006*. 22 Sept. 2009. Web. 17 May 2012.

Statistics Canada. *Women in Canada: A Gender-Based Statistical Report*. Ottawa: Minister of Industry, 2006. Web. 17 May 2012.

St. Denis, Verna. "Feminism Is for Everybody: Aboriginal Women, Feminism and Diversity." *Making Space for Indigenous Feminism.* Ed. Joyce Green. Halifax: Fernwood, 2007. 33–52. Print.

Tuck, Eve. "Breaking Up with Deleuze: Desire and Valuing the Irreconcilable." *International Journal of Qualitative Studies in Education* 23.5 (2010): 635–50. Print.

———. "Suspending Damage: A Letter to Communities." *Harvard Educational Review* 79.3 (2009): 409–27. Print.

Tuhiwai Smith, Linda. *Decolonizing Methodologies: Research and Indigenous Peoples.* London: Zed Books, 1999. Print.

Urquijo, Covadonga Robles, and Anne Milan. "Female Population." *Women in Canada: A Gender-Based Statistical Report July 2011.* Ottawa: Statistics Canada, 2011. 5–19. Web. 17 Sept. 2012.

Vizenor, Gerald. *Fugitive Poses: Native American Indian Scenes of Absence and Presence.* Lincoln: U of Nebraska P, 1998. Print.

———. *Manifest Manners: Narratives on Postindian Survivance.* Middleton: Wesleyan UP, 1994. Print.

Ward, Jane Victoria, and Beth Cooper Benjamin. "Women, Girls, and the Unfinished Work of Connection: A Critical Review of American Girls' Studies." *All About the Girl: Culture, Power and Identity.* Ed. Anita Harris. New York: Routledge, 2004. 5–28. Print.

Wilson, Daniel, and David Macdonald. *The Income Gap Between Aboriginal Peoples and the Rest of Canada.* Ottawa: Canadian Centre for Policy Alternatives. 2010. Web. 17 Sept. 2012.

CHAPTER 6

Girls' Texts, Visual Culture, and Shifting the Boundaries of Knowledge in Social Justice Research

The Politics of Making the Invisible Visible

Claudia Mitchell

This chapter takes up the critical role of the visual in deepening an under-standing of the experiences of girls and young women, as well as the pol-itical project of addressing the invisibility of girls across a broad range of sectors. For close to two decades I have been studying various aspects of girls' lives, including barriers to their education, particularly in sub-Saharan Africa and in the context of such critical issues as poverty and gender-based violence; the significance of girls' voices and their participation more gen-erally in informing policy about their own lives; and girls' popular culture, including digital media. Increasingly, I have found that working with girls through their photographs, drawings, and video productions has contrib-uted to what can be described as a "shifting" of the "boundaries of know-ledge" (see Marcus and Hofmaener). In this chapter I highlight some of the ways that this shifting can take place, and why it needs to be an important component in also shifting the agenda for work with girls more broadly.

This visual project of girlhood, as I think it could be described, has a number of different facets, reflecting a body of literature that in and of itself is complex and made up of separate yet interrelated areas. While I identify a number of these here as an indication of a typology of sorts, the list is by no means complete. Consider, for example, the photographic and other visual images of girlhood that are produced by adults, as can be seen in Sally Mann's dramatic and controversial photographs of her young daughters as "the new mothers," explored by Anne Higonnet in her book *Pictures of Innocence*; in Mann's *At Twelve* work with early adolescent girls; and by authors such as Loren Lerner in her study of girlhood in paintings, "Adolescent Girls, Adult Women." A second area of study on visual representations of girlhood, also produced by adults, relates more to media depictions, ranging from Patricia Holland's work *Picturing Childhood*, which looks at everything from Hallmark greeting card images to international non-governmental organization (NGO) child rescue images, to the more deliberately constructed social justice images compiled in *Broken Bodies, Broken Dreams* (see Ward), to work that critiques the images of girlhood used in reports and other policy documents produced by NGOs (see Magno and Kirk). A third area of girlhood and visual study can be seen in the self-reflexive analysis of family photographs that some feminist scholars have taken up in their own memory studies of girlhood. These include Valerie Walkerdine's auto-ethnographic study of a photograph of herself as a little girl dressed up as a fairy in *Schoolgirl Fictions*, Annette Kuhn's analysis of herself as an eleven-year-old in her new (and socially uncomfortable) school uniform in *Family Secrets*, and Jo Spence's schoolgirl staging work (in collaboration with Rosy Martin) in *Cultural Sniping*, as a way of reconstructing the family album.

Then there are the visual images of girlhood produced by girls and young women. These include the work of young women as artists, as can be seen in Sadie Bening's video work. As Nicholas Paley describes it, when Bening was fifteen years old, her filmmaker father gave her as a Christmas present a Fisher-Price Pixelvision video camera (Paley 69). While she was horrified to receive an $89.95 child's toy, it was this toy that launched her career as a video artist. At the other end of the spectrum are the images that girls and young women produce within their own DIY digital media culture and which freely circulate as avatars or other visual representations on Facebook and other social networking sites, and which are independent of adult-run galleries or studios (Morrison).

Finally, and as the focus of this chapter, there are the images that girls themselves have produced through their own photographs, drawings, and video-making in community-based participatory research and interventions. While these visuals sit alongside the work of Sadie Benning or the

DIY images noted above, they are typically produced within adult-organized projects.[1] Depending on the reach of the project, they may end up being seen primarily in local community or school settings, or they may become part of larger exhibitions. This last body of work includes the video-making studies *Girl Making*, by Gerry Bloustien; *Girls Make Media*, Mary Celeste Kearney's work with girls and media-making; and the photo work of Kamina Walton with primary school girls focusing on sexual harassment in "Creating Positive Images"; along with the body of work that my colleagues and I have been developing through the Centre for Visual Methodologies for Social Change at the University of KwaZulu-Natal in South Africa. Our work involves video, photography, drawings, and the study of the image-making process, with girls in Rwanda, Ethiopia, Swaziland, and South Africa (see Mitchell, *Doing Visual Research*; de Lange, Mitchell, and Stuart).

At the centre of this work is one critical question: How can girls and young women "see for themselves" the issues (and as such take on agency), and at the same time make visible to the community, policy-makers, and others the issues that need changing? This question is located within what Patricia Maguire in *Doing Participatory Research* refers to as feminist participatory research, an approach to research that acknowledges girls and women as more than "subjects," and in so doing recognizes the perspectives of girls and women in identifying both the issues that concern them and possible solutions at the community level. Caroline Wang's innovative photovoice work with rural Chinese women in the 1990s remains an inspiration for the girlhood visual project.

In this chapter, I take the study of girls' engagement through participatory visual research one step further by looking at the ways in which girls can be both cultural producers (creating images through video, photography, and drawings), as well as interpreters of their own work through a process of participatory analysis. This "shifting the boundaries of knowledge" approach refers to transforming what is typically a top-down process of research and knowledge production into what might be described as a grassroots, "from the ground up" approach (Choudry and Kapoor). Indeed, as Susan Sontag writes, "[t]he task of interpretation is virtually one of translation" (89). Her point serves to underpin my interest in "translation" and meaning-making with girls through a process of participatory analysis, or working in participatory ways with girls and their own visual data. The analytic voices of participants may, of course, show up when they curate an exhibition, or select images for a website. An area that is under-studied in the work of participatory studies and community-based research, however, relates to a more explicit consideration of how participants themselves contribute to making meaning of the data beyond the initial eliciting of data. One of the challenges in participatory visual research is making explicit the process. Because so much of this work involves interactive workshops and, ideally, engagement over a period of time, and because there are limits to what can be represented in an article or book chapter, it is sometimes difficult to give the full story. The question of what one does with the photos, videos, drawings, data, and so on, is one that is frequently asked and one that often implies that, once the visual data have been collected, the next step is for the researcher to embark upon the analysis (in whatever way that might be) in some sort of solitary way that is separate from the community. Few published studies have looked at how to engage participants in generative ways beyond the initial stages of documenting the issues in their lives. Thus, I explore "the next step" by drawing together examples of visual work with girls between ten and fourteen years of age in order to look at the possibilities for participatory analysis and ultimately the idea of shifting the boundaries of knowledge.

Girls and Participatory Analysis

This section is not about the theories behind or the "how to" of photovoice, participatory video, or using drawing in visual research. These are all areas that are written about extensively elsewhere (see, for example, Pink; Banks; Rose). I also do not highlight the obvious interpretive lens that the girls I discuss in this chapter are already using by virtue of taking the pictures in the first place. Arguably, choosing what to photograph or to represent visually is in some ways already part of data analysis, in that the girls have made some decisions about what to draw, photograph, or film in their environment. It is also not about how researchers can do their own analysis of data. Although this remains an area in which there is much more to be written, there are nonetheless writings and analytic schemes within fieldwork studies that inform researchers' analyses of data (Clark-Ibáñez).

What this section *is* about is how girls have been and could be involved in analyzing and interpreting their own visual data after the photos have been taken, or, in other words, how girls have worked with their data. Drawing from four case studies on participatory visual research with girls in Ethiopia, Canada, South Africa, and Rwanda, I argue that engaging girls in the process of translation and interpretation of their own visual data is the obvious next step in making this work more participatory. And although, as

I point out in a section at the end of the four case studies, this work is not without its challenges and limitations, participatory analysis can build on the reflexivity—as Joan Solomon says, "ourselves to ourselves" (10)—that is already embedded within much work with girls and visual culture.

Case Study 1: Growing Up as a Girl in the Land of Coffee (Ethiopia) Photo Analysis

"This one is perhaps not the best photo; it is a little blurry but it shows the way over-cutting has contributed to soil erosion here, and why we need to do something," says Bizeyeu, age thirteen, of rural Ethiopia. Bizeyeu is offering to a group of peers a poster presentation of the photographs that she and fourteen other girls working in groups of five produced in response to a very simple prompt: "picture growing up as a girl in the land of coffee." Part of the "Wake Up and Smell the Coffee" module of a larger study,[2] in this photovoice component two groups of girls—the group Bizeyeu belonged to and living in a town, and another group about twenty kilometres away and in a deeply rural area—participated in a one-day photo shoot using digital cameras. In a follow-up session, the members of each small group were given colour prints of their photos, markers, press stick, and a poster board sheet, with the very broad prompt: "work with 10–15 of your photos and your poster board." We avoided asking participants to "tell a story" or "to analyze the photos," with the idea that groups could choose how they might want to work with their photos. Once the small groups had finished creating their poster, each group presented their poster to the larger group. The posters were taped on the wall so that the group as a whole could do a walk-about and look at the posters closely. The idea of engaging in photo analysis through the production of poster narratives has been tested in other settings with adults (de Lange et al., "Seeing"). Here I am making explicit each aspect of the process in order to frame the production of these posters as analysis (see fig. 6.1, 6.2, and 6.3):

- The selection process (which ten to fifteen photos to choose from a collection of thirty or more and why?)
- Participatory coding (which photos go together and why?)
- Making and rationale for decisions about the physical/aesthetic arrangement of the photos on the poster board
- The use of symbols showing relationships between and among photos
- Coming up with a title

FIGURE 6.1 • Creating captions (Ethiopia). Photograph: Author's collection.

FIGURE 6.2 • Presenting the analysis to the larger group (Ethiopia). Photograph: Author's collection.

FIGURE 6.3 • Three posters (Ethiopia). Photograph: Author's collection.

As with the feminist researcher group process described by Caroline Ramazanoğlu and Janet Holland in *Feminist Methodology*, the interpretive work comes out of discussion and debate. The resulting posters speak to a number of critical issues, ranging from the environmental issues raised by Bizeyeu's group, to findings in another group focusing on the differing forms of oppression for boys and girls growing up in the land of coffee, through to the gendered landscape of coffee growing (see fig. 6.4 and 6.5).

FIGURE 6.4 • Girls' group poster (Ethiopia). Photograph: Author's collection.

FIGURE 6.5 • Gender analysis: Close-up of a poster (Ethiopia).
Photograph: Author's collection.

Case Study 2: Which One Is Not Like the Others? What Do Our Photos Have in Common? (Canada)

A group of twenty fifth- and sixth-grade girls (ten to twelve years old) in a multi-ethnic and multilingual Montreal school are involved in a photovoice project where they take photos of "feeling safe and feeling not so safe" and "feeling strong and not so strong." The girls, as part of a lunch-break project in their school, volunteer to participate in a girl-focused project as something special in a school that primarily has boy-focused and sports projects only. Over a period of four weeks, they brainstorm issues that are of significance to them, learn how to use cameras, and each take their own photos in their everyday home and community environments; then they select photos and develop captions for each of their works, and identify several photos with captions that they would like to have in a school exhibit.

Building on the idea of what seems like a version of the simple *Sesame Street* compare-and-contrast game—"which one is not like the others"—and engaging in close readings of photos, the project organizers involve the girls in viewing their own photos displayed alongside photos produced by girls in Swaziland, Rwanda, and South Africa, who also worked with the prompts "feeling strong and feeling not so strong" and "feeling safe and feeling not so safe."[3] As part of the compare-and-contrast process, the girls have a chance to view all the photos and then each select two photos—one of their own or one of their classmates' photos, and one of the photos from Swaziland, Rwanda, or South Africa—to write about and present to the whole group (see fig. 6.6).

While the two sets of photos are quite different, not least because most of the photos from the African context are rural and the Montreal girls live in an urban environment, the girls themselves see many similarities, particularly in relation to "feeling strong" (for example, having friends and family, sticking together). And although the girls see that gender violence is more prominent in the photos from Africa, they too draw attention to some of the dangers around them ("my stepfather hits me with his slippers"), and then highlight new forms of danger, such as the busy highway that runs in front of the apartment buildings where many of them live.

FIGURE 6.6 • Girls looking at photographs (Canada). Photograph: Author's collection.

Case Study 3: Girls and Video-Making (South Africa)

In a participatory video project in rural KwaZulu-Natal in South Africa, groups of young people, teachers, parents, and community healthcare workers produce short "no editing required" videos (see Mitchell and de Lange). These productions follow an "in my life" prompt where the participants brainstorm, create storyboards, plan out their videos, do film shoots, and screen their productions to the whole group in a one-day workshop. Most of the videos produced by the various groups rely on some aspect of fictional practice to convey a message, and almost all the videos produced by young people have something to do with gender violence. One group of girls creates a short video called *Vikea Abantwana* (or "Protect the Children: A Story about Incest").[4] Their three-minute video dramatically draws together a number of critical issues about sexual abuse. In the video, the girls tell the story of Philendelini, a young girl who is found crying in the classroom by her best friend. As she reveals her story, we learn that she has been raped by her father, and that though she has tried to tell the various women in her community, no one is willing to pass the information on to her mother. When she is eventually taken to a doctor who confirms that she has been raped and also that she is pregnant, her mother bursts into tears, and the story ends with Philendelini's father behind bars in a jail. The video highlights the ways in which adult women who are part of the lives of such girls are often silent. For example, Philendelini confides in the housekeeper but the housekeeper feels that she cannot directly confront her boss, Philendelini's mother, and so she passes the information on to a neighbour whom she hopes will then inform the mother. It is also interesting to note the initial denial on the part of the mother in the video. There is also something alarming about the ways in which the various women in Philendelini's life wonder whom else she has told, as though they think that she should keep the information to herself—a point that is reinforced by the father, who cries out at the end that this should be kept in the family. Through the voices of the various girls and women represented in the video there is also the idea that what has happened to Philendelini is not really true: they say, "That cannot be. You are lying, neighbour," and, "Honestly, she says she was also there when this happened but she is afraid of tell you because you will dispute it." The truth, it seems, is unbelievable, to all but Philendelini. One of the clear messages in the story is that the girls feel that adults do not listen to them when they report rape and other sexual abuse. Although Philendelini has tried to tell so many of the women around her who should care about her welfare, she has been let down by them, as they take no action on her behalf.

Clearly, the visual production, in and of itself, might be viewed as an analysis of a situation, which for this group of girls is about the silences in their community about sexual abuse. Working with video production as a group process—from initial concept through to storyboarding, planning shots, shooting, and initial screening—offers participants access to a type of socially constructed knowledge that is particularly significant in addressing themes which have often been taboo or unspeakable. The group chooses the themes, decides on the images, constructs the stage, and so on. In the case of video (as compared to live performance), a whole array of techniques are available that expand the possibilities for constructedness: from shot angles to dialogue to theme music. Participants can stop the process, view, and re-view the work. Each frame is considered and reconsidered. In the case of *Vikea Abantwana*, a fascinating process is operating whereby the girls take the opportunity to voice silence. The girls' brainstorming notes, and the storyboard they produce, can already be taken as evidence of their analysis.

At a second level of analysis, a post-screening small-group session takes place several weeks later where each group gets to sit and watch their video on their own, something that is very important since it is the first time that the group gets to really look at their own video separate from the celebratory event of screenings at the end of the video-making workshop. A set of generic reflexive questions frame the analytic process as the producers re-view their videos:

- What did you like about your video?
- What are some of the images that stay in your mind about the issue you were addressing?
- If you could change something in your video what would it be?
- Who would you like to see your video and why?
- How do you think it could help address the issues (gender-based violence)?
- What would help you in the school and community to address the main issue in this video?

Although these questions come from our research team rather than from the girls themselves, they are representative of the questions that have come up in our video work with other young people, and are, as I argue elsewhere, the stuff of research (Mitchell, "Taking Pictures" 232). It is worth noting that all the video-making groups (adults and young people) in their analysis wanted their videos to be viewed by others in the community.

Case Study 4: Participatory Archiving–A New Direction in Girls' and Participatory Analysis?

This section speaks more to the future and ways of drawing on digital technology to engage girls in participatory analysis. In particular, it addresses moving from low tech (drawings) to high tech (a participatory digital archive). Adolescent girls in various regions of Rwanda have produced drawings in relation to the prompts "what does gender-based violence look like?" and "what can be done?" Their drawings, produced as part of several projects—one a consultation process on addressing violence against women and children, and one a project to study the use of participatory methodologies with children in identifying and addressing violence in and around schools (see Mitchell and Kanyangara)—poignantly depict the critical issues that confront many girls and young women: poverty, food insecurity, violence, and unwanted pregnancy. These images sit alongside the statistics and other data, such as police reports collected by the Rwandan police (see fig. 6.7 and 6.8). While the use of children's drawings is a common participatory activity used by many researchers and NGOs (Clacherty), these images too often remain in file cabinets in offices or appear as decoration on the covers of reports. In this chapter, I am interested in how these texts can find their way back into communities, not only for interpretation from insider perspectives, but also ultimately for their use in informing policy within the community.

In his essay "Reading the Archive," Allan Sekula notes that archives are far from neutral, and cites numerous examples of the ways in which both the content and the management of archives shape what and whose knowledge is stored, how it is coded and categorized, how it can be retrieved, and who has access to the archive. Embedded in Sekula's work is the question of ownership and who can participate in constructing and using archives. The idea of the participatory archive, as Isto Huvilo (16) and Katie Shilton and Ramesh Srinivasan (91) term it, makes it possible for community members to participate in identifying content, engaging in coding, and working with archival material in creative ways. As these authors observe, the reason for creating a new participatory method is to prevent, as much as possible, the distortion of cultural histories of marginalized populations. A

FIGURE 6.7 • Drawing of pregnant girl (Rwanda). Photograph: Author's collection.

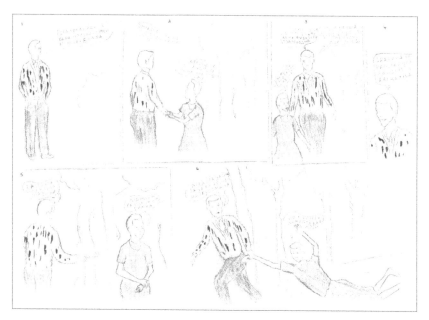

FIGURE 6.8 • Drawing of a boy propositioning a girl (Rwanda). Photograph: Author's collection.

good example of this can be seen in the gay and lesbian archive project set up at the University of the Witwatersrand in South Africa (see "GALA"). While much of the work related to participatory archives focuses on the use of public archives in such settings as libraries and universities, the nature of interactivity offers promising developments that could be incorporated into the participatory work of community-based archives in new ways. Work on digital archives of local photo data, for example, highlights the possibility for community members to be more directly engaged in contributing to an analysis, management, and dissemination of the data/knowledge production.[5]

As a work in progress, my colleagues and I are building a girl-focused digital archive using the extensive collection of drawings on gender violence. The archive in itself is important in terms of preserving the data. Indeed, in the context of childhood, it speaks to the significance of the voices of children as witnesses to abuse. As Sarah Henry points out, such collections of children's drawings highlight the ways in which children move from being the observed to the observers:

> Children are among history's most elusive witness. Museums and libraries are full of objects and documents that appear to tell the stories of childhood but are actually the creations of adults. The books, toys, clothes, and child-rearing manuals that inform what we think we know about childhood tell us much more about what society wanted children to be than what children actually saw, heard, believed, or felt. Thus children are more often than not the observed, rather than the observers, of history.
>
> This gap in the historical record troubles historians of childhood and leaves the rest of us with a seriously impoverished understanding of our own history. For when we do have the opportunity to listen to children, their testimony is powerful. And art is one of the most compelling ways children have of expressing what they have experienced. (18)

But beyond the construction of the digital archive for preservation purposes and for the use of researchers, our interest is in the development and application of interactive digital formats (within the archive) for girls to work with, remix, and rework the visual data (the collections of drawings), so that the archive can be fully explored. Digital media offer a particularly hopeful platform in terms of partnership development in working with girls and can be regarded as an important component of girl-focused social movements. Grassroots human rights organizations are increasingly active in incorporating new digital and mobile platforms within their education programs in order to strengthen community-based projects and initiatives, and a recent report resulting from Plan International's *Because I Am a Girl* campaign notes that "access to technologies can help towards the achievement of the Millennium Development Goals, counter gender inequality and build adolescent girls' assets" (105). The idea that girls could themselves participate in studying the cultural production of other girls offers a critical and important perspective on their role in participatory analysis.

Shifting the Boundaries of Knowledge?

The case studies above, focusing on the use of various visual data sources, suggest different ways in which girls can engage in knowledge production through participating in analyzing and interpreting their own visual data. But the inclusion of girls in participatory analysis also carries with it various challenges, including the challenge of considering whether this type of work can really shift the boundaries of knowledge, or whether such a shift is only something that is part of the hope of do-good researchers. Caitlin Cahill, in her chapter "Participatory Data Analyses," looks at some very practical aspects of participatory work with community groups, noting that participatory analysis may require specific training, and that it can be tedious. Is this something that is feasible with ten-to-fourteen-year-olds? In the examples above, the interpretive process was simply part of a participatory project and, although it may be that more could have been done (and the "more" could require training and be tedious), generally the girls seemed quite willing and able to engage with their own productions in an interpretive way. We might look to the work of Suzanne de Castell and Jennifer Jenson, who highlight the ways that digital play and gaming could become part of the interpretive process in their article "Serious Play," on youth, sexuality, and HIV and AIDS. Cahill also notes that it can be difficult for participants to review data that present them (or their situation) in a negative light (185). In the case of the drawings from Rwanda, for example, which all depict examples of violence in schools, working with the data could be very painful. I became particularly aware of this in an earlier component of the project when, while working with a group of university students as data collectors in rural schools, I realized that to have these students spend such intensive time on such a painful topic was far from easy for them, and potentially invoked their own autobiographies (Mitchell and Kanyangara). Building in a debriefing is indeed a concern, and the idea of turning the interpretive process into an interactive supportive environment could be important.

Joe L. Kincheloe and others have written about the risk of romanticizing the participant's voice (Kincheloe 119–20). Speaking of Participatory Action Research (PAR) techniques, Kincheloe observes:

> Too many contemporary advocates of PAR have failed to ask hard questions about the nature of participation. Without such complex and intense questions, PAR too often migrates to one of two positions: a research method/design that (1) romanticizes and essentializes the perspectives of the oppressed and fails to question the diversity of viewpoints among subjugated groups; (2) embraces facile notions of participation that serve as new and more hegemonically sophisticated modes of exclusion. (119–20)

Alongside the broader issues that Kincheloe raises, there are of course questions about the voices of girls (and children) more specifically, and whether, as with the critique of a children's voices discourse, this is simply another type of tokenism and colonization. In the case of tokenism and children's voices, if there are platforms for speaking but no platforms for being heard, the charge is legitimate. In the case of girls and participatory analysis, arguably a component of the work on children's voices, there are a number of questions that could be used to evaluate the doing and the success of these approaches, starting with a consideration of the overarching one: Where in a participatory research project with girls is there a space for girls to be engaged in the interpretive process? And if girls are included in the process, how do the various relations of power, for example, between adult researcher and girl, figure into the analysis? Questions could include the following:

- Is participatory analysis an afterthought, or is it built into the project from the beginning?
- To what extent does the interpretive work of the girls appear in the research analysis?
- How do the girls themselves feel about the process of participatory analysis?
- How do we as researchers consult and follow up with girls in order to find out what they think of participatory analysis?

But to go back to the idea of "disclos[ing] ourselves to ourselves" (Solomon 10), we are interested in whether there any special observations to make about participatory analysis and girls' visual culture—particularly arts-based creations such as photos, drawings, or video production. As noted above, Cahill refers to the fact that participants may not want to "go there" in relation to confronting issues that they might perceive to be negative about themselves (186–87). But will there be any self-consciousness about interpreting the artwork itself? Bizeyeu's earlier comment about the blurriness of her group's photograph shows a remarkable maturity, which enables her to step beyond form/aesthetics in favour of content and the message they were trying to convey.

In this chapter, I have argued for an insider perspective on girls' lives and experiences, both through the images they produce but also through their insider perspectives on interpreting the images. I regard this point about interpretation as particularly critical based on my experiences of working with various outsiders to the project. A few summers ago, for example, I worked with a conscientious research assistant at McGill who was keen to examine the collections of drawings produced by Rwandan girls (see MacEntee and Mitchell). She digitized them and then tried to sort them according to different thematic areas, but in the end she confessed that it was all very frustrating. As she expressed it:

> My ability to read scenes of men and girls with cars and cells phones as prostitution was inhibited by lack of familiarity with this type of exchange in my urban North American childhood where cell phones and cars are a "natural" part of middle-class life. So too was my ability to interpret scenes of children in forests as a commonplace threat to a Rwandan child's safety impeded by my cultural estrangement from having to cross wide-open, un-policed spaces daily without the provision of a trusted adult. (Personal communication [anonymous], email, 19 September 2010)

Her honesty and forthrightness in explaining why she had so much difficulty highlighted her outsider position as someone who had never travelled to Rwanda and whose childhood was quite unlike the images she was seeing in the girls' drawings. In working with young research assistants in Rwanda who had been born and had grown up there, I found, however, that there were other barriers to interpretations. As part of the same project where schoolgirls had been asked to draw what they saw as violence, I worked with a group of university students who acted as data collectors and then later as interpreters of the data. Although they were only a few years older than the girls who had produced the drawings, the researchers also confessed that they experienced difficulties in the interpretive process. In some cases, the data collectors were young men and, although they were very understanding, they sometimes found themselves getting angry at the males who were responsible for the acts of gender violence, and it became difficult for them to code the data. They found it difficult to carry out something that seemed somewhat technocratic, when what they really wanted to do was talk about how they felt about such horrific acts of violence. Alternatively, several of the young women who had themselves grown up in Rwanda also found it difficult but for different reasons, not the least of which were their own memories as girls who had gone to these same schools. Where possible we had data collectors working in the same area of the country where they had grown up (although in some cases the data collectors were young women who were from the capital city of Kigali, which has a population of over one million, and who thus felt lost in a rural area). It was also the case that fourteen or more years after the Rwandan genocide, which was part of the lived experience of all the data collectors, these issues remained difficult to confront. For example, some of the children had drawn pictures of men with machetes, something that they were too young to have experienced during the genocide, but that was at the centre of the childhoods of the data collectors. I do not want to argue against the value of distance, or that only those who have experienced something can interpret the data; rather, my point in listing these issues is to point to the limits of being an outsider (or different types of outsiders), and perhaps also the rich potential for involving insiders. If we want to interpret the data on gender violence in Rwanda experienced by fourteen-year-old girls, should we not see what they make of the data that they themselves produce? Framing participatory analysis in this way suggests that we need to see it as central to new work in the area of participatory visual methodologies with girls.

Notes

1 The images that are presented in this chapter were collected as part of four separate research projects. Study 1 was conducted in 2011 under the auspices of the PostHarvest Management to Improve Livelihoods project, and ethical clearance was granted by Jimma University and McGill University. Study 2 was carried out in 2009 in Montreal, and ethical clearance was granted by McGill University. Study 3 was carried out in 2006 as part of the Learning Together project at the University of KwaZulu-Natal, with ethical clearance granted by UKZN. Study 4 was carried out in 2005 in collaboration with UNICEF in Kigali, Rwanda, and all procedures of ethical clearance were

carried out under the auspices of the Ministry of Youth and Sport and the office of UNICEF.

2 The photo work is part of a project funded by the Canadian International Development Agency and undertaken by the Nova Scotia Agricultural College, McGill University, and Jimma University. See "Post-Harvest Management to Improve Livelihoods."

3 For further photovoice work on the prompt "feeling safe and feeling not so safe," see Mitchell et al., "Why We Don't Go to School on Fridays"; Mitchell, "Geographies of Danger."

4 This particular video is also described in Relebohile Moletsane, Claudia Mitchell, Ann Smith, and Linda Chisholm's *Methodologies for Mapping a Southern African Girlhood*.

5 For an example of this, please see the following works, which all relate to the "giving life to data to save lives in the age of AIDS" studies, based on setting up a digital archive made up of community-based visual data: de Lange et al., "Giving Life to Data"; Mnisi; and Park, Mitchell, and de Lange.

Works Cited

Banks, Marcus. *Visual Methods in Social Research*. London: Sage, 2001. Print.

Bloustien, Gerry. *Girl Making: A Cross-Cultural Ethnography on the Processes of Growing Up Female*. Oxford: Berghahn Books, 2003. Print.

Cahill, Caitlin. "Participatory Data Analysis." *Participatory Action Research Approaches and Methods: Connecting People, Participation and Place*. Ed. Sara Kindon, Rachel Pain, and Mike Kesby. London: Routledge, 2007. 181–87. Print.

Choudry, Aziz, and Dip Kapoor, eds. *Learning from the Ground Up: Global Perspectives on Social Movements and Knowledge Production*. New York: Palgrave Macmillan, 2010. Print.

Clacherty, Glynis. *Refugee and Returnee Children in Southern Africa: Perceptions and Experiences of Children*. Pretoria: UNHCR, 2005. Print.

Clark-Ibáñez, Marisol. "Inner-City Children in Sharper Focus: Sociology of Childhood and Photo-Elicitation Interviews." *Visual Research Methods: Image, Society, and Representation*. Ed. Gregory C. Stanczak. Los Angeles: Sage, 2007. 167–96. Print.

de Castell, Suzanne, and Jennifer Jenson. "OP-ED: Serious Play." *Journal of Curriculum Studies* 35.6 (2003): 649–55. Print.

de Lange, Naydene, Claudia Mitchell, Relebohile Moletsane, Jean Stuart, and Thabisile Buthelezi. "Seeing with the Body: Educators' Representations of HIV and AIDS." *Journal of Education* 38.1 (2006): 45–66. Print.

de Lange, Naydene, Claudia Mitchell, and Jean Stuart. *Putting People in the Picture: Visual Methodologies for Social Change.* Rotterdam: Sense, 2007. Print.

de Lange, Naydene, Thoko Mnisi, Claudia Mitchell, and Eun G. Park. "Giving Life to Data: University-Community Partnerships in Addressing HIV and AIDS through Building Digital Archives." *E-learning and Digital Media* 7.2 (2010): 160–71. Print.

"GALA: Gay and Lesbian Memories in Action." *GALA.* N.d. Web. 30 April 2011.

Henry, Sarah M. "Children as Witnesses to History." *The Day Our World Changed: Children's Art of 9/11.* Ed. Robin F. Goodman and Andrea Henderson Fahnestock. New York: New York U Child Study Center and Museum of the City of New York, 2002. 18–22. Print.

Higonnet, Anne. *Pictures of Innocence: The History and Crisis of Ideal Childhood.* London: Thames & Hudson, 1999. Print.

Holland, Patricia. *Picturing Childhood: The Myth of the Child in Popular Imagery.* New York: IB Taurus, 2004. Print.

Huvilo, Isto. "Participatory Archive: Towards Decentralised Curation, Radical User Orientation, and Broader Contextualisation of Records Management." *Archival Science* 8.1 (March 2008): 15–36. Web. 12 Oct. 2012.

Kearney, Mary Celeste. *Girls Make Media.* London: Routledge, 2006. Print.

Kincheloe, Joe L. "Critical Complexity and Participatory Action Research: Decolonizing 'Democratic' Knowledge Production." *Education, Participatory Action Research, and Social Change: International Perspectives.* Ed. Dip Kapoor and Steven Jordan. New York: Palgrave Macmillan, 2009. 107–21. Print.

Kuhn, Annette. *Family Secrets: Acts of Memory and Imagination.* London: Verso Books, 1995. Print.

Lerner, Loren. "Adolescent Girls, Adult Women: Coming of Age Images by Five Canadian Women Artists." *Girlhood Studies* 1.2 (2009): 1–28. IngentaConnect. Web. 12 Oct. 2012.

MacEntee, Katee, and Claudia Mitchell. "Lost and Found in Translation: Participatory Analysis and Working with Collections of Drawings." *Picturing Research: Drawing as Visual Methodology.* Ed. Linda Theron, Claudia Mitchell, Ann Smith, and Jean Stuart. Rotterdam: Sense, 2011. 89–102. Print.

Magno, Cathryn, and Jackie Kirk. "Sight Unseen: *Re-viewing* Images of Girls' Education." *Girlhood Studies* 3.1 (2010): 9–33. *IngentaConnect.* Web. 12 Oct. 2012.

Maguire, Patricia. *Doing Participatory Research: A Feminist Approach.* Amherst: Centre for Educational Research, 1987. Print.

Mann, Sally. *At Twelve: Portraits of Young Women*. Turin: Aperture, 2005. Print.

Marcus, Tessa, and Alexandra Hofmaener, eds. *Shifting Boundaries of Knowledge: A View on Social Sciences, Law and Humanities in South Africa*. Pietermartizburg: U of KwaZulu-Natal P, 2006. Print.

Mitchell, Claudia. *Doing Visual Research*. London: Sage, 2011. Print.

———. "Geographies of Danger: School Toilets in Sub-Saharan Africa." *Ladies and Gents: Public Toilets and Gender*. Ed. Olga Gershenson and Barbara Penner. Philadelphia: Temple UP, 2009. 62–74. Print.

———. "Taking Pictures, Taking Action: Visual Arts-Based Methodologies and Research as Social Change." *Shifting Boundaries of Knowledge: A View on Social Sciences, Law and Humanities in South Africa*. Ed. Tessa Marcus and Alexandra Hofmaener. Pietermartizburg: U of KwaZulu-Natal P, 2006. 227–41. Print.

Mitchell, Claudia, and Naydene de Lange. "Community-Based Participatory Video and Social Action in Rural South Africa." *The SAGE Handbook of Visual Research Methods*. Ed. Eric Margolis and Luc Pauwels. London: Sage, 2011. 171–85. Print.

Mitchell, Claudia, and Patrick Kanyangara. *Violence against Children and Young People in and around Schools in Rwanda: Through the Eyes of Children and Young People*. Kigali: National Youth Council and UNICEF, 2006. Print.

Mitchell, Claudia, Jean Stuart, Relebohile Moletsane, and Callistus Bheka Nkwanyana. "'Why We Don't Go to School on Fridays': On Youth Participation through Photo Voice in KwaZulu-Natal." *McGill Journal of Education* 41.3 (2006): 267–82. Print.

Mnisi, Thoko. "Beyond Visual Data: How Educators Use Metadata to Help Learners Understand Issues on HIV and AIDS Stigma." Diss., U of KwaZulu-Natal, 2010. Print.

Moletsane, Relebohile, Claudia Mitchell, Ann Smith, and Linda Chisholm. *Methodologies for Mapping a Southern African Girlhood in the Age of AIDS*. Rotterdam: Sense Publishers, 2008. Print.

Morrison, Connie. *Who Do They Think They Are? Teenage Girls and Their Avatars in Spaces of Social Online Communication*. New York: Peter Lang, 2010. Print.

Paley, Nicholas. *Finding Art's Place: Experiments in Contemporary Education and Culture*. London: Routledge, 1995. Print.

Park, Eun, Claudia Mitchell, and Naydene de Lange. "Working with Digital Archives: Photovoice and Meta-analysis in the Context of HIV and AIDS." *Putting People in the Picture: Visual Methodologies for Social Change*. Ed. Naydene de Lange, Claudia Mitchell, and Jean Stuart. Amsterdam: Sense, 2007. 163–72. Print.

Pink, Sarah. *Visual Interventions: Applied Visual Anthropology*. New York: Berghahn Books, 2007. Print.

Plan International. *Because I Am a Girl: The State of the World's Girls 2010: Digital and Urban Frontiers, Girls in a Changing Landscape*. London: Plan International, 2010. Print.

"Post-harvest Management to Improve Livelihoods." Ethiopia UPCD. *NSCA International*. N.d. Web. 30 April 2011.

Ramazanoğlu, Caroline, and Janet Holland. *Feminist Methodology: Challenges and Choices*. London: Sage, 2002. Print.

Rose, Gillian. *Visual Methodologies: An Introduction to the Interpretation of Visual Materials*. London: Sage, 2001. Print.

Sekula, Allan. "Reading an Archive: Photography between Labour and Capital." *The Photography Reader*. Ed. Liz Wells. New York: Routledge, 1993. 443–52. Print.

Shilton, Katie, and Ramesh Srinivasan. "Participatory Appraisal and Arrangement for Multicultural Archival Collections." *Archivaria* 63 (2008): 87–101. Print.

Solomon, Joan. "Introduction." *What Can a Woman Do with a Camera? Photography for Women*. Ed. Jo Spence and Joan Solomon. London: Scarlet Press, 1995. 9–14. Print.

Sontag, Susan. *Against Interpretation and Other Essays*. New York: Farrar, Straus & Giroux, 1966. Print.

Spence, Jo. *Cultural Sniping: The Art of Transgression*. London: Routledge, 1995. Print.

Walkerdine, Valerie. *Schoolgirl Fictions*. London: Verso Books, 1991. Print.

Walton, Kamina. "Creating Positive Images: Working with Primary School Girls." *What Can a Woman Do with a Camera? Photography for Women*. Ed. Jo Spence and Joan Solomon. London: Scarlet Press, 1995. 153–58. Print.

Wang, Caroline C. "Photovoice: A Participatory Action Research Strategy Applied to Women's Health." *Journal of Women's Health* 8.2 (1999): 185–92. Print.

Ward, Jeanne. *Broken Bodies, Broken Dreams: Violence against Women Exposed*. Nairobi: Kenya, 2005. Print.

CHAPTER 7

"Doing Their Bit"

The Great War and Transnationalism in Girls' Fiction

Kristine Moruzi

Girls' fiction published in England, the United States, Canada, and Australia during and immediately after World War I produces a transnational subject that transcends domestic roles and national boundaries. This literature reflects a patriotic fervour that extols imperialist greatness and transnational allegiances alongside a strong national pride, where girls are encouraged to understand and to accept their responsibilities to family, community, and nation in their support of the war effort. These heroic models of femininity encompass both the courage and the patience required to keep the home fires burning and the bravery associated with active participation on the front. Texts such as Mary Grant Bruce's Billabong series, Angela Brazil's *A Patriotic Schoolgirl*, Jessie Graham Flower's *Grace Harlowe Overseas*, and L.M. Montgomery's *Rilla of Ingleside* contain models of female support for the war that encourage girls to think of themselves as active wartime participants even as they also consider their "sisters" in other countries that were similarly supporting the war. Because girls' wartime texts were published, advertised, and distributed throughout the British Empire and the United States, girl readers encountered representations of wartime girlhood that encouraged a global sisterhood, promoted allegiances across borders, and encouraged their participation in national, transnational, imperial, and gender-based communities.

Girls' fiction produced in England, the United States, and the former colonies during and immediately after the war is a vital source of inquiry because this body of texts, small though it may be, reflects a formative moment in the development of transnational ideologies of girlhood. Texts written about the war reflect various nationalisms, yet these national girlhood identities are also simultaneously superseded by transnational ideas of war, duty, and courage. These girls' texts represent the early development of a transnational female subject, as girl readers found similar expectations of duty, patriotism, and bravery in their fiction, regardless of the author's, or the protagonist's, nationality. British, American, Canadian, and Australian girls support their brothers and their suitors in their wartime duty, since to do less would be unpatriotic and cowardly. This fiction also shows how the experiences of wartime enabled girls' maturation as they took on new responsibilities while waiting for the war's end and their loved ones' return. Coming of age is a transnational phenomenon, especially in texts where the romantic plot enables marriage.

The consistency across girls' wartime texts is remarkable, particularly given the often fiercely patriotic and nationalist rhetoric found in these novels. Michael Paris has noted that, for authors of juvenile war fiction, "patriotism was not just a popular theme that sold books, but a deeply held conviction, a credo that informed their work" (11). Yet nationality is not the primary marker of girlhood in wartime texts. Instead, a transnational ideal of girlhood emerges out of girls' shared identity and responsibility in wartime. While not all girls wished to go to the front—although some did participate actively as nurses and ambulance drivers—they were nonetheless all part of the war effort, which was unified in its opposition to the Germans and their reported atrocities.

Elements of this transnational girlhood undoubtedly emerge out of the imperialist rhetoric that was popular at the time. In American texts, imperial rhetoric is replaced by republicanism, yet the ideals of American girlhood remain consistent with those found in British and colonial texts. Wartime girlhood reflects a feminine ideal of sacrifice and maturity, not only because the ideology of girlhood was similar across nations, but also because girls' texts travelled across national borders, thereby creating a reading environment where ideals of girlhood transcended national frameworks and became transnational.

A Transnational Approach

The transnational girl is made visible through a comparison of the models of femininity appearing in girls' wartime texts. Nation-based studies, which address the specificities of national, social, political, cultural, and economic concerns, tend to ignore the universalities of wartime girlhood. Historian Ann Taylor Allen, in her chapter "Lost in Translation? Women's History in Transnational and Comparative Perspective," explains that "[t]he underlying assumption of a national history is that each nation—its landscape, its cultural and political self-expression, its rise and fall—is unique and distinctive. But without comparing it to others, the historian cannot assess what is distinctive to the nation and what it shares with others" (95). A transnational examination of the fiction of wartime girlhood can identify unifying features of girlhood that would otherwise be missed in a nation-based study. The development of a transnational model becomes possible when narratives from different nations are placed alongside one another and examined both for their unique depictions of wartime conditions for girls and for their similarities. As Clare Bradford writes in *Unsettling Narratives*, however, "universalizing readings that forget the local and the particular in their desire for order and consistency" (5) can produce inaccuracies. In this context, it is crucial to clarify that my argument is limited to Western, white, middle-class girlhood. The protagonists in these girls' texts come from similar, relatively privileged, middle-class backgrounds. Even stories that feature factory workers, who historically and traditionally would have been working class, do not always contain working-class girls.[1]

The transnational girl subject emerges from white settler colonies like Canada and Australia that actively demonstrated their imperial connections to England during wartime. As historian Jonathan Vance explains, "[t]he children of Mother Britain have been scattered around the globe yet remain tied to England by bonds stronger than steel. When the call goes out in August 1914, they all answer 'Ready, aye, ready' and come running to the aid of Mother Britain" (150). Yet the depiction of American girls engaged in similar models of girlhood suggests a transnationalism extending beyond the imperial connections of the early twentieth century. The models of wartime girlhood envisioned in girls' print culture present an "imagined community" (Anderson, *Imagined Communities* 46) of girls, based on age, race, class, and gender, who are brought together through a shared understanding of the necessity of the war and their determination to support the men at the front.

When gender is included within the structures of globalization, the idea of transnational girlhood becomes more visible.[2] Anthropologist Carla Freeman writes about the significance of this inclusion:

> A gendered understanding of globalization is not one in which women's stories or feminist movements can be tacked onto or even "stirred into" the macropicture; rather, it challenges the very constitution of that macropicture such that producers, consumers, and bystanders of globalization are not generic bodies or invisible practitioners of labor and desire but are situated within social and economic processes and cultural meanings that are central to globalization itself. (1010)

By including gender as a category for analysis, an entirely different model of transnationalism is created, one in which the production, distribution, and consumption of girls' texts are situated within global processes of print culture and book history. Using this model allows the literary historian to demonstrate the extent to which girls were able to consume texts written in countries other than their own and the degree to which the ideologies found in those texts were consistent. The expectations of girls in wartime and the models of femininity that appear in girls' fiction of this period suggest how ideologies of girlhood transcend national boundaries.

Crucial to the construction of this transnational girlhood is the reiteration of these transnational models of femininity. Gender theorist Judith Butler examines the repeatability of gender acts, drawing on Derrida's notion of iterability to assert that gender performativity "must be understood not as a singular or deliberate 'act,' but rather as the reiterative and citational practice by which discourse produces the effects that it names" (2). By reiterating the norms associated with female participation in wartime, girls' fiction produces a model of transnational girlhood in its pages.

More broadly, transnational girlhood is enabled through the circulation of ideas, people, and commodities such as books and magazines. As literary critic Paul Jay argues in *Global Matters: The Transnational Turn in Literary Studies*, "globalization is characterized by complex back-and-forth flows of people and cultural forms" that complicate the centre–periphery model, which sees "power, commodities, and influence flowing from urban centres" such as London "to a peripheral developing world" (3) like the British colonies and the United States. The wartime texts read by girls were written, often in highly nationalistic terms, in Canada, Australia, the United States, and England, and then shared across borders through the circulation of print culture. A comparison of texts from different nations demonstrates that girls were invited to respond in very similar ways to the challenges of wartime. Whether readers responded to this invitation to consider themselves transnational is outside the scope of this chapter; instead, I wish to show how these models of girlhood can be read alongside each other to potentially produce a model of transnational girlhood.

An examination of these texts brings constructions of wartime girlhood to the forefront. Writing in 1994, Donna Coates explains how women's wartime activities have been obscured "because participation in war has traditionally been considered an exclusively male experience and, by extension, the narration of that experience, the genre of war literature, has been a male-dominated field, with tales of the battlefield privileged, and thus canonised" (120). Recent examinations of women writers and the war have begun to write the history of women's contributions to wartime literature.[3] Yet, as Trudi Tate and Suzanne Raitt explain, "some feminists are becoming slightly uneasy about writing separately about women as if women were a unified group, requiring special pleading; or as if 'woman' were an unproblematic category for organizing knowledge" (2). Until girls' wartime texts are positioned alongside one another, the complexities of girls' wartime roles are not obvious. Girlhood as represented in these texts clearly has national qualities such as a specific allegiance to nation, but transnational qualities such as bravery, courage, honour, and morality supersede a nationalistic framework.

The Production, Reception, and Dissemination of Wartime Texts

Critics remain divided over the importance of wartime fiction for girls. Mary Cadogan and Patricia Craig conclude in their book *Women and Children First: The Fiction of Two World Wars* that "girls' wartime fiction was not particularly impressive . . . [because] girls were simply encouraged to worship the male heroes at the front, and to knit comforts for them" (59). Their critique fails to acknowledge the significance of these texts in constructing models of wartime girlhood. More recent scholars like Jane Potter, however, emphasize the importance of popular fiction for children, and especially girls, because it "reinforced the existing war effort" where "fictional representations . . . drew on increasingly familiar and instantly recognizable images: wounds, khaki, women in uniform, public mourning, family grief" (7).[4] Perhaps unsurprisingly, women were the authors of the girls' wartime texts under consideration here, yet these texts have received little critical attention. In one study, David Walker concludes that reviewers ignored the first war novels of Mary Grant Bruce and Ethel Turner, despite the already impressive reputations of these Australian authors, in part because of their gender.[5] Yet these novels played an important role in the construction of adolescent identities by revealing what their authors felt "were the particular disadvantages of being female [and] the qualities they expected to find in young men during a national crisis," preoccupations that were "woven in to the more complex pattern of class, national and imperial loyalties" and that informed the lives "of those called upon to respond to the outbreak of the war" (Walker 297).

Understanding the globalized production, dissemination, and reception of girls' wartime texts is crucial to the development of a model of transnational girlhood. Literary critic Graham Huggan notes that Australian literature "has always been shaped as much by external market forces as by internal producers and commentators," owing to its "small domestic market with offshore titles that made up the bulk of book sellers' lists" (6). At the same time, the status of English as a global language "presented the possibilities of a market that spanned the world" (6). Not only were girls' texts already travelling throughout the British Empire and America, but the market for (and marketing of) children's books was increasing. In this context, it is reasonable to conclude that girls were encouraged to read texts from other countries and, therefore, that the transnational features of the texts to which girls had access between 1914 and 1920 are important aspects of their meanings.

An examination of the publication, advertising, and reviews of girls' texts demonstrates the porous nature of national boundaries. Girls' novels were often published by companies with extensive international networks, thereby enabling wide distribution throughout English-speaking countries. In addition, a book was not always first published in the author's home country. The economics of book publication meant that colonial writers in particular often made arrangements to have their books published in larger metropolitan cities like London, New York, and Boston. For example, Ward, Lock and Co. of London published Australian author Mary Grant Bruce's Billabong series, and Canadian author L.M. Montgomery's *Anne of Green Gables* appeared under the Boston imprint L.C. Page in 1908 and was published later that same year by British publisher Isaac Pitman.[6]

The reviews of girls' war fiction reflect the transnational appeal of these texts. The *Spectator*, a British weekly periodical interested in providing a wide range of material, often included reviews of literature for young people.

Its 9 December 1916 issue discusses gift books for girls and includes brief reviews of Marchant's *A Girl Munition Worker* and Bruce's *Jim and Wally*. The review begins by noting that "[t]here is an abundant supply of new stories for girls this season, and many of them are very readable. The war of course enters more or less directly into a number of these stories, but we are inclined to think that most young girls will prefer the unwarlike domestic variety" ("Gift-Books" 737). Whether or not girls preferred domestic fiction to war fiction, the presence of two books featuring models of wartime girlhood—one by a British author, the other by an Australian author— appearing alongside each other in a British review suggests that readers could, and should, read both books. Undoubtedly, their presence in a British periodical was facilitated by Bruce's British publisher.[7] Ward, Lock and Co., which published Mary Grant Bruce, frequently advertised in the pages of the *Spectator*. One advertisement notes that Bruce is a contributor to the October 1915 number of *Windsor Magazine*. Another advertisement for Ward, Lock and Co.'s 1924 Autumn List includes Bruce as the author of popular gift books by Australian writers. In this case, Bruce's nationality as an Australian is presented as a selling point to attract British buyers.[8] Ward, Lock and Co. clearly felt that Bruce's Australian series would appeal to British readers. It advertised *From Billabong to London* in the *Athenaeum*, a weekly periodical similar to the *Spectator*, in November 1915.

The popularity of Australian fiction in England was in part a result of a history of strong support for colonial print culture. For example, in the 30 August 1913 number of *The Academy: A Monthly Record of Literature, Learning, Science and Art*, A. G. Rosman contributes "A Sketch of New Literature in Australia," where she comments on the "delightful bush stories of Mary Grant Bruce" (277). Similarly, the February 1929 issue of *The Bookman: A Literary Journal* includes W. T. Allison's "Canadian Literature of To-Day." Allison, professor at the University of Manitoba and the leading book critic of the influential *Winnipeg Tribune*, observes that "[a] woman novelist who has also been specially loved by young people is Lucy M. Montgomery, whose stories of Prince Edward Island have had an enormous circulation in Canada and the United States" (272). Allison's reference to the circulation of the Anne of Green Gables books through-out Canada and the United States once again suggests the transnational appeal of at least some girls' fiction. A 26 November 1921 *Spectator* adver-tisement for *Back to Billabong* makes the transnationalism of print culture more explicit when it includes a quotation from the *Melbourne Argus* daily newspaper which states that "[t]here can be no doubt about the success of

Miss Bruce" because she elicits "real pathos which gets hold of the reader, and her effects are obtained in a natural way that makes them all the more telling" (723). By quoting an Australian review in a British periodical, Ward, Lock and Co. may simply be taking advantage of a positive review. Yet the publisher may also be leveraging an "authentic" Australian reviewer's view that Bruce's representations of Australian bush and culture are "natural" and realistic. The *Spectator*'s review, appearing a month later on 17 December 1921, reinforces this perspective, describing the story as "highly interesting and cheerful" and concluding that "Mrs. Bruce writes of what she knows well" ("Fiction" 831).

In the British press, the colonial children's author is a breed apart, connected to and yet distinct from British writers for children. The *Spectator*, in its 6 April 1918 review of Montgomery's *Anne's House of Dreams*, writes that this novel

> furnishes a strong confirmation of Mr. Stephen Leacock's view . . . that Canadian literature, like Canadian journalism, education, and culture, approximates more nearly to the type and standard of the United Status than to those of Great Britain. Miss Montgomery reminds one far more of Miss Alcott, Miss Wilkins, and Kate Douglas Wiggin than of any English writers; though in saying this we intend no disparagement—rather the reverse. The note is different, but the results are refreshing and delightful. ("Fiction" 376)

The reviewer suggests that Montgomery's style is akin to that of American writers for girls, implying a degree of cultural affinity among North American writers that reduces the significance of the imperial connections between Britain and its colonies. At the very least, the importance of geographic ties, rather than national or imperial ties, cannot be underestimated in the construction of ideologies of girlhood.

Inheritances from the International Women's Movement

The transnationalism of wartime girlhood emerges in part from the history of the international women's movement, which began in the 1830s as a loosely organized group of feminists from England, France, Germany, and the United States who shared information and strategies to improve the condition of women. As feminist historian Bonnie Anderson observes, events that historians had previously viewed as local phenomena "really occurred within the matrix of a feminism that transcended national bound-aries" (2). Leila J. Rupp similarly comments that the roots of this movement "can be traced to a variety of connections forged across national boundaries, creating what social movement scholars call a 'preexisting communications network'" (14) created via the contacts that women made as travellers, missionaries, migrants, and writers. One of the earliest and most impres-sive examples of the transnational women's movement emerges from the International Women's Congress for Peace, where participants from both neutral and warring nations met in The Hague from 28 to 30 April 1915 to suggest ways to protest against the war. The idea that women from different, even warring, nations came together to work toward a common goal dem-onstrates that women's war work could, and did, cross national boundaries.

The importance of women's war efforts is reflected elsewhere in the print culture of the period. For example, suffragette and British govern-ment employee Helen Fraser argues for the transnational aspects of World War I in her book, *Women and War Work*, based on her government-sponsored propaganda tour of America in 1917.[9] In the preface to the book, Fraser writes:

> The women of all the allies are one in this great struggle. Our hopes and our fears, our anxieties and our prayers, our visions and our desolations, are the same.
>
> Our work is the same task of supporting and sustaining the energies of our men in arms and of our nations at home. All the allied women know more of each other than they ever did before, and this is all to the good.
>
> The task of women in this struggle and in the reconstruction to come after, are great tasks, and the world needs in every country not only the wis-dom and knowledge of its own women but the strength in them that comes from being one of a great world-wide group and conscious of the unity of all women. (n. pag.)

Fraser limits her transnational community to Allied women who must work together under the "same task" of supporting the troops and their nations, while acknowledging that "the strength" of women emerges from their shared understanding of the "great world-wide group" of unified women. This idea is reinforced in the book's title page, which includes an excerpt from Rudyard Kipling's "For All We Have and Are" (1914), a war poem in which the need for "iron sacrifice" is required of "all," not just men.[10] Fraser's overt emphasis on the transnational unity of women is central to her belief in the importance of women's work during the war. She provides examples of the many different kinds of work in which British women are engaged, such as building airplanes and working in munitions factories, in the hopes of encouraging American women to become similarly involved. In the fictional examples of American girlhood that appeared in 1917 and 1918, particularly in girls' series, girls and women responded enthusiastically to this type of rhetoric, suggesting that these books may have had similar propagandist objectives.

Girlhood Before World War I

Prior to the advent of World War I, girls' texts show girls being offered a wider range of educational and employment activities. Girls were increasingly seen as modern figures in this period. The *Girl's Realm*, a popular British middle-class girls' magazine, for example, used current events to fashion girlhood as a time of bravery and courage. The girls in its pages were educated and feminine, and positioned as heroes. In its coverage of the Second Boer War, the *Girl's Realm* guided girls toward appropriate wartime behaviours that position duty and sacrifice as crucial to a girl's maturity.[11]

The landscape of girlhood prior to World War I shifted as girls were defined based on their age and yet also assumed to be part of an undifferentiated readership based on gender. For example, the *Girl's Realm* merged in 1915 with the adult magazine *Woman at Home* because of wartime paper shortages. Editor S. H. Leeder appealed to his readers to continue purchasing the magazine, claiming, "[t]his is the day of patriotism, loyalty, and sacrifice" ("Important" 4). Historian Jane Potter explains that "[j]ust as the press helped to 'sell' the War, the War helped to sell papers. These periodicals did not question but appropriated the conflict for their own ends, to sell copy and to encourage readers in the imperial mission" (14). In the case of the *Girl's Realm*, the editor included a "Special Supplement," in which he responds to pleas from his readers about how they can help in the war effort. Having "made inquiries at the proper authorities" ("The War" 1), Leeder provides an extremely narrow range of activities for girls: nursing or sewing. By expanding the periodical to contain not only entertainment, but also specific, practical details of possible wartime contributions girls can make, the *Girl's Realm* presumably hoped to attract a wider readership while also demonstrating its commitment to girls' concerns.

In the fictional accounts of wartime, a much wider variety of girlhoods are represented, but these, as in the *Girl's Realm*, consistently emphasize the importance of supporting the soldiers in their battle against the Germans. Girls' stories, like much of the popular adult wartime fiction, were designed for escapist entertainment—where readers could forget some of the grim realities of trench warfare—and to reassure readers that supporting the boys was the right thing to do. They also provided important information about why the war needed to be fought. The 15 October 1914 *Times Literary Supplement* commented on the need for war literature: "A great national service is performed by writers who set forth in clear popular language the reasons why we have gone to war and the vital character of the struggle" (Collett 455). The *Times Literary Supplement* positions these texts as part of national propaganda employed to educate its citizens about the necessity of the war.

Yet these fictional accounts also performed an important function by modelling appropriate wartime behaviours for girls, behaviours that transcended national boundaries. Girls are informed about the importance and propriety of supporting the war by assuming increased domestic responsibilities such as childcare, supporting brothers and friends as they went to war, and fundraising. The form of this transnational support for the war emerges on a variety of fronts. Young men and young women are encouraged to "do their bit," but girls' texts acknowledge that not everyone can support the war effort in the same way. Some girls were best suited to remain within the home, while others were encouraged to perform their support in more public ways through nursing, ambulance driving, and factory work.

The Home Front

Girls were encouraged to "do their bit" in many ways, but one of the most important was to stay at home and keep the home fires burning. In *Death So Noble*, Jonathan Vance describes the two groups of Canadians who were memorialized after the war. The first, of course, is those men and women who appeared on the nation's service rolls. The second refers to "those people who, because of age or infirmity, could not themselves go to France and so were forced to stay at home and support the troops in spirit . . . people whose conduct and public statements left no doubt about their whole-hearted support for the war effort" (126). While Vance fails to mention gender as a specific category for memorialization, girls' war novels situate the role of girlhood differently, expecting girls to support their brothers and fathers and to keep the domestic space ready for their return. For girls who were encouraged by the narratives directed at them to consider themselves as brave and heroic figures, the idea of remaining at home must have been a bitter pill to swallow.

Yet, as Marjorie realizes in Angela Brazil's *Patriotic Schoolgirl* (1918), even a school provides models of feminine wartime accomplishment. In this story, war is a distant concern, although Marjorie's father and brothers are at the front. Her brother refuses to tell her "everything" that he does out in France because "you wouldn't like to hear everything . . . it's not fit for your ears. Be glad that you in England don't see anything of the war" (ch. 23). Girls at home are to be protected from the violence and horror of the war, and Marjorie understands her role in the war effort. Her letters and descriptions of her activities at school provide an escape for her father while he is at the front. He writes, "Tell me about your doings. I love to have your letters, even though I may not have time to answer them" (ch. 7). Marjorie acknowledges her responsibility to her father, and responds promptly and positively to his requests for news and information about her experiences at school. A girl's cheerfulness and resilience is an important component of her wartime duty.

At the same time, Marjorie also wishes to participate more actively when her schooling is complete. She wants "to help with the war, if it isn't over. I'll nurse, or drive a wagon, or ride a motor-bike with dispatches" (ch. 7). Marjorie has clear expectations about the possibilities available to her as a girl and feels no hesitation about the appropriateness of such activities. The possibilities for girls are reinforced when Winnifred, the head girl of Brackenfield School, encourages them to think about their future roles as wives and mothers:

> We are only schoolgirls now, but in a few years we shall become a part of the women of the nation. In the future Britain will have to depend largely on her women. Let them see that they fit themselves for the burden! . . . The watchwords of patriotic women at present are 'Service and Sacrifice'. In the few years that we are here at school let us try to prepare ourselves to be an asset to the nation afterwards. Aim for the highest—in work, games and character. (ch. 12)

Winnifred's rhetoric is patriotic and also somewhat revolutionary. She envisions a future where Britain depends "largely on her women" because they have shown themselves equal to the burden and have demonstrated their ability to support England in its time of need through "service and sacrifice." This echoes the rhetoric of the social purity movement of the late nineteenth and early twentieth centuries, "a loose national network of powerful religious lobby-groups that sought to reinforce Christian norms of sexuality, marriage and family life through a series of demands for enhanced moral legislation issued from the pulpit and the press" (Morgan 151–52). Winnifred extends the range of women's capability to include more active responsibilities of nationhood, such as farming (ch. 12), at a time when women did not yet have suffrage.

Even girls in school, with little money, agency, or autonomy, can help in the war effort, or at least plan for a future when they will be able to contribute more actively. Winnifred invokes an "old American" saying—"Hitch your wagon to a star," a quotation from Ralph Waldo Emerson—"because it's better to attempt big things, even if you fail, than to be satisfied with a low ideal" (ch. 12). To encourage the girls to do their best, the head girl provides a list of all the Brackenfield girls who are doing things to help their country, including nursing, cooking, driving, translating, typewriting, and quartermastering at a Red Cross hospital. One former student, with two young sons, is mentioned for the loss of her husband, who died from enemy fire. In addition to active roles, girls are also intended to marry, have children (significantly, in this case, sons who might grow up to fight another war), and, possibly, to sacrifice their husbands.

The domestic responsibilities of girls during wartime are further emphasized in an American series about the war, the Outdoor Girls, a product of the Stratemeyer Syndicate, published under the pseudonym Laura Lee Hope between 1918 and 1921.[12] *The Outdoor Girls in Army Service* emphasizes the importance of the home fires, and the gendered roles of wartime. On hearing the news that the Germans have sunk an American ship, Betty wishes she could fight: "Oh, if I were only a man . . . I'd fight until there wasn't one German left on the face of the earth" (ch. 12), but the boys tell her that they will handle the fighting. The group of friends sing a collection of popular war songs until Betty's suitor, Allen, asks her to sing "Keep the Home Fires Burning" by herself. For both Allen and Betty, this song is a public declaration of his commitment to the war effort and her determination to keep the home fires burning "til the boys come home."

This sentimental war tune gained rapid popularity among Allied servicemen and those they left behind to serve on the front. As Jane Potter explains, the romantic sensibility associated with maintaining the domestic front was an important part of wartime propaganda: "This model of domestic bliss has important implications for the events to come. It provides the stability that survives the upheaval of war" (97). The presence of this British song in an American text reinforces the transnationalism of wartime girl-hood, since these sentiments of home are relevant around the world. It also emphasizes the transnational circulation of a range of texts, including musical recordings and sheet music. Betty stumbles on the lines "[t]hough our lads are far away/[t]hey think of home" as "tears blinded her eyes, her voice quivered, and she had to stop" (ch. 12). She tries to complete the song three times before she finally gives up. Her girlfriends run to her, "while the boys turn away to hide their own emotion" (ch. 12). Both men and women are affected by the sentiment of the song, reinforcing the idea that everyone, everywhere, is aware of the importance of the boys going to fight and of the girls staying home. Literary historian Sharon Ouditt explains how roman-tic love helps to support this domestic ideology. She writes that "if women were to keep the home fires burning, that fire was to be as alive in their hearts as it was in their hearths. Romantic love seemed to offer both sol-diers and civilians some continuity and order to their lives" (*Fighting Forces* 89). The heterosexuality promoted in the Outdoor Girls helps to reinforce gender norms of female passivity and male action despite the girls' various adventures, including capturing spies and finding long-lost relatives.

In Mary Grant Bruce's Billabong series, Norah Linton also under-stands her domestic responsibilities. In the wartime novels *From Billabong to London*, *Jim and Wally*, and *Captain Jim*, published between 1914 and 1916, Norah Linton re-creates the home front in England for soldiers of all nationalities. In the earliest books in the series, Bruce establishes the timeless world of the Australian bush, but with the advent of the war the children can no longer remain on the cusp of adulthood. Jim, Wally, and Norah must answer the Empire's call and courageously respond to the need for soldiers and caregivers. While the boys are at the front, Norah and her father decide to set up a "Home for Tired People" in England for soldiers who lack connections or family during their leave and need a place to relax and recuperate from the horrors of war, so that they can return to the front as "cheery men, rested and refreshed and keen" (*Captain Jim* 25).

This wartime experience undoubtedly reflects traditional gender roles, where Jim and Wally demonstrate their willingness to serve the Empire's cause and Norah understands her role as caregiver. David Walker explains that "[i]t was part of the burden of being a woman in wartime that Norah was unable to participate in this unique experience as fully as Jim and Wally" (303). Although Bruce positions women's work as vital to the war effort, "equally . . . the war demanded more from men than from women. Those women who wanted to participate to the full were forced to endure a life removed from the centres of conflict" (306). While the boys are doing their bit by fighting at the front, Norah's Home for Tired People allows her to learn the skills she needs to manage a household and to perform her duty as caregiver and surrogate mother to boys in need of her attention. As the moral centre of the home, she is also responsible for maintaining the way of life that the men at the front are fighting to preserve.

In addition to the specific domestic and caregiving responsibilities assigned to girls in these texts, they also assisted in the war effort more directly through financial means. In *Mary Louise and the Liberty Girls* (1918) by Edith Van Dyne (pseudonym of Frank L. Baum), for example, girls are effective fundraisers.[13] As Van Dyne explains in the preface,

> The object of this little story is not especially to encourage loyalty and devotion to one's country, for these are sentiments firmly enshrined in the hearts of all true American girls. It is rather intended to show what important tasks girls may accomplish when spurred on by patriotism, and that none is too humble to substantially serve her country. (n. pag.)

Van Dyne emphasizes the importance of patriotism to "one's country," and the Liberty Girls raise funds specifically for American soldiers. Yet the international scope of the conflict complicates a simple reading of these efforts, since the Americans were part of a coalition of Allied forces. Nonetheless, the fierce patriotism of this novel is reinforced through the accompanying illustration of the Liberty Girls (see fig. 7.1), where the Liberty Girls are depicted in their Stars-and-Stripes dresses. The protagonist, Mary Louise, positions the girls' duty as lying on "a higher plain" than knitting and sewing, for, as she explains, "we're going to get money to enable Uncle Sam to take care of our soldier boys" (ch. 3).

Involvement in fundraising is a common theme in girls' wartime texts because girls' persuasive, fervent, and feminine patriotism enables them to quickly raise significant amounts of money. As Mary Louise meets with business leaders in the community and attempts to convince them of the legitimacy of her cause, she herself is amazed: "she felt she was the mouthpiece of the President, of the Nation, of worldwide democracy" (ch. 3). Although she solicits funds specifically for American troops, she simultaneously sees herself as part of a transnational community of democratic supporters. Her grandfather similarly positions her within an international community of women, where the war "is bringing the women of all nations into marked prominence" (ch. 4). His comment implies that women, in

FIGURE 7.1 • Illustration from *Mary Louise and the Liberty Girls*, by Edith Van Dyne [Frank L. Baum], illustrated by Alice Carsey. Copyright © 1918.

fictional texts and elsewhere, are raising funds for the war effort, helping the troops and contributing to the Allied success. This work is also taken up in girls' books from other countries, such as Montgomery's *Rilla of Ingleside*, in which she must put aside differences with other girls to make a fundraising performance successful.

At the Front

Despite Peter Hunt's conclusion that the patriotism included in children's literature "was kept in line with suitable sex-roles" (198), some girls' wartime texts unreservedly encourage more active contributions from girls, even when those actions put their lives at risk. In *Grace Harlowe Overseas*, for example, Grace Harlowe joins a Red Cross unit. This book is part of a lengthy American series written by Josephine Chase under the pseudonym of Jessie Graham Flower, chronicling the adventures of Grace Harlowe and her schoolgirl friends.[14] In the novel immediately preceding the first Overseas book, Grace has married Tom Gray. As soon as Tom leaves for the front (after some concern about Tom's loyalty and bravery as he delays enlisting until he can settle his business affairs), Grace is invited to become part of a Red Cross unit. Although she writes to Tom for permission, the irregularities of wartime correspondence mean that she makes her own decision to accept the invitation. Within the space of this 250-page novel, the ship on which she travels to France is sunk by a German submarine, her accommodation in Paris is bombed, she foils a plot by a French countess to give away troop locations, she is arrested as a spy and then released as a patriot, and she delivers much-needed supplies to the front after almost being killed by German artillery. In the meantime, she comforts American soldiers with dancing, chocolates, and quiet conversation while anxiously awaiting word from her husband.

The image of this adventurous girl, who remains calm and womanly throughout the novel, is markedly different from the frontispiece illustration of Grace, which is captioned: "A Picture That Tom Gray Never Forgot" (see fig. 7.2). Grace is standing on a veranda, surrounded by foliage, looking serene and pure in a long dress, wearing a hat to shade her face. This illustration is quite different from the illustration on the front cover (see fig. 7.3), where Grace is behind the wheel of a truck, looking sombre and serious in her uniform. These two images of Grace, one immortalized in her husband's memory and one depicting her active wartime contributions, suggest the challenges of having two very different feminine ideals (the domestic, maternal figure of home and the active war supporter) embodied within a single girl.

A Picture That Tom Gray Never Forgot.

Frontispiece.

FIGURE 7.2 • Frontispiece from *Grace Harlowe Overseas* by Jessie Graham Flower [Josephine Chase]. Copyright © 1920.

In some ways, the patriotism and dedication of *Grace Harlowe Overseas* is to be expected, given that it was published in 1920. By that point the war was over, and the American troops had been instrumental in its conclusion. In contrast, Margaret Vandercook's 1916 *The Red Cross Girls in the British Trenches*, published prior to the American involvement in the war, is more surprising for its timing. The sentiments in the novel are connected to the international campaigns for women's suffrage. For example, Mildred gains permission from her father to join a Red Cross unit, persuading him that girls are "making something of their own lives," "doing something useful," and "following their own consciences" (49). As the four American girls travel to England, they discuss their eagerness to meet Dr. Louise Garrett

FIGURE 7.3 • Cover from *Grace Harlowe Overseas* by Jessie Graham Flower [Josephine Chase]. Copyright © 1920.

Anderson, "the woman who has done more for nursing among the British soldiers than any other woman in this war" (127). Barbara comments on the return of Dr. Anderson to London, where she has been made a major, "the first woman ever given military rank in the British Army!" (127). Anderson is an important historical figure, not only as a former member of the militant Women's Social and Political Union agitating for women's suffrage, but also as one of the founders, alongside Dr. Flora Murray, of Endell Street Military Hospital, a Paris hospital founded and run by women to care for wounded British soldiers. When the decision was made to care for wounded soldiers in England, Anderson and Murray were invited to run a large military hospital in London. As neuropathologist Jennian Geddes notes, "[e]ntirely staffed by women, and the only women's unit run by militant suffragists," Endell Street Military Hospital "was one of the most remarkable hospitals of the war" (79). The Red Cross girls in Vandercook's novels have the opportunity to visit the hospital and meet its founder, thus aligning their efforts with British suffragettes and women who were already doing their part to support the war effort. Barbara makes this connection explicit when she says, "When one considers the Englishman believes 'a woman's place is the home,' it is hard to tell how he is going to reconcile what women are doing to help in this war, men's work as well as their own. But I'll bet you the English won't give the women the vote when the war is over, just the same" (127–28).[15] This explicit connection between American girls and the British women's movement is another aspect of the transnational femininity operating in these girls' wartime texts.

In addition to its connections with the British suffrage campaign, the Red Cross girls embody feminine ideals of bravery and heroism found in other girls' wartime texts. For example, when Barbara's friend lies injured on the battlefield, she quickly moves to rescue him because, "in moments of great peril, as we all know, a courage is born which one does not have in the lesser moments of life" (241). Vandercook reinforces Barbara's bravery by noting her unusual heroism: "Curious that Barbara, who had been so fearful of the horrors of war, should be so fearless now! But it did not occur to her that she was in equal peril there by the body of her wounded friend. The gun fire which might again strike him was equally apt to choose her for a victim" (250). Barbara is momentarily resentful that her injured friend, Dick, has risked his life at the front even though, as an American, he owes "no duty to another country" (252). Yet the war is meant to be fought by both men and women and by people of all nations who reject the German cause: "Were not men and women fighting for the right, brothers and sisters in the divinest sense?" (252). The image of Barbara pulling Dick to safety (see fig. 7.4) embodies this shared responsibility. He has been injured driving an ambulance, and her role is to help those who are injured. Each must courageously perform the task he or she has been asked to do.

IT DID NOT OCCUR TO HER THAT SHE WAS IN EQUAL PERIL.—(*See page 250*)

FIGURE 7.4 • Illustration from *The Red Cross Girls in the British Trenches* by Margaret Vandercook. Copyright © 1916.

Although relatively few texts contain girls on the front, the idea that both men and women could do their bit in the war effort appears elsewhere in girls' wartime fiction. In Bessie Marchant's *A V.A.D. in Salonika* (1917), for instance, Joan Haysome volunteers in a hospital as part of a Voluntary Aid Detachment, but her skill as a mechanic and a driver is put to good use. Similarly, Norah in Bruce's *From Billabong to London* discovers the German spy during the voyage to London and helps Jim and Wally capture the German submarine off the coast of England. While most of these stories are obvious escapist fantasies designed to allow girls to dream of adventure, they also provide a different perspective than wartime fiction, where girls' contributions are characterized by domestic concerns.

Coming of Age in Girls' War Texts

The importance of wartime conditions to girls' maturity into young womanhood is another crucial similarity that crosses national boundaries. In *A V.A.D. in Salonika*, Joan Haysome's duty in a Voluntary Aid Detachment in Salonika is vital to her maturity from girlhood into young womanhood. Joan is initially spoiled, petulant, and snobbish, and her unwillingness to sacrifice her own desires results in German spies obtaining British secrets and in the demotion of the British soldier assigned to guard those secrets. Only through her time in Salonika is she able to atone for her mistakes on both personal and national levels.

Similarly, in L.M. Montgomery's *Rilla of Ingleside*, Rilla begins by spending all her money on a foolish hat, but develops into a more mature, thoughtful young woman during the war years; she adopts a war baby, finds a suitor of her own, and supports her mother through difficult times as her brothers go off to war and are injured or killed. As literary scholar Andrea McKenzie describes,

> Suffering, sacrifice, and self-denial temper Rilla's personality: as the War unfolds, she will shed (or purge) herself of her frivolity, like her soldier-brother counterparts. Their maturity stems from their battlefield and trench experiences; her equivalent maturity results from grief, loss, and responsibility. Her brother Walter's enlistment and death are the catalysts that cause her full adulthood, but it is her (adoptive) motherhood that transforms her into the idealized metaphor representing the future of the young Canada. (97)

This story is clearly domestic, since Rilla remains at home and within her community during the entire period of the war. Although sometimes active duty might be necessary for the growth of emotional maturity in these fictional characters (as in the case of Joan), in many cases the reality of wartime conditions was sufficient to prompt this coming of age. As literary scholar Elizabeth Rollins Epperly explains, "*Rilla of Ingleside* is about heroism and womanhood. The novel is invaluable as a social record, but it is also a wonderful study of psychology—of what the women left behind use to support themselves, what fictions they create to make the days and months and years bearable" (114). The seemingly secondary role that girls and women occupy at home is essential to the war effort and, "equally importantly, to the continuation of a life of values and vision after the war" (114). Rilla is an active, engaged young woman whose "heroism is impressive and inspiring because it grows with her" (115). Moreover, *Rilla of Ingleside* is the embodiment of Montgomery's myth of Canada "as a unified nation born out of the sacrifices and fires of war," based on "*female* sacrifice during wartime" and the "forging of a new nation based on *shared* sacrifice and *shared* suffering" (McKenzie 83–84). Rilla symbolizes the new young nation of Canada, just as Norah in the Billabong novels represents young Australia. Both girls embody the cheerful resilience and steadfast courage required of girls supporting the war effort.

In Norah's case, she leaves Australia as a daughter and sister, but returns to take her place as a young woman who understands her role in constructing the future of Australia. Her wartime experiences are fundamental to her maturity and development as a young woman. In Bruce's novels, "the war called upon qualities which were integral to life on Billabong station" (Walker 305). Having left Australia as children, Norah, Jim, and Wally return as adults, newly independent within the stable structure of the Billabong station. Coates argues that Norah and other Australian female protagonists achieve little through their wartime adventures, affecting "only flights of escape, not acts of rebellion. Rather than moving towards emancipation or autonomy, they merely tread water, and hence cause scarcely a ripple in the surface of the patriarchal structures which keep them submerged as subordinates in the war effort" (121). While this reading accurately points to Norah's position within the patriarchal structures of Billabong, it neglects the ways in which her wartime action enables her maturation and development as a young woman. Her ability to cope with Jim's death, in particular, is a turning point.

In texts that focus most obviously on coming of age, a clear connection exists between the protagonists and nationalism. As the voices of young nations, Rilla and Norah tell a story of youth, adventure, and patriotism that is part of each country's mythology of nation-building. Yet, the ideology of girlhood transcends this framework if we look beyond these national paradigms. World War I was a total war that encompassed young men *and* young women from many nations, and consequently Norah and Rilla, as well as other girls like Marjorie and Grace, are more than mere tools in the national propaganda to support the war effort. The similarities between girls of different nationalities are elided by closely associating femininity and colonial nationhood. The protagonists in these texts demonstrate the range of feminine models available to girl readers and suggest a range of possibilities for contributing to the war effort, from keeping the home fires burning to performing dangerous feats of heroism. While not all of these possibilities are equally likely, they offer heroic models of femininity that transcend national boundaries and encourage girls to think of themselves as active participants in the war and also as transnational subjects. Moreover, the publication, advertisement, and distribution of these texts invites a new conception of girlhood that facilitates a model of transnational girlhood as a motivational force for global citizenship, promotes allegiances across borders, and encourages ties simultaneously to national, transnational, imperial, and gender-based communities.

Notes

1 In Bessie Marchant's *Girl Munition Worker* (1916), for example, an upper-class girl sets new standards for production while working in a munitions factory. In Brenda Girvin's *Munition Mary* (1918), working-class Mary's romance with the nephew of the factory owner suggests her class situation may be fluid.

2 Although "globalization" was first used only in 1930 and did not enter popular debate until the 1980s, globalizing movements and politics preceded the invention of the term and of theories relating to the phenomenon.

3 Sharon Ouditt's *Fighting Forces, Writing Women: Identity and Ideology in the First World War* (1994) and her extensive bibliographic work, *Women Writers of the First World War: An Annotated Bibliography* (2000), demonstrate the extent of British women's wartime writing and examine "the literary and political capital made from the idea of 'femininity' in a historically turbulent situation" (*Fighting* 4). Other important studies include Nosheen Khan's *Women's Poetry of the First World War* (1988), Claire Tylee's *The Great War and Women's*

Consciousness (1990), Dorothy Goldman's edited book *Women and World War I* (1993), and Angela K. Smith's anthology *Women's Writing of the First World War* (2000).

4   Michael Paris's study of British wartime fiction emphasizes the importance of popular juvenile texts. He stresses the significance of this fiction because of its "exciting images of war" and because the "patriotic sentiment" it aroused "encouraged readers to enlist" (xii). Unfortunately, Paris conflates "the young" with "boys and young men" (xi) in his introduction, implicitly excluding girls and young women and ignoring the fact that girls, as well as boys, were reading the war stories he discusses, as well as the adventure fiction that predates them.

5   See Walker. Bruce's first war novel was *From Billabong to London* and Ethel Turner's was *The Cub.*

6   See Cecily Devereux's discussion of the publishing history of *Anne of Green Gables* for more details.

7   The reviewer does not note the nationality of the writers, although the Australian setting of the Billabong books is mentioned.

8   Australian writers were regularly featured in British girls' periodicals such as the *Girl's Own Paper*, which published several of Ethel Turner's stories and included contributions about life in the Australian bush.

9   Fraser began working for the British government after the war began and had worked for the non-militant National Union of Women's Suffrage Societies under the leadership of Millicent Garrett Fawcett.

10 The lines from Kipling's "For All We Have and Are" are as follows:

No easy hopes or lies
Shall bring us to our goal:
But iron sacrifice
Of Body, Will, and Soul
There's but one task for all:
For each one life to give,
Who stands if Freedom fall (lines 33–39)

11 See Moruzi for further details.

12 The four wartime novels are *The Outdoor Girls in Army Service* (1918), *The Outdoor Girls at the Hostess House* (1919), *The Outdoor Girls at Bluff Point* (1920), and *The Outdoor Girls at Wild Rose Lodge* (1921). These novels were all written by Elizabeth Duffield.

13 *Mary Louise and the Liberty Girls* is part of the Bluebird Books series, published between 1916 and 1924. Baum wrote numerous books for girls under his female pseudonym.

14   Grace Harlowe features in two earlier series, the High School Girls Series
(four books published in 1910–1911) and the College Girls Series (seven
books published between 1914 and 1917). There are six books in the Overseas
Series, all published in 1920: *Grace Harlowe Overseas*, *Grace Harlowe with the
Red Cross in France*, *Grace Harlowe with the Marines in Chateau Thierry*, *Grace
Harlowe with the Yankee Shock Boys in St. Quentin*, and *Grace Harlowe with
the American Army on the Rhine*.

15   Barbara would, of course, be proven wrong. Women over thirty were granted
the franchise in 1918. Universal suffrage for all adults over twenty-one years
of age was granted in 1928.

Works Cited

Allen, Ann Taylor. "Lost in Translation? Women's History in Transnational and
Comparative Perspective." *Comparative Women's History: New Approaches.*
Ed. Anne Cova. Boulder: Social Science Monographs, 2006. 87–115. Print.

Allison, W. T. "Canadian Literature of To-Day." *Bookman* Feb. 1929: 270–74.
Print.

Anderson, Benedict. *Imagined Communities: Reflections on the Origin and Spread
of Nationalism.* 2nd ed. London: Verso, 2006. Print.

Anderson, Bonnie S. *Joyous Greetings: The First International Women's Movement,
1830–1860.* Oxford: Oxford UP, 2000. Print.

Bradford, Clare. *Unsettling Narratives: Postcolonial Readings of Children's
Literature.* Waterloo: Wilfrid Laurier UP, 2007. Print.

Brazil, Angela. *A Patriotic Schoolgirl.* London and Glasgow: Blackie & Son, 1918.
Project Gutenberg. Web. 5 Aug. 2010.

Bruce, Mary Grant. *Captain Jim.* London: Ward, Lock and Co., n.d. Print.

———. *From Billabong to London.* London: Ward, Lock and Co., n.d. Print.

Butler, Judith. *Bodies That Matter: On the Discursive Limits of "Sex."* New York:
Routledge, 1993. Print.

Cadogan, Mary, and Patricia Craig. *Women and Children First: The Fiction of Two
World Wars.* London: Victor Gollancz, 1978. Print.

Coates, Donna. "Guns 'N' Roses: Australian Women Writers' Bold-and-Not-So-
Bold Journeys into the Great War." *Proceedings of the Association for the Study
of Australian Literature, July 3–8, 1994.* Ed. Susan Lever and Catherine
Pratt. Campbell: Association for the Study of Australian Literature, 1995.
120–26. Print.

Collett, Anthony Keeling. "War Pamphlets." *Times Literary Supplement* 15 Oct.
1914: 455. Print.

Devereux, Cecily. "A Note on the Text." *Anne of Green Gables*. L. M. Montgomery. Ed. Cecily Devereux. Peterborough: Broadview P, 2004. 42–50. Print.

Epperly, Elizabeth Rollins. *The Fragrance of Sweet-Grass: L. M. Montgomery's Heroines and the Pursuit of Romance*. Toronto: U of Toronto P, 1992. Print.

"Fiction." *The Spectator* 6 April 1918: 376. Print.

———. *The Spectator* 17 Dec. 1921: 831. Print.

Flower, Jessie Graham [Josephine Chase]. *Grace Harlowe Overseas*. Philadelphia: Henry Altemus, 1920. Print.

Fraser, Helen. *Women and War Work*. New York: G. Arnold Shaw, 1918. Print.

Freeman, Carla. "Is Local:Global as Feminine:Masculine? Rethinking the Gender of Globalization." *Signs* 26.4 (Summer 2001): 1007–34. Print.

Geddes, Jennian F. "Deeds *and* Words in the Suffrage Military Hospital in Endell Street." *Medical History* 51 (2007): 79–98. Print.

"Gift-Books: Stories for Girls." *The Spectator* 9 Dec. 1916: 737–38. Print.

Girvin, Brenda. *Munition Mary*. London: Humphrey Milford, 1918. Print.

Goldman, Dorothy, ed. *Women and World War I: The Written Response*. Basingstoke: Macmillan, 1993. Print.

Hope, Laura Lee [Elizabeth Duffield]. *The Outdoor Girls in Army Service, or Doing Their Bit for the Soldier Boys*. New York: Grosset and Dunlap, 1918. *Project Gutenberg*. Web. 5 Aug. 2010.

Huggan, Graham. *Australian Literature: Postcolonialism, Racism, Transnationalism*. Oxford: Oxford UP, 2007. Print.

Hunt, Peter. "Retreatism and Advance (1914–45)." *Children's Literature: An Illustrated History*. Ed. Peter Hunt. Oxford: Oxford UP, 1995. 192–224. Print.

Jay, Paul. *Global Matters: The Transnational Turn in Literary Studies*. Ithaca: Cornell UP, 2010. Print.

Khan, Nosheen. *Women's Poetry of the First World War*. New York: Harvester Wheatsheaf, 1988. Print.

Kipling, Rudyard. "For All We Have and Are." *The Times* 2 Sept. 1914: 9. Print.

Leeder, S. H. "Important Notice to Readers." *Girl's Realm* 16 (1914): 4. Print.

———. "The War: How Girls May Help in Practical Ways." *Girl's Realm* 16 (1914): 1–4. Print.

Marchant, Bessie. *A Girl Munition Worker*. London: Blackie and Son, 1916. Print.

———. *A V.A.D. in Salonika*. London: Blackie and Son, 1917. Print.

McKenzie, Andrea. "Women at War: L. M. Montgomery, The Great War, and Canadian Cultural Memory." *Storm and Dissonance: L. M. Montgomery and Conflict*. Ed. Jean Mitchell. Newcastle: Cambridge Scholars, 2008. 83–108. Print.

Montgomery, L. M. *Rilla of Ingleside*. New York: A. L. Burt, 1921. Print.

Morgan, Sue. "'Wild Oats or Acorns?' Social Purity, Sexual Politics and the Response of the Late-Victorian Church." *Journal of Religious History* 31.2 (June 2007): 151–68. Print.

Moruzi, Kristine. "Feminine Bravery: The *Girl's Realm* (1898–1915) and the Second Boer War." *Children's Literature Association Quarterly* 34.3 (Fall 2009): 241–54. Print.

Ouditt, Sharon. *Fighting Forces, Writing Women: Identity and Ideology in the First World War*. London: Routledge, 1994. Print.

———. *Women Writers of the First World War: An Annotated Bibliography*. New York: Routledge, 2000. Print.

Paris, Michael. *Over the Top: The Great War and Juvenile Literature in Britain*. Westport: Praeger, 2004. Print.

Potter, Jane. *Boys in Khaki, Girls in Print: Women's Literary Responses to the Great War 1914–1918*. Oxford: Clarendon P, 2005. Print.

Rosman, A. G. "A Sketch of New Literature in Australia." *The Academy: A Monthly Record of Literature, Learning, Science and Art* 30 Aug. 1913: 277–78. Print.

Rupp, Leila J. *Worlds of Women: The Making of an International Women's Movement*. Princeton: Princeton UP, 1997. Print.

Smith, Angela K., ed. *Women's Writing of the First World War: An Anthology*. Manchester: Manchester UP, 2000. Print.

Tate, Trudi, and Suzanne Raitt. "Introduction." *Women's Fiction and the Great War*. Ed. Suzanne Raitt and Trudi Tate. Oxford: Clarendon P, 1997. 1–17. Print.

Turner, Ethel. *The Cub*. London: Ward, Lock, and Co. 1915. Print.

Tylee, Claire. *The Great War and Women's Consciousness*. Basingstoke: Macmillan, 1990. Print.

Vance, Jonathan F. *Death So Noble: Memory, Meaning and the First World War*. Vancouver: UBC P, 1997. Print.

Vandercook, Margaret. *The Red Cross Girls in the British Trenches*. Philadelphia: John C. Winston, 1916. Print.

Van Dyne, Edith [Frank L. Baum]. *Mary Louise and the Liberty Girls*. 1918. *Project Gutenberg*. Web. 5 Aug. 2010.

Walker, David. "War, Women and the Bush: The Novels of Mary Grant Bruce and Ethel Turner." *Australian Historical Studies* 18.71 (1978): 297–315. Print.

"Ward, Lock & Co.'s List." *Athenaeum* 27 Nov. 1915: 408. Print.

"Ward, Lock & Co.'s List." *Spectator* 20 Sept. 1924: 408. Print.

"Ward, Lock & Co.'s Xmas List." *Spectator* 26 Nov. 1921: 723. Print.

CHAPTER 8

Bollywood as a Role Model

Dating and Negotiating Romance

Kabita Chakraborty

This chapter demonstrates how Bollywood guides young women in their quest for romantic love in the *bustees*, or urban slums, of Kolkata. Bollywood is the popular Hindi- and Urdu-language cinema of India, and this research shows how unmarried Muslim women in the *bustees* use popular Bollywood culture as a role model to understand what to expect and how to perform on dates, and acceptable kinds of romantic relationships. The context of this research is the rapidly changing *bustees* and a globalizing India, where the possibilities of romantic love are expanding as a result of greater education, employment, and social mobility (see Kapur; Netting; Patel; Jeffrey; Srivastava; Grover, *Marriage, Love, Caste*; Grover, "Lived Experiences"; Lukose).

The research presented here has been drawn from a large study on the changing lives of young Muslim women in a globalizing India. The research took place over a seventeen-month period; twelve months were spent in the *bustees* over 2005–2006, two months in 2007, and three months in 2011. The chapter represents participatory work with over twenty-five young Muslim women between the ages of fourteen and twenty-two and living in two *bustees* in Kolkata. The participants are all unmarried Muslim women, and are school students, engaged in full-time household duties, or involved in paid home-based work. All the young women are literate and all have some secondary schooling experience.[1]

The *bustees* are interesting and productive sites of analysis, presenting a non-hegemonic view of the social and cultural impact of economic liberalization and globalization on lower-class Indians. The *bustees* in which this research was conducted are two large slum communities (2.5 square kilometres with a population of over 250,000) which are home to mostly migrant and displaced Muslim populations. Migrants are predominantly from within India, especially Bihar state. Intermixed with this majority Muslim population are pockets of Christian and SC/OBC[2] populations, some from migrant backgrounds. Residents live mostly in large extended families, with many generations within a one-room home. The *bustees* are also characterized by class- and caste-specific occupations, including rubbish and scrap collectors and tannery workers. The bulk of the participants in this research live in the established interior of the slums, where there are thousands of one-room *bustee* homes, most sharing one wall. Residents are first-, second-, and third-generation migrants who live in brick (permanent) dwellings, and most have access to public taps, toilets, and (often illegal) electricity connections. The peripheries of the slums include areas around a large garbage dump, two rail lines, and several sewage canals. The peripheries house some first-generation and recently arrived migrants living in more temporary dwellings. Most young women who participated in this research are from the established centres of the slums; they represent a more privileged population than the residents living on the margins of the communities.

My role as a researcher was made possible through partnership with a local NGO, Azeem,[3] which supported my research in the slums by giving me two separate spaces in which to conduct participatory research: an art class and a girls' class. The classes both used art and other creative methods to talk about young women's lives, and became spaces where young women came to hang out, chat with their friends, and talk about their experiences. The *bustees* have very few public social spaces for young unmarried women, so the sessions were all well attended, with consistent female participants and numerous fluctuating participants.

The *bustees* are considered by the media and popular discourse in Kolkata to be a conservative space. The community is home to many orthodox religious organizations, and the cultural fabric of the slums is highly regulated by social and religious expectations that police the public behaviour of men and women. The conservative nature of the slums obviously influences the type of information young people can and do reveal in public and private. Because matters like mixed-sex relationships, romance, and sex are difficult to discuss with young women in general, a participatory approach was deployed, which made room for young women to participate only when and how they decided.

Child rights scholars have made a strong call for more participatory research with children and young people to understand their lives. Judith Ennew, for example, has argued that children and young people must actively participate in research which affects or has the potential to affect them. To accurately tell their stories, multiple data collection methods must be employed. These multiple methods need to take into account the various capacities of young people, including their verbal, creative, and technical literacies and abilities. Multiple appropriate methods ensure children and young people have numerous ways to express themselves. Moreover, Article 13 of the United Nations Convention on the Rights of the Child (1990) specifically states that children and youth have the right to use and have access to multiple methods of expression in order to share their voice and give their opinions. In the research outlined in this chapter, young people contributed to the research process by formulating topics for discussion, engaging in discussions about what methods should be used, and conducting peer interviews. Within each class, multiple qualitative research tools were employed, including interviews, art, yoga, photography, and focus groups. I have written about the participatory processes involved in this research elsewhere (Chakraborty, "The Good Muslim Girl").

This project made it easier for young people to talk about love and romance because of its use of Bollywood popular culture. As Anvita Madan-Bahel found while using Bollywood films to teach South Asian youth sex education in the diaspora, popular cinema helps South Asians locate individualized sex and romance within culturally specific frameworks. For young people in the *bustees*, romance is normalized within the context of Bollywood. It is through Bollywood that young people see their first (almost always) heterosexual romantic date, hand-holding, and kissing. Similarly, in the *bustees* young women use Bollywood texts to talk about romance through Bollywood film characters. Talking through popular culture does not directly implicate them and thus provides a safer avenue to reveal their own desires and romantic practices (Chakraborty, "The Sexual Lives"). In addition to films, other Bollywood-inspired media were also used. As Ashish Rajadhyaksha has commented, Bollywood culture can encompass a myriad of popular entertainment in India. Thus clips of stylized television programs, Bollywood-themed reality television shows, various forms of advertising, music videos, film magazines, and, of course, popular films and music were all used to talk about sex and romance in this community.

Love and Romance in a Globalizing India

The strategy of using Bollywood to enable young women to talk about and recount their experiences is particularly important because individually directed romance and love contrasts with the dominant arranged marriage system found in many parts of India. The arranged marriage system understands that marriage is a union that relies on the compatibility of two families. In this system, romantic love is not a precursor to marriage, and a woman and man are matched based on individual and familial compatibility. In most of India, after an arranged marriage, a young woman leaves her natal family to join her partner and in-laws in their home. Importantly, the partnership between husband and wife aims to produce offspring to continue the social duties and responsibilities of the family. Traditional academic analysis of love and arranged marriages places these social unions at polar opposites. Recent work suggests, however, that young people in India are combining and blending their relationships with these two seemingly opposite systems in complex ways, and with greater frequency than ever before (Netting; Kapur). Indeed, romance among youth in India is a burgeoning field of investigation (Abraham, "Redrawing the *Lakshman Rekha*"; Donner; Grover, "Lived Experiences"; Grover, *Marriage, Love, Caste*; Mody, "Kidnapping, Elopement and Abduction"; Patel).

This growing academic attention to love and romance practices addresses a clear Western bias relating to studies of romance, as William Jankowiak and Edward Fischer have pointed out. Their classic analysis of cross-cultural views of romantic love argues that the "study of romantic (or passionate) love is virtually nonexistent due to the widespread belief that romantic love is unique to Euro-American culture. . . . Underlying these Eurocentric views is the assumption that modernization and the rise of individualism are directly linked to the appearance of romantic notions of love" (149). Their observations dismiss the work of prominent sociologists who have tried to make theoretical links between individualization, romance, modernity, and globalization. In *The Transformation of Intimacy*, Anthony Giddens, for example, has argued that the individualistic process of romantic love, as well as self-identity developed as a result of this process, has been a key factor in the rise of the bourgeoisie in the West, a claim supported by previous studies (see Beck; Beck-Gernsheim and Beck).

Some Indian scholars have shown that, in a globalizing India, individually directed romances are not the norm for many young people. Steve Derné's work with middle-class young men in Northern India reveals how young men view Bollywood romance through the lens of fantasy ("The [Limited] Effect of Cultural Globalization in India"). Although popular culture tantalizes young men into fantasizing about individually directed romantic love, their commitment to arranged marriages remains strong. Caroline and Filipo Osella also show that arranged marriages, joint family systems, and the dominance of hetero-normative social systems in middle-class India remain firmly in place. Like Derné, they point to the status and power gained by arranged unions, as opposed to love unions, for both young men and women. Love marriages in many communities can have an impact upon one's public reputation. For example, Osella and Osella point to the ways in which communities can view a young woman entering into a love marriage as being too much of a "modern girl" (*Social Mobility* 107). Her marriage pathway implies a lack of both parental control and self-control. Shalini Grover adds to these discourses by highlighting the importance of the kinship ties gained through arranged marriages (see "Lived Experiences"; *Marriage, Love, Caste*). In a country that offers few state-provided services for childcare and the unemployed, love marriages may result in potentially relinquishing pivotal family support following marriage.

Many scholars, including Steve Derné and Grover, describe how this traditional arranged way of linking families helps to re-create and reinforce an Indian patriarchy that continues to favour working men and their families. Their respective works explicitly reject the assertions of Ulrich Beck, Elisabeth Beck-Gernshiem and Ulrich Beck, and Giddens that, in a modern world, individualized romantic love will grow and that this will break down arranged marriage culture, communal families, and the dominance of hetero-normative social systems. While there is no shift toward the pure-individualized relationship as Beck and Giddens have discussed, there is evidence in the slums of changing relationship formations, in particular new technology and greater mobility impacts upon relationship creation and maintenance. For many young people in the slums, Bollywood, new technologies, and new mobilities present new types of relationships, including online and migration-specific relationships (Chakraborty, "Virtual Mate-Seeking"; Douglass). This speaks to Arun Appadurai's thesis that as a result of increased transnational cultural flows associated with migration, tourism, and mass media, young people now consider a wider set of possible lives than they ever did before (52). But like Grover and Osella and Osella, I do agree that in the slums many are reluctant to shift traditional marriage systems, and that communities are not in the process of transforming into an individually directed "risk society" (see Beck) with greater emphasis on the individual, egalitarian unions and nuclear family systems. While the *bustees* are far from becoming highly individualized spaces, the realities of young Muslim women's lives in this community complicate the often polarized discussions around arranged marriages and self-directed love marriages.

Bollywood as a Dating Role Model

There are many young women in the slums who strive for and indeed achieve premarital romance, and various local NGOs estimate that love marriages constitute between 40 and 80 percent of all nuptials. Young women's desire and pursuit of love, however, is complicated by the normative construction of the "good Muslim girl." The normative expectations of and for young women instruct them to play by the rules of a dominant femininity that dissuades them from premarital romantic pursuits. A good Muslim girl should not stray from the expectations of arranged marriage, female chastity, and modest public behaviour (Chakraborty, "The Good Muslim Girl"; Bennett). Rules around premarital intimacy are deeply rooted in selected reading of Islamic text, in which sexual and mixed-sex relations are considered to be sacred and special, and as such should take place only within the confines of a heterosexual marriage. I have detailed elsewhere that transgressing the rules which apply to the good Muslim girl can result in violence, slander, and other risks (Chakraborty, "The Sexual Lives"). As a result, the mobility of young women in the *bustees* is strictly monitored, and *purdah*, the public separation of the sexes, is enforced to ensure that immoral premarital contact between men and women is curtailed. As detailed by scholars such as Shanti Rosario, Sajeda Amin, Feldman and McCarthy, and Diia Rajan, Deepa Dhanraj, and K. Lalita, *purdah* in South Asia usually designates public space as male space, and domestic space as female space. In the slums, *purdah* results in women having limited access to public space, especially after attaining puberty. When women do use public space, modesty and embodied *purdah* (including the use of the *burqa*) is expected and often enforced through gossip and monitoring by family and community members.

Scholars throughout India note, however, that the possibilities of mixed-sex romance are certainly not diminished by these rules. Rachel

Dwyer and Francesca Orsini have detailed how Indian culture is rich with stories and tales of religious, family, and romantic love. Scholars like Nancy Netting, Henrike Donner, Cari Constanzo Kapur, and Reena Patel have argued that what has changed, especially after economic liberalization in the 1990s, is that many ordinary Indians have had increased opportunities to find premarital romantic love.

Schooling in particular is the way young women are able to develop partnerships in the *bustees*. To prevent misuse of the freedoms of mobility associated with schooling, many young women are escorted to and from school and wear the *burqa* to embody *purdah* in public space. Parents and community members are well aware of the risks of schooling; as one parent explained to me, "she should not think that just because we let her go to school the door will open to other things [boyfriends]." Parents struggle to decide if the freedom to pursue studies is worth the risk of increased public mobility. But, as Craig Jeffrey, Patricia Jeffery, and Roger Jeffery argue, in a globalizing India, educational capital is seen as a necessity for all youth; thus schooling opportunities for Muslim women in the *bustees* continue to grow.

In line with parental fears, it is during their time at school that all young women in this research develop relationships with boys. Young women purposefully skip school and tuition classes to meet boyfriends in shopping centres, parks, and other social centres away from the slum. Romantic love between a girlfriend and boyfriend, then, must grow and develop in these new geographies. As the logistics governing the occurrences and development of love change, so do role models of romance. The stories of neighbours and families whose love grew from within an arranged marriage do not prepare young women for their romantic escapades. Folk tales that depict arranged unions where the patient wife lives through years apart from her spouse, finally being rewarded with love at the end—do not sound very appealing to young women, either. Thus, young women turn to new role models; the cinematic tales of Bollywood romance are seen by many to be inspiring. Gone are Lala and Majanu, star-crossed lovers similar to Romeo and Juliet; in the Kolkata communities in which this research was conducted, it was Shah Rukh Khan (SRK) and Kajol, two popular actors who have played romantic lovers in films, and whom many describe as the "ideal loving couple" and "the best match," that the girls turned to.

Almost all young women mention that SRK and Kajol's love story in the film *Dilwale Dulhania Le Jayenge* (*DDLJ*, or *The Big Hearted Man Will Take the Bride*, 1995) is a great mix of romantic love, understanding and patience, and, eventually, family approval. In *DDLJ* actors Kajol and SRK play two non-resident Indian (NRI) characters in the UK who meet each other while pursuing independent travel with friends. This travel is won by Kajol's character as a reward for being a "good girl"—specifically, for doing well in school and agreeing to an arranged marriage. In contrast, SRK is a spoiled young man whose silly antics on the trip are an extension of his carefree lifestyle. Upon being granted permission to travel, Kajol and her girlfriends take a train around Europe, where they meet SRK and his group of male friends. While Kajol's character is initially displeased with SRK's indulgent ways, the two protagonists eventually fall in love.[4]

After the trip, Kajol's character is swiftly taken back to India for her arranged nuptials after her father overhears that she fell in love with a stranger on the trip. SRK's character follows Kajol's character to India in order to marry her, and he disguises his identity in order to gain the trust and friendship of her family. He repeatedly meets with Kajol, explaining that he will find a way to convince her family to let them marry. Kajol's mother discovers the lovers' history and is sympathetic to their plight, even suggesting they run away together. SRK, however, disagrees, stating that he will marry her only once he obtains everyone's approval. When Kajol's father eventually finds out that SRK is Kajol's lover from the trip, he becomes so enraged that he begins to slap SRK. Kajol, witnessing SRK being abused, breaks up the fight and argues with SRK that they should have run away and eloped. SRK sticks by his position that they should marry only with parental permission, and tells Kajol's father that he will respect Kajol's arranged marriage before leaving the house. While waiting at the train station to leave town, SRK meets Kajol's arranged husband-to-be and they get into a violent altercation; SRK is badly beaten by the enraged future spouse and his gang of friends. Kajol and her family come to the train station to witness the conflict, and Kajol's father sees how much SRK's character truly loves his daughter. The film ends with Kajol's father agreeing that the two should marry, after being convinced that no other man could love his daughter like SRK's character. He encourages Kajol's character to jump onto the train and find happiness with SRK.

The young women I interviewed in the *bustees* spoke about this film as a good example of a successful romance, and all desired such a love story; as Aysha, fifteen years old, explains, "I hope I can achieve such a love match in my life." Young women acknowledge that for romantic love to be truly successful within the context of the *bustees*, it needs to play by the communal rules of the community, and thus must be approved by both families. When asked about romantic love in their community, young women were quick to share tales of heartbreak and hurt as a result of ill-conceived love. All the participants could name multiple peers who fell in love, but were unable to continue their relationship with "their one true love" because of a lack of family support or parental interference. Some also spoke of love marriages that suffered as a result of poor family support. Here it is useful to draw on Osella and Osella's and Grover's work, which suggests that romantic unions struggle without family and community support. Kinship support, they argue, often keeps partnerships together through hard times, including after childbirth and during economic hardship (Osella and Osella, *Social Mobility*; Osella and Osella, *Men and Masculinities*; Grover, "Lived Experiences"; Grover, *Marriage, Love, Caste*). What makes SRK's character an ideal partner for young women in this community is his ability to love within a communal system. Raya, sixteen years old, describes to me SRK's "deep love" and "patience," which gives him the strength to wait for parental approval.

Bollywood film heroes are not only viewed for their relationships with women, but provide good aesthetic role models as well, as Raya describes of her ideal man: "Salman Khan's body is very fine. I like John's height, but not his hair. I love everything about Shah Rukh. His lips, eyes, clothes, dance and acting. And Raj's deep love. I also like Hiten's face." Raya's ideal man is a mix of different Bollywood stars and popular characters: here, Raj is SRK's character in *DDLJ*, and Hiten Tejwani is a popular television actor. Interestingly, Raya's description of an ideal man does not include popular music singers, sports personalities, or models. When asked about this, she responded that she can tell a good man only by his interactions with females and this can be viewed only in popular culture. Although Bollywood provides visions of ideal handsome men, the true beauty of these men comes from the romantic interactions that young women observed.

The propensity for young women to view and idolize movies stars as romantic partners is certainly not a novel phenomenon, but, in a changing India in which individually styled romance is growing, idolizing a celebrity plays an important role in young women's newly developing romantic identities. Yuna Engle and Tim Kasser's critical analysis of why young women idolize celebrities makes the important link between a young woman's developing romantic identity and male stars. They show that

[f]or many adolescents, identity is partially constructed by interacting with popular media, which of course includes many celebrities. . . . [I]dolization is an avenue through which girls explore romantic views and attitudes toward

interpersonal relationships. . . . Thus, celebrity idolization may relate to the types of relationships girls form. (264–65)

All the young women with whom I worked in the *bustees* idolize particular stars with attractive screen characters, and reject popular characters who have bad relationships with women on screen. Mumtaz, fifteen years old, explains, "Emraan Hashmi is just a disgusting man, he is the worst character, he takes advantage and behaves badly with women." Emraan Hashmi, an actor popularly known as the "kiss-king," plays a Casanova-type character in most films, having intimate relations with many female actors on screen. All the young women I spoke with rejected Emraan Hashmi as an ideal man because of his perceived womanizing ways, even though they all agreed he was handsome. Similarly, Rachel Karniol finds that Israeli girls who had boyfriends or who wanted boyfriends chose to idolize male celebrities who were perceived to be masculine and datable.

Relationships in the *Bustees*

I found that, similar to Leena Abraham's research with young people in Bombay, young women in the *bustees* can participate in a variety of relationships with young men: *Bhai-behen* ("brother and sister–like"), romantic "true love," and transitory and sexual "time-pass" relationships ("Bhai-Behen" 337; "Risk Behaviour" 75). For a relationship to become a romantic relationship, or "true love," it often needs to go through several stages, and these stages are also greatly influenced by popular culture. First, to win spaces for romance, young women skipped classes and tuition classes (Chakraborty, "The Good Muslim Girl"; Chakraboty, "The Sexual Lives") to meet up with their friends and lovers outside the home. Like Kajol's character in *DDLJ*, it is through manipulation of the image of the "good girl" who is an earnest school student that young women gain freedom to go to school. They use this time to hang out with their peers and lovers without adult supervision. Young women spend a lot of their time socializing in same-sex peer groups before, during, and after school. As Abraham found, mixed-sex peer groups in Bombay are not as common as same-sex friendship groups ("Risk Behaviour"), a trend I found in the *bustees* as well. Even when meeting same-sex friends, finding romance is a key concern. Indeed, it is during time spent with girlfriends that young women have the greatest opportunity to meet eligible young men in alternative middle-class spaces like shopping centres.

Upon skipping school, young women and their friends can go on small excursions to shopping centres, parks, or a *mela* (the local fair). Here they spend time eating, gossiping, and talking. As young women's pocket money is limited, these spaces are not always sought out for their consumption possibilities; rather they are considered "cool" hangouts, places that have been identified within Bollywood culture as acceptable middle-class haunts where love occurs. Mixed-sex interactions occur in these spaces when one or more of the girls within the group meet a boy of interest, or when the group itself meets similar all-boy cliques that have come to hang out (see Chakraborty, "The Sexual Lives"). Meeting up with boys while in a same-sex group begins the first phase of the dating process for most couples, and even upon maturation of a romantic relationship it is not uncommon for couples to go on group dates.

Group dates are supported by popular Bollywood culture, which often depicts mixed-sex group social outings, as seen in *DDLJ*. In India this group socializing can even occur when a newlywed couple goes on holiday; in the slums it is not uncommon for a couple to take a close family member with them on their honeymoon. In the film *Hum Saath Saath Hain* (*We Are All in It Together*, 1999), a newly married couple goes on a group honeymoon with their extended family; young women saw this film as a "great" (using the English word) example of a group date. For young women fun is accentuated when together with friends. According to many participants, romance is also easier to develop when they are in a space that is fun. Group dating creates "less tension," and having friends around often puts young women at ease. Giddens argues that individually styled romantic practices highlight agency and desire and can help to undo traditional commun-al-based social systems (*The Transformation*). We can see that young women in the *bustees* create for themselves individually styled love, which grows within and through communal systems, and that, in fact, young women use communal structures to develop their individual desires for love. Rather than shifting communal and joint-family systems, young women negotiate individualization within these systems.

The young women with whom I spoke greatly enjoy the group dating experience. Group settings decrease the pressures of one-on-one conversa-tions and the fear of possible intimacy, and thus afford an ideal opportunity to meet up with boys in whom girls might be interested. Boyfriend–girlfriend relationships are further developed within these group interactions when young men and women break off into couples within the vicinity of the group. Young women extract information from Bollywood to glean how to conduct themselves in these more intimate situations. Dating sequences in popular culture are viewed with great excitement, and young women admit that they watch these events to gain information on what to expect on dates, and what is expected from them on dates. Heera, twenty years old, explains that "it is from these films we learn what is a date and what to do on them. Before, how would you know, it is not like they teach you these things in school [laughs]." However, their relationship with film in the arena of love is complex; as Shirzad, sixteen years old, explains,

> You don't want anyone to think you are so uneducated that you don't know about these matters [of love] and that you need some television serial to help you with problems with your boyfriend . . . it's fake, just timepass. Even though we all know that Tulsi[5] gives good advice, you won't tell anyone you take it seriously or they might think you don't have your own personality.

Shirzad's comments are supported by Shakuntala Banaji's findings among middle-class young people in Bombay and London. Banaji shows that there is a sense of shame among young South Asians in admitting that they are influenced by the media ("Intimate Deceptions"; "Loving with Irony"; *Reading "Bollywood"*). Shirzad echoes this sense of shame in her assertion that people in the slums who follow the admittedly sound advice of popular characters are devoid of their "own personality."

Young women, however, need Bollywood to prepare them for dating, especially when visiting new spaces like theme parks and large shopping centres. Here we see how class intersects the dating process, since in the slums young women are very aware of their own poor and marginalized status within Kolkata. They often speak of the opportunities that "girls from good neighbourhoods" (middle and upper classes) have to familiarize themselves with spaces like Nicco Park, a large amusement park. When girls from the *bustees* first venture to these middle-class spaces, Bollywood dating sequences provide insight into how to correctly behave. Shirzad best explains this when describing a date at a shopping centre. At the mall, she was taken to a food court for the first time by a boy she liked. In this space she was initially confronted with all the choices available to her: "I wanted to try everything it seemed! But I knew I had to pick one and I was watching the price as well . . . but everything like burgers and pizzas and sandwiches is all something I wanted to get, I just couldn't make up my mind!" Most of the foods from which she had to select were international foods, and she confided in me later that she had never had the chance before this date "to actually eat what is called a burger or pizza," foods often featured in Bollywood films.

Although Shirzad could have chosen regional food at the food court, when she was out with a boy she wanted to impress, she chose to perform an identity that appreciated international food, and more importantly, understood international foods; in other words, she was keen to exhibit a modern middle-class identity. Here it is helpful to heed food sociologist Pasi Falk, who suggests that food as a commodity is consumed not just for nutrition or to stave off hunger, but because of the cultural values that surround it and the persona presented when consuming it (40). Shirzad finally decided on a chicken burger, which had been "indigenized" with chili sauce and lots of onions (see Jackson). She later admitted that the burger lacked flavour, and "could have used more chili." But she did not regret her decision, commenting that the experience of being in a food court and choosing from the neat rows of indoor food stalls was "just like the films." Her sentiment that the experience was more important than the food aligns with Deborah Lupton's understanding that "when food is consumed symbolically, its taste is often of relatively little importance: it is the image around the food product that is the most important" (23).

Toward Love-cum-Marriage Unions

The desire for romantic love before marriage, the urge to develop premarital romance, and the goal for romantic love to lead to marriage are growing occurrences within the *bustees*. There are many reasons young people long for, and enact, premarital romantic unions. Obviously, we cannot underestimate the power of romance and the feelings of love that develop within a romantic relationship. The euphoria, the tenderness, and the trust that develop in a romantic union are some of the feelings human beings of all backgrounds can experience when in love. Many young women in this research, however, articulate that the "best" kind of boyfriend is one who is willing to take dating into marriage, and protect his partner in a joint family unit. Layla, twenty years old, explains, "A really good boy is the one who tries to work hard and find a separate place for his wife so that she does not have to put up with abuse from his family." Here Layla describes how after courtship and marriage a young woman may be the subject of violence in her in-laws' home. Violence post-marriage, especially around poor dowry or extramarital affairs, is a common problem in the slums.

Layla envisions that the nuclear family system protects young women from difficulties associated with the "burden" of the position of daughter-in-law, and that, by relying on love, women can obtain protection in the form of a separate living situation with their husbands. Her understanding of a problem-free nuclear family is highly influenced by popular culture, as she explains that, in film, "when the couple finds love and lives on their own do you ever see a wife being set on fire?" Similarly, Netting's work in Gujarat shows how young women "felt that a self-chosen marriage would alleviate the danger, as a loving, egalitarian husband would help preserve a woman's rights within the man's family" (720). For many young women, romantic love is viewed as a protective factor against the potential ills of arranged marriages and joint family living.

This certainly does not mean that young women accept individually directed romance and nuclear family systems as a future goal. Some of the most appealing films and Bollywood-inspired serials are the ones that "combined love with the family" (Medena, 14). Medena and other respondents were critical of the en masse individualization depicted in recent Bollywood films, such as the romantic film *Neal 'n' Nikki* (2005). In this film a young NRI man, Neal, desires to meet, and sleep with, as many young women as he can before his upcoming marriage later in the month. On his quest he meets Nikki, a young NRI woman, who is "modern" in her desire for fun, drink, and dance. Nikki initially suspects Neal of taking advantage of her when she was drunk one night, but soon after vows to assist him on his romantic quest. She ends up inadvertently ruining all his opportunities to complete his mission, and during the course of the month she also finds herself falling in love with him. Young women in the *bustees* disliked this film for its depictions of gratuitous intimacy. They were exceptionally critical of Nikki, disappointed that "as a woman" she was "as loose" as Neal. Unlike Shakuntala Rao's respondents in middle-class India, who felt excluded from Bollywood images of middle-class consumption and grossly individualized behaviours, young women in the *bustees* pick and choose aspects of a film they agree with, and discard those they do not. The nuclear family system in response to family conflict is thus acceptable in times of conflict, while unjustified individualization is not.

Much research shows how extended family systems continue to be dominant in a globalizing India. Grover, Donner, and Osella and Osella explore how the traditions of arranged marriage are strong within middle-class communities. Their collective work reminds us that links to kinship support are critical in a country where bureaucracy is mandatory, and it is usually through connections that things get done quickly. Although in the *bustees* there is an undercurrent of individually directed romantic relationships among young people, I concur that these romantic directions do not always lead to marriage, nor do couples in love partnership move toward a more egalitarian relationship, as Osella and Osella and Grover have all found in their work as well.

In many parts of India the reality of romantic love is very far from the fantasies presented in Bollywood. Grover shows that, when a couple marries for romantic love in Delhi, they may face uncertain and uneven support in their post-marriage life, unlike many couples whose families approve and arrange their children's unions. True love unions that do not obtain support can result in difficult marriages in comparison, and thus Grover suggests that arranged marriages are a protective factor from the neglect and rejection felt by many young women in love marriages (see Grover, "Lived Experiences"; Grover, *Marriage, Love, Caste*). There is strong evidence, however, that a middle ground between the highly individualized romantic love/nuclear family unit and the arranged-marriage/communal unit is emerging as a contemporary marriage strategy in India. As Netting and Perveez Mody both note, a "love-cum-arranged" marriage (Mody, "The Intimate State" 158) is increasingly an acceptable strategy. Here a romantic partnership first is created, then subsequent family support is sought. Once approved, the couple marry and live within the joint family. These unions are developing as a bridge between two different marriage systems. In the *bustees* love-cum-marriage unions are understood by young women to be a satisfactory way to protect oneself from the potential harms of joint family living, but are regarded as not always ideal. Like respondents in Netting's and Grover's work, young people are wary of the adjustments they have to make in their new home, and are skeptical of their partners' ability to protect them over the long term.

While the importance of Bollywood popular culture in India has been recognized within academic studies, there is a dearth of research that understands how Bollywood popular culture influences young people's everyday lives in India. In this chapter, I have shown how young women living in the *bustees* use Bollywood culture as a role model when pursuing an individually directed love life. I have explored how young people pick and choose different aspects of Bollywood culture to inform their dating processes and romantic lives. Unlike Rao's respondents in middle-class India who felt excluded from Bollywood images of love, consumption, and middle-class life, young women in the *bustees* felt there was valuable information to take away from Bollywood. They selected particular information to help inform and prepare themselves for potential and actual romantic encounters. They also obtained information from Bollywood texts in order to gain confidence in middle-class arenas. For many young people in the *bustees*, Bollywood culture allows them to write their identities as modern youths in a globalizing India, and provides a window to the changing world (Nandy).

Notes

1   Secondary school refers to class 7 to class 10, with students technically between the ages of twelve and fifteen, but it is important to acknowledge the varied dropout rates and fail rates of students. In the slums, college-going individuals can be described as both pre-college (class 11 to 12) and university or technical college, which can include degree, diploma, and certificate levels of study.
2   "Scheduled Castes and Other Backward Castes"; these are historically marginalized populations in India.
3   All names, including names of people, organizations, and localities, have been changed to protect the identities of participants in the study.
4   Young women in the community sometimes, and especially when discussing films, conflated actors' and characters' names. In contrast, they very rarely referred to television actors by their given names, using instead their characters' names.
5   A character in a popular television series, *Kyunki Saas Bhi Kabhi Bahu Thi*.

Works Cited

Abraham, Leena. "Bhai-Behen, True Love, Time Pass: Friendships and Sexual Partnerships among Youth in an Indian Metropolis." *Culture, Health and Sexuality* 4.3 (2002): 337–53. Print.

———. "Redrawing the *Lakshman Rekha*: Gender Differences and Cultural Constructions in Youth Sexuality in Urban India." *South Asia* 24.1 (2001): 133–56. Print.

———. "Risk Behaviour and Misperceptions among Low-income College Students of Mumbai." *Towards Adulthood: Exploring the Sexual and Reproductive Health of Adolescents in South Asia*. Ed. Sarah Bott, Shireen Jejeebhoy, Iqbal Shah, and Chander Puri. Geneva: World Health Organization, 2003. 73–77. Print.

Amin, Sajeda. "The Poverty-Purdah Trap in Rural Bangladesh: Implications for Women's Roles in the Family." *Development and Change* 28.2 (1997): 213–33. Print.

Appadurai, Arun. *Modernity at Large: Cultural Dimensions of Globalization.* Minneapolis: U of Minnesota P, 1996. Print.

Banaji, Shakuntala. "Intimate Deceptions: Young British Asian Viewers Discuss Sexual Relations On and Off the Hindi Film Screen." *South Asian Popular Culture* 3.2 (2005): 177–92. Print.

———. "Loving with Irony: Young Bombay Viewers Discuss Clothing, Sex and Their Encounters with Media." *Sex Education* 6.4 (2006): 377–91. Print.

———. *Reading "Bollywood": The Young Audience and Hindi Films.* London: Palgrave-Macmillan, 2006. Print.

Beck, Ulrich. *Risk Society: Towards a New Modernity.* London: Sage, 1992. Print.

Beck-Gernsheim, Elisabeth, and Ulrich Beck. *The Normal Chaos of Love.* Cambridge: Polity P, 1995. Print.

Bennett, Linda Rae. "Zina and the Enigma of Sex Education for Indonesian Muslim Youth." *Sex Education* 7.4 (2007): 371–86. Print.

Chakraborty, Kabita. "The Good Muslim Girl: Conducting Qualitative Participatory Research to Understand the Lives of Young Muslim Women in the *Bustees* of Kolkata." *Children's Geographies* 7.4 (2009): 421–34. Print.

———. "The Sexual Lives of Muslim Girls in the *Bustees* of Kolkata, India." *Sex Education* 10.1 (2010): 1–21. Print.

———. "Virtual Mate-Seeking in the Urban Slums of Kolkata, India." *South Asian Popular Culture* 10.2 (2012): 1–20. Print.

Derné, Steve. *Globalization on the Ground.* New Delhi: Sage, 2008. Print.

———. "The (Limited) Effect of Cultural Globalization in India: Implications for Culture Theory." *Poetics* 33 (2005): 33–47. Print.

———. *Movies Masculinity and Modernity: An Ethnography of Men's Filmgoing in India.* Westport: Greenwood Press, 2000. Print.

Dilwale Dulhania Le Jayenge. Dir. Aditya Chopra. Perf. Shah Rukh Khan, Kajor, Amrish Puri, and Aunpam Kher. Yash Raj Films, 1995. Film.

Donner, Henrike. *Domestic Goddesses: Maternity, Globalization and Middle-Class Identity in Contemporary India.* London: Ashgate, 2008. Print.

Douglass, Mike. "Global Householding in Pacific Asia." *International Development Planning Review* 28.4 (2006): 421–45. Print.

Dwyer, Rachel. *All You Want Is Money, All You Need Is Love: Sex and Romance in Modern India.* London: Cassell, 2000. Print.

Engle, Yuna, and Tim Kasser. "Why Do Adolescent Girls Idolize Male Celebrities?" *Journal of Adolescent Research* 20.2 (2005): 263–83. Print.

Ennew, Judith. *The Right to Be Properly Researched: How to Do Rights-Based, Scientific Research with Children.* Bangkok: Knowing Children, 2010. Print.

Falk, Pasi. *The Consuming Body.* London: Sage, 1994. Print.

Feldman, Shelley, and Florence E. McCarthy. "Purdah and Changing Patterns of Social Control among Rural Women in Bangladesh." *Journal of Marriage and the Family* 45.4 (1983): 949–59. Print.

Giddens, Anthony. "Family." *BBC Reith Lectures.* BBC. 1999. Web. 9 Sept. 2012.

———. *The Transformation of Intimacy: Sexuality, Love and Eroticism in Modern Societies.* Cambridge: Polity, 1992. Print.

Grover, Shalini. "Lived Experiences: Marriage, Notions of Love, and Kinship Support amongst Poor Women in Delhi." *Contributions to Indian Sociology* 43.1 (2009): 1–33. Print.

———. *Marriage, Love, Caste and Kinship Support: Lived Experiences of the Urban Poor in India.* New York: Social Science P, 2010. Print.

Hum Saath Saath Hain. Dir. Sooraj Barjatya. Perf. Salman Khan, Krishma Kapoor, Saif Ali Khan, and Tabu. Rajshri Productions, 1999. Film.

Jackson, Peter. "Local Consumption Cultures in a Globalizing World." *Transactions of the Institute of British Geographers* 29.2 (2004): 165–78. Print.

Jankowiak, William, and Edward Fischer. "A Cross-cultural Perspective on Romantic Love." *Ethnology* 31.2 (1992): 149–55. Print.

Jeffrey, Craig. "Timepass: Youth, Class, and Time among Unemployed Young Men in India." *American Ethnologist* 37.3 (2010): 465–81. Print.

Jeffrey, Craig, Patricia Jeffery, and Roger Jeffery. "'A Useless Thing!' or 'Nectar of the Gods?' The Cultural Production of Education and Young Men's Struggles for Respect in Liberalizing North India." *Annals of the Association of American Geographers* 94.4 (2004): 961–81. Print.

Karniol, Rachel. "Adolescent Females' Idolization of Male Media Stars as a Transition into Sexuality." *Sex Roles* 44.1–2 (2001): 61–77. Print.

Kapur, Cari Costanzo. "Rethinking Courtship, Marriage, and Divorce in an Indian Call Center." *Everyday Life in South Asia.* Ed. Diane P. Mines and Sarah Lamb. Indiana: Indiana UP, 2010. 50–61. Print.

Lukose, Ritty A. *Liberalization's Children: Gender, Youth, and Consumer Citizenship in Globalizing India.* Durham: Duke UP, 2009. Print.

Lupton, Deborah. *Food, the Body and the Self.* London: Sage P, 1996. Print.

Madan-Bahel, Anvita. *Sexual Health and Bollywood Films: A Culturally Based Program for South Asian Teenage Girls.* Amherst: Cambria P, 2007. Print.

Mody, Perveez. *The Intimate State: Love-Marriage and the Law in Delhi.* London: Routledge, 2008. Print.

————. "Kidnapping, Elopement and Abduction: An Ethnography of Love-Marriage in Delhi." *Love in South Asia: A Cultural History*. Ed. Francesca Orsini. Cambridge: U of Cambridge Oriental P, 2006. 207–21. Print.

Nandy, Ashis, ed. *The Secret Politics of Our Desires: Innocence, Culpability and Indian Popular Cinema*. New Delhi: Oxford UP, 1998. Print.

Neal 'n' Nikki. Dir. Arjun Sablok. Perf. Uday Chopra and Tanisha. Yash Raj Films, 2005. Film.

Netting, Nancy S. "Marital Ideoscapes in 21st-Century India: Creative Combinations of Love and Responsibility." *Journal of Family Issues* 31.6 (2010): 707–26. Print.

Orsini, Francesca, ed. *Love in South Asia: A Cultural History*. Delhi: Cambridge UP, 2007. Print.

Osella, Caroline, and Filippo Osella. *Men and Masculinities in South India*. London: Anthem Press, 2006. Print.

————. *Social Mobility in Kerala: Modernity and Identity in Conflict*. London: Pluto Press, 2000. Print.

Patel, Reena. *Working the Night Shift: Women in India's Call Center Industry*. Stanford: Stanford UP, 2010. Print.

Rajadhyaksha, Ashish. "The 'Bollywoodization' of the Indian Cinema: Cultural Nationalism in a Global Arena." *Inter-Asia Cultural Studies* 4.1 (2003): 25–39. Print.

Rajan, Diia, Deepa Dhanraj, and K. Lalita. "Bahar Nikalna: Muslim Women Negotiate Post-Conflict Life." *Inter-Asia Cultural Studies* 12.2 (2011): 213–24. Print.

Rao, Shakuntala. "The Globalization of Bollywood: An Ethnography of Non-Elite Audiences in India." *Communication Review* 10.1 (2007): 57–76. Print.

Rosario, Shanti. "The New Burqa in Bangladesh: Empowerment or Violation of Women's Rights." *Women's Studies International Forum* 29.4 (2006): 368–80. Print.

————. *Purity and Communal Boundaries: Women and Social Change in a Bangladeshi Village*. London: Zed, 1992. Print.

Srivastava, Sanjay. "Revolution Forever: Consumerism and Object Lessons for the Urban Poor." *Contributions to Indian Sociology* 44.1–2 (2010): 103–28. Print.

United Nations. *Convention on the Rights of the Child*. New York: United Nations, 1990. *Office of the United Nations High Commissioner for Human Rights*. Web. 6 Sept. 2012.

III

Settling and Unsettling Girlhoods

CHAPTER 9

· · · · · · · · · · · · · · · ·

Movable Morals

Eighteenth- and Nineteenth-Century
Flap Books and Paper Doll Books for
Girls as Interactive "Conduct Books"

Jacqueline Reid-Walsh

Today children play with numerous interactive media texts both online, on websites and through multiplayer games, and on stand-alone devices such as consoles, iPads, and mobile phones. Many of these texts reproduce the binary gendered world of Western children's popular culture: a domestic, hyper-feminine domain for girls and a rugged, action-based universe for boys (see Cassell and Jenkins). These narrow depictions of the feminine in girls' media is of concern to feminist scholars who interrogate, for instance, Barbie, Polly Pocket, and doll-maker websites as instructional sites of conventional femininity (see Cassell and Jenkins; Reid-Walsh, "Playing"; Willett). In engaging with such online games and other activities, girl users are invited through play to perform conventional behaviours that revolve around clothing and domestic activities and are set in bedrooms and kitchens. At the same time, the capabilities of the digital interface may allow small spaces where girls can play in resistant or even parodic ways, despite the fact that game design tends to reinforce a limited number of options (Willett).

While there has been continued debate about this aspect of interactive texts, there is little awareness of the longevity of these representations in children's texts, particularly regarding their long-established connections with interactive media. In this chapter, I consider how Anglo-American girlhood is constructed in multimodal texts and how design may both reinforce the conventional and also provide spaces where girls can resist, negotiate, or subvert the aims of these texts. I analyze popular, interactive texts directed to Anglo-American girls in the late eighteenth and early-nineteenth centuries. I focus on two texts in particular: an eighteenth-century flap book or turn-up book entitled *The Moralist: Or Entertaining Emblems for the Instruction and Amusement of Young Ladies* (1768), and an early-nineteenth-century paper doll book called *The History of Little Fanny* (1810). Both were produced by enterprising British publishers who worked within the dominant trend for didactic children's literature, but decided to transmit their messages differently by utilizing a paper media format directed to younger children, the movable book. The intent is that a girl would play herself into good behaviour.

My primary questions concern how moral girlhood is constructed in these interactive texts. For example, are the texts similar or are there significant changes in depiction between the late eighteenth century and early nineteenth century? What genres do the flap book and paper doll book use to achieve their didactic aims? How does design reinforce and/ or enable different types of engagement by the girl? Furthermore, what can we extrapolate about the position of girls of the middling classes in Anglo-American culture? Are there aspects that can be compared to today's multimedia texts for girls? In order to answer these questions, I engage in a multimodal textual analysis that interprets the words, images, and interactive design in the light of ideas from comparative media studies. Before beginning my analysis, though, I would like to clarify what I mean by the terms "movable books" and "conduct books," and to describe my analytical and theoretical approach.

Movable Books

As the term "movable books" suggests, movability and the ability to make changes or transformations are at the core of the definition. Bibliographically, these are texts in codex form in which some of the words and/or illustrations are presented in the format of a mechanical device such as a wheel, tab, slat, or flap. The genre has an ancient history across cultures; in the West, movable books predate the invention of printing and were used by early thinkers in science, philosophy, and divination. One of the earliest books to use movable parts was created in the thirteenth century by the Catalan poet and mystic Ramon Llull of Majorca, who used a revolving disc or volvelle to illustrate his theories. From the fourteenth century onwards, layers of flaps were used to illustrate anatomical treatises. After the invention of the printing press, books with movable components continued to be made for scholarly purposes and for religious and moral education.

Movable books came to be associated with children in the period of burgeoning commercial publishing for children during the Enlightenment, partly through the popularity of John Locke's ideas concerning the importance of visual images and playthings in the promotion of literacy. Movable books meet these requirements since they are hybrid artifacts that combine aspects of a book with those of a picture or print and a toy or game (Hurst). To "read" a movable book, a person has to engage in several actions or activities: reading the words, looking at the images, and moving the components. In each case the movable parts depict change or movement. Movable books became more elaborate in the Victorian period when improvements in paper technology allowed for the development of precursors of the "pop-up" and other effects. They continue to be published today by artists and paper engineers and are achieving more and more spectacular effects (McGrath).

In this essay, the early examples I am analyzing predate the pop-up and are simpler in design. The eighteenth-century flap book consists of one or two pieces of paper cut and folded into flaps. The piece of paper is folded like an accordion, while the hinged flaps are folded vertically, meeting in the middle. As a consequence, the reader engages in two types of actions: a horizontal unfolding of the artifact into sections, and a vertical turning of the flaps up and down. Flap books were produced commercially in the mid seventeenth century as religious texts directed to a wide, semiliterate audience. In the 1760s early English publishers such as Robert Sayer and the Tringham family started to create different types of flap books—first moral narratives and then stories based on the pantomime, called harlequinades. In *The Moralist*, the flaps meet over the mid torso of the figure's body, as in the earliest known seventeenth-century texts.

In contrast to the flap books, which had an inclusive readership, by 1810–1811 movable books such as paper doll books and toy theatres were being produced which were directed toward specific genders and ages of middle-class children. Paper doll books were invented by S. and J. Fuller, sellers of art instruction for ladies (McGrath 14), in London between 1810 and 1816. Consisting of seven to nine coloured cut-outs—mostly clothes, props, or accessories (such as dolls, baskets, or swords); occasionally transport; a head on a tab; and a storybook, all in a case—the books told brief stories usually in verse centred on a character represented by the paper doll. As the story progressed, the child reader was intended to dress the doll in the appropriate attire. Most of the paper doll books feature child protagonists, while a few have teenage heroines or heroes. Selling for a price from five to eight shillings each, the books would have been marketed to the affluent and, as inscriptions in extant copies indicate, were probably intended as gifts.

The two texts I analyze are significant bibliographically as each forms part of a gendered pair of publications. *The Moralist* for girls follows a text with the same title for boys, published three months earlier. These rare, little-known texts are some of the earliest known extant flap books directed specifically to a child audience. *The History of Little Fanny* is the first of a two-book set, the companion volume being *The History of Little Henry*, which together started a vogue for the paper doll book in the early nineteenth century. Accordingly, while my main focus is on the texts for girls, comparisons with the paired books for boys, which reveal different patterns of logic concerning gendered conduct, throw the girls' texts into sharp relief.

Conduct Books as Advice Literature

Advice literature is an ancient yet vital genre for children and young adults. In the eighteenth century, with the burgeoning of the middling classes bent on self-improvement, the conduct book began to emerge. These were gendered texts in which boys were informed about how to succeed in work and in social or political life, while girls were educated in the cultivation of morals, manners, appearance, and a strict code of behaviour. This last theme proliferated in the nineteenth century (Zipes et al. 1417). The best-known examples of advice literature were directed toward the adolescent girl and written by influential writers such as the Rev. James Fordyce (*Sermons to Young Women*, 1766) and Dr. John Gregory (*A Father's Legacy to His Daughters*, 1774). The intended readers were young women about to enter society and the marriage market, where their appearance, actions, and social performance were to be subjected to strict scrutiny by social arbiters. In this select social space, young women were understood as texts to read: every external action was interpreted as directly transmitting their inner morals in an allegorical logic (Reid-Walsh, "She Learned Romance" 216–17). Contemporary women novelists such as Frances Burney and Jane Austen examined many of these issues in fictional form, the former developing the "conduct book novel" and the latter both mocking and exploring the strictures in her juvenilia, and in her early novels such as *Northanger Abbey* and *Pride and Prejudice*.

The conduct book was also directed to young middle-class girls who were "not out" in society and who lived a circumscribed existence at home and school. One popular manual for this age group was *The Polite Academy* (1762), in which there is abundant advice about how to behave in many social situations. The opening passage focuses on the importance of self-regulation of behaviour and particularly of her body:

> A Young Woman of Virtue and good Sense, will never think it beneath her Care and Study to cultivate the Graces of her outward Mien and Figure, which contribute so considerably towards making her Behavior acceptable: For as from the happy Disposition of the Hands, Feet, and other Parts of the Body, there arises a genteel Deportment; so where we see a young lady standing in a genteel Position, or adjusting herself properly in Walking, Dancing, or Sitting, in a graceful Manner, we never fail to admire that exterior Excellence of Form, and Disposition, suited to the Rules of Decency, Modesty, and good Manners. (vi)

Again, this focus on posture and deportment as the outward or visible indicator of the girl's inner moral nature indicates that her appearance and physical movements were considered to be an allegory of her soul, in a strict one-to-one relation. In this essay I am interested in how the mores of the conduct book are transmitted through the interactive design of the movable books. I consider whether there is a focus on the importance of regulating the girl's body in the words, images, and movement of the books, and how the body is represented differently in the two types of movable books—those using flaps and those with paper doll figures.

Theoretical Approach

My research for this essay is based on primary materials consulted in rare books rooms in Canada, the United States, and England, and my theoretical approach draws from book history and comparative media studies. Taking concepts and terms that are used most often in relation to digital media, I apply them to these early interactive paper media texts. I draw centrally on the idea of textual remediation. This refers to the process whereby a text, here the movable book, "remediates" or formally refashions other media forms (either earlier ones or concurrent ones) and in so doing reworks social, economic, and political beliefs (Bolter and Grusin 273, 277). I consider that each type of movable book seeks to transmit the message of teaching proper conduct to girls by being a remediation of other earlier or concurrent media forms: the emblem book and the paper doll, respectively. In my analysis I consider how the texts are addressed to specific child interactors, and how the designs of the movable books suggest certain affordances. Here I adapt reader-response theorist Wolfgang Iser's concept of the "implied reader," and combine this with Janet Murray's idea of the "interactor" to refer to the relation of the user to narrative in computer games. Since the child engaging with a movable book plays several roles—reader, viewer, and player, similar to a game player—the girl possesses the ability for multiple actions or "activity" and/or autonomous actions or "agency" (Murray 126–29; Iser).

In terms of the interactive design of the movable books, each type affords a set of implied interactions for the interactor. The term "affordances" is adapted from the ideas of James Gibson, who uses the term to refer to the action possibilities perceived by an actor based on the physical properties of an environment (Gibson). In computer game design, the term refers to how particular objects or computer interfaces not only make particular actions possible but also seem to suggest particular actions (see Wardrip-Fruin et al.). In a similar fashion, with movable books this concept refers to what is facilitated and what is restricted by the design and structure of the movable components. This includes intentional and unintentional reading, viewing, and playing paths that may either accord or contradict the stated intent of the narrative.

Flap Books as Remediating the Emblem Book:
The Moralist: Or Entertaining Emblems for the Instruction and Amusement of Young Ladies (1768)

The Moralist consists of a sequence of coloured emblematic images with accompanying morals contrasting images of good and bad girls—first a schoolgirl then a young woman—organized loosely by the topos of the "ages of woman." The girl's fall into bad behaviour is depicted in terms of moral and religious absolutes, and the message is unremittingly deterministic: a bad girl, unless she repents, will become a wicked woman who will suffer for eternity. At the same time, the details in the illustrations depict an affluent late-eighteenth-century girl's domestic life. The schoolgirl is shown with an array of toys ranging from ball and stick, to a puppet of Punch on a stick, to a fashion doll. It is useful to consider these activities through a class and gendered lens: some of the toys and activities such as ball and stick are traditional activities engaged in by boys and girls, like those depicted in Newbery's *A Pretty Little Pocket Book*, while others such as the fashion doll are tied to the emerging commercial toy market with gendered products (Burton).

In my analysis I explore how the affordances of the flap book animate the message and whether there are possibilities for subversion, or only double layers of hectoring. I consider how the book transmits the message through a formal refashioning of the emblem book. I am interested in what the relation is between the movable parts and the girl's body, given the placement of the flaps, and how the movability of the flaps enables the implied interactor to achieve motion or stasis.

It is significant that the subtitle states that this is a book of "emblems," for the form influences the choice of pictorial images and the overall design, and it implies specific interactive relations with the reader/viewer. Emblem books were a product of European Renaissance culture, drawing on traditions in rhetoric, and in the fine and decorative arts. In England, two types dominated: the religious and the moralizing. Typically each page consisted of three parts: a symbolic image at the centre of the page, a sententious motto above, and a verse application below. The effect is striking. A number of motifs commonly occur, including children's activities and religious conventions such as the *disjecta membra*, or images of dismembered legs, arms, and especially hearts and eyes to indicate intense religious belief (Bath 168). The images were recognizable at the literal level, but the challenge was to interpret the allegorical dimensions. In the Renaissance they were seen as riddles or hieroglyphs; the emblem was intended to arrest the senses and draw the onlooker into the text, creating a slow and thoughtful pondering of the relationships ("The English Emblem Book Project"). When adapted to books for children, such as the seventeenth-century Puritan text by Benjamin Keach *War with the Devil, or, the Young Man's Conflict with the Powers of Darkness* (1693), the oppositional pairing of bad and good youth with appropriate emblematic illustrations reinforces the message (Demers 61–62).

When the emblem is remediated into the flap book, the layout and design suggest that the intended reading path is to read the verse at the top of the page, look at the complex image with the moral application, and then lift the flaps up and down to see the consequences of the behaviour.

The act of lifting the flaps progressively transforms each half of the picture. The design of the flap is ingeniously adapted to both the allegorical and representational aims of the book. The verse accompanying the illustrations refers to important details and explicates the emblematic significance to the reader. The relation of an allegorical, one-to-one correspondence between image and moral or religious interpretation is maintained. The placement of the images is such that the reader is impelled to turn the flaps out of curiosity to see the changes or results in the character. The sequences follow one after the other in an apparently relentless manner, facilitated by the child reader-viewer herself. The design is such that, even if a reader lifts the flaps out of order in specific episodes, at the end the same consequences occur, reinforcing the apparent inexorability of the logic. Since the act of turning the flap up or down can effectively depict different ages in the same figure, it seems that the interactor is the cause of the depiction, creating a close relation between the implied reader/viewer and the subject depicted.

The first two episodes of *The Moralist* focus on the schoolgirl: one who appears to be well behaved and then one who is obviously not. In the first set, the girl stands holding a case in one hand and a book in the other. When the second flap is lifted, we see that toys are strewn at the girl's feet, ignored, along with a little dog on a pillow (see fig. 9.1). The verse links schoolwork and moral behaviour, implying that a girl is not studious for the sake of learning but for the sake of being good. The moral states: "Learning and goodness go together, / And each alike support each other" (n. pag.). The second set depicts the converse. Here the girl dresses fashionably, holding a fashion doll on a string, and all her schoolwork and needlework are strewn at her feet. When the upper flap is lifted she is dishevelled with her hair straggling down, wearing a dunce's cap. Yet she is resistant. While she is about to be physically chastised, raising the lower flap reveals that she has stuck her foot out from under her dress and placed it on a page of paper with the inscription "Learning & Advice" (see fig. 9.2). The warning is severe: she is called a "wicked creature" (n. pag.) and the determinist moral predicts a lifetime of thoughtlessness.

The last two episodes depict the fate of the good and bad girl as an adult, and employ the conventions of the *disjecta membra* to convey their message. The third set begins with a fashionable young woman praying on a cushion in a chapel. Turning up the flap, the reader sees that she is now standing, looking straight out with one hand out and the other one held over her heart in a dramatic pose (see fig. 9.3). There is a burning heart on the table and an angel from above bringing down a wreath of flowers. When the flap is turned down, under the inscription "The Reward of Virtue," a serpent and a feather are seen lying at her feet. In contrast to the powerful iconography of the burning heart as signifying Christian devotion, the moral is vague and flat: "Who ever does the moral scan / Will find that virtue is the plan" (n. pag.).

In keeping with the theme of an eternal present and the determinism of a girl's actions, the final sequence presents different ages out of chronological order. When the flaps are closed, the top flap displays an image of an old woman dressed elaborately with flowers in her hair and holding a fan—she looks coquettish. On the ground are dice, cards, and flowers. She seems to

FIGURE 9.1 • Page spread from *The Moralist*, Cotsen Children's Library. Department of Rare Books and Special Collections. Princeton University Library. Reproduced by permission of Princeton University Library.

be holding a string with a bird, and the word "rue" is written in capital letters beside her. Over her is an angelic figure dressed as a young lady, and next to her is a tree with a bird and the word "chatter," while a peacock stands on her other side. When the flap is raised, she is metamorphosed into a girl in the cave of wretchedness (see fig. 9.4). The final sequence creates a dramatic verbalization and visualization of the bad girl's fate, the poem reading:

> The cave of wretchedness behold,
> An object tatter'd poor and cold,

Crown'd with a fools Cap what a Face,
As void of meaning as of grace.
The Rods you fee. difplay'd to view.
Shews very plainly whats her due .
Moral
Shun folly 'tis a dangerous thing,
For naught that's good can folly bring .

Ah! me behold the wicked creature
How fhocking to a virtuous nature
Learning the faireft Child on earth
Is Trod on as of little worth
Moral
A Thoughtlefs Girl you'll find it true
Will make a thoughtlefs Woman too

FIGURE 9.2 • Flap from *The Moralist*, Cotsen Children's Library. Department of Rare Books and Special Collections. Princeton University Library. Reproduced by permission of Princeton University Library.

The great reward behold in view,
A Crown to virtue only due,
Who would not then be good and wife,
To gain fuch favour from the Skies .
Moral
Let every pretty. Mifs proceed,
Like this and gain the Crown decreed .

The wily Serpent wifdom is
And fhews the mind of pretty Mifs
The Feather fhews how that's defpif'd
Which is alone by folly priz'd
Moral
Who ever does the moral fcan
Will find that virtue is the plan

FIGURE 9.3 • Flap from *The Moralist*, Cotsen Children's Library. Department of Rare Books and Special Collections. Princeton University Library. Reproduced by permission of Princeton University Library.

But yet behold above from thence,
The watchful Eye of providence.
> Moral
Let not one despair of Heaven
But all repent and be forgiven. (n. pag.)

The image shows a girl in a cave in an attitude of beseeching repentance, with her hands clasped in prayer. The eye of providence is drawn in the top of the cave, and around it is inscribed "repent and be forgiven." The

FIGURE 9.4 • Flap from *The Moralist*, Cotsen Children's Library. Department of Rare Books and Special Collections. Princeton University Library. Reproduced by permission of Princeton University Library.

illustration of the eye recalls the eyes used in the emblem books, such as "The Meditative Eye of the Mind" in George Wither's *Emblems* (1635), to signal intellectual contemplation. Yet, in this remediation of the device for the moral flap book, the context of the eye is altered significantly in order to relay its message to the girl reader. The eye is drawn not as an organ linked to the eternal power of a radiant God but as an external one, unattached to the girl, depicting the eye of God watching and judging her ill behaviour. The design of the disembodied eye is thus used here to transmit its message through a dire prediction of the future for vain and frivolous girls. At the same time, this disembodied watching eye could be interpreted as being a literal representation of the metaphorical social eye prevalent in eighteenth-century conduct books, where the "eye of the world" observes and judges the behaviour deportment of young ladies (Reid-Walsh, "Eighteenth Century Flap Books" 765). As noted above, when the flaps are opened in sequence, an old woman transforms backwards in age into a young girl. If the flaps are lifted out of order, the girl transforms into an old woman. The reverse chronology of images creates a disturbing sense of fusion of time in female experience. This visual presentation is reinforced by the allegorical one-to-one logic of the verse, whereby a girl is presented as equivalent to an old woman and the reverse.

Throughout, the changes that are achieved emphasize shifts in bodily position and large body movement such as shifting the torso, turning, and standing. The emphasis is not on the images in motion but on one static or completed image, one after the other. This stasis is in keeping with the emblem book tradition in that the images and words are meant to be spurs for reflection. At the same time, the impression of stasis is reinforced by the polished positions assumed by the girl as a young woman. This is particularly the case with the religious postures when the figure is praying or raising her arms in supplication. These dramatic stances recall the frozen "attitudes" popular in dramatic prints of the day and in magazine illustrations such as in the *Lady's Magazine* (Reid-Walsh, "Eighteenth Century Flap Books" 771, note 301).

In this way, the aim of the flap book appears to be to remediate the iconography and logic of the emblem book for specific moral purposes and to frighten the girl into submission. The use of the flaps to shift from one attitude to the other effectively suggests the timelessness of the intended message. At the same time, the implied girl interactor could perhaps find some limited playful applications by playing with the flaps while ignoring the words. The two images of the young obstinate girl are amusing, especially in her stubborn action—literally standing on learning—while the slow standing up of the good young woman is elegantly performed, so she could be moved up and down repeatedly. Yet, this playful potential is severely curtailed by the total design of the artifact since the girl's activity of moving the flaps means that she has been the motor for propelling the inexorable, determinist logic along.

Paper Doll Books as Remediating Paper Dolls: *The History of Little Fanny: Exemplified in a Series of Figures* (1810)

Paper doll books are a hybrid form, tapping into the popularity of paper dolls, the didactic children's story, and gendered play patterns—for example, doll play for girls and theatrical play for boys (Speaight 89–90)—that were emerging during this period. Paper dolls were produced in England from the 1790s onwards and were modelled on the shapely form of the expensive three-dimensional fashion doll. About eight inches high, they initially cost three shillings but, due to large production runs, were soon reduced to a few pence; as inexpensive commodities, they appealed to all classes and ages of girls and women (Mitchell and Reid-Walsh 176–77). The paper doll figures in these texts remediate or refashion the shapely design of fashion paper dolls, for they tend to show girls' or boys' undeveloped forms. They are also constructed differently, for each set does not consist of bodies that are dressed but of a head and neck that has multiple dressed bodies. The neck serves as a tab that slides into slots in the backs of the elaborate outfits.

The narratives are usually didactic, many using the home-away-home pattern (Nodelman and Reimer 201). Some are retellings of the "prodigal son plot" where a disobedient child leaves or is forced to leave home, suffers reversals of fortune, has adventures, repents, and is restored to the family (see Immel). This basic plot is strongly inflected by gender and genre. Narratives featuring heroines tend to be miniature conduct book novels. Two types of heroine were popular: the naive "reformable" heroine who is shown learning from her mistakes, as in the early novels of Frances Burney and in Jane Austen, and the "exemplary" heroine who models correct behaviour, as in the novels of Maria Edgeworth and later Burney (Spencer 140–42). Paper doll books about young girls such as Little Fanny are of the first type, while books featuring adolescent heroines are of the second. On the economic level, the narratives are about middle-class girls and the tenuousness of their status, which is dependent on their conventional behaviour. On the ideological level, the lesson is about the dangers of female vanity, frivolity, and fashion. By contrast, the narratives featuring boys tend to incorporate little didacticism and concern real or imagined adventures. The only overtly educational book for boys, *St. Julien, the Emigrant: or Europe Depicted* (1812), was published by the map- and puzzle-maker Wallis and teaches geography.

Some of the paper doll books featuring boys establish a link between play as activity and play as theatre. A book displaying the legitimate theatre of tragedy and serious drama is *Young Albert, the Roscius, Exhibited in a Series of Characters from Shakespeare and Other Authors* (1811), based on an actor who was a child prodigy. The text consists mainly of key dramatic monologues and the costumes include those for Othello, Hamlet, Falstaff, and Douglas. Significantly, in order to enable boys to play all the roles, the book includes both a white head and a black head. The figures are set in dramatic postures with suggestions of scenery as partial backdrops. At the other end of the theatrical and class spectrum is *Frank Feignwell's Attempts to Amuse his Friends* (1811). This concerns an affluent Regency boy engaging in amateur theatricals by dressing up in different costumes to entertain his house party. Roles include a King; "Rolla," a Peruvian hero; a barber; and Harlequin (Reid-Walsh, "Harlequin" 78).

Based on the design, format, and narrative, the intended manner of engagement for the child player of the paper doll books appears to be a set of interrelated activities: taking the precut figures, which were originally interleaved into the appropriate section of the story (Rickards and Twyman 221), matching the costumes to the narratives by inserting the heads into the appropriate figures, and arranging them while reading the stories. The exception is *Lucinda* (1812), the figure of which is a truncated shapely fashion paper doll ending at the hips, like a dressmaker's mannequin. Her clothes are presumably laid on her flat and she is provided with a stand so that she (and her clothes) can be placed upright.

In *The History of Little Fanny*, the conduct book message is remediated through a modified paper doll, and the design enables or restricts certain types of play. For instance, the design of the insertable head is intriguing in terms of the affordances of the play it enables in comparison to the conventional paper doll. With the latter, unless children used a gummy substance to attach the clothes to the body, much paper doll play would have to take place on a flat surface, since most required clothes to be placed onto the body (there were no tabs, as in modern paper dolls). By contrast, the movable head enables multiple play patterns for the girl interactor of paper doll books. Since the doll components are made of card, inserting the head into the dressed bodies creates a sturdy format that can be held up or inserted into a block. This turns them into actors—two-dimensional action figures, as it were. Toy theatres were being developed in England during this period and consisted of elaborate sets and characters with costumes that were held upright by metal slides or slotted grooves in the stage floor. These were popular with middle-class boys (Speaight 85–90). The play affordances of the design of the Fuller paper dolls might be related to this contemporary type of inventive play.

The plot of *Little Fanny* is a tale that shows how a little girl comes to realize the errors of her ways by experiencing the consequences of her actions. It combines the conduct book type of the reformable heroine with the children's moral tale, such as was promoted by Maria Edgeworth, where the child is shown coming to her own realization of her errors, not through fear of punishment (as in *The Moralist*). Indeed, Fanny's adventures of losing her class status and having to work as a beggar and then as a respectable poor girl end with her fortuitously being sent to her mother's house, so the consequences of her adventures are not as dire as they seem. When all is resolved and Fanny has learned her lesson, the reader realizes that Fanny's mother has engineered the entire experience: "Had she but known her mother's watchful eye / Follow'd her close and was for ever nigh" (11). Here, the disembodied eye is used not, as in *The Moralist*, as the judgmental eye of God linked to the scrutinizing societal eye, but rather as an omnipotent maternal eye that serves the role of panopticon. Fanny was never in danger for long, if at all!

At the same time, since the paper doll is a means to transmit fashion, the clothing Little Fanny wears at home is the height of modernity for young affluent girls of the early nineteenth century. The plot concerns fashion as well, for Fanny has to learn how to wear the appropriate garb at the appropriate times. There is also the dictum against vanity in clothes, a concern that Maria Edgeworth expressed in her treatise *Practical Education* in regards to girls and doll play (Edgeworth and Edgeworth 3–4; Field 44). In the course of the narrative, Fanny has to wear different costumes connected with the different classes, from the poorest poor to the respectable poor, before being welcomed home and "return'd to what she ought to be " (*The History of Little Fanny* 15), again exquisitely dressed.

In considering the relations between the narrative and the figures, there are intriguing gaps. One way to make the connections between the story and the paper doll figures is to follow the narrative. Each of the seven episodes or scenes tells the child player how to dress the doll for the adventure, complete with emblematic props. Beginning with the frivolous girl obsessed with playing with dolls (see fig. 9.5), like the one in *The Moralist*, "Fanny dressed in a white frock, and pink sash, with a doll in her arms" (n. pag.). The pantalettes Fanny wears beneath the dress are the height of fashion, having been assumed in this period first by small girls and then later by older ones (Marshall 238). Since she is holding a doll, Fanny is also wearing playing garb, the pantalettes perhaps allowing more vigorous play (Calvert 101). At the end (see fig. 9.6), the restored Fanny is "modestly dressed in a coloured frock, with a book in her hand" (n. pag.). The longer dress Fanny wears, while equally fashionable, also suggests her newfound maturity. Notably in both cases, after being allowed some modest tribulations outside the home, she is inside the house, standing still.

In the middle episodes, the props are less emblems of virtue than markers of status and professions, presented in a theatrical way: beggar girl with hat in hand, errand girl for a fish shop with a fish basket on her head, carrying milk and eggs, and so on. The selection of objects recalls popular prints for children such as the *Street Calls of London*, while the clothes, such as a red cape or a blue apron, suggest theatrical costumes that might have been used in such period dress-up play as children's masquerades or home theatricals. Fanny as an impoverished girl wears a red cloak in several scenes (see fig. 9.7). Anne Buck notes that, in the early nineteenth century, scarlet cloaks, which had once been worn by the gentry, remained a prized

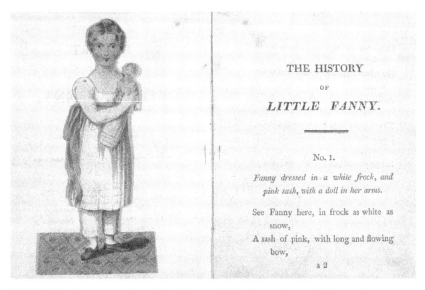

FIGURE 9.5 • Page spread from *The History of Little Fanny*, Cotsen Children's Library. Department of Rare Books and Special Collections. Princeton University Library. Reproduced by permission of Princeton University Library.

item of clothing for the unfashionable as their good or Sunday wear (193). The repeated cloak image may also be a visual allusion to the fairy-tale heroine Little Riding Hood. In *The Trials and Tribulations of Little Red*

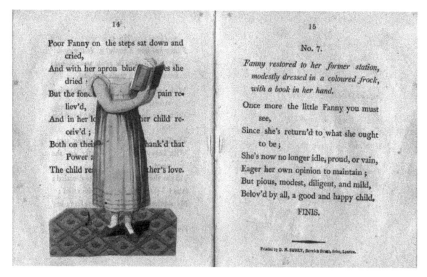

FIGURE 9.6 • Page spread from *The History of Little Fanny*, Cotsen Children's Library. Department of Rare Books and Special Collections. Princeton University Library. Reproduced by permission of Princeton University Library.

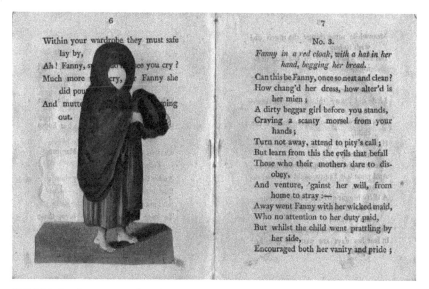

FIGURE 9.7 • Page spread from *The History of Little Fanny*, Cotsen Children's Library. Department of Rare Books and Special Collections. Princeton University Library. Reproduced by permission of Princeton University Library.

Riding Hood, Jack Zipes notes the popularity of Perrault's version of the tale (translated by Robert Samber in 1729) in the eighteenth and nineteenth centuries, where the spoiled girl's red cape suggests her vain nature (26, 31).

The separate coloured figures are placed in poses of modest action: Fanny stands still, facing front in the first and last episode, but otherwise her well-shod, bare, and roughly shod feet tend to be shown in motion, with either a heel raised ready to move or a foot raised walking. These are not theatrical attitudes (as in *The Moralist*) but natural-looking positions. These figures of Fanny in motion contain their own possibilities of narrative beyond the confines of the domestic moral narrative. Since there is a physical separation between the paper doll figure and the scripted narrative, the paper figures have their own potential life as toys that could extend or subvert the story.

Gendered Play and Playing Gender: Activity and Agency in Movable Books

As mentioned, both *The Moralist* and *Little Fanny* form halves of paired volumes directed toward girls or boys. This gendered dimension had already occurred as a marketing device in one of the earliest texts for children, John Newbery's *Pretty Little Pocket Book* (1744), where his address to the child from Jack the Giant Killer exists in two forms—for girls and boys. The advice, however, is the same (Zipes et al. 132–33). The tie-in toys are gendered as well, for there is a ball for boys and a pincushion for girls, emblems of how middle-class children were intended to spend their time. By contrast, with both the flap books and paper doll books, the message is gendered to the degree of being oppositional.

The two flap books have almost identical titles: *The Moralist: Or Entertaining Emblems for the Instruction and Amusement of Young Gentlemen* and *The Moralist: Or Entertaining Emblems for the Instruction and Amusement of Young Ladies,* the book for boys being published three months prior to the one for girls. In both a similar trajectory of behaviour occurs, the boy starting out as a good schoolboy, then devolving into a bad one. In each case, similar emblems are used but with a different inflection: the good boy reads a book but, when the flap is lifted, he literally and allegorically wins over ignorance (his foot rests on the head of Punch on a stick) (n. pag.). In the second episode, he has regressed into playing, and the emphasis when the flaps are lifted is on corporal punishment. The moral is pragmatic, ending, "[b]e good or dread like him a beating" (n. pag.). The bad boy is not wicked but stupid. The same practical focus continues as the grown-up good young man displays the positive effects of becoming a genius: emblems of the laurel leaf and of future fame abound. The inscription on the statue reads "[t]he reward of merit" balanced against "the reward of virtue" in the text for girls (n. pag.). The alternative negative ending presents failure solely on an economic plane, for the boy is shown with an empty purse, in ragged clothes. His ultimate fate when the flaps are lifted is to have a fool's cap descend on his head, and to be laughed at by everyone. The focus is on economic success breeding social success for the boy, and there is no comparison to the punishment meted out to girls. All the didactic emphasis is on the boy as a possible viable "economic man," as Beth Tobin observes (179–97)—a type emerging in the eighteenth century and exemplified in Jane Austen's novels by the independent farmer Mr. Martin in *Emma*.

Similarly, *The History of Little Fanny* is paired with *The History and Adventures of Little Henry*. Looking at the titles, it is apparent that Little Fanny has a "history" while Little Henry has a "history" and "adventures." This distinction hearkens back to the conduct book novels where respectable young females had only histories, not adventures, notably expressed in the subtitle of Frances Burney's conduct book novel *Evelina: or the History of a Young Lady's Entrance into the World* (1778). In order to read and play the miniature adventure plot of *Little Henry*, as with all the paper doll books, the child interactor inserts Henry's head into a set of dressed bodies, beginning with a wealthy young boy and then suffering a societal fall into beggarhood. Unlike the girl figures, which have only rudimentary backgrounds of carpet, brick, or dirt, the backgrounds of the boys' figures are filled in and the card paper is formed into elaborate cut-out shapes. These changing backgrounds could be seen as miniature stage sets, each in a different locale. Similar to *Little Fanny*, some locales stress the economic status (or the inverse) of the hero—a Pemberly-like estate (see fig. 9.8), his beggarhood, his status as a chimney sweep. However, unlike Fanny, Henry's economic fall is not his own fault but comes through the error of a lower-class woman. His achievements, however, are his own. He serves in a variety of professions, ultimately rising through the scale of the navy as drummer boy, cadet, and midshipman. The coloured figures tend to show him in vigorous action, carrying a bag of soot, playing a drum, and so on. In the last scene he is seen with one foot raised on a foreign landscape, leading his men (see fig. 9.9). In comparison to the *Moralist* for boys, where the position indicates an allegorical stance of triumph over ignorance, here it is used in a narrative context of territorial conquest. Notably, Henry returns home only when he is famous as a war hero, but still a boy.

FIGURE 9.8 • Page spread from *The History and Adventures of Little Henry*, Cotsen Children's Library. Department of Rare Books and Special Collections. Princeton University Library. Reproduced by permission of Princeton University Library.

FIGURE 9.9 • Page spread from *The History and Adventures of Little Henry*, Cotsen Children's Library. Department of Rare Books and Special Collections. Princeton University Library. Reproduced by permission of Princeton University Library.

Little Henry's narrative could be seen as a very early, miniature precursor of the boy's adventure story later popularized by Robert Louis Stevenson. The genre of the adventure story itself can be understood as a boy-directed conduct book—an interpretation that is backed up by Jean-Jacques Rousseau, who in his *Emile, or on Education* (1762), places *Robinson Crusoe* as the sole book in Emile's childhood library (Zipes et al.). There has been much discussion of the Robinsonade and the colonial expansion fantasies promulgated by these texts, but of particular interest in relation to Little Henry's story is Rousseau's description of the boy's fantasy play derived from reading the book:

> I want his head be full of it, and for him to be ceaselessly busy with his castle, his goats, his plantations. Let him figure out in detail, not from books but from things, all that is necessary in such a case. Let him think he is Robinson himself; let him see himself dressed in skins, wearing a tall cap, a great sword. . . . I want him to anxiously consider what measures to take if this or that happens to be missing, to examine his hero's conduct, to search for things he might have omitted or that he might have done better. (Rousseau sec. 648)

Rousseau creates an evocative image of a young boy playing adventure-story dress-up, the child's self-reflective fantasy enacting a program for creative learning. Rousseau elides activity and agency, as philosopher John Locke had done previously (Reid-Walsh, "Activity and Agency"), but focuses on the physical realm of play and permits fantasy play. Like Locke, Rousseau values the importance of physical freedom (albeit restricted to well-off children, particularly preadolescent males). At the same time, Rousseau presents this play as a model for moral conduct since the child reflects on and interrogates Crusoe's behaviour and compares himself to the hero. In this case, boys' play activity is the same as agency.

Rousseau's evocation of boys' omnipotent, self-aware play stands in sharp contrast to his description of a girl's play with a fashion doll as obsessive, unthinking activity:

> The doll is the girl's special plaything; this very obviously shows her instinctive taste for her life's purpose. The physical aspect of the art of pleasing is found in one's dress, and this physical side of the art is the only one that the child can cultivate. Watch a little girl spend a day with her doll, continually changing its clothes, dressing and undressing it, trying new combinations of

trimmings either well or poorly matched. Her fingers are clumsy, her taste is crude, but already a tendency is shown in this endless occupation. . . . "But she is dressing her doll, not herself," you will say. Of course; she sees her doll, she cannot see herself; she cannot do anything for herself, she has neither the training, nor the talent, nor the strength. So far she herself is nothing, she is engrossed in her doll and all her coquetry is devoted to it. This will not always be so; in due time she will be her own doll. (Rousseau sec. 1290–1291)

Doll play is thus a destiny narrative. Rousseau uses the same deterministic logic as in *The Moralist,* whereby a girl's actions predict, prefigure, and are treated equally with those of a woman. Unlike boys, girls seem not to possess a reflective capacity nor the ability to alter their fate.

With this background and context, it is intriguing to speculate where this situates a nineteenth-century girl interactor who may have access to both *Little Fanny* and *Little Henry,* and perhaps others in the series. In terms of play paths, the plots are presented as options for a child, particularly since the size of the heads and bodies is almost identical in all the books. This type of play is suggested by the merchandizing of the books. If the paratextual information on the back covers and paper cases of the first editions is examined, it becomes apparent that the books were sold as a gendered pair, each being described "as a companion" to the other one. While *Little Fanny* was probably published first (Aldersen and Oyens 130–31), since no day of publication is given, it might be that both were published close together, employing a "breeder" strategy of marketing not usually considered to have been used in children's publishing until the twentieth century.

All the Fuller books tie in to a contemporary fad for masquerade play engaged in by adults and children of both genders, which involved playing both genders. The Fullers also published artifacts of this sort, some very expensive and beautiful, for an adult market. In the case of the pair of *Little Fanny* and *Henry,* these books enable a girl to engage in fantasy adventure play herself by inserting the head of the doll into either the girl's or boy's body and thereby creating an avatar for herself in different exciting locales. Significantly, the movable heads of both Fanny and Henry have the short hair that became fashionable for both girls and boys of the middle class by the turn of the nineteenth century (Buck 200), and the features appear similar—the gender is not demarcated by the "loose" heads, but only by the gendered fashionable dress to which they are literally and metaphorically anchored. In this way, the design feature of the movable head provides a simple means for a girl to escape the rigid gender-genre links in the conduct book. The play affordances of the design of the paper doll books, in other words, contain the mechanisms for their own undermining of the narrow didactic narrative by the child reader-viewer-player.

In this chapter, I have contrasted two different types of movable books, a flap book and a paper doll book, that seek to convey their message of promoting proper girls' conduct by remediating two other media forms, in the first case the earlier genre of the emblem book and in the second case the concurrent genre of the paper doll. Both are stylish in terms of design, and the girl figures are always in decorous or elegant postures, no matter what the message of the narrative is in terms of addressing the girl reader. The contrast between the two is quite startling. The 1768 flap book, with its remediation of the emblem book, looks antique. A reworking of the Renaissance form of the emblem, the appearance suggests that of an object earlier than the date of the artifact. By contrast, the 1810 paper doll book looks more modern. If we consider the paper doll figures as action figures, they could almost be contemporary "historical" paper dolls comparable to the American Girl paper dolls or the Tierney paper dolls for adults.

In terms of the affordances of interactive play, a contrast exists as well. *The Moralist* seems to turn the possibilities of the flap book for horizontal and vertical movement against itself. The harsh determinist message in word and image seems to disavow or severely limit subversive play. On the other hand, *Little Fanny* with her movable head offers trajectories of play outside of the individual didactic text. The design thereby allows a player to engage with all the other texts in the paper doll series, and thus enables play crossing gender, class, age, and race boundaries. In this way, the girl could play with the components of the entire series of Fuller Paper dolls as a large, multifaceted "cumulative cultural text" (Mitchell and Reid-Walsh 189), of which the initial book is only the enabler for the wider play.

Comparing the design and intended aims of these two eighteenth- and nineteenth-century movable books directed toward girls to interactive media today, it is apparent that the conduct book dimension and the stress on domestic scenes for proper, contained girls' play continue to be emphasized. Girls (and boys) are in many cases still playing long-established gender-genre patterns, except that they are now remediated into digital media texts. At the same time, as with these early texts, the design of contemporary digital texts may have affordances that allow degrees of play which enable the child interactor to subvert, or even invert, the didactic and restrictive messages. There have been many anecdotal and documented cases of girls playing with Barbie, Polly Pocket, or Bratz virtual dolls in unintended ways, such as whirling the dolls until the viewer becomes dizzy, and jumping from one virtual domain to another to create a hybrid play environment tailored to their likes and dislikes, or pushing the Sims' characters to their breaking point in their virtual dollhouses (see Reid-Walsh, "Playing At and With"). Girls now, like girls in the past, can seize on the affordances of the interactive design to create their own modified texts where they have more agency and control of the narratives, so that they can experience "adventures" as well as "histories."

Works Cited

Alderson, Brian, and Felix de Marez Oyens. *Be Merry and Wise: Origins of Children's Book Publishing in England, 1650–1850*. New York: Pierpont Morgan Library, 2006. Print.

Bath, Michael. *Speaking Pictures: English Emblem Books and Renaissance Culture*. London: Longman, 1994. Print.

Bolter, Jay David, and Richard Grusin. *Remediation: Understanding New Media*. Cambridge: MIT P, 1999. Print.

Buck, Anne. *Clothes and the Child: A Handbook of Children's Dress in England 1500–1900*. New York: Holmes & Meier, 1996. Print.

Burton, Anthony. *Children's Pleasures: Books, Toys and Games from the Bethnal Green Museum of Childhood*. London: V&A, 1996. Print.

Calvert, Karin. *Children in the House: The Material Culture of Early Childhood, 1600–1900*. Boston: Northeastern UP, 1992. Print.

Cassell, Justine, and Henry Jenkins, eds. *From Barbie to Mortal Kombat: Gender and Computer Games*. Cambridge: MIT P, 1998. Print.

Demers, Patricia, ed. *From Instruction to Delight: An Anthology of Children's Literature to 1850*. 2nd ed. Toronto: Oxford UP, 2004. Print.

Edgeworth, Maria, and Richard Edgeworth. *Practical Education*. 1798. Introd. Gina Luria. New York: Garland Publishing, 1974. Print.

"The English Emblem Book Project." *Penn State University Libraries*. 2004. Web. 21 Aug. 2005.

Field, Hannah. "'A Story, Exemplified in a Series of Figures': Paper Doll versus Moral Tale in the Nineteenth Century." *Girlhood Studies: An Interdisciplinary Journal* 5.1 (2012): 37–56. Print.

Gibson, James J. "The Theory of Affordances." *Perceiving, Acting and Knowing: Towards an Ecological Psychology*. Ed. Robert Shaw and John Bransford. Hillsdale: Lawrence Erlbaum, 1977. 67–82. Print.

The History of Little Fanny: Exemplified in a Series of Figures. London: S. and J. Fuller, 1810. Print.

Hurst, Clive. *Early Children's Books in the Bodleian Library.* Oxford: Bodleian Library, 1995. Print.

Immel, Andrea. "Fuller, Samuel, and Joseph Fuller." *Oxford Encyclopedia of Children's Literature.* Ed. Jack Zipes. Oxford: Oxford UP, 2006. 109–10. Print.

Iser, Wolfgang. *The Implied Reader: Patterns of Communication in Prose Fiction from Bunyan to Beckett.* Baltimore: Johns Hopkins UP, 1974. Print.

Lucinda the Orphan, or, the Costumes: A Tale. London: S. and J. Fuller, 1812. Print.

Marshall, Noreen. *Dictionary of Children's Clothes: 1700 to Present.* London: Victoria & Albert, 2008. Print.

McGrath, Leslie. *This Magical Book: Movable Books for Children, 1771–2001.* Toronto: Toronto Public Library, 2002. Print.

Mitchell, Claudia, and Jacqueline Reid-Walsh. *Researching Children's Popular Culture: The Cultural Spaces of Childhood.* London: Routledge, 2002. Print.

The Moralist: Or Entertaining Emblems for the Instruction and Amusement of Young Gentlemen. London: Wm. Tringham, 1768. Print.

The Moralist: Or Entertaining Emblems for the Instruction and Amusement of Young Ladies. London: Wm. Tringham, 1768. Print.

Murray, Janet M. *Hamlet on the Holodeck: The Future of Narrative in Cyberspace.* New York: Free P, 1997. Print.

Nodelman, Perry, and Mavis Reimer. *The Pleasures of Children's Literature.* 3rd ed. Toronto: Allyn and Bacon, 2003. Print.

The Polite Academy. London: R. Baldwin, 1762. Rpt. in *The Hockliffe Project.* De Montfort University. Web. 17 Sept. 2012.

Reid-Walsh, Jacqueline. "Activity and Agency in Historical 'Playable Media': Early English Movable Books and Their Child Interactors." *Journal of Children and Media* 6.2 (2012): 164–81. Print.

———. "Eighteenth Century Flap Books for Children: Allegorical Metamorphosis and Spectacular Transformation." *Princeton University Library Chronicle* 68.3 (2007): 751–90. Print.

———. "Harlequin Meets the SIMS: A History of Interactive Media for Children and Youth from Early Flap Books to Contemporary Multimedia." *The International Handbook of Children, Media and Culture.* Ed. Sonia Livingstone and Kirsten Drotner. London: Sage, 2008. 71–86. Print.

———. "Playing At and With Popular Teen Culture on 'Girl' Websites: The Case of Alice." *Growing Up Online: Young People and Digital Technologies.* Ed. Sandra Weber and Shanly Dixon. London: Palgrave Macmillan, 2007. 181–94. Print.

———. "'She Learned Romance as She Grew Older': From Conduct Book Propriety to Romance in *Persuasion*." *Persuasions* 15 (1993): 216–25. Print.

Rickards, Maurice, and Michael Twyman. *Encyclopedia of Ephemera: A Guide to the Fragmentary Documents of Everyday Life for the Collector, Curator, and Historian*. New York: Routledge, 2001. Print.

Rousseau, Jean-Jacques. "Emile, or On Education." *Institute for Learning Technologies of Columbia University*. Columbia U, n.d. Web. 17 Sept. 2012.

Speaight, George. *The History of the English Toy Theatre*. London: Studio Vista, 1969. Print.

Spencer, Jane. *The Rise of the Woman Novelist: From Aphra Behn to Jane Austen*. Oxford: Basil Blackwell, 1986. Print.

Tobin, Beth Fowkes. "Arthur Young, Agriculture, and the Construction of the New Economic Man." *History, Gender, and Eighteenth-Century Literature*. Ed. Beth Fowkes Tobin. Athens: U of Georgia P, 1994. 179–97. Print.

Wardrip-Fruin, Noah, Michael Mateas, Steven Dow, and Serdar Sali. "Agency Reconsidered." *Proceedings of the DIGRA: Breaking New Ground: Innovation in Games, Play, Practice and Theory Conference, September 2009*. London: Brunel U, 2009. 1–9. Web. 17 Sept. 2012.

Willett, Rebekah. "Consuming Fashion and Producing Meaning through Online Paper Dolls." *Growing Up Online: Young People and Digital Technologies*. Ed. Sandra Weber and Shanly Dixon. London: Palgrave Macmillan, 2007. 113–28. Print.

Zipes, Jack. *The Trials and Tribulations of Little Red Riding Hood*. London: Routledge, 1993. Print.

Zipes, Jack, Lissa Paul, Lynne Vallone, Peter Hunt, and Gillian Avery. *The Norton Anthology of Children's Literature: The Traditions in English*. New York: Norton, 2005. Print.

CHAPTER 10

Wild Australian Girls?

The Mythology of Colonial Femininity in British Print Culture, 1885–1926

Michelle J. Smith

Until the end of the nineteenth century, British emigrants to Australia, totalling approximately three million, outnumbered people of British descent who were born in its six colonies (Denoon 63). The early twentieth century, marked by Australia's federation in 1901, is a critical moment at which to consider how Australian identity was figured as entwined with and yet differentiated from British identity. This chapter focuses on British girls' novels that were published in the first several decades of the twentieth century, and that generate an imagined picture of Australian girlhood. It analyzes girls' fiction in particular because of the liminality and resultant freedoms ascribed to girlhood in the late nineteenth and early twentieth centuries (Mitchell, "Girls' Culture" 245). These books were written by British authors, primarily for the consumption of British girls, but were also read by Australian girls, as most Australian children's books were sourced from Britain well into the twentieth century. Literary critic and journalist Brenda Niall suggests that by the 1890s, with the establishment of several agencies for British publishing houses in Australia, a "double readership could be assumed" (27).[1] The dual audience of these fictions therefore enables us to consider how these texts open up the possibility for readers from different national contexts to respond to Australian girl protagonists who are, as I shall argue, clearly differentiated from British fictional girls and championed for their heroism. The major, and often comical, differences in Australian heroines reveal how the figure of the Australian girl is mobilized by British authors of this period not only to celebrate a mythical version of colonial femininity, but also to perform wider ideological work through critiques of the British class system and affirmations of imperial identity.

British emigrants to Australia attempted to replicate aspects of home in a new and vastly different land, with women expected to re-create British domestic situations. As Janet C. Myers argues in developing the concept of "portable domesticity," British women in the colonies both performed the work of domesticity and embodied it (8–11). Nevertheless, the new generation of Australian-born girls were not necessarily constrained by a need to rehearse British feminine and domestic norms in the same ways as British women emigrants were. Both fictional examples and contemporary British periodicals outline a generally consistent model of the Australian girl as embodying a distinct type of femininity characterized by physical strength, bravery, lack of regard for class-based conventions, and selfless concern for others.

Girlhood and Colonial Identity in the Periodical Press

The perception that Australian girls differed from their British counterparts can be related to broader notions of colonial identity that circulated within and between the imperial centre and its outposts. Despite this common perception, though, Australian identity remained entangled with British identity. Andrew Hassam proposes that to have a British identity did not necessarily require one to live in Britain, but that "being British but not of Britain meant that Australians were and were not British. They were the same and yet different" (27–28). The British periodical press imagined these differences as inspired by the hardships of colonial life. While anthropologists disputed such ideas, the *Times* reported perceptions of different national "types" in 1919. A march of troops from Australia, Canada, and New Zealand showed the Australian to be "a fine fellow physically, [who] had a countenance which would look well on an old Roman coin, there being about him a suggestion of beaked nose and ancient Imperialism. The Canadian, on the other hand, was more English in his traits and, but for a certain breadth of feature might make an excellent Cockney" ("Dominion Faces" 9). The perceived physical difference between the English and the residents of the dominions is particularly marked with the Australian man, as if Australians have rapidly evolved the greatest physical difference from the English.

Australian novelist and traveller Mary Gaunt similarly distinguished between the English and colonial settlers in the *Times*, pointing to the physical prowess and mental strength of successful male and female settlers who left the comfort of "old England":

> These new countries were not won without hardship, and nowhere does individuality tell more markedly than in the immigrant to a new country. The man or woman who can adapt themselves to the new conditions is likely to do well; the man or woman who cannot beg help to go from State to State and finally beg their way home filling the air with their wailings. "No English need apply," is often the cry in Canada and Australia, and can one wonder when one reads such accounts of fecklessness and help-lessness? (6)

The idea that Britain was home to individuals who were spoiled by its com-forts and who had not been encouraged to develop the same physical and mental strength that colonial life inspired was also promoted by British writers. A 1924 *Times* article entitled "Women as Empire Settlers" sug-gests that living in the dominions, with "simpler conditions" and with "less rigid conventions," prevented "individuals from being hampered and restricted by constant subservience to a tradition: and promoted 'above all the greater important of the individual'" (9). The article also highlights the essential contribution of women to the development of the Empire, their responsibility for which was potentially "even greater than the man's" (9). The attribution of great imperial responsibility to women was an extension of late-nineteenth-century calls for female emigrants to travel to the col-onies.[2] In 1894, for instance, Flora Shaw pointed out that the colonies were suffering from a scarcity of women, provoking an undesirable situation in which men were required to perform domestic tasks and were inclined to "recklessness" (11). Like Gaunt, Shaw praises the girl who can marshal her energies to create a home in difficult circumstances: "No healthy, sensible girl fears work. It is the dullness of the left-behind which makes so many of those whose circumstances are not altogether prosperous discontented" (11). There emerges a sense that safe, routinized British life can induce laz-iness of spirit and faults in character, whereas the hard-working girl is more inclined to embrace the challenges of settler life.

An article on colonial life in the popular magazine the *Girl's Own Paper* in 1891 reads effectively as pro-emigration propaganda, talking up the potential for self-improvement, health, and freedom, particularly that afforded by horse riding, in Australia. Emigration is introduced as a particularly suitable venture for working-class or poor girls who might be suffering on low wages with polluted air and subsisting on little food. In contrast, in "Brighter Britain," as Australia is described by author Adelaide Ross, there are "boundless resources" awaiting these girls (487). Ross makes reference to the purported frequency with which the magazine receives letters from girls who have emigrated from Britain, the writers of which she represents as declaring, "I have grown so strong and stout you would not know me. None of the clothes I took out fit me any longer" (487). Amid the propagandistic elements of the article are clear signs of how the picture of colonial Australian girlhood was emerging in British eyes as strong, healthful, and independent, at least where it concerned working-class girls who were not prospering in Britain.

These aspects of the imagined Australian girl are also emphasized in British publications intended for an adult readership. An article in *John Bull* in 1885 records the thoughts of British journalist George Augustus Sala about the girls of Sydney after his visit of the same year. He observes that the young ladies "run tall" due to their outdoor exercise and their training to be "skilful and fearless horsewomen," and that the younger girls of twelve or thirteen look "slightly too old for their age" ("Mr Sala on the Australians" 581). He asks, "Is it climate, or democratic institutions, or the greater or smaller independence from parental control engendered by such institutions, that has been the cause why so many Australian little girls have so grave and resolved an expression of countenance as to resemble facially so many little women?" (581). In the article "The Land of the Wattle" in *All the World* in 1892, there is a similar sense that Australian children grow prematurely or "shoot up like mushrooms" (892). In this article, Australian boys and girls are said to be "men and women of society long before their ancestors had left the schoolroom," though this does not indicate a compliment about superiority, as the Australian youth also spends surplus time in "pleasure rather than profit" (892). The author observes that women's rights in Australia are well sustained because of "a Colonial girl's natural independence of character and partly because of their good sense" (892). Despite fears of the upheaval that might be provoked by greater freedoms and rights for British women, the Australian woman is repeatedly admired for managing the peculiarities of colonial life while demonstrating qualities such as intellectual practicality.

The stereotypical tropes of Australian femininity popularized in the British periodical press were intimately related to women's suffrage. As women's suffrage was achieved in New Zealand and Australia in 1893 and 1902 respectively, antipodean femininity acquired an air of progressiveness and modernity. Angela Woollacott proposes that attaining the right to vote led Australian women to perceive themselves as "politically more modern than even British and American women" ("White Colonialism" 50), a thesis borne out by the British periodical press. The *Times* of 1911 noted a deputation by Vida Goldstein on behalf of the Australia and New Zealand Woman Voters' Committee concerning the loss of status of a woman "who came to this unenlightened country where women did not vote" ("Australian Women" 16). In the same year, a speech by Australian prime minister Andrew Fisher was reported in the *Times* with especial interest shown in female questioners on women's suffrage and the subsequent establishment of a minimum wage for women. Fisher believed that Australian women visiting England "would feel degraded at losing their citizen rights, and most of them, if they were true Australians, would make a few remarks about it" ("Woman Suffrage" 7). "True" Australians, including women, do not remain silent at the sight of a perceived injustice. The association of the Australian woman with progressive femininity is also evident in a *Punch* cartoon from 1900 depicting Australia as a girl holding a "latch key": a sign of the freedoms of the New Woman of the *fin de siècle* and also of Australia's growing freedom as a nation, one year before its federation (Tenniel 299). The trope of independence is firmly entrenched in fictional depictions of the Australian girl, and, like the New Woman, she is variously admired and occasionally mocked for her abilities to fend for herself.

Australian Girls in British Fiction

Historically, the term "girl" might refer to any female from a prepubescent child to an unmarried woman of twenty-four or twenty-five years of age. Nevertheless, studies of the representation of the figure of the Australian girl do not consider young people's texts, but examine Australian novels and periodicals targeted solely at an adult readership.[3] In her examination of Australian women's relationship to modernity and colonialism, Woollacott describes the "Australian Girl" as a counterpart to the Australian bushman, a figure of female independence that stood in contrast to the masculine pastoral economy. Woollacott argues that the Australian Girl was "a vehicle for combatting English condescension to colonials. Her emergence marked, as well, a shift from colonial to national identities" (*To Try Her Fortune* 159). Such a figure arises in answer to British femininity being championed as the model for Australian femininity, against which the Australian was necessarily inferior,[4] and points toward the use of girl figures to debate imperial belonging and national identity. In the sources for adult readers that Woollacott examines, the Australian girl stands for a modern, independent identity that works synecdochically for the nation itself. The Australian girl, in other words, answers perceived and actual critiques of Australia's lack of development and sophistication.

British authors producing girls' fiction did not use Australian girls for the same purpose with which Woollacott associates the trope in Australian literature. Instead, these fictional representations by authors, most of whom had never even visited Australia, perform several cultural functions that both critique aspects of Britishness and reinforce imperialism. Specifically, the Australian girl in girls' fiction is variously used as a tool by which to mount a critique of the English class system, to define the limits of femininity in racial terms, to support continued emigration to former colonies, and to affirm imperial identity through the incorporation of colonial stereotypes into the accepted definition of British femininity. These British novels do not privilege British femininity as the standard, perpetuating notions of British superiority that shaped reactionary depictions of the Australian girl in Australian fiction. Instead, the imagined characteristics of the Australian girl are usually celebrated in ways that support the British Empire and, specifically, that reassert the strength of imperialism in the face of the real movement in Australia from colonial to national identifications.

The novels considered in this chapter can be defined according to four broad categories. The first depicts Australian girls who must travel to England for their schooling, including E. L. Haverfield's *Dauntless Patty* (1909) and Ethel Talbot's *That Wild Australian School Girl* (1925). The second, a rarer reverse scenario in the school story genre, concentrates on an Australian girls' school in which an English girl must adapt to colonial life, an example of which is Violet Methley's *The Bunyip Patrol* (1926). The third is the adventure story set in Australia, exemplified by Bessie Marchant's novels *The Black Cockatoo: A Story of Western Australia* (1910), *The Ferry House Girls: An Australian Story* (1912), and *Sally Makes Good: A Story of Tasmania* (1920). The final unique example is Haverfield's *Queensland Cousins* (1908), in which a British young woman visits her Australian relatives and the family, including its four Australian-born children, returns to England partway through the narrative. All four of these scenarios contrast the differences between Australian and British girls, on home soil, in the unfamiliar motherland, or in both places. The first sub-group works against the idea that British women represent the apogee of femininity by linking the misfit identities of Australian heroines with the greatest successes of the closures of the novels, closures that usually encompass saving the school or saving the lives of others. These scenarios enable critique of British class and gender norms, while also emphasizing the primacy of imperial belonging. The second and third scenarios show British girls, or girls of British parentage, soon adopting idealized Australian heroism: this trope supports the continued emigration of British subjects to its former colonies by demonstrating the ease with which girls can adapt and assume a colonial identity. The final scenario, however, presents Australian life as replete with hardships that make it an inferior place in which to live, and engages the heroine in a battle of domestic knowledge in order to demonstrate the potential for Australians to return to and settle in England. While *Queensland Cousins* is this scenario's lone example, the ease with which the children in this novel can discard their Australian identity likewise contributes to a broader notion of imperial identity superseding that of nation.

Transforming the Generic Conventions of the School Story

From the late nineteenth century onwards, school stories became one of the most popular genres for girl readers across the British Empire. Alastair Fowler argues that genres "are actually in a continual state of transmutation" and that it is primarily through their modification "that individual works convey literary meaning" (24). Australian girl protagonists in British girls' school stories are often used in alterations to the well-known trope of the middle-class Edwardian school story written by the likes of Angela Brazil, in which a girl outsider must be tamed and disciplined to suit the norms of an English school. This is most often achieved through the use of an Irish protagonist or a motherless child of Empire who has not yet learned appropriate feminine ways. One of the most frequently discussed examples is L. T. Meade's *Wild Kitty* (1897), which depicts an Irish girl who is accustomed to hunting and experiencing the outdoors on her father's estates and never submits to discipline. Sally Mitchell proposes that "outsiders" such as Kitty can be admired even though they are passionate and undisciplined, but "the same characteristics would fatally mar a respectable English girl" (*The New Girl* 95). Girls who remain within England, such as the eponymous heroine of Angela Brazil's *The Fortunes of Philippa* (1906), cannot stay untamed. Philippa, who has been raised in Argentina among black servants, is transformed through her English schooling from "a tropical blossom into an English rose" (208). In the two examples of Australian schoolgirls in Talbot's and Haverfield's fictions, however, their distinctly colonial ways—namely their willingness to trust and their concern for others—are shown to be superior, leading to favourable outcomes for the school and for the protagonists' English friends. These Australian protagonists, in other words, suggest a transformation in the generic model of the school outsider who must learn to conform. In particular, the acceptance of feminine behaviours that do not fit the English model typically reinforced in stories in this genre conveys a sense of imperial belonging, in which the eccentricities of the Australian girls can be reasonably accommodated within England.

In addition, the inclusion of Australian girls within the school story also permits its British readers a vicarious experience of freedom from the constraints imposed upon girls who were not colonial-born. The genre is often interpreted as fantasy, with a minority of actual children experiencing in reality the kind of schools rendered within the novels. For instance, Mitchell argues "the boarding-school fantasy lets girls imagine being free of parental control while not yet burdened by the hard work of supporting themselves" (*The New Girl* 95). Moreover, she suggests that these stories "use a patently unreal world to expose desires and dreams about a real world" (99). Kate Flint observes that theories of women's reading of romance novels similarly fixate on the idea of escapism "into imagined lives more active and interesting than the reader's own, and into fictional spaces where 'feminine' values are granted more weight than is often the case in 'real' life" (32). Flint argues, however, that romance novels enable more than the pleasure of fantasies in which feminine values are elevated to a higher position: women readers can enter a world that might "free" them "from the immediate and particular pressure to live up to such values" (32). Using Flint's argument to read school stories, we can speculate that British readers might be freed momentarily from gender and class restraints through their identification with an Australian heroine. At the same time, the smaller segment of Australian girl readers would have been able to see the triumph of Australian values over antiquated class and gender norms, as the Australian girls within the story act in ways that make visible the limits of the British class system.

Nevertheless, these narratives did not present the return of Australians to Britain as unproblematic. By 1887, Australian arrivals in Britain, including short-term British visitors and migrants returning home, numbered only ten thousand, predominantly from the middle classes. The first mass opportunity for the working classes to travel to Britain did not come until World War I, when 330,000 Australian men served in Europe (Hassam 23). Myers has noted a double standard with regard to emigration in the Victorian period. She argues that, "[w]hile the potential for social mobility, whether through economic success or marriage, often featured prominently in propaganda about Australia, such mobility was valued only if it did not reinfiltrate established British social systems" (81). That is, such advancement was meant to occur in the colonies and not return to problematize or contaminate class norms in the metropolitan centre. An ambivalent welcome to Britain might result from such a problematic return. According to Myers, Australian emigration and return "undermines the British family, and by extension, the nation, by importing the fluidity associated with colonial identity into the supposedly stable British home" (78).

In the school stories set in England, skepticism toward the Australian girl is initially evident, particularly because of her lack of awareness of and respect for class boundaries. The heroine of Ethel Talbot's *That Wild Australian School Girl* is an Australian heiress called Peggy (her given name is actually Margaret) who holds the promise of assisting the English Dalkieth family because they are in financial straits. She initially causes a stir by bringing a girl whom she befriends on the ship journey with her to the Dalkieths' home, and haughtily declares that if her friend Ermyntrude is "not fit to have tea" with the family, then she is not either (13). British girl characters are shown as wary of the poor, especially beggars, gypsies, and sundowners, whereas Australian girls cannot restrain their concern for others, despite British middle-class social customs. These itinerant groups are threatening in part because they are not contained within the domestic sphere, and thus in turn are located "outside of the nation" in British discourse, as Myers suggests (7). That the Australian girl brings with her traits that are transgressive of British domesticity and class norms presents her as more willing to put herself out for others in need, including others who share her location outside the nation.

That Australian girls are located outside of the nation and outside of the home is signified in these texts by wildness and wilderness. Peggy's "wildness" is initially indicated through her affinity with horses. She declares that she would rather travel on a "bush pony" than in a "prim and proper" fashion, and equates the orderliness of the school to which she is sent with being treated as a farm animal or "penned in like a lamb," presenting her freedom as a higher form of being (23). One incident early in the narrative clearly establishes Peggy's dissatisfaction with British order and civility. She decides to visit Ermyntrude in London on horseback, and the reader is told: "There is no bylaw which forbids Londoners to ride horse-back to their destinations. That few of them do it is due, among other reasons, to the fact that very few of them could. To Peggy, a horsewoman from her cradle, the journey seemed a very ordinary and everyday occurrence" (39). Peggy's horse panics and takes off on busy Charing Cross Road and almost runs over a "small brown sticky urchin," age two (30). While her travel preferences and impulsive desire to help others do not accord with the workings of the city, Peggy is nevertheless courageous in her response, heroically scooping up the child and sparing him from injury.

The illustration (see fig. 10.1) comically shows that Peggy's Australian identity, which is closely associated with animals, is incongruous with modern London, rendering her quite distinct from the Australian girl who appears in the Australian fiction that Woollacott studies, and who stands for modernity in contrast with the iconic bushman figure who represents the older pastoral economy (157). In British print culture, the Australian girl is frequently associated with horse riding, in which she is able to outpace men, especially British men. Stories in which Australian girls demonstrated proficiency on horseback were even published in the *Boy's Own Paper*, which, though sometimes read by girls, almost always published fiction about male heroism. In W. H. Timperley's "Bush Luck: An Australian Story" (1890), for example, differences in Australian femininity are explained in the suggestion that women's saddles can be scarce in the country and that girls often have to do the work of a young man. Australian femininity, in other words, strays into masculinity in ways not necessary within England, especially not within middle-class families. A sub-narrative within the story describes an Australian girl who loses an English gentleman in the thick bush on horseback. She then offers to outride him again after exchanging saddles. The new arrival to Australia laughs at the prospect and imagines that the girl will surely fall. After the exchange of saddles, "they had not gone far when the man was unseated, and the young lady galloped after the riderless steed and brought it back to her somewhat crestfallen cavalier" (273). In this serial story, the horse-riding Australian girl takes on a heroic, admirable form for her physical capabilities, as does Peggy in *That Wild Australian School Girl*. In the school story, however, these qualities are accommodated within Britain, rather than appreciated from a distance as a colonial necessity.

The incorporation of what are marked as Australian traits into Britain accommodates and supports the notion of an imperial identity: "colonial" traits are not "civilized" within Britain but necessary to it. In a convoluted plotline, Peggy prevents the school from being foreclosed on by saving the life of the landlord's son. Rather than taming her through the regulation of routinized lessons and surveillance, as is typical in the genre, the school community becomes respectful of Peggy, with her being declared the "Princess of the School" who will carry out the school motto *Noblesse*

Frontispiece

In a stream of taxis and 'buses.

FIGURE 10.1 • Frontispiece from *That Wild Australian School Girl*, by Ethel Talbot, illustrated by G. P. Micklewright. Copyright © 1925.

oblige (279), an honour that sees her accepted in class terms despite her transgressions. Because she escapes punishment and is not subject to any attempts to transform her behaviours, Peggy's transgressions of class norms are given tacit approval.

In Haverfield's *Dauntless Patty* (see fig. 10.2), Australian femininity is similarly associated with a critique of class through the heroine's drive to help others regardless of the polite norms of British society. Colonials returning to Britain were often regarded as being motivated by "pure sentiment" with no knowledge of "home" ("Women's Work" 6). To counter this ignorance of British customs and locations, the Victoria League operated

FIGURE 10.2 • Cover image from *Dauntless Patty*, by E. L. Haverfield, illustrated by Dudley Tennant. Copyright © 1909, reproduced by permission of Oxford University Press.

to provide hospitality to hundreds of colonials returning to England who found themselves in "what is to all intents and purposes a foreign country" (6). Similarly, in both school novels, Australian girls are initially perceived as sufficiently foreign as to not understand British social mores. Recalling the way in which Peggy is initially feared to be "colonial in her ways" in Talbot's novel (13), Patty's English cousin Marjorie, who mixes in good society, is concerned that she will be disgraced by her cousin's "lack of knowledge" (Haverfield, *Dauntless Patty* 11).

The equivalent to Peggy's transgression of city norms on horseback occurs in Haverfield's novel when Patty misses the train to her new English school because she is determined to assist an elderly lady on the platform.[5] Marjorie has already warned Patty of the danger of exercising her natural inclination to help beggars, of leaving doors open when leaving home, and of speaking to people without introduction, but Patty nevertheless is kind to the stranger, a kindness that contributes to her attempting to walk the long distance to school. She enjoys the outdoors after feeling constrained in London, but cannot help but entangle herself in the lives of others after stopping a runaway horse and cart and saving a child (again like Talbot's heroine), and later rescuing a cat caught in a trap. Contrary to Marjorie's admonition never to speak to people without an introduction, Patty is helped by strangers for her good deeds, and she lodges with them for the evening after her eventful journey. These people seem as if they might be Australian to Patty because of their willingness to help, implying a critique of British customs that foster suspicion of others (57). Patty is unable to fit in with the girls at her school, and until the close of the narrative, thinks that she is unattractive and disliked—in part because of the behaviours of the other girls at the school, and in part because, in the most unlikely turn of the narrative, she has been temporarily blinded after bragging about her tennis abilities. After recovering from her brush with blindness, however, Patty resourcefully rescues her adversary Kathleen from drowning, cutting her petticoat with a penknife in an exhibition of the daring attributes of Australian femininity. The novel concludes with Patty's ultimate acceptance into the school, including the major coup of an invitation to join the school's secret society. Both school stories therefore represent transformation in the conventions of the genre through allowing their protagonists to remain "untamed" in comparison to their British counterparts. Moreover, they champion the qualities that distinguish the protagonists from British girls. Both heroines remain in England, rather than returning to Australia, suggesting that, while Australian femininity might be imagined as different in certain ways, it can readily be accommodated within Britain.

British Girls "Down Under"

Violet Methley's *The Bunyip Patrol*, in which a British girl, Rae Raeburn, must adapt to an Australian school setting, also minimizes the difference between Australian and British girls and reinforces the notion of imperial identity. Rae is a fifteen-year-old British girl and a former Girl Guide. Her arrival in Australia does not prompt an initial assessment of her own behaviour or her ability to comply with Australian norms as does the arrival of Australian girls in England in Talbot's and Haverfield's novels. Instead, the narrative tension concerns the British girl's prejudices about Australians, especially as Rae does not expect that the Australian girls would be "quite so English—and . . . ordinary" (16). The novel mocks the stereotypes that form the basis of the "fish out of water" scenarios that are seen in the school stories set in England, in order to emphasize the ease with which a British girl might adapt to life in a white settler colony.

This plot type affords the opportunity for the Australian girl to show off her capacity for independence and bravery within an imagined Australian environment. Australia has typically evoked the imagined threat of deadly native animals; *The Bunyip Patrol* plays on this fear when Rae falls victim to a shark attack. Australian girl Mavis rescues Rae by distracting the shark. Climactically, it seems as if Mavis has lost her foot in the efforts to save Rae, but in an unlikely and convoluted explanation, the Australian girl has actually been concealing that she wears an artificial foot after losing her own during her travels with her uncle in Samoa, where she was pricked in the foot by a poisonous thorn. This fanciful explanation provides further evidence of the extent to which Australian girls are depicted as distinctly adventurous and brave in British girls' fiction in the first quarter of the twentieth century. Moreover, Mavis's perilous travels to Samoa also reinforce the "English—and . . . ordinary" characterization of Australia by displacing its exoticism, from a British perspective, on to Samoa, another colonial site.

Transformation works in reverse in this novel, as Rae learns to become self-sufficient in the harsh Australian environment. After her helpless near-death experience with the shark, Rae concludes the novel by fighting a bushfire for a period on her own, attempting to beat it out with a large tree bough, while sparks and charred wood fall around her. Eventually she assists in forming a chain of girls hauling water in buckets, showing her integration with the heroic Australian girls. Rae's hair is burnt in the process, and another girl declares that the style is no longer a "shingle" but "an Eton crop" (178). This popular 1920s hairstyle not only has masculine connotations in its association with the boys' school, but also connects Rae's heroic qualities with modern femininity. Rather than suggesting that Rae has regressed by adopting colonial attributes, her heroically earned hairstyle echoes the British periodical press's emphasis on Australian women's modernity in response to women's suffrage. Through the ease with which Rae takes on the attributes of the heroic Australian girl, *The Bunyip Patrol* does not enforce an impermeable barrier between British and Australian identity, but rather positions the British girl reader to see herself as a potential emigrant to Australia and a hero to Australia.

Few records exist of how Australian and British girls responded to these fantasies of Australian life, but we can derive a sense of how Australian girls might have taken different meanings from these texts from local reviews. Bessie Marchant, the author of more than a hundred adventure novels, never travelled outside England, and several of her titles set in Australia—for example, *The Black Cockatoo* and *The Ferry House Girls*—were problematically received by Australian reviewers. In the revealingly titled "An Unfamiliar Australia" (1910), the reviewer of *The Black Cockatoo* finds many aspects of Marchant's story implausible, believing it to be a "pity" that "people should write about a place with which they have no acquaintance, though that will have little to do with the interest of the story to the general reader outside Australia" (5). The reviewer highlights the problem that readers outside Australia, likely British, will not recognize inaccuracies that may be jarring to Australians, for whom the descriptions of the land and customs may not ring true. A later review of Marchant's *The Ferry House Girls* suggests that her envisioning of Australia is a mythical, historical one: "Either the period is not in this century, or the author's ideas are still a little vague, for bushrangers ride gaily over the pages" ("A Book List" 570). The reviewer describes the book as a "colonial" rather than an "Australian" story (570) because it does not present the increasingly nationalistic identity that Woollacott argues corresponded with the emergence of the literary figure of the modern Australian girl. British girl readers would likely not recognize the anachronism of Marchant's bushrangers, while Australian girls, especially the majority who lived in its capital cities, might have viewed her fictions as historical adventures that celebrated an idea of femininity largely dissimilar to their own experience.

Marchant regularly differentiates colonial girls from British girls in her fiction, celebrating protagonists who adapt to, or already possess, self-sufficiency and physical strength, rather than offering up British femininity as the norm within the former colonies. For instance, in *Sally Makes Good: A Story of Tasmania* (1920), the sisters of an emigrant family contrast genteel British femininity with more resourceful colonial femininity. Only one of the daughters in the family adapts to Australian life, the heroine, Sally, who is the most useful of the sisters, and with whom the implied British reader is positioned to identify and admire. While the other two daughters throw up their hands in despair at the prospect of having to wash clothing, Sally approaches the task practically, rather than lamenting the move to the Australian country. She responds quickly to danger and threats to the family property, and, to her surprise, she is chosen ahead of her sisters for marriage because of her greater suitability to be a wife to an Australian man (245).

However, unlike *Sally Makes Good*, the two Marchant novels cited in the newspaper reviews above depict Australian-born girls. The heroine of *The Ferry House Girls*, Victoria Holmes, displays a number of the ideas developed in British periodicals about Australian femininity, such as the belief that colonial life sped up feminine development: Victoria is seventeen years old but carries herself as if she is twenty-five. In Marchant's adventure novels, girls frequently demonstrate their full capabilities when their father is called away on urgent business, and they must assume all tasks necessary for tending the property and protecting it from external threats. These tests of imagined Australian girlhood are achieved in *The Ferry House Girls* when Victoria and her sister, having being left under the charge of an old man, are separated from their guardian during a run of misfortune when the river floods and there is a bushranging gang on the loose. The girls go to extreme lengths to protect their father's money, attempting to outride the gang on their horses, with Victoria wielding a gun (though she only ever aims for the men's legs).

This behaviour is not depicted as a transgression, nor is the ability of the heroine to catch horses and kill snakes; rather, such competent femininity is presented as a distinctive element of pride within Australian national identity. If her father could see his daughters in action, Victoria believes that "[h]e would say 'Advance, Australia! And declare that we were worthy daughters of the Southern Cross." In contrast, "only the English misses . . . sit still and wait to be spoken to" (98). Apart from this reference, there is no further explication of how Australian femininity differs from what is acceptable in Britain. This lack of differentiation suggests that these adventure fictions for a largely British girl readership were not preoccupied with demarcating the bounds of the fantasy of comparatively uncontained femininity, but with promoting imperial femininity.

Marchant's *The Black Cockatoo: A Story of Western Australia* (see fig. 10.3) utilizes the Australian girl for another ideological purpose: to mark out the racial limits of imperial femininity. Aimed at a younger readership than the other novels considered in this chapter, *The Black Cockatoo* incorporates a rare portrait of an Indigenous Australian girl in a British girls' novel of the

FIGURE 10.3 • Illustration from *The Black Cockatoo*, by Bessie Marchant, illustrated by Lancelot Speed. Copyright © 1910, reproduced by permission of the Lutterworth Press.

period. The protagonists are the Payntter children, Tom, age nine, and Ellie, age eleven. When the pair go missing in the bush, they are entirely unable to survive and will no doubt die in the elements, but after they pray for help, Yarra, an Aboriginal girl, comes upon them. Though the other Australian girls I have discussed in this chapter sometimes display masculine traits and are willing to get their hands temporarily dirty when a situation requires it, their dress is ordinarily described and depicted in illustrations as traditionally feminine. In contrast, Yarra's appearance is recounted in abject terms. She is clad in a man's ragged shirt and is dirty, clearly suggesting that she is not entirely feminine and that indigeneity is not encompassed within the idealization of Australian femininity identified in other texts. While Yarra gives the children three roasted frogs and finds water for them, saving their lives in the process, as the children have no knowledge of the land and how to survive on it, unlike the other heroic girls mentioned in this chapter, Yarra is not celebrated as a heroine, and there is absolutely no recognition of her rescue as a demonstration of Indigenous knowledge or of her capability as a young girl able to live from the land. Instead, it is the Payntter children "who taught Yarra to give thanks also for an escape as great as theirs, and the black girl was quick to respond to the teaching she received" (282). The bringing of Christianity to Yarra is simultaneously a triumph of religious norms that is to be expected in a title published by the Religious Tract Society, and an erasure of Indigenous knowledge which marks out a limit to the admiration of Australian femininity evident in British girls' fiction.

Leaving and Returning "Home"

Several of these fictions present Australian characters as dually identifying with Australia and Britain. Talbot's Peggy describes herself as "a bit of each" (110), meaning both Australian and English, while an Australian teacher in *The Bunyip Patrol* remarks that "we still call England 'home,' even though we've never been there, and perhaps never shall" (78). In Haverfield's *Queensland Cousins*, however, the Orban children feel no attachment to Australia and describe England as their "real 'home'" (191) and "our country" (98) because of the sense of belonging engendered by their mother's stories of her life there. The Australian girl is mobilized in this novel to support the idea of imperial identity through the successful return and reincorporation of an Australian family in Britain.

The novel's implied reader is British, as becomes clear through the narrator's repeated use of "our" to connote English beliefs and notions of superiority, such as, for example, a remark concerning the Australian children that notes "the common things of our everyday existence were marvels to them" (16). The eldest girl of the family, Nesta, is enamoured with the idea of England, remarking that "English stories always make me ache to go there" (17), which, predictably, is exactly the effect conveyed by the novel, with persistent emphasis on the hardships and dangers of Australia contrasted with the desirable qualities of England. Mrs. Orban finds life on the north Queensland sugar plantation distressing, but must remain because work for her husband is not as readily found in England. Nesta's brother Eustace, on whom most of the Australian section of the narrative rests, is assigned the protective role over their mother in their father's absence on business travel. His protection is required because of the threats of wild Indigenous neighbours and a thief who has been stealing from the property, who turns out to be the stablehand, Manuel. Manuel's acts, which throw the family into a panic in the absence of Mr. Orban, also highlight the Orbans' experience of the unsettling presence of Chinese and Malay field hands with no "white neighbours" in close proximity to them (22). Twenty-three-year-old Aunt Dorothy from England visits her relatives in the midst of this fear of invaders, and she effortlessly lames the stableboy intruder with a shotgun. Despite her quickness to protect herself and the Orban family, however, Dorothy is nevertheless frightened of large Australian spiders and remarks, "A poor, ignorant Englishwoman isn't expected to be brave when she sees a spider as big as a penny bun, with furry legs in proportion, trying to sit on her knee" (154).

In addition to positioning implied British readers to understand the Australian landscape and fauna as unnatural, the narrative also encourages the reader to share the perspective of the Orbans' English relatives, such as their class-inflected judgment of how the Orbans appear in photographs as "pasty-faced, spiritless beings. The prints that the girls were dressed in were rather washed out; Peter had outgrown his suit. They were ill-clad, shy and awkward" (95). Haverfield's *Queensland Cousins* works against the myth-ology present in British and Australian print culture of Australian life as provoking health and vigour, such as in the pro-emigration propaganda in the *Girl's Own Paper* where these benefits are emphasized for working-class girls. The negative perception of Australian life in *Queensland Cousins* rests largely on the middle-class English family viewing their relatives as hav-ing fallen below their station because of the threats to domesticity and to firm class boundaries encouraged by colonial labour. Unlike the first two novels I considered, which use the Australian girl to critique class norms,

Queensland Cousins upholds the values of class and positions the Australian girl as desirous of acceptance into that system.

Hassam suggests that when colonial Australians visited Britain, the "desire for recognition and incorporation" prevailed (4). The remainder of the narrative of *Queensland Cousins* shows the Orban children's struggle to be welcomed "home" to England by their cousins, Herbert and Brenda Dixon, who are horrified by Australian customs and act as gatekeepers of the incorporation that was eagerly desired by colonial returnees. The Orbans' failure to adhere to class or age distinctions through work on their sugar plantation is of particular offence to Brenda: "The thought of her uncle going daily to his work in shirt-sleeves; of her aunt helping in housework; her cousins brought up just anyhow, without a governess or any schooling, shocked her sensibilities" (189). The real debate that occurs between the cousins relates to the domestic space of Maze Court, the Dixons' home. The British cousins suggest that the Australian children eat with their servants, drawing attention to their lack of knowledge about the class divisions within the middle-class English home, and snobbishly remind the Orban children that people dress for dinner in England, unlike "savages" (189). These slights and the resulting arguments provoke the children to engage in a battle of domestic knowledge on a tour of the house.

Where Eustace was pre-eminent as the protector of the Australian homestead in the narrative segment set in Australia, in the segment set in England, his sister Nesta comes to the fore in the domestic realm. As Herbert shows the Orban children around the family home and introduces each room, Nesta repeatedly interrupts, demonstrating her knowledge of this English family domicile and taking up the challenge to demonstrate Australian civility and domestic knowledge. Nesta wins out over her British cousin Brenda when she demonstrates her fuller knowledge of family history in correctly identifying the portrait of an ancestor. Nesta is annoyed by her brother's failure to join the task of showing the refinement of the Australians. The difference between the brother and sister is symptomatic of the novel's division of Australian masculinity and femininity along traditional lines, divisions that are not replicated in other British girls' fictions that celebrate adventurous and heroic Australian girls.

The initial conflict between the cousins and the reluctance shown by the Australians to remain in England is largely due to the mistaken belief that their aunt Dorothy had drowned on the ship journey back to England.

When she miraculously returns, the unease dissolves: "The change was something like a fairy tale to the Bush children; every one seemed suddenly 'magiked' into different beings. This, then, was home as mother had known it" (235). The transformation to contented British children is achieved instantaneously, with any sense that the children might wish to return to Queensland neatly quashed and Australian identity instantly erased. *Queensland Cousins* uniquely shows a young British woman as more capable of self-defence within Australia than her aunt or cousins who have been raised in the bush, thereby rewriting popular conceptions that saw Australian femininity as distinct from, and in several aspects superior to, British femininity. Furthermore, the novel suggests that ties to Australian identity are easily broken, particularly in light of the obvious superiority of British life, again reinforcing the primacy of imperial, rather than national, identity.

British girls' fiction in the early twentieth century uses the figure of the Australian girl in distinctly different ways to Australian literature in the late nineteenth and early twentieth centuries. While the figure in Australian literature is seen as a modern, nationalistic answer to colonial stereotypes, in British girls' fiction the Australian girl is frequently used to perpetuate ideas of colonial femininity to enact a range of cultural functions. The Australian girl is marked as different, especially in class terms, but can always be subsumed into British femininity. The fact that this difference can be so easily accommodated within Britain, or that transformation for a British girl in Australia can be so simply performed, erases the significance of national differences in such a way as to promote the idea of an overarching imperial identity, even in the face of the independence of many former British colonies. For Australian girl readers, this trope may have fulfilled their fantasies of incorporation and acceptance in Britain. For British girl readers, we can read this erasure of difference as part of a continued call for female emigration to British dominions and an assertion of the continued relationship between Britain and its former colonies. All of these fictions had very little grounding in the actual lives of Australian girls, but instead were built on the mythology formulated in print culture of the late nineteenth and early twentieth centuries that imagined the unique qualities of Australians. Ultimately, these positive traits were seen as issuing from British settlement. As a result, the Australian girl in British fiction of this period provides reassurance to both British and Australian girls as to the continued coherence of the British Empire.

Acknowledgements

I would like to thank Professor Mavis Reimer and Professor Clare Bradford for their invaluable and detailed comments on several drafts of this chapter.

Notes

1 Niall argues that this "view from Britain" provided to colonial Australian child readers helped to shape Australian self-perception (20).

2 The Girls' Friendly Society (GFS) was a Christian organization that assisted girls emigrating to Britain's colonies and dominions, as well as the United States, to take up domestic work. The GFS had an Australian branch, with two lodges established by 1909, and its organ *Friendly Leaves* regularly included emigration news for girls seeking assisted passage to New South Wales, Western Australia, Victoria, and Queensland. Nevertheless, from the late nineteenth century on, *Friendly Leaves* rarely discussed Australian life, as far more of the GFS's travelling parties, and all its large parties, were organized for other locations. Indeed, in 1908 *Friendly Leaves* referred to emigration to Canada and the United States as "the great exodus" ("Emigration News" 91). This trend is also reflected in its occasional articles about "what women do in Canada" (Mercier) and fiction about a girl living in the Rocky Mountains (West), as well as letters and reports from GFS members in Canada ("Letter from a G.F.S. Member"; "Christmas in British Columbia").

3 Tanya Dalziell's *Settler Romances and the Australian Girl* examines the figure of the Australian girl in Australian newspapers and journals of the late nineteenth and early twentieth century. See also Sharyn Pearce, "The Best Career Is Matrimony."

4 Beverley Kingston suggests that the consequence of the British standard of femininity "was a widespread sharing and reinforcement of the notion that Australian women were second-best, not quite up to the real 'ladies' of London, inevitably colonial in their views. Their outlook, their experience" (27).

5 Haverfield's *The Girl from the Bush* (1920) similarly shows an Australian girl placing the needs of others first. The heroine, Hilary Walford, is an orphan who finds herself alone in England, but she is temporarily taken in at a small boarding school. Hilary is unwaveringly loyal to a sick girl whom she meets outside the grounds of the school, and repeatedly sneaks out at night to comfort her, despite the problems that this transgression of school rules causes for her.

Works Cited

"Australian Women and Naturalization." *Times* 17 June 1911: 16. Print.

"A Book List for Young People." *Register* [Adelaide] 15 Dec. 1923: 570. Print.

Brazil, Angela. *The Fortunes of Philippa*. London: Blackie and Son, 1906. Print.

"Christmas in British Columbia." *Friendly Leaves* Jan. 1909: 47. Print.

Dalziell, Tanya. *Settler Romances and the Australian Girl*. Crawley: U of Western Australia P, 2004. Print.

Denoon, Donald. *Settler Capitalism: The Dynamics of Dependent Development in the Southern Hemisphere*. New York: Oxford UP, 1983. Print.

"Dominion Faces. Theory of Distinct Types." *Times* 6 May 1919: 9. Print.

"Emigration News." *Friendly Leaves* Feb. 1908: 91. Print.

Flint, Kate. *The Woman Reader, 1837–1914*. Oxford: Oxford UP, 1995. Print.

Fowler, Alastair. *Kinds of Literature: An Introduction to the Theory of Genres and Modes*. Oxford: Clarendon P, 1982. Print.

Gaunt, Mary. "Married Immigrants in Australia." Letter. *Times* 29 March 1910: 6. Print.

Hassam, Andrew. *Through Australian Eyes: Colonial Perceptions of Imperial Britain*. Carlton South: Melbourne UP, 2000. Print.

Haverfield, E. L. *Dauntless Patty*. London: Humphrey Milford, 1909. Print.

———. *The Girl from the Bush*. London: Collins' Clear-Type Press, 1920. Print.

———. *Queensland Cousins*. London: Thomas Nelson and Sons, 1908. Print.

Kingston, Beverley. "The Lady and the Australian Girl: Some Thoughts on Nationalism and Class." *Australian Women: New Feminist Perspectives*. Ed. Norma Grieve and Ailsa Burns. Melbourne: Oxford UP, 1986. 27–41. Print.

"The Land of the Wattle." *All the World* 1 May 1892: 892. Print.

"Letter from a G.F.S. Member." *Friendly Leaves* Aug. 1908: 275–76. Print.

Marchant, Bessie. *The Black Cockatoo: A Story of Western Australia*. London: Religious Tract Society, 1910. Print.

———. *The Ferry House Girls: An Australian Story*. London: Blackie and Sons, 1912. Print.

———. *Sally Makes Good: A Story of Tasmania*. London: Blackie and Sons, 1920. Print.

Mercier, Anna. "What Women Do in Canada." *Friendly Leaves* Aug. 1906: 272–74. Print.

Methley, Violet M. *The Bunyip Patrol: The Story of an Australian Girls' School*. London: Pilgrim Press, 1926. Print.

Mitchell, Sally. "Girls' Culture: At Work." *The Girl's Own: Cultural Histories of the Anglo-American Girl, 1830–1915*. Ed. Claudia Nelson and Lynne Vallone. Athens: U of Georgia P, 1994. 243–58. Print.

———. *The New Girl: Girls' Culture in England, 1880–1915*. New York: Columbia UP, 1995. Print.

"Mr Sala on the Australians." *John Bull* 3.381 (1885): 581. Print.

Myers, Janet C. *Antipodal England: Emigration and Portable Domesticity in the Victorian Imagination*. Albany: State U of New York P, 2009. Print.

Niall, Brenda. *Australia through the Looking-Glass: Children's Fiction 1830–1980*. Carlton: Melbourne UP, 1984. Print.

Pearce, Sharyn. "'The Best Career Is Matrimony': First-Wave Journalism and the 'Australian Girl.'" *Hectate* 18.2 (1992): 64–78. Web.

Ross, Adelaide. "Life in the Colonies." *Girl's Own Paper* 12 (1891): 487. Print.

Shaw, Flora L. "Miss Shaw on the Australian Outlook." *Times* 10 Jan. 1894: 11. Print.

Talbot, Ethel. *That Wild Australian School Girl*. London: Robert South, 1925. Print.

Tenniel, John. "Advanced Australia!" *Punch, or the London Charivari* 25 April 1900: 299. Print.

Timperley, W. H. "Bush Luck: An Australian Story." *The Boy's Own Paper* 577 (1890): 273–75. Print.

"An Unfamiliar Australia." *West Australian* 24 Oct. 1910: 5. Print.

West, Noel. "Susie's Mistake." *Friendly Leaves* Jan. 1898: 42–46. Print.

"Woman Suffrage in Australia. Speech by Mr. Fisher." *Times* 3 June 1911: 7. Print.

"Women as Empire Settlers: Conditions of Life Overseas." *Times* 27 Feb. 1924: 9. Print.

"Women's Work for the Empire." *Times* 2 July 1910: 6. Print.

Woollacott, Angela. *To Try Her Fortune in London: Australian Women, Colonialism and Modernity*. Oxford: Oxford UP, 2001. Print.

———. "White Colonialism and Sexual Modernity: Australian Women in the Early Twentieth Century Metropolis." *Gender, Sexuality and Colonial Modernities*. Ed. Antoinette Burton. London: Routledge, 1999. 49–62. Print.

CHAPTER 11

Dynamic (Con)Texts

Close Readings of Girls' Video Gameplay

Stephanie Fisher, Jennifer Jenson, and Suzanne de Castell

Video games are important cultural texts that have become increasingly central to youth and entertainment culture over the last two decades. Driven primarily by the interests and pocketbooks of the male consumer, the video game industry has become one of the largest entertainment industries worldwide (Siwek). Within the last decade, and particularly over the last few years, the games industry and its consumers have moved well beyond the boundaries of console- and computer-based play, extending to other platforms like mobile devices, as well as to other media such as film (*Tomb Raider*, *Resident Evil*, *Prince of Persia*, *Tron: Legacy*), music (symphonies), social media games (especially social networking games), and merchandising (Pokémon, Angry Birds, and Club Penguin plush toys). Throughout these expansions, mainstream games culture specifically and computing culture more generally continue to be realms dominated by men and boys. Marketing tactics remain clearly demarcated along gender lines, as there is continued hypersexualization and a relative absence of playable, main female characters in video games, and a parallel paucity of women working in the games industry in the real world (Fron et al.; Jenson and de Castell, "Girls@Play").

The ongoing expansion of gaming to different forms, platforms, and devices—in particular, to mobile devices like smartphones and tablets and to social networking sites like Facebook—could provide additional entry points into gaming culture. This could, in turn, open up that culture to groups previously marginalized and disenfranchised, to the extent that previous notions of what it means to play games and to be a gamer nowadays might be changing, making this an appropriate time to examine, and to help to create, a more level playing field. Notwithstanding this positive outlook on the possibilities and potentials for girls and gaming, it continues to be a struggle to examine and talk about girls' participation in gaming culture as equal members, not as "girl gamers," or as a group that is somehow different from, and disadvantaged relative to, their male counterparts. That this divide is still very much in place is evidenced in current news stories on the creation of "games for girls" (see, for example, Silicon Sisters' game *School 26*), and in the ongoing policing and outright hostility that women who play games continue to face (see the blog *Fat, Ugly or Slutty*).

In this chapter we report on one year of a multi-year project on gender and gameplay, detailing the progression of girls from "outsider" video game players to "insider" status as the girls became more expert in playing, and as they appropriated and developed fluency in gamer discourse. Drawing upon Jean Lave and Etienne Wenger's work on communities of practice, we describe the processes by which this group of girls moved from peripheral participation in the community (not to be confused with legitimate peripheral participation, a significant distinction), to fostering their own community of praxis that legitimated and supported their play. Lave and Wenger describe how a peripheral member of a community is introduced by degrees to a larger community of practice through a set of what they call legitimate (and legitimizing) roles. Their accounts focus primarily on documenting how a nonexpert gradually becomes more expert through "legitimate peripheral participation" in a given community.

In the case we describe here, the participation is indeed peripheral, but, as we will show, given the larger game community, far from "legitimate" (37). We begin by providing an overview of the status and experiences of girls and women in game culture generally, explaining how they are othered, how their participation and expertise are consistently rendered illegitimate, and how sex-based stereotypes are re-invoked in the service of policing a masculine culture of gameplay. Next, we describe our three-year study of girls and digital gameplay, "Smarter Than She Looks," where we intentionally created gameplay spaces that could challenge persistent cultural notions about what and how girls prefer to play. We then move to a reading of the texts that girls produce while they play, demonstrating how girls' gaming preferences can and *do* change with experience and over time. By examining character selection and other play patterns, we track the ways in which participants' own conceptions of their gaming identity are fluid and subject to change with changing contexts and conditions. We conclude by discussing the importance of undertaking feminist intervention projects that seek to *transform*, not just rediscover or reproduce, well-established stereotypes regarding girls and gameplay.

Girls and Gaming Outsiders

Although we are now nearly twenty years beyond the original "girl games" movement, during which mavericks like Brenda Laurel, who worked in her early career with Seymour Papert on Logo programming in schools and defined the landscape for girls' digital gameplay, very little has changed in terms of how the video games industry perceives girls as consumers and players of games. In the 1990s, Laurel's answer to the question of "what girls want" in video games was to create games with non-violent settings (for example, schools) that featured social interaction as the main gameplay mechanics. In 2011, Brenda Bailey Gershkovitch's answer to the very same question is eerily similar: she created an iOS game for girls, *School 26*, where players solve interpersonal problems by answering quizzes and playing card games. While these carefully targeted games are more thoughtful than the crass rebranding of gaming products into pink packages to sell to girls, such as the pink "girls' versions" of the Nintendo DS and the PlayStation Portable, the thought behind them is no less problematic: their girl-friendly designs are based on a binary gendered framework that supports and upholds two constructions—"gamers" (boys/men) and "girl gamers"—that promote stereotypical characteristics and practices of gendered play. These stereotypes have been and continue to be echoed in research on gender and gameplay, which positions girls/women as preferring to play non-violent, prosocial cooperative games (Graner Ray).

From the outset, female gamers have occupied a subordinate position within gaming culture, due in part to socio-cultural assumptions of what activities and interests are suitable for and appeal to girls and women, and in part to the economic resources differentially available to male and female players across the age range from children to adults, making male players a more profitable target demographic. A masculinist "hardcore gamer" sub-culture has become the yardstick for assessing the legitimacy of a player's claim to gaming culture membership. The term "hardcore gamer" refers not only to a person who plays games frequently, enthusiastically, and intensively for long periods of time, but also to a particular type of person, typically male, who plays particular types of games: typically first-person shooter or other battle-based games. Writing about how technological, commercial, and cultural power structures have dominated the develop-ment of the digital game industry over the past thirty-five years, Janine Fron, Tracy Fullerton, Jacquelyne Ford Morie, and Celia Pearce describe the hardcore gamer as "characterized by an adolescent male sensibility that transcends physical age and embraces highly stylized graphical violence, male fantasies of power and domination, hyper-sexualized, objectified depictions of women, and rampant racial stereotyping and discrimination" (7). Because this group is considered the de facto target demographic for the games industry, it largely informs the development and marketing of commercial games and heavily influences cultural perceptions of gamers, in effect excluding players who do not fit the hardcore gamer demographic from making legitimate claims to membership in this culture (Fron et al.; Jenson and de Castell, "Girls@Play").

So, despite recent initiatives to open up game culture to those on the outside, the majority of bestselling games are still primarily developed for and directly marketed to those on the inside, or, in other words, to boys and men. Not surprisingly, it is largely men who respond positively to these marketing tactics and schemes, demonstrating their enthusiasm and dedi-cation to their hobby by lining up outside stores for hours to be the first to own and play highly anticipated games. Photographs of gamers out-side stores on the release dates for *Call of Duty: Black Ops* (2010) or *Halo: Reach* (2010), both incredibly successful first-person shooter franchises, show queues of men wrapped around the store, ecstatic as they approach the checkout counter with their limited or collector's edition bundles, and socializing while playing with replica weapons or other special artifacts brought in for the launch event. In these public spaces and in market-ing campaigns, female participation is rendered invisible by comparison. Although a retail store is not a public gaming site per se, these observations align with studies that show that female participation within mainstream gaming culture in public game events is largely invisible and, when it is visible, it is often in hyper-stereotypic or marginalized ways (Beavis and Charles; Taylor, Jenson, and de Castell).

Writing about the marginalization of females in competitive gaming spaces, Nicholas Taylor, Jennifer Jenson, and Suzanne de Castell point out how female participation is primarily read in sexualized terms in these male-dominated spaces: "female players risk being labelled as '*Halo* hoes,' mothers at events describe themselves as 'cheerleaders,' and promotional models become 'booth babes'—all supportive, subordinate roles" (243). This is also seen in our own research with after-school video game clubs where preteen girls primarily described their gameplay at home as supportive to their brothers' play: reading manuals, pointing out incoming enemies or valuable items, or informing their brothers when they were running low on health or other crucial resources (Jenson and de Castell, "Girls@Play").

The practice of casting women as non-gamers is reinforced in advertising, where women are rarely shown as consumers of big-budget, hardcore games (Chess). The TV commercial for the bestselling 2010 PlayStation game *God of War III*, for example, features a woman in her late twenties complaining to a male PlayStation executive about her boyfriend's neglectful behaviour toward her since he started playing the game. The complaint, however, falls on deaf ears when she is further ignored by the executive, who is also too captivated with playing *God of War III* to pay attention to her, validating her boyfriend's actions through this mimicry. While the commercial is humorous to anyone who has experienced immersive gameplay, it communicates and naturalizes a female inability to understand the appeal of playing video games, and specifically the high-budget AAA titles that are enjoyed by the hardcore crowd.

This is not to say that women and girls do not play these games or play them well, as some most certainly do. Public gameplay by women creates opportunities to challenge the binary gendered framework of mainstream gaming culture. Here, female players may take advantage of their othered identities to reformulate or disrupt notions about girls' lack of interest or skill in playing video games (Beavis and Charles). While the presence and active participation of skilled female players may be instrumental in creating an illusion of balance, there are limited opportunities for showcasing female gaming talent under conditions that do not already mark them as subordinate.

A well-known example of "levelling the playing field" is a group of female *Halo* players who refer to themselves as the Frag Dolls, and who are consistently referred to as the exception to the general rule that women cannot skilfully play hardcore games. The Frag Dolls are a good example of a disruption of the normalized gender order of game culture that is (re)bounded by hyper-femininity and fits all too neatly into hetero-normative masculine desires. The fact that the Frag Dolls, and other groups like them, promote their gaming competency as an anomaly—contrasting or disassociating their gameplay or motivations to play from notions about stereotypical girl gamers, who are characterized as relatively unskilled in comparison—actually *reinforces* normative gamer categories. By invoking the girl gamer stereotype in contrast to their gameplay, these skilled female players reinforce and re-inscribe the binary framework of gender even as they seek to disrupt it.

Female players who *challenge* the binary gender order also receive attention and are often targets for misogynist remarks or sexualized discourse, especially when engaging in online play or posting on discussion boards. One public example of this is the blog *Fat, Ugly or Slutty*, which was started in early 2011 in an effort to publicly "shame the Johns." On this blog, female gamers post screenshots of the sexual, misogynist hate speech that is directed to women who play in online spaces, in this case, mostly Xbox Live, but also massively multiplayer online games (MMOGs) like *World of Warcraft*. Male players in these games sometimes react to female transgressors in ways and with words that are generally unacceptable in real-life scenarios, for example, "make me a sandwich, ho," "get back in the kitchen," or explicitly sexual remarks, such as "are you a naughty girl?" or "wanna suck me?" General hate speech abounds: "stupid whore stop playing Xbox fat bitch" and "kill urself cunt" are only two of the egregious examples available. Our point here is not to re-invoke the kind of violence that is inherent in these speech acts, but to take a closer look at what amounts to hate speech against women, using a medium that is very difficult to trace, given that user accounts permit players to choose pseudonyms or handles that allow them to play relatively anonymously.

A similar kind of documentary practice exists on YouTube, in the many videos uploaded by both male and female gamers. Here, males overwhelmingly insist that females do not have the natural abilities to keep up with the boys in gameplay, and women and girls speak out against the inequitable treatment they receive when their sex becomes known in-game. In their videos, female gamers talk about how males gang up on them during gameplay, simply because they are identified as female and are often outnumbered. Many of these women and girls say they just leave the channel or game out of frustration, as they feel that there is no point in defending themselves against these abusive tactics that seek to undermine female participation. In other words, even when women are full and not just

peripheral participants in gamer culture and its practices, they are invariably denied legitimacy. We can attribute the construction of the long-held
cultural assumption of naturalized female inferiority with regard to gaming
skill to a male-dominated history of technological production and consumption practices (de Castell and Bryson); this same rhetoric continues
to be invoked to explain the relative absence and apparent low skill level
of females in games and in computing culture in comparison to their male
counterparts. Meanwhile, the games industry, viewing the hardcore gamer
as their target demographic, responds to, reinforces, and capitalizes on the
notion of sex-based difference through their construction of an alternative
identity and genre exclusive for female consumers: the girl gamer.

"Girl Gamers": Marginalized and Pinkified

As already noted, in their efforts to expand the market to new types of
players, game developers continue to design games specifically targeted at
female game players and, in the process, construct the public image of the
girl gamer. Ironically, rather than opening up video game culture to female
players, these actions tend to validate female participation in a way that
is limiting and subordinate to the gamer stereotype—in other words, the
male gamer—thus ghettoizing and delegitimizing female participation in
that culture.

Of the more recent video games that are directly marketed to girls,
most show a girl as the main player, use different shades of pink (the signifier of any and all things feminine), and promote stereotypically feminine activities. Ubisoft's *Imagine* series[1] for girls ages six to fourteen, for
example, offers over thirty occupational role-playing games to choose
from, including fashion designer, babysitter, movie star, figure skater,
teacher, master chef, wedding designer, party planner, makeup artist,
salon stylist, ballet star, boutique owner, cheerleader, gymnast, and even
sweet-sixteen birthday girl. At the time of publication, the only available roles that are relatively gender neutral are soccer captain, reporter,
detective, family doctor, and zookeeper. Gender-normative activities are
also promoted in Ubisoft's *Ener-G* series of sports video games for girls.
Professional sports video games have been, and continue to be, a staple
gaming genre, with franchises like *Madden NFL* or *FIFA Soccer* releas-
ing new titles on an annual basis since the late 1980s or early 1990s, and
selling over 85 million and 100 million units respectively as of summer
2010 ("EA SPORTS"; Molina). Like gaming, the world of professional

sports is an overwhelmingly masculine domain that marginalizes female participation (Taylor et al.). In seeking to create sports games meant to be played primarily by girls, Ubisoft had a golden opportunity to shake up the culturally assumed gender-normative roles in both domains; however, instead of challenging the status quo by creating female-oriented equivalents of bestselling sports franchises like *Madden* or *FIFA*, with *Ener-G*, the company opted to present activities that were, again, stereotypically female, such as horseback riding, gymnastics, and dancing.

Ubisoft recognizes that its products and packaging contribute to stereotypical constructions of girl gamers, but insists that the decision to develop these games is based on consumer demand, that is, on market surveys of "what girls want" ("Ubisoft"). Others within the industry use bolder tactics to market to female players. In February 2011, for example, Evil Controllers, a company that manufactures customized controllers for PlayStation 3 and Xbox 360 consoles, announced that February was "girl gamer month": "Let it be a month to celebrate a gaming population that frequently goes unrecognized and under-appreciated! This month will be all about women's empowerment—and, with a few new developments from within the Evil Labs, Evil Controllers hope to do just that—to find a way to empower any girl's game" ("Evil Controllers"). This empowerment came, predictably enough, in the form of specially designed pink camouflage controllers—in other words, regular controllers in modified pink casings. On gaming blogs and forums, consumer reactions to Evil Controllers' promotion and proclamation were mixed, with some female gamers expressing enthusiasm for the girl gamer bundle and others questioning exactly how using a pink controller is empowering. These more critical posters argued that, because they had smaller hands, a more appropriate way to assist women and girls in improving their gaming skills would be to modify the size, not the colour, of a standard controller.

In these ways the game industry, in effect, patronizes female gamers, prescribing for them what they should play and what appeals to them instead of seriously considering how females might participate in mainstream gaming culture *beyond* these designations. Of the growing body of research that has documented girls and women playing, and sometimes making, games, much of it continues to reproduce stereotypical gendered accounts of what women and girls want, prefer, and like when it comes to video games (Jenson, Fisher, and de Castell). Consistent in such work is a predominant, indeed, almost intuitive, reflex to crudely demarcate difference along male/female sex binaries. This reflex presents itself no less persistently in research that sees itself as assiduously attempting *not* to re-invoke gender- and sex-based stereotypes (Walkerdine; Williams et al., "Looking for Gender"; Winn and Heeter). For example, in their study of leisure time and time spent playing digital games, Jillian Winn and Carrie Heeter frame female under-participation in gaming as a lack of interest that is sex based. They argue that women are drawn to and will continue to play casual games[2] over hardcore games that require a commitment and investment of time, even when these women have the available leisure time to play them. They conclude that, to close the gender gap in gaming, game designers should target women by developing more games that can be played in less than half an hour. By presenting their findings as sex-based preferences for gameplay (in that women always prefer to play casual games), this study contributes to the body of literature that explains and compresses gendered behaviours into sex-based difference that is necessarily coded as male or female. Winn and Heeter thus fail to take seriously the fact that women (and girls) enjoy far less control over their own time than do men and boys, it being presumed that women and girls are always on call and infinitely interruptible to attend to domestic duties as and when required by partners and families (Smith).

"Smarter Than She Looks": An Interventionist Study of Girls and Gaming

The biggest pitfall of gender and gameplay studies to date[3] has been the reporting of results in such a way that gender performances, which are always already contextually situated, are reduced to a reinforcement of gendered stereotypes. It is no great intellectual feat simply to describe stereotypical patterns and choices, and then explain them by reference to stereotypes. If we are interested in research that supports changing female marginalization in game culture, we need to pay closer attention to methodology. Now more than ever it is important to consider different approaches to performing gender and gaming research, and to be surprised by findings (Jenson and de Castell, "Theorizing Gender"). Perhaps the most obvious way to do this is to stop looking for or using gender difference as a rationale or a starting point for research.

In our own study, "Smarter Than She Looks" (STSL), we used feminist theory—notably, notions that gender is socially and culturally constructed (Butler; Foucault; Haraway; Smith)—to inform our methods and as one way to attempt to resist the hegemonic gender double-bind that guides previous work in the field. In particular, we mobilize Butler's analysis of gender performativity, which distinguishes between what *appears* to be an essential or inner truth about gender from performances of gender conventions that, through their repeated embodiment in actions and self-representations, *make* those conventions appear both necessary and natural. What we sought to do in STSL was to conduct an empirically grounded investigation of digital gameplay that not only takes into account differing levels of gameplay (from novice to expert), but also examines it as a performance, one that is just as important as the performance of knowledge and/or skill.

To do this type of work requires a level playing field between male and female players. As the previous section highlights, however, a physical or virtual space where male and female players are equally enfranchised members of gaming culture would be a rare find or, arguably, non-existent. Because equality for females in games culture does not exist, it has to be invented (Jenson and de Castell, "Theorizing Gender"). This charges the researcher to go beyond simply observing and reporting on girls' gameplay in the typical context of gameplay, where males have the advantage, and intervene to disrupt the "business as usual" practices and power relations that maintain inequality between sexes. In STSL, our intervention strategy was to construct a space that privileged, encouraged, and supported female players' development of gaming skills and competencies—essentially an inverse scenario to the typical contexts of gameplay. Interventions such as these, we argue, are among the ways out of the methodological and conceptual stranglehold that continues to define girls and gaming research, since such interventions provide opportunities for new observations and findings to be constructed.

To disrupt the notion that there is an innate female style or preference for playing video games, we ran one such interventionist video game club in a Toronto elementary school, one of several similar disruptive projects within the larger STSL study. This gaming club took place in the school library during lunch and after class over the 2008–2010 academic years. The library is a large open space, providing an ideal setting to host multiple screens and consoles for gameplay. Because the club took place in a school, all the games that were played were rated "E" for everyone, with the exception of some of the music titles that were often rated "T" for players over the age of thirteen because of the song lyrics.

In the first year of the video game club, both boys and girls were allowed to join, and they played together in the same space, giving us a rich baseline of normative mixed gender relations in play at this site. There is little doubt that the boys dominated the gaming club in this first year: they monopolized the newest and latest games (whereas the girls played with the leftovers), extended their turns by restarting levels, pronounced their achievements frequently and loudly, and sometimes outright refused to give up their controller until forced to by an adult. The boys outnumbered the girls fourteen to four and thus had critical mass, but we argue that these behaviours are also a result of the context of play. For example, it is of no small significance that two male gamers and a female non-gamer ran the club. The boys would leverage this disparity to assert their perceived natural right to govern the space, which they demonstrated through these performances. When the girls did get a chance to play the games that the boys had been hogging, we observed very little difference between girls and boys in terms of their actual play. This is consistent with our findings from similar research projects (Jenson and de Castell, "Fair Play"; Jenson and de Castell, "Theorizing Gender"), which found that players of the same skill level, regardless of sex (that is, female expert and male expert), play in more similar ways than players who are of the same sex but at differing skill levels (for example, male novice and male expert).

In year two, again, far more boys than girls wanted to join the club (over forty boys, only fifteen girls). To accommodate the overwhelming demand from the boys and maintain our primary commitment to providing a supportive game space for the girls, the first four months of the club were exclusive to the fifteen girls and the club was run by two female research assistants. During this time the girls divided into two distinct groups: a dominant group of girls whose behaviours were very similar to the boys' in year one (in that they felt entitled to control and take up space) and a more passive group of girls who had limited agency or power in this space (for example, they had to enlist the help of the research assistants if they wanted to ensure they got a turn playing the more popular games). After four months of the all-girls club, we split the club to form two new clubs. One remained an all-girls space populated by the more passive girls, and the other became a mixed club for boys on the waiting list and the more dominant girls. Interestingly, what we observed in the mixed club was an inverse scenario to year one. The newly empowered girls saw the creation of a mixed club as an invasion of what they viewed as *their* space by boys and took measures to protect it from these outsiders. Ironically, they did this through the same kinds of performances and behaviours exhibited by the boys in year one, which resulted in the boys' participation resembling the experience of the passive year-one girls. As we expected, these girls, initially passive, developed a range of gaming skills rather quickly once they were able to play freely, without impositions or restrictions.

This study demonstrates how the context one creates in research, from the research assistants to the participants, shapes the kinds of results reported. For example, the boys' dominance in year one was not the result of a natural male inclination to dominate and take control of video game-play, any more than it was for girls in year two. Instead, the choices we made about who participated in the project, who was present on a daily basis to oversee the research and interact with participants, and how those participants were recruited *differently* in years one and two influenced the behaviour we observed. This demonstrates how research design constructs results. We might have a very different research story to tell if we had not changed the operation of the clubs and counted on reproducing our findings from year one in year two. However, what we were able to show, strikingly, is that, when we changed the conditions and the actors, we radically altered our research results, destabilizing the male/female gamer binary perpetuated by gender and gaming research and used by gaming companies. This argument can be illustrated through a close reading of player activities and attitudes toward gaming culture over a period of time.

Games as Texts

One way of analyzing video games is to view them as cultural texts that can be read and interpreted, typically through theories of narrative, semiotics, and rhetoric (Aarseth; Bogost; Frasca). Indeed, browsing through the Digital Games Research Association's online database demonstrates the myriad ways that game studies scholars have analyzed games as texts. This chapter contributes to this body of work by analyzing a relatively under-studied area of narrative: the *out-of-game* narratives that players construct when talking about their play.

It has been previously argued that embodied identities and positions within real-world power structures and discourses are always in play when interacting in virtual spaces (Balsamo; Haraway; Plant; Stone; Taylor). Similarly, within a co-constructed[4] game text, players' actions can be interpreted as a reflection of their perceived identity or position within the space in which this text is produced—for instance, as a novice, expert, non-gamer, hardcore gamer, girl gamer, and so on. The choices that players make within a game will also reflect the cultural values they subscribe to, in particular their own ideas regarding their access to and status within gaming culture—as a fully enfranchised member, an outsider, a transgressive girl gamer, and so on. If these in-game choices and out-of-game narratives are indeed reflections of the ways real-life embodied players understand their relationship with video games and their broader culture, an examination of these gaming texts over time ought to be able to demonstrate how players' dispositions change as they transition from novice to more expert players.

One anecdotal example of this kind of transition is James Paul Gee's elucidation of his and his son's play, which he uses as a platform to theorize the way in which learning is scaffolded by games. In Gee's account of that play, his narrative about himself as a player in relation to the games he is describing alters over time, from someone who is somewhat outside the game looking in, to someone who has transitioned to becoming a more skilled player. Gee refers to those cultures and communities who share goals and practices (game driven, in this case) as "affinity groups" (27). Similar to Lave and Wenger's community of practice, affinity groups teach newcomers the practices that are valued and reproduced in the community. Over time, one transitions from outsider to insider by learning the expected and acceptable social practices and identities in response to the affinity group. This status as an insider or outsider is conferred by other members, but also self-determined, as one chooses the degree to which one publicly demonstrates one's understanding of these practices and identities.

If we view the girls' interweaving of their own real-life narratives of identity with their often interpretive (and reconfigured) in-game narratives as an expression of "who they are," we can then track their beginning and developing engagement with/in game culture and gamer identity over time. In the section that follows, we examine the narrative accounts that girls produced both inside and outside the game, using player narratives to show how our modest intervention—a change in the conditions and contexts of girls' play—could enable them to transition from gaming novices to more expert players. We show that, as these girls became more skilled, the narratives they constructed about their own play and the larger text of the game they were playing began to break away from, and then to reject, the stereotypical characteristics of girl gamers as these girls reconstructed their identities as players of games.

Disrupting Ideas of "What Girls Like to Play" through Textual Analysis of Character Choices

Character or avatar choice in games and virtual worlds (like Second Life, Habbo Hotel, or Club Penguin) is typically the point of entry for a player and can be a site of playfulness, deliberation, and careful selection (Kafai; Yee et al.). In our own research, we have noted the time, energy, and consideration that players give to character selection within a game (even if this is simply a matter of selecting which car a player is controlling). Deciding who or what will represent a player in a video game and the process by which they come to this decision can be seen as a kind of self-characterization, providing insight into how players view themselves or want to be viewed by other players (whether these are strangers online or other players in the room). Accordingly, in games where there is a hierarchy of characters, we have observed players selecting characters based on how they perceived their own skill level, with self-proclaimed experts wanting to play only as leaders—refusing to play if they could not play with a leader character or demanding that less-skilled players play with characters positioned lower within the hierarchy of the game (Jenson, Fisher, and de Castell). So character selection is one way we can observe and monitor over time how players' notions of themselves as gamers—that is, how they identify with or position themselves within the game and broader game culture—can change. Before turning to an analysis of character selection by our young female players over time, we want to emphasize the importance of bearing in mind that female characters in video games are under-represented in comparison to male characters (Williams et al., "The Virtual Census"), and that, when female characters *do* appear in video games, they are more likely to occupy secondary roles than primary ones.

The initial character selection pattern of the girls in our study appears to reinforce sex-based claims that girls prefer to play with female characters (Bryce, Rutter, and Sullivan; Graner Ray; Williams et al., "The Virtual Census"; Yee et al.). For example, in the many Mario franchise games[5] that were played by the girls, there were a limited number of female characters to choose from (see fig. 11.1). This led to the girls calling dibs on or arguing over who gained control over what was often the only female character. When female characters were not available to play with, the girls consistently selected asexual characters. These characters were neither human nor easily categorized as male or female and were described by the girls using infantilizing terms such as "small," "cute," and "happy." In the case of

Mario games, these were Toad (a mushroom), Yoshi (a dinosaur or dragon), and Koopas (turtles). They also, when possible, avoided playing with recognizably strong male characters such as Mario, Luigi, Wario, Waluigi, Bowser, or Donkey Kong. These characters were described in undesirable and unfavourable terms ("ugly," "fat," "big," and so on), and it was not unusual for the girls to vocalize their disgust at even the *idea* of using these characters, usually through negative comments such as "ew" and "no way" when the selection tool would pass over these characters in the menu. In these early sessions, the girls rejected playing with characters that were identifiably masculine and instead chose either female or gender-neutral anthropomorphized characters.

Based on the conversations the girls had about their selected characters, it appeared important to them that others who might be watching their play (other players, researchers, students passing by) would view, understand, and acknowledge that their selected character was female. This is illustrated, for example, by the girls' choice to play with only one version of Samus, a playable female character in *Super Smash Bros. Brawl* and the main character of Nintendo's *Metroid* franchise. In the *Metroid* games, Samus typically wears a futuristic suit of armour that hides any defining feminine features and a helmet that covers her entire head (see fig. 11.2). As a result of this attire, as well as the masculine overtone of her name,

FIGURE 11.1 • Screen capture of characters from *Super Smash Bros. Brawl*, by Nintendo. Uploaded to the Naruto forum by member UzumakiNaruto0095.

the default male status of main characters in video games, and the girls' lack of knowledge of the *Metroid* series in general, the girls automatically assumed that Samus was a male. This presumption continued until one of the research assistants unlocked Zero Suit Samus in *Super Smash Bros. Brawl*, where she trades in her armour for a light-blue, skin-tight one-piece wetsuit that clearly displays her long blond hair and feminine figure (see fig. 11.3). To play as this version of Samus, the player must first select the regular, Powersuit-wearing Samus from the character roster and then perform a special "final smash" action in the game to activate the transformation to Zero Suit Samus. Although one could now play as either version of Samus, the girls repeatedly chose to play only with the identifiably female Samus, performing the final smash as soon as they were in the game. It appeared that knowing that Samus was a female underneath her armour was not enough; her femininity had to be displayed visually. Whereas selecting regular Samus often prompted the girls to provide an explanation for their choice ("she's actually a girl"), this was unnecessary when played as the Zero Suit version.

These explanations and rationalizations of the girls' choices of characters were regularly observed when the girls played with an anthropomorphized,

FIGURE 11.2 • Screen capture from *Metroid*, by Nintendo.
Copyright © *Super Smash Bros.* official website.

gender-neutral character like the *Super Mario Bros.* Toad or Yoshi. Interestingly, this group of female players began to construct feminized background stories for their androgynous characters as a way of rewriting the game text to suit their own needs, and to make even more evident the plausible femininity of these otherwise ungendered characters. For instance, during a game of *New Super Mario Bros. Wii*, one of the participants explained to the research assistant that she and her friend were playing with the toadstool characters, who were "twin sisters playing against the boys" (Mario and Luigi, who were being controlled by two other female gamers).[6] The pair followed up this explanation with comments such as "help me, sister" or "sisters forever" while playing, affirming the toadstools' femininity as well as their own. For years, the sex of the toadstool characters in Mario games was indeterminate until Nintendo introduced Toadette,

FIGURE 11.3 • Screen capture from *Super Smash Bros. Brawl*, by Nintendo. Copyright © *Super Smash Bros.* official website.

the female counterpart to Toad, whose gender is made explicit through her hairstyle (plaited pigtails) and clothing (pink dress). Toadette was a well-known playable character in several of the games played during the club, but is not available in *New Super Mario Bros. Wii*, so this statement was not simply a consequence of mistaken gender identity. Rather, we view this alternative narrative as a means for the players of the toadstools to reaffirm their commitment to their own femininity while participating in a very male activity, and to make visible their desire to project the appropriate gender performance to others who might be watching or listening to them play.

In another instance, this time with a group of girls playing *Mario Party 7*, three of the four players chose the three female characters available in the game (Peach, Daisy, and Toadette) and the fourth player selected Yoshi. When the female research assistant (and club leader) came to watch them play, the fourth participant told her that Yoshi was female. This is noteworthy because characters represented as gender neutral are typically presumed to be male (Martins et al.) and certainly not female, likely because female characters are invariably marked with hyper-feminized attributes (pink hair bows, long eyelashes, and so on) to communicate their sex. When the research assistant asked the player how she knew Yoshi's sex, she replied with a confident "because I said so." It was well known in the club that the research assistant was herself a skilled gamer, and she was viewed by the girls as a resource they could consult for video game knowledge. Much to the (unintended) embarrassment of the girl controlling Yoshi, the research assistant candidly responded that, since it is impossible to determine Yoshi's sex concretely, it was probably more appropriate to refer to Yoshi as a sort of "genderless dragon." This statement (that Yoshi was not a girl, despite the player's confident claim) caused the girls who were controlling the undeniably female characters to erupt in uncontrollable laughter and teasing directed at the girl who was controlling Yoshi for about a minute before resuming their game. For the remainder of the session, the Yoshi participant played unenthusiastically and quietly. It is of no small significance that the other girls had chosen female characters, a privileged choice that may have reflected these girls' relative status outside of the game world, and this was likely the reason why the fourth player felt compelled to feminize Yoshi, as a way to minimize, and to equalize, the status difference among the four characters.

It would be convenient to echo the usual conclusions that attribute these selections to the players' sex (that girls want to play with female characters). Observations of these same girls playing the same games a few months later, however, revealed significant changeability in avatar selection, and suggested reasons for those altered choices. As these girls became more skilled in their gameplay, they expanded their repertoire of playable characters to include the male characters they had initially rejected, like Mario, Luigi, Boo, Pit, Ike, Link, and Bowser. When asked why they were now choosing these characters, they rationalized their decisions by citing the affordances of the character (for example, what bonuses or unique abilities the male character offered), their familiarity with controlling that character (knowing "how to use" a particular character), or the character's status within gaming culture (wanting to "be Link," a gaming icon from the popular *Legend of Zelda* franchise). We view this radical change of thinking around character selection as an effect of the girls' growing familiarity with these games and gaming in general, enculturation within the gaming community, and further development in gameplay skill. After playing these games for several months, the girls now had a firm understanding of their win conditions, and thus adjusted their character selection criteria to increase their chances of winning. It could also be the case that these girls, in building more confident player identities, felt that they no longer needed to assert the real-world fact that they were girls by making girl-appropriate avatar selections, because they began to participate *legitimately* in this particular community of practice.

From the outset we observed male club members applying the same criteria—function, familiarity, and status—that the now more skilled-up girls employed when selecting *their* characters. The majority of boys in the study were experienced gamers with access in their homes to the same consoles and games played at the club. Many broadcasted and positioned themselves as gaming experts and used the club as a forum to demonstrate this self-proclaimed expertise, as a sort of proving ground. In contrast, the majority of the girls in the club were novices who did not enjoy the same level of access to gaming technologies as the male club members did. In fact, for most of the girls, their only opportunity to play video games was during the club. So, in the early sessions, because they had very little experience with playing games, the girls did not identify as gamers or show any inclination to identify as such. Rather, the girls' initial considerations for character choice appear to reflect a desire to project (and perhaps also to protect) their femininity while engaging in a traditionally masculine activity.

In the later months of the club, however, being female in the game was no longer a priority. It was replaced, in one sense, by the girls' desire to now identify and be recognized as gamers. This shift in identity projection and criteria for selecting characters can be illustrated through an analysis of the play of two club members and best friends, Ali and Elise. Upon joining the club as novices, the girls announced their close friendship to the research assistants, who made note of how these two girls always played together and also sometimes referred to themselves as sisters, even though they were not actually related. *New Super Mario Bros. Wii* was Ali and Elise's favourite game, and they played it every day the club was held. When they first started playing the game, the duo would select the toadstool characters as their avatars. As mentioned earlier, they reappointed the toadstool characters as twin girls, imposing their close real-world relationship and sex onto these characters. In later sessions, however, Ali and Elise began to choose Mario and Luigi instead. They would refer to each other as "brother" during play (for example, "wait up, brother!" and "thanks, brother!"), appropriating Mario and Luigi's fraternal bond to continue to signify their close real-world friendship.

In later sessions, wanting to remain feminine or to project a feminine identity was further deprioritized and replaced by a desire to appear as skilled gamers. Now the girls always attempted to secure the Mario and Luigi characters for their play and rejected the toadstools. Interestingly, in *New Super Mario Bros. Wii*, the four playable characters (see fig. 11.4) are equal in terms of abilities, so playing as Mario is actually no different from playing as a toadstool. Since playing as Mario or Luigi does not provide any additional benefits (that is, you cannot jump any higher or run any faster), this shift in character preference, however much it may have been cast in the girls' accounts as a functional choice maximizing their chances to win, more likely represents a reflection of their growing comfort with

FIGURE 11.4 • Screen capture from *New Super Mario Bros. Wii*, by Nintendo. Uploaded to Flickr by user Crash Cortex.

and enculturation into gaming as fully legitimate players. Ali and Elise were now considering the characters' symbolic status in game lore and culture. As *the* brothers of the Super Mario Bros. franchise, Mario and Luigi are a recognizable, iconic team even to those who do not play video games. Accordingly, they are at the top of the character hierarchy within their franchise, whereas the toadstools occupy a subordinate position by comparison. Moreover, Ali and Elise were now in fact embracing masculinity as part of their identity in the club. Their use of the word "brother" when talking to each other about their play continued to signify their close real-world relationship, where they described themselves as "closer than siblings." This way of managing the incursions of real-world identity or position upon game-world character selection is a far cry from their initial rejection of and visible disgust at the thought of playing with male characters in earlier sessions.

That is not to suggest that the girls in the club necessarily believed that they needed to sacrifice their femininity to be recognized as skilled gamers. Katrina, for example, was a female club member in the mixed gender club who enjoyed playing the game *Super Smash Bros. Brawl* and became very good at controlling the character Pit, a male warrior from Nintendo's *Kid Icarus* series. After a particularly intense round where she had successfully beaten the three boys she was playing with, one of the boys lamented, "Aw, we lost to Pit," to which Katrina replied, "That's *Ms.* Pit to you." Katrina's comment here can be interpreted in several ways. The most superficial reading is that she wanted to retain her femininity while engaging in a male activity with males. However, as she was one of the more skilled and outspoken club members, we think that she viewed this as an opportunity to remind (and educate) the players around her that being a girl *and* a skilled gamer are not mutually exclusive identities, so that her statement represented an authentic move toward disruption, not recitation, of the gender order. Her reminder to the boys seemed to us to be less about wanting to be seen as feminine in the game space, and more about attempting to claim respect from her recently defeated opponents, a demand that they acknowledge that she is a girl, and that she just kicked their asses.

These clear shifts in criteria for character selection coincide with the girls' increasing skill level and expertise, and also, importantly, their growing sense of entitlement to participate in this and other public gaming spaces, where they no longer seemed to need to assert their femininity in order to participate because of their enhanced familiarity and skill. These readings of player narratives in and around their gameplay suggest that players' character preferences may have less (or nothing) to do with their real-world sex and more to do with their position in the hierarchies of expertise, knowledge, and status within the game and its broader player culture. In this case, because the male club members had more gaming experience and knowledge from playing video games outside the club, they entered the space with a set of gaming competencies and understandings that enabled them to use these selection criteria *earlier* than the girls, who had to skill up and become familiar with the games first. However, once the girls increased their gaming skills and their knowledge base, they moved away from playing in the ways that are often expected of female game players and started to play as gamers, not as girl gamers.

What this work highlights is the importance of studying players and their play *over time* and *across contexts*, especially if what is being documented at the outset is novice gameplay. As expertise is gained, not only do play styles, avatar choices, and general vocabulary for speaking about the game shift, but what also shifts is how players read the game—that is, how they narrate and navigate it, what depths they sound, the sites of play to which they return, what they choose to replay, with whom they play, and so on. It is therefore important to document shifting identities and their different contexts. As this work demonstrates, examining the gaming texts and out-of-game narratives that players construct over time is one way to track these shifting identities. This approach—examining dynamically constructed identity-texts over time—may also prove to be useful for examining other aspects of girls and gaming, such as designing and developing games. For example, we suspect that, if we examined the games that girls create using game design software, the games that they create as beginners may be very different from the games they create a year later. Research that chooses to focus not how things "are" but how they can and do change when it comes to girls and gaming can provide more nuanced, and far more disruptive, theory-building with respect to questions about differences between girls' and boys' play. These theories would be useful indeed for designing equity-oriented interventions in policy, pedagogy, or practice.

Notes

1   Games in the *Imagine* series were released in 2008. Ubisoft continues to develop and release *Imagine* games and has also launched an online virtual world, *Imagine Town*.

2   Casual games are digital games that are primarily played on web browsers or mobile devices, have simple rules and gameplay mechanics, require no long-term time commitments or special skills to play, and have comparatively lower productive and distribution costs in comparison to hardcore games.

3   See, for example, Bryce and Rutter; Carr; Jenkins and Cassell; Graner-Ray; Schott and Kambouri; Walkerdine; and Winn and Heeter.

4   A video game is a text that is half-written and positions players as authors as they make their way through the game. Henry Jenkins views this as the co-construction of two narratives: "one can imagine the game designer as developing two kinds of narratives—one relatively unstructured and controlled by the player as they explore the game space and unlock its secrets; the other pre-structured but embedded within the mise-en-scene awaiting discovery" (126).

5   Members of the gaming club had access to and played a number of popular Nintendo games that featured characters from the Mario franchise, including *Mario Party 7*, *Mario Party 8*, *Mario Kart Double Dash*, *Mario Kart Wii*, and *New Super Mario Bros. Wii*.

6   *New Super Mario Bros. Wii* had just been released and was a very popular game to play in the club. This meant that, despite their feelings about playing with male characters, two out of the four girls playing necessarily had to play as either Mario or Luigi, or not play at all. As already noted, quarrels over who got to play as the toadstools (the preferred androgynous characters) were frequent in the earlier sessions.

Works Cited

Aarseth, Espen J. *Cybertext: Perspectives on Ergodic Literature*. Baltimore: Johns Hopkins UP, 1997. Print.

Balsamo, Anne. "Reading Cyborgs Writing Feminism." *The Gendered Cyborg: A Reader*. Ed. Gill Kirkup, Linda Janes, Kathryn Woolard, and Fiona Hovenden. London: Routledge, 2000. 148–58. Print.

Beavis, Catherine, and Claire Charles. "Would the 'Real' Girl Gamer Please Stand Up? Gender, LAN Cafes and the Reformulation of the 'Girl' Gamer." *Gender and Education* 19.6 (2007): 691–705. Print.

Bogost, Ian. *Persuasive Games*. Cambridge: MIT P, 2007. Print.

Bryce, Jo, and Jason Rutter. "Gendered Gaming in Gendered Space." *Handbook of Computer Game Studies*. Ed. Joost Raessens and Jeffrey Goldstein. Cambridge: MIT P, 2005. 301–10. Print.

Bryce, Jo, Jason Rutter, and Cath Sullivan. "Digital Games and Gender."

Understanding Digital Games. Ed. Jason Rutter and Jo Bryce. Thousand Oaks: Sage, 2006. 185–204. Print.

Butler, Judith. *Gender Trouble: Feminism and the Subversion of Identity.* 1989. New York: Routledge, 1999. Print.

Carr, Diane. "Contexts, Gaming Pleasures, and Gendered Preferences." *Simulation and Gaming* 36.4 (Dec. 2005): 464–82. Print.

Chess, Shira. "A 36-24-36 Cerebrum: Productivity, Gender, and Video Game Advertising." *Critical Studies in Media Communication* 28.3 (2011): 230–52. Print.

de Castell, Suzanne, and Mary Bryson. "Retooling Play: Dystopia, Dysphoria, and Difference." *From Barbie to Mortal Kombat.* Ed. Justine Cassells and Henry Jenkins. Cambridge: MIT P, 1998. 232–61. Print.

"EA SPORTS FIFA Soccer Franchise Sales Top 100 Million Units Lifetime." *Business Wire.* 4 Nov. 2010. Web. 10 Dec. 2010.

"Evil Controllers Announces Girl Gaming Month." *Evil Controllers.* 26 Jan. 2011. Web. 10 Feb. 2011.

Fat, Ugly or Slutty. N.d. Web. 9 Sept. 2010.

Foucault, Michel. *The History of Sexuality.* Vol. 1. New York: Vintage, 1990. Print.

Frasca, Gonzalo. "Simulation vs. Narrative: An Introduction to Ludology." *The Video Game Theory Reader.* Ed. Mark Wolf and Bernard Perron. New York: Routledge, 2003. 221–35. Print.

Fron, Janine, Tracy Fullerton, Jacquelyn Ford Morie, and Celia Pearce. "The Hegemony of Play." *Situated Play: Proceedings of the Digital Games Research Association, September 24–27, 2007.* Sept. 2007. Web. 9 Sept. 2010.

Gee, James Paul. *What Videogames Have to Teach Us about Learning and Literacy.* New York: Palgrave Macmillan, 2003. Print.

Graner Ray, Sheri. *Gender Inclusive Game Design: Expanding the Market.* Hingham: Charles River Media, 2004. Print.

Haraway, Donna. "A Cyborg Manifesto: Science, Technology, and Socialist-Feminism in the Late Twentieth Century." *Simians, Cyborgs and Women: The Reinvention of Nature.* New York: Routledge, 1991. 149–81. Print.

Jenkins, Henry. "Game Design as Narrative Architecture." *First Person: New Media as Story, Performance, Game.* Ed. Noah Wardrip-Fruin and Pat Harrigan. Cambridge: MIT P, 2004. 118–30. Print.

Jenkins, Henry, and Justine Cassell. "From Quake Grrls to Desperate Housewives: A Decade of Gender and Computer Games." *Beyond Barbie and Mortal Kombat.* Ed. Yasmin B. Kafai, Carrie Heeter, Jennifer Y. Sun, and Jill Denner. Cambridge: MIT P, 2008. 5–20. Print.

Jenson, Jennifer, and Suzanne de Castell. "Fair Play: Gender, Digital Gaming and Educational Disadvantage." *Human Perspectives in the Internet Society: Culture, Psychology and Gender.* Ed. K. Morgan, C. A. Brebbie, J. Sanchez, and A. Voiskounsky. Boston: WIT P, 2004. 227–34. Print.

———. "Girls@Play: An Ethnographic Study of Gender and Digital Gameplay." *Feminist Media Studies* 2.11 (2011): 1–13. Print.

———. "Theorizing Gender and Digital Gameplay: Oversights, Accidents and Surprises." *Eludamos: Journal for Computer Game Culture* 2.1 (2008): 15–25. Print.

Jenson, Jennifer, Stephanie Fisher, and Suzanne de Castell. "Disrupting the Gender Order: Leveling Up and Claiming Space in an After-School Gaming Club." *International Journal of Gender, Science and Technology* 3.1 (2011): 149–69. Web. 15 May 2011.

Kafai, Yasmin B. "Gender Play in a Tween Gaming Club." *Beyond Barbie and Mortal Kombat.* Ed. Yasmin B. Kafai, Carrie Heeter, Jennifer Y. Sun, and Jill Denner. Cambridge: MIT P, 2008. 111–24. Print.

Lave, Jean, and Etienne Wenger. *Situated Learning: Legitimate Peripheral Participation.* New York: Cambridge UP, 1991. Print.

Martins, Nicole, Dmitri C. Williams, Kristen Harrison, and Rabindra A. Ratan. "A Content Analysis of Female Body Imagery in Video Games." *Sex Roles* 61.5–6 (2009): 824–36. Web. 10 Dec. 2010.

Molina, Brett. "Eleven Things You Didn't Know about 'Madden NFL 11.'" *USA Today.* 11 Aug. 2010. Web. 9 Sept. 2010.

Plant, Sadie. *Zeros and Ones.* London: Fourth Estate, 1997. Print.

Schott, Gareth, and Maria Kambouri. "Social Play and Learning." *Computer Games: Text, Narrative and Play.* Ed. Diane Carr, David Buckingham, Andrew Burn, and Gareth Schott. Cambridge: Polity P, 2006. 119–32. Print.

Silicon Sisters. *School 26.* Silicon Sisters, Inc. 2011. iOS and Android devices.

Siwek, Stephen E. "Video Games in the 21st Century: The 2010 Report." *Entertainment Software Association.* N.d. Web. 7 Sept. 2010.

Smith, Dorothy E. *The Everyday World as Problematic: A Feminist Sociology.* Toronto: U of Toronto P, 1987. Print.

Stone, Allucquère Rosanne. "Will the Real Body Please Stand Up? Boundary Stories about Virtual Cultures." *Cyberspace: First Steps.* Ed. Michael L. Benedikt. Cambridge: MIT P, 1991. 81–118. Print.

Taylor, Nick. "Periscopic Play: Re-positioning 'the Field' in MMO Studies." *Loading* 2.3 (2008): n. pag. Web. 15 Dec. 2010.

Taylor, Nicholas, Jennifer Jenson, and Suzanne de Castell. "Cheerleaders/Booth Babes/*Halo* Hoes: Pro-Gaming, Gender and Jobs for the Boys." *Digital Creativity* 20.4 (2009): 239–52. Print.

"Ubisoft Unveils Imagine Video Game Series for Girls." *Ubisoft.com*. Ubisoft, 12 July 2007. Web. 10 Dec. 2010.

Walkerdine, Valerie. *Children, Gender, Video Games: Towards a Relational Approach to Multimedia*. New York: Palgrave Macmillan, 2007. Print.

Williams, Dmitri, Mia Consalvo, Scott Caplan, and Nick Yee. "Looking for Gender: Gender Roles and Behaviors among Online Gamers." *Journal of Communication* 59 (2009): 700–25. Print.

Williams, Dmitri, Nicole Martins, Mia Consalvo, and James D. Ivory. "The Virtual Census: Representations of Gender, Race, and Age in Video Games." *New Media Society* 11.5 (August 2009): 815–34. *SAGE Journals*. Web. 10 Dec. 2010.

Winn, Jillian, and Carrie Heeter. "Gaming, Gender, and Time: Who Makes Time to Play?" *Sex Roles* 61.1–2 (2009): 1–13. Print.

Yee, Nick, Nicolas Ducheneaut, Mike Yao, and Les Nelson. "Do Men Heal More When in Drag? Conflicting Identity Cues between User and Avatar." *Proceedings of the Annual Conference on Human Factors in Computing Systems, May 6–12, 2011*. New York: ACM, 2011. 773–76. Web. 5 Jan. 2012.

CHAPTER 12

Reading Smart Girls

Post-Nerds in Post-Feminist Popular Culture

Shauna Pomerantz and Rebecca Raby

Introducing the New Smart Girl

A new kind of smart girl has emerged in popular culture. No longer nerdy, dowdy, and ostracized for her intelligence, this post-nerd smart girl is attractive, capable, and sexually desirable. She is clever and sexy, brainy and beautiful, and, though she may not always be popular, she has the power and confidence to build her own world. This smart girl can also be athletic, tough, and cool, showcasing a range of possibilities that were previously presented as antithetical to smart girls of the past. In short, this smart girl has it all, including a bright future, dates with boys, and a "can-do" attitude. In contrast, the classic female nerd of the 1970s, 1980s, and 1990s has been criticized for presenting a bookish, one-dimensional character (Conaway). Sporting glasses and a gawky demeanour, girl nerds were generally portrayed as being at the mercy of popular girls and shallow boys who taunted them for their good grades and quirky personalities. Social status eluded girl nerds, who usually had one or two friends, but still yearned for social recognition from the popular group.

Yet, while new representations of smart girls seem to depict a wider range of performances of femininity, sexuality, and power (Inness), they remain concerning. We argue that these contemporary portrayals of smart girls are not as powerful or progressive as they appear and are, instead, examples of post-feminism in popular culture (see Kelly and Pomerantz). Emerging in the 1990s in conjunction with girl power rhetoric (see Currie, Kelly, and Pomerantz), post-feminism is the widespread belief that feminism is no longer necessary as gender equality has been achieved (see McRobbie, *The Aftermath*). Angela McRobbie notes in her 2009 book *The Aftermath of Feminism* that modern-day girlhood is now defined by individualism, consumerism, hypersexuality, and the belief that girls can do, be, and have anything they want without fear of structural inequalities such as sexism, racism, or homophobia interfering with their individual efforts to achieve success. As a consequence, such structural inequities have now come to be seen as individual rather than social problems. Post-feminism is further reinforced by the broader trend of neo-liberalism, an approach to politics and the economy which advocates individual responsibility, free-market capitalism, consumerism, and a dismantling of social safety nets and services (Gill and Scharff). These political, economic, and social developments have combined, shifting the way girls are viewed and valued in Western society (see Aapola, Gonick, and Harris; Harris; Walkerdine, Lucey, and Melody). From these perspectives, gender inequality is no longer relevant—and, as girls are now equal to boys, they are no longer viewed as needing specialized curricula, social programs, or government support (see Francis and Skelton). Girls are also newly framed as not only equal to boys, but surpassing them in every way, constructing girls as either privileged or ideal global subjects (Harris).

Anita Harris argues that a certain kind of (middle-class, white, and heterosexual) girl has been constructed as the "vanguard of the new subjectivity" (1) of global neo-liberalism. In order for global capitalism to thrive, it needs versatile, independent go-getters who can adapt to ever-changing workplaces and flexible, contractual work without recourse to social supports. The "future girl" fills this need (Pomerantz and Raby; Harris; Walkerdine, Lucey, and Melody). Through the overlapping and mutually informing discourses of post-feminism and neo-liberalism, successful "future girls" are well positioned to do, be, and have anything they want (Harris). But, as Harris soberly emphasizes, this girl is a construction used to obscure ongoing structural inequalities and to justify a political and economic paradigm that is routinely described as ruthless, competitive, and dehumanizing, and as exacerbating inequality (see also Gill and Scharff).

Jessica Ringrose and Valerie Walkerdine argue that this supergirl phenomenon depicts girls with "masculine" confidence alongside "feminine" responsibility as they strive for success in school, work, family, and social life. An oft-cited article in the *New York Times*, for example, explores the supergirl phenomenon by highlighting girls "by the dozen who are high achieving, ambitious and confident" (Rimer; see also Chaudhry; Kindlon). Rimer interviews so-called supergirls to learn more about girls "who have grown up learning they can do anything a boy can do, which is anything they want to do." But interestingly, these girls also discuss the perils of being a supergirl by noting that, in order to maintain their "perfect" or "amazing" status, they must also be thin, pretty, and "effortlessly hot" (Rimer).

In this chapter we critically explore the post-nerd terrain by first describing the characteristics of the classic girl nerd. We then highlight the emergence of the post-nerd girl in popular culture by exploring three contemporary examples of smart supergirls: Rory from *Gilmore Girls* (WB and CW, 2000–2007), Gabriella from *High School Musical* (Disney Channel Original Movie, 2006), and Veronica from *Veronica Mars* (UPN and CW, 2004–2007).[1] After describing these three examples, we analyze how these representations signify the intersection of post-feminism and neo-liberalism. At first glance, the smart supergirl seems to offer a positive example for smart girls looking to popular culture for available subject positions, an example that far surpasses the classic nerd. After all, smart girls can now be pretty, fashionable, popular, and talented in extracurricular activities, rather than socially awkward and marginalized nerds. But while there may be some benefits for girls who are inspired by the post-nerd icon, we argue that such representations demand closer scrutiny, particularly within the problematic contexts of post-feminism and neo-liberalism.

Smart Performances: Cultural Studies and Feminist Post-structuralism

Given our interest in representations of smart girls, we situate our study in the multidisciplinary field of cultural studies, which focuses on meaning-making through cultural texts and practices (During, *The Cultural Studies Reader*; Storey). As Simon During notes in *Cultural Studies: A Critical Introduction*, this broad definition of cultural studies is rooted in its threefold engagement with contemporary culture. First, cultural studies is a form of political analysis that aims to undermine hegemonic structures that perpetuate power imbalances in society. Second, cultural studies asks how things come to have meaning to particular people at particular times. Third, cultural studies is committed to viewing "culture as a part of everyday life" (1), highlighting an engagement with cultural forms that have previously been considered too pedestrian to be valid objects of study. The insistence in cultural studies that everyday life is filled with meaningful texts and practices has made the study of popular culture a legitimate pursuit.

Our interest in popular culture is rooted in its power to construct girls' lives through the "project of representation" (Nash 4). Stuart Hall defines representation as "the production of meaning through language" (16), where language is broadly construed as anything that can be "read," including writing, visual images, the spoken word, and body language. Representations, Hall explains, are thus ways of symbolizing or standing in for "a wider set of meanings" (16). But as Hall also notes, representation produces meaning through subjective links between signifiers (images, words, sounds) and signifieds (the concepts that images, words, and sounds invoke) that are informed by dominant relations of power. These links then "fix" meaning, making arbitrary associations appear natural.[2]

Representations are not a transparent reflection of the "real" world "out there"; instead, representations help to manufacture reality. For example, glasses in popular culture have typically been a signifier for a particular kind of girl: one who is shy, mousey, intellectual, and sexually repressed—a real "librarian" type (Radford and Radford). Glasses do not have any intrinsic meaning in and of themselves, other than helping people to see well. Yet, as Roland Barthes notes, glasses are instilled with ideological or mythological significance that becomes a taken-for-granted "truth." According to Barthes, such mythologies need to be excavated in order to bring to light the way that representations perpetuate ideological assumptions that support dominant power structures—and in the case of glasses, operate to make the subject position associated with the smart girl seem unattractive not only to boys but to girls as well.

Seen through a feminist post-structural lens (Weedon), representation is part of discourse, or culturally, socially, and historically produced stories, beliefs, and knowledges that take on the status of Truth (Burr; Fraser). Rather than reflecting reality, discourses have the constituting power to produce the very things they seek to describe. As Michel Foucault suggests in *The Archaeology of Knowledge*, the power of discourse is derived not from what is said per se, but from how discourses congeal as truth over time and space. Through repetition and circulation, discourses outline the boundaries of good and bad, normal and abnormal, safe and dangerous, and sacred and profane. Discourses are thus productive in that they "articulate objects and subjects in their intelligibility" (Butler, "For a Careful Reading" 138). Judith Butler calls the reiterative power of discourse "performativity," or "a set of repeated acts within a highly regulatory frame that congeals over time to produce the appearance of a substance, of a natural sort of being" (*Gender Trouble* 33). Performativity describes the process by which girls "do" girlhood (Butler, *Undoing Gender*; see also Currie, Kelly, and Pomerantz). But the "doing" of girlhood is not meant to suggest free will or unlimited choice. Instead, theorists of performativity regard gender as a form of improvisation within wide-sweeping social, cultural, and historical constraints (Butler, *Undoing Gender*). Representations of girls in popular culture contribute to these discursive constraints by helping to regulate the boundaries of ideal girlhood.

The smart supergirl is represented as ripe with endless possibility and laden with responsibilities: brilliance, beauty, heterosexual dating success, and a multitude of extracurricular skills. Within post-feminist and neo-liberal contexts, such representations reproduce a particular kind of girlhood that resignifies structural inequities as individual problems that girls must conquer single-handedly. The post-nerd supergirl is thus constructed as a beautiful and brilliant workhorse who is an idealized citizen within neo-liberal global capitalism. Yet, as we will argue in this paper, the supergirl icon is actually quite a narrow representation of successful girlhood; few actual girls can take up the subject position of the supergirl, as it necessitates emulating white and middle-class values that are elusive to girls who fall outside of these regulatory boundaries.

Because so few representations of alternative or subversive girlhood exist in popular culture (Kelly and Pomerantz; Willis), representations of supergirlhood require interrogation as social regulations that "fix" how girls should be. As Sandra Conaway suggests, Butler's theory of performativity "helps to explain how girls learn to behave according to our culture's rules for appropriate girlhood" (23)—and how others expect them to act. A feminist post-structural lens within a cultural studies framework enables us to take seriously forms of popular culture that are often written off as mere entertainment. We thus critically explore discourses that have emerged surrounding smart girls, and consider how these discourses contribute to girls' performances of gender identity and the depoliticization of girlhood within post-feminist and neo-liberal contexts. We now turn our attention to the particulars of these discourses, beginning with the classic girl nerd and then focusing on the smart supergirl.

Desperately Seeking Popularity: Classic and Makeover Nerds Vie for Social Intelligibility

The "nerd" stereotype is a time-honoured tradition in popular culture. For boy nerds, this iconic trope is humorously and cruelly juxtaposed to the brawny jocks who rule the school: the jocks embody hegemonic masculinity (Connell), and the nerds embody an abject form of masculinity that is signified as feminine and/or homosexual (Pascoe).[3] Similarly, the female nerd has historically been characterized by her own set of entrenched traits. From the 1970s until the late 1990s, smart girls were almost always represented as klutzy, mousey, overly responsible, and concerned with doing the right thing. The classic girl nerd wore glasses, dressed unfashionably, and was unattractive by conventional standards. But, above all, she was intensely intelligent, and this intelligence prevented her from being anything other than a nerd.

An example of the classic girl nerd is the smart yet socially unsavvy Lisa Simpson of the long-running cartoon sitcom *The Simpsons* (Fox, 1989–present), who, though a member of Mensa with an IQ of 159, remains an outsider. Occasionally self-righteous and addicted to grades, Lisa struggles with her lack of popularity and desire for recognition from boys, creating a binary opposition between academic and social success. She is also an easy target for the popular girls, Sherri and Terri, who tease her for being a teacher's pet, having a "big butt," and being socially undesirable. Isolated and often withdrawn, Lisa finds no solace at home, where Homer and Bart ridicule her intelligence. Another example of the classic girl nerd is from the 1980s cult classic sitcom *Square Pegs* (CBS, 1982–1983), starring a young and very unfashionable Sarah Jessica Parker. Best friends Patty and Lauren endeavour to transition from nerd to cool by tirelessly courting the popular crowd. The dialogue just before the opening credits explains their plan:

> *Lauren:* Listen. I've got this whole high school thing psyched out. It all breaks down into cliques.
>
> *Patty:* Cliques?
>
> *Lauren:* Yeah, you know, cliques—little in-groups of different kids. All we have to do is click with the right clique, and we can finally have a social life that's worthy of us.
>
> *Patty:* No way! Not even with cleavage.

Lauren: I tell you, this year we're going to be popular.

Patty: Yeah?

Lauren: Yeah, even if it kills us. ("Pilot")

Unfortunately for Lauren and Patty, their plan never takes root. Depicted as having an "inner nerdiness" that holds them back, they cannot overcome their looks, intelligence, and cultured attitude in order to be seen as one of the "in-crowd."

As exemplified by Lisa, Lauren, and Patty,[4] classic nerds do not have the social capacity to be transformed into sexy and attractive popular girls. But if a classic girl nerd is willing to put her intelligence on hold and dutifully practise emphasized femininity (Connell), particularly in relation to wearing the "right" clothes, having the "right" hair, and baring the "right" amount of skin, she may be lucky enough to transition into popularity through a makeover. Makeover nerds fulfill the alluring fantasy of moving from the ghetto of academic invisibility to the promised land of popularity by both "dumbing down" and "sexing up" (Conaway).

An example of the makeover nerd fantasy is the 1999 film *Never Been Kissed*, a romantic comedy starring Drew Barrymore as the socially awkward Josie Geller. Josie, a journalist in her early twenties, is sent back to high school by her editor in order to gather information on what it is like to be a teenager "today." While undercover, Josie initially relives her horrible high school experience as a classic girl nerd, but eventually learns to shed her "Josie Grossie" past and is made over into the most popular girl in school. This transformation takes place through a change in dress and hair, but also through the suppression of her academic abilities. Another example of the makeover nerd occurs in the 1999 romantic comedy *She's All That*, starring Freddie Prinze Jr. and Rachael Leigh Cook. Cook's character, Laney Boggs, undergoes a makeover transformation when a popular athlete, Zack Siler, bets his friends that he can turn a smart, nerdy, unattractive girl into the most sexually desirable girl in school. When his friends doubt that such a feat is possible, Zack accurately predicts, "give her the right look, the right boyfriend, and bam. In six weeks she's being named prom queen."

These classic and makeover nerd representations suggest that intelligence and popularity are mutually exclusive, reinforcing the idea that "it is impossible for girls . . . to [both] position themselves within discourses of academic success and femininity" (Niemi 485). While gender success is off limits to the classic nerd, as the makeover nerd shows, one can achieve such success by suppressing intellect, changing a look, and capitulating to the desires of boys. These representations serve to reproduce traditional gender norms, which essentialize girls as sexual objects without independent worth. They also work to discursively produce smartness as a non-feminine pursuit. As Conaway notes, they teach girls "that they must perform their gender appropriately, or suffer the consequences of being invisible and unpopular" (23).

Smart, Sexy, and Socially Astute: Post-Nerds Vie for Supergirl Status

While representations of classic and makeover nerds are easy to critique, several recent representations of smart girls in the twenty-first century offer a greater challenge. At first glance, the smart supergirl in the post-nerd landscape seems to constitute a quantum leap forward; as we describe below, characters like Rory, Gabriella, and Veronica offer girls a much more dynamic and exciting example of how a smart girl can be, look, and act. But as our analysis of these representations illustrates, the post-nerd is a problematic, apolitical, and individualized character.

The Golden Girl: Rory Gilmore

When we first meet Rory Gilmore (played by Alexis Bledel) in the television show *Gilmore Girls*, she is a sixteen-year-old high school student who is about to start her first day at an elite prep school. Entrance into Chilton Academy is the first step in Rory's plan to eventually attend Harvard, and it is this Ivy League ambition that becomes one of the staples of this fast-talking drama, where smart girls and women of various kinds permeate the post-feminist storylines. Rory's intelligence is clearly marked by her high grades, her academic determination, and her need to study. In an episode entitled "The Break Up, Part 2," Rory is invited to a Chilton party. Rather than socializing like all the other teens, Rory sits quietly in a chair with her book. When Tristan, a popular boy who has a crush on her, says, "Great party, huh?" Rory responds, "Not bad. Gave me a chance to catch up on my reading." But rather than making Rory an outcast, her academic drive enhances her worth on the social scene. In an episode entitled "Like Mother, Like Daughter," the popular clique invites her into "the Puffs," a secret Chilton sorority. However, Rory rejects the invitation because the Puffs' interests are antithetical to her own. Instead, she prefers to sit alone in the cafeteria reading and listening to music on her headphones.

While portrayed as smart and highly ambitious, Rory is also classically beautiful. Waif-like, wide-eyed, and innocent, Rory is the girl next door who attracts attractive young men, including Tristan, the most popular boy in school; Dean, the nice guy who worships the ground she walks on; Jess, the troubled youth from the big city; and Logan, the heir to a newspaper dynasty. Rory has romantic experiences that were elusive to classic nerd characters and granted to the makeover nerd only if she was able to downplay her intellectual abilities. Rather than hindering her romantic success, however, Rory's intelligence is essential to her representation as a complete "package." In the pilot episode, Dean makes clear that he has fallen for Rory because she is beautiful *and* smart.

> *Dean:* After school, you come out and you sit under that tree there and you read. Last week it was *Madame Bovary*. This week it's *Moby Dick*. . . .
>
> *Rory:* But why would you . . .
>
> *Dean:* Because you're nice to look at and because you've got unbelievable concentration. . . . I thought, "I have never seen anyone read so intensely in my entire life. I have to meet that girl."

This quotation clearly exemplifies Rory's charm as being tied to her intelligence. Dean is drawn to her not just because she is "nice to look at," but also specifically because she is both attractive and bookish. While the latter quality would have made her undesirable by traditional nerd standards, in this post-feminist landscape, Rory is shown to effortlessly "have it all."

Throughout the series, Rory's dating success is mirrored by her extracurricular achievement. In an episode entitled "Hammers and Veils," Rory becomes aware of the importance of outside-school pursuits to distinguish herself from the hundreds of other Harvard applicants. Worried by her lack of involvement, Rory volunteers to build a house for Habitat for Humanity. Later she is recruited to run for Chilton student council; she also reports for the *Franklin*, Chilton's student newspaper, a journalistic experience that precedes her editorship of the *Yale Daily News*. Attractive, quirky, determined, and media savvy, Rory is a new kind of smart girl who cares more about doing well in school than popularity. As Karin Westman suggests, *Gilmore Girls* presents education as something cool and important by showcasing an assortment of smart women who get what they want by aiming high and trying hard. In the next example, we see a similar representation in smart girl Gabriella, whose extracurricular talents and quiet determination earn her the attention of the most popular boy in school.

The Quiet Girl: Gabriella Montez

When we first meet Gabriella Montez (played by Vanessa Hudgens) in the made-for-television movie *High School Musical*, it is New Year's Eve at the ski lodge where she and her mother are on holiday. Gabriella is reading quietly when her mother admonishes her to put down her book and join the festivities on their last night of vacation. We are immediately cued that Gabriella is smart, demure, and shy. She reluctantly closes her novel and, at her mother's insistence, attends a youth party hosted by the resort. There she meets Troy Bolton (played by Zac Efron), a very attractive boy with whom she is paired for a karaoke performance that brings the house down. Gabriella displays an amazing talent for performing, and she and Troy learn that they not only love to sing, but they love to sing together.

When Gabriella becomes the new transfer student at Troy's school after vacation ends, the principal remarks on her astounding academic record. Gabriella is quick to respond that she does not want to be "the school's freaky genius girl again." At her old school, Gabriella won first place in the chemistry competition and was labelled a "whiz kid" in the local paper. In order to protect herself from the possibility of negative attention, she opts to "lay low" at East High. But, despite her best intentions to keep her intelligence a secret, when her teacher incorrectly writes an equation on the board, Gabriella cannot help but correct her: "Ah, shouldn't the second equation read sixteen over pi?" Taylor, the head of the scholastic decathlon team, pushes for Gabriella to join them for their first competition of the year, but she refuses for fear of being teased. News of her academic success continues to spread, however, when singing rivals Sharpay and Ryan reveal to the entire school that she is an "Einsteinette."

At the same time as Gabriella's intelligence becomes the talk of the school, she also becomes well known for her budding romance with Troy. Gabriella attracts the attention of Troy, the captain of the basketball team, with her singing and her conventional beauty. She is petite, thin, and voluptuous. Her name, dark hair, and slightly darker skin tone denote that she is Latina, though her ethnicity is not mentioned in the film, nor written into the script as a part of her identity. Because there are so few smart girls of colour in popular culture (Conaway),[5] it is tempting to read Gabriella as a challenge to the racial and ethnic homogeneity of much popular culture.

But since her ethnicity is obscured, her character reproduces a hegemonic view of success rooted in emphasized femininity as it intersects with whiteness and middle-class values (Bettie). Her ability to fit in at her new school, both academically and socially, suggests that she possesses the kind of cultural capital typically reserved in popular culture for those fluent in the language of the dominant youth culture, including knowledge of current trends, colloquialisms, and styles (Bettie; Lareau).

The Rebel Girl: Veronica Mars

Like Rory and Gabriella, Veronica (played by Kristen Bell), the star character of the television show *Veronica Mars*, is also a smart supergirl—but with a rebel streak. Veronica's diverse range of skills is showcased early in the first season when she is presented as an accomplished private investigator who learned the trade from her father. From the beginning of the series, it is established that Veronica is smart academically, and especially technologically:

> *Ms. Dent:* This is a 35-millimetre camera. Now my suggestion as you're starting out is just to set it on auto and that way you—
>
> *Veronica:* I'd really be more comfortable if I could just use my own camera. Um, the swivel LCD really comes in handy when you're doing overhead shooting or ground-level macro shooting.
>
> *Ms. Dent:* Right . . .
>
> *Veronica:* The optical zoom actually goes up to 71.2 millimetres and it's good to have the raw file option because you can mess with the images post-exposure without nearly the loss of image quality you'd get with a JPEG file.

In this exchange with her journalism teacher in the pilot episode, Veronica illustrates her familiarity with photography and her confidence in demonstrating this familiarity to the teacher. In addition to being an ace with a camera, Veronica doctors videos, plants bugs, dismantles computers, and locates confidential information through the Internet. She has a phenomenal memory, a knack for creative sleuthing strategies, and an ability to impersonate a range of personalities when necessary. As Conaway notes, Veronica "is smarter than everyone around her, does well enough in high school to just miss becoming valedictorian, and is such a good student in her college criminology class that her teacher recommends her for an

internship at the FBI" (238). Veronica also possesses a range of characteristics that neither Rory nor Gabriella possesses, making her unique in the
genre of smart supergirls: toughness, indignation, and fearlessness in the
face of authority.

Veronica also has social intelligence, although her relationship to popularity is complicated, in part due to the show's dominant plot line in the
first season. In her recent past, she was a part of the wealthy in-crowd at
her school, despite her relative poverty, but, because her father accused the
patriarch of the most powerful family in Neptune of murder, she became
ostracized by this popular crowd. Despite these events, Veronica's confidence
and willingness to help other students faced with injustice foster a circle
of supportive friends from different groups in the school, and a grudging
respect from many others. Veronica's social success is also about her conventional attractiveness. She is slim, blond, athletic, and fashionable with a
funky, somewhat sporty look. Veronica is considered to be "hot," as two boys
at school comment in an episode entitled "Meet John Smith":

Owen: Eight and a half. That's my final offer.

Justin: Dude. She's that smokin' and a private eye? That's gotta make her at
least a nine.

Like Dean's less objectifying assessment of Rory, this quotation suggests
Veronica's charm lies in her "total package" persona. Being both beautiful
and talented makes her all the more desirable. As a result, Veronica has
little trouble attracting muscular, popular boyfriends, including popular,
rich Duncan Kane; Leo, a hunky young police officer; and the dysfunc-
tional, but handsome and rich, Logan Echolls.

Veronica is certainly not a nerd in the classic or makeover sense. She
can pretend to be nerdy if necessary, but her persona is smart, hip, and sexy,
and in the series she is clearly represented as someone who understands
herself in this way. In "You Think You Know Somebody," her friend Wallace
calls her "Velma," the classic girl-nerd in the cartoon *Scooby-Doo.* Her
response—"It's Daphne, thank you very much"—makes it clear that she
would prefer to be associated with the pretty yet ditzy character, rather than
with the klutzy yet brilliant one. However, in "Blast from the Past," she says
to her boyfriend, "You're here for your looks; why don't you leave the heavy
thinking to me, sugar-pants? Now go make yourself pretty." Viewers see
Veronica confidently embrace her own sexuality and her own intelligence.

Despite positioning Veronica as an outsider to some extent, the series also positions her as someone who is both smart and socially successful; her intelligence is, in fact, part of what is attractive about her to friends and lovers. Her cleverness does not undermine her but, rather, makes her more powerful.

Analyzing the Post-Nerd: Intersections of Post-feminism and Neo-liberalism

The post-nerd presents a complex and attractive representation of smart girls in popular culture. The figures of Rory, Gabriella, and Veronica clearly challenge representations of classic and makeover nerds by illustrating that academic success is not antithetical to sexual desirability, social success, or extracurricular talent. On the contrary, Rory, Gabriella, and Veronica are depicted as intelligent, and this intelligence is an advantage on the social and dating scene. All three smart girls manage to attract the popular boys at their school because they stand out from the "typical" girl who focuses on cheerleading and makeup. They are also shown to be strong in their ability to go against the grain, rather than follow the in-crowd. What makes these representations so commanding is that each girl is able to achieve success at anything to which she puts her mind. For young people watching, Rory, Gabriella, and Veronica offer exciting examples of multitalented female subjects who are also beautiful, stylish, funny, and refreshing. While seemingly positive, however, these representations add to a girl-power version of girlhood that is grounded in the depoliticizing discourses of post-feminism and neo-liberalism.

Girl power began as a declaration of power by Riot grrrl bands in the mid-1990s, with "girl power" shorthand for "a sexy, brash, and individualized expression of ambition, power, and success" (Harris 17; see also Currie, Kelly, and Pomerantz; Gonick, "Between 'Girl Power'"). Yet as Harris notes, girl power was quickly and easily co-opted by marketers as a "discourse of choice and focus on the self," making it the defining feature of girls who are "self-inventing, ambitious, and confident" (17). Girl power became a highly lucrative branding strategy in the late 1990s and early 2000s, celebrated through merchandise, celebrities, and plot lines that epitomized female independence, consumerism-as-power, sexual prowess, and the narrative of reinvention, all set against the backdrop of presumed gender equality. In this way, girl power has become a post-feminist discourse in its celebration of girls' individualism and its negation of gender inequality. Angela

McRobbie describes how post-feminism becomes visible in popular culture, when "female freedom and ambition appear to be taken for granted, unreliant on past struggle . . . and certainly not requiring any new, fresh political understanding, but instead merely a state into which young women appear to have been thrown, or in which they find themselves" ("Notes on Postfeminism" 6).

Rory, Gabriella, and Veronica exist in a post-feminist universe, where feminism is entirely unnecessary. While feminism is mentioned in the pilot episode of *Gilmore Girls*, it never surfaces as a key discourse, even though Rory is raised by a single mother who left an oppressive home to live on her own terms while working as a maid. Though viewers might logically expect Rory's mother to be a feminist in this context, Rory is depicted as facing a range of choices, easily and independently achieving her goals, and never encountering sexism either in her dating life or in the academic worlds of her private high school or at Yale. Similarly, Gabriella offers no critique of gender constructions, even though East High revolves around the worship of its basketball team, which is so heterosexist and hegemonically masculine that the mere thought of its star player wanting to sing in a musical threatens to unravel the entire school. Though Gabriella clearly lives in a sexist social world, neither she nor anyone else in the film acknowledges this gender inequality. Instead, commensurate with a post-feminist landscape, Gabriella exists as if the school were absolutely gender and race neutral. Gabriella performs white girl femininity and middle-class academic, extracurricular success without ever engaging with the complex intersectionality of her identity as both female and Latina (Bettie; Gonick, *Between Femininities*).

While *Gilmore Girls* and *High School Musical* are set against a backdrop of post-feminism, it is *Veronica Mars* that presents the clearest post-feminist plot line when, in its third season, Veronica tries to solve the mystery of multiple rape cases on her college campus. While fraternity boys foil her at every turn, it is the group of feminists from "Lilith House"—represented as the very worst kind of "femi-nazis"—who truly work against her; in their obsessive desperation to have the fraternities on campus outlawed, they fake the occurrence of at least one rape. While Rory and Gabriella exist in a world that is presumed to be devoid of gender trouble, Veronica battles misogynist sexual violence but never names these battles as examples of disturbing gender inequality. Instead, she independently deals with individual "assholes" one at a time while also battling feminists. In their analysis of post-feminism in teen films, Deirdre M. Kelly and Shauna Pomerantz call this lack of structural insight a closed loop (xiv) that causes female characters to blame individuals rather than implicate broader constructs of power and inequality. Girls in film and television are not granted access to a language of opposition that would enable them to name structural inequities, such as sexism, racism, homophobia, ageism, or ableism in order to understand and challenge their experiences.

Dawn H. Currie, Kelly, and Pomerantz note that girl power has become a highly diversified representational strategy, generating multiple discursive meanings that define girl power in relation to meanness, hyper-sexuality, new feminine toughness, rebellion, and the pursuit of perfection. The last signification best exemplifies neo-liberal effects on representations of smart girls. While the classic and makeover nerds were concerned with climbing up from the lowest rung on the social ladder in order to attract a boyfriend, the post-nerd is concerned with perfection. As Rory, Gabriella, and Veronica show, smart supergirls excel at everything from school and extracurricular activities to dating and their consuming body projects (Brumberg). Harris's depiction of the "can-do" girl similarly describes girls striving for supergirl perfection. These girls, both real "can-do" girls and media supergirl characters, shape themselves into ideal, flexible, capable, and confident students, consumers, and workers, all in agreement with the demands of global neo-liberalism.

The post-nerd is a punishing role model for girls looking to popular culture for acceptable subject positions. Such representations suggest that perfection is attainable to any girl who tries hard enough with a "can-do" attitude, regardless of the structural inequities that stand in her way. Similarly, if a girl fails, such representations suggest that it is the girl's fault alone (Harris; see also Pomerantz and Raby). Rory, Gabriella, and Veronica all display a bootstrapping mentality; they convey the idea that girls of all races, ethnicities, classes, and sexualities exist on a level playing field and, therefore, have equal chances for success, yet at the same time privilege and emulate white middle-classness. The producers of *High School Musical* present Gabriella, one of the few smart girls of colour in popular culture, as a symbol of meritocracy as she walks into a new school and quickly attains the highest level of success in academic, social, and extracurricular areas. Yet this is not the reality for most girls. As Harris makes clear, "there are many young women who are not succeeding, both those who are structur-ally disadvantaged by poverty and racism, as well as those who are far more privileged and yet cannot cope with the enormous pressure on them to achieve" (34). In a *Gilmore Girls* episode entitled "The Incredible Shrinking

Loreleis," Rory comes close to the latter description. Her professor asks her to drop a class at Yale because she is on the verge of failing. Since failure has never been in her lexicon, she berates herself for not being "perfect" enough. Sobbing on Dean's shoulder, she explains, "It's a *really* big deal. I'm not supposed to drop a class. I'm not the drop-a-class person. I get good grades. I—*handle* things." While the episode gestures toward the enormous stress of being a smart supergirl in the world outside the text, Rory recovers herself in time to continue her pursuit of perfection in the next episode, when her balance is magically restored.

As Rory's character illustrates, individualism goes hand in hand with girl power's pursuit of perfection, where girls "handle things" on their own. The smart supergirl fends for herself and relies as little as possible on others for help. While Rory, Gabriella, and Veronica are supported within networks of family and friends, they all come to a point when they feel they must triumph over some significant obstacle alone. For Veronica, individualism means conducting many sleuthing operations without her dad's knowledge and letting her friends in on her investigations only when she needs their skills. Veronica even attempts to single-handedly restore her dad's reputation. Like Buffy, her vampire-slaying predecessor, Veronica is surrounded by family and friends, yet remains alone: stoic, responsible, and unable to ask for help. Veronica maintains her cool exterior in the face of heartbreak and disappointment; she exposes anxiety and stress only when alone, thus protecting others from worrying about her.

Individualism is further emphasized in the way that the smart supergirl characters achieve success, represented in the texts through personal tenacity; bodily composure; a keen sense of style; a fit, sexy body; and the assumption through narrative logic that each of these girls *will* succeed no matter what comes their way. The viewer never doubts the girls' abilities to rise above any problem, which is always represented as personal rather than structural. Rory is a perfect example of this individualized success. While her mother is not rich, her grandparents are, and they provide Rory with tuition to Chilton and Yale, a car, dorm room furniture, and all the spending money she needs for clothes and a social life. Rory benefits enormously from her grandparents' desire to see her succeed, but the show does not link Rory's academic success to her grandparents' fortune. Rather than acknowledging how this economic capital might have made Rory's life easier and offered her the kind of cultural capital necessary to succeed (Lareau), the show focuses specifically on Rory's individual determination in spite of her grandparents' wealth, her refusal to take "too much," and her mother's estranged relationship with her parents as evidence that Rory did it "all by herself." The financial support from Rory's grandparents thus functions as icing on the cake, but never as the actual reason why Rory is so successful at both school and the work life alluded to in the series' final episode.

Classic and makeover nerd characters are portrayed through a narrow kind of gender performativity. They are presented to viewers as one-dimensional characters without sass, savvy, or sexual desirability. In contrast, the post-nerd characters we have analyzed here are tightly wound perfectionists whose personal struggles are never connected to sexism, racism, heterosexism, and other social inequities. While these characters are constructed as girls who have it all, we conclude our chapter by problematizing this representation for what it may mean in the lives of actual girls and speculating as to what kind of representations would make for more liberating examples of smart girls.

Packaging the Smart Girl

The smart supergirl is portrayed in popular television texts as *almost* perfect, with intelligence, desirability, talent, and a fulfilling social life. Though the characters of Rory, Gabriella, and Veronica all experience challenges, heartache, and disappointment, their framing as likeable leads in highly rated popular cultural texts showcases their lifestyle as worthy of emulation. But while success for Rory, Gabriella, and Veronica hinges on smartness and other talents, it is also importantly defined through their attractiveness to hegemonically masculine boys. Also, though heterosexual "hotness" and normative beauty are key to these girls' success stories, we never see them working out, worrying about what they eat, or dieting. Post-nerd representations thus contain smart girls by restricting their intelligence through a non-threatening package of seemingly easy attractiveness. As Westman contends in her analysis of *Gilmore Girls*, "feminine beauty allows [smart women] to 'pass,' to be accepted by both the geek subculture and popular culture." Westman argues that this acceptance effectively "contains their brilliance" (16) and their independence within a form of feminine attractiveness and sexuality that is appealing to young, straight men, and therefore more palatable to those who espouse patriarchal ideals. As Naomi Wolf similarly argues in *The Beauty Myth*, as women gain power in other arenas, standards of female beauty intensify. Representations of the smart supergirl thus constrain girls' performances of smartness by insinuating that intelligence must be performed within the boundaries of impossible standards of slim, sexy attractiveness. Given that conventionally "hot" and "sexy" bodies are the only bodies linked to smart supergirl representations, we can ask, along with Butler, "how bodies which fail to materialize provide the necessary 'outside,' if not the necessary support, for the bodies which, in materializing the norm, qualify as bodies that matter" (*Bodies That Matter* 16). The racialized, working-class, and non-hypersexualized bodies that are absent in these popular cultural texts emphasize the "normal" status of the white and middle-class (or emulating white and middle-class), hypersexualized, feminine bodies. As a result of these presences and absences, such bodies become the only bodies that matter in smart girl representations.

Performances of success are constructed through narrow, conventional terms. For the smart supergirl in popular culture, success is always about achieving As in school, attending a good university, and attaining an ambitious career. Reflecting girl power rhetoric, characters' achievements of these kinds of goals are portrayed as "deftly pursuing middle-class avenues and definitions of success, namely conventional forms of academic, athletic, artistic, and interpersonal achievement as well as community service" (Currie, Kelly, and Pomerantz 40; see also Bettie; Walkerdine, Lucey, and Melody). We do not see smart supergirls challenging dominant social structures or dropping out of an oppressive education system that cannot cater to their needs, nor do we see alternative versions of success that might revolve around non-Western ideals. Part of the problem with the perfectionism of smart supergirls is that, while they are intelligent, they are also confined to the narrow representation of the middle-class dream: college and successful employment, conventional dating, beauty, and the consumer habits that necessarily accompany these hegemonic expectations. Extrapolating from Öslem Sensoy and Elizabeth Marshall's theory of missionary girl power, the smart supergirl thus exports the idea that the way to be smart is to emulate white, straight, and middle-class girlhood. For girls of poor or working-class backgrounds, and for girls who are not white or straight, this representation can be read as a directive to reproduce dominant power structures in order to achieve success—academic or otherwise—in life.

Performing Smartness and Girlhood Differently

Given the way that representations of the post-nerd circumscribe an idealized girlhood, our chapter concludes by asking whether the smart supergirl nonetheless offers a broader range of possibilities to viewers than the classic girl nerd. The classic girl nerd is frequently portrayed as lonely and desperate to fit in. She is an abject figure who is often subject to teasing by her peers. While some girls may secretly embrace the classic girl nerd for her intelligence, independent path, and distinct identity, the classic nerd is not rewarded in popular culture. In contrast, the post-nerd reflected in characters such as Rory, Gabriella, and Veronica is comfortable with her smartness, confident, befriended by others, and loved by handsome young men. But these post-nerd representations are also ironically elusive to real girls who do not meet their ambitious, narrow, and normative expectations for femininity and success. The post-nerd reifies the consumerist, individualized, and hypersexualized ethos of girl power, while also signalling to girls that intelligence is not enough—they must also be hot, thin, stylish, and entangled in a heterosexual dating matrix in order to be seen as successful (see Renold; Renold and Allan; Ringrose). Given how oppressive this model for success is, what other representations are out there in mainstream popular culture that better nurture self-acceptance for different kinds of girls?

While characters like Rory, Gabriella, and Veronica appear to be flawless examples of success, they also experience themselves as independent outsiders. Rory intentionally separates herself from many of the other students at her school, recognizing her difference from them and enjoying her solitude. Gabriella is drawn reluctantly into the academic sphere of her school, as she sees the need to protect her smart girl identity from other students, but also values her more nerdish smart girl friends. Veronica aspires to be in the popular crowd, but also savours her unique status as a smart sleuth, embraces various unique friends, and experiences herself as a loner. It may be in these small fissures that othered smart girls can find more liberating models. Yet, while there are fissures in how smart girls are constructed, opening up possibilities for viewers to eschew hegemonic norms (Butler, *Bodies That Matter*), we certainly see room for improvement in how smart girls are portrayed in popular culture.

One example of a less conventional smart girl representation is the character of Juno MacGuff from the critically acclaimed 2007 film *Juno*. When a popular jock teases Juno about how "ugly" she is, her voiceover comically notes just the opposite:

> The funny thing is that Steve Rendazo secretly wants me. Jocks like him always want freaky girls. Girls with horn-rimmed glasses and vegan footwear and goth makeup. Girls who, like, play the cello and read *McSweeney's*, and wanna be children's librarians when they grow up. Oh, yeah, jocks totally

eat that shit up. They just won't admit it because they're supposed to be into the perfect cheerleaders.

Juno sees herself as a "freaky girl," and she is on the social margins of her school—a position that is reaffirmed through her decision not to have an abortion when she becomes pregnant. Juno, while white and slim, spends much of the film big with her pregnancy and is far from a conventionally feminine dresser. She is also very clearly located as working class and chooses a feminine, "emo" boy as her sexual partner rather than the Steve Rendazo jocks of her school. In all these ways Juno does not fit the post-nerd trope. And yet Juno has a confidence and a satisfaction with her world-view that helps her deal with the challenges of her situation. As Wesley Morris writes, "'Juno' serves cool, intelligent girls something they rarely see in a movie: themselves."

Another powerful example of less conventional smart girlhood can be found in the critically acclaimed Fox musical comedy-drama, *Glee* (Fox, 2009–present). Rachel Berry (played by Lea Michele) is a highly complex character who vacillates between selfish narcissist and dedicated team player throughout the course of most episodes. Rachel is the Glee Club's prima donna lead female singer who is unbearably ambitious and determined to succeed in all pursuits, musical or otherwise. The daughter of a same-sex, interracial couple, Rachel, who is Jewish, is ostracized for her lack of cultural capital, her pursuit of academic achievements, and her overbearing personality. But like Juno, what makes Rachel so interesting is her refusal to conform to conventional girlhood. Her style is unfashionable and she is often shown to actively alienate her classmates. Rachel prefers to stand on the periphery of her school's social world because she feels this social position offers her the freedom to follow her perfectionist pursuits in school and extracurricular activities. Rachel's powerful and determined nature mark her as a radically unfeminine subject by classic and post-nerd standards. She quite simply refuses to repeat "nice" girl normative behaviour. Yet these quirky traits eventually attract the love of the school's quarterback and fellow Glee Club member, Finn, who admires her power and talent. Finn, while typically masculine on the surface, also performs a non-normative identity as a jock with a deep and sensitive soul, and as the lead male in the Glee Club.

We advocate for producers, directors, and screen writers to diversify the portrayal of smart girl performativity in order to include complex characters, such as Juno and Rachel, who are not conventionally beautiful, but who are still able to maintain satisfying social lives. We would like to see girls who are realistically aware of their racialized, cultural, and class backgrounds, and other social positionings, which may impede or contribute to their academic success. And, of course, we would like to see smart girls who are able to connect with political action and social justice, thereby offering real girls much-needed access to a language of opposition, such as feminism and anti-racism. But instead of such intersectional characters, the more dominant post-nerd supergirls we have analyzed in this chapter flourish alongside lingering classic nerds (for example, Alex from *Modern Family*, ABC, 2009–present). Post-nerd representations thus accomplish two less positive, contradictory aims: they fulfill the problematic post-feminist, neo-liberal vision of a society free of gender and other inequalities in which individuals either fail or succeed on their own merit, and they contain smart girls' brilliance in pretty, sexualized packages that remain palatable to the masses. Given these characteristics, the smart supergirl of early-twenty-first-century popular culture may be merely an illusion of feminist progress.

Notes

1 Our chapter analyzes two television shows and one made-for-television movie, which have smart high school girls as the lead characters. The texts were chosen for their target teen and tween girl audience, commercial success, and cultural impact.

2 While it is widely acknowledged within cultural studies that people do not read signs the same way, Hall notes that representations offer a preferred reading that limits the possibility for alternative understandings.

3 For good examples, see *Revenge of the Nerds*, *The Breakfast Club*, and *Freaks and Geeks*.

4 For an extensive list of classic girl nerds in popular culture, see Conaway.

5 Another exception to this pattern is the elementary school character Akeela, who shines in a spelling bee in *Akeela and the Bee*.

Works Cited

Aapola, Sinikka, Marnina Gonick, and Anita Harris. *Young Femininity: Girlhood, Power and Social Change*. London: Palgrave, 2004. Print.

Akeelah and the Bee. Dir. Doug Atchinson. Lion's Gate Films, 2006. DVD.

Barthes, Roland. *Mythologies*. Paris: Editions du Seuil, 1957. Print.

Bettie, Julie. *Women without Class: Girls, Race, and Identity.* Berkeley: U of California P, 2003. Print.

"Blast from the Past." *Veronica Mars.* Dir. Harry Winer. Warner Home Video, 2007. DVD.

The Breakfast Club. Dir. John Hughes. Universal Pictures, 1998. DVD.

"The Break Up, Part 2." *Gilmore Girls.* Dir. Nick Marck. Warner, 2007. DVD.

Brumberg, Joan Jacobs. *The Body Project: An Intimate History of American Girls.* New York: Random House, 1997. Print.

Burr, Vivien. *An Introduction to Social Constructionism.* London: Routledge, 1995. Print.

Butler, Judith. *Bodies That Matter: On the Discursive Limits of "Sex."* New York: Routledge, 1993. Print.

———. "For a Careful Reading." *Feminist Contentions: A Philosophical Exchange.* Ed. Seyla Benhabib, Judith Butler, Drucilla Cornell, and Nancy Fraser. New York: Routledge, 1995. 127–44. Print.

———. *Gender Trouble: Feminism and the Subversion of Identity. 1989.* New York: Routledge, 1990. Print.

———. *Undoing Gender.* New York: Routledge, 2004. Print.

Chaudry, Lakshmi. "The Supergirl Syndrome." *The Nation.* 1 May 2007. Web. 17 Sept. 2012.

Conaway, Sandra B. "Girls Who (Don't) Wear Glasses: The Performativity of Smart Girls on Teen Television." Diss. Bowling Green State U, 2007. Print.

Connell, Robert W. *Gender and Power.* Stanford: Stanford UP, 1987. Print.

Currie, Dawn H., Deirdre M. Kelly, and Shauna Pomerantz. *"Girl Power": Girls Reinventing Girlhoods.* New York: Peter Lang, 2009. Print.

During, Simon. *Cultural Studies: A Critical Introduction.* New York: Routledge, 2005. Print.

———. *The Cultural Studies Reader.* 3rd. ed. London: Routledge, 2007. Print.

Foucault, Michel. *The Archaeology of Knowledge.* London: Tavistock, 1972. Print.

Francis, Becky, and Christine Skelton. *Reassessing Gender and Achievement: Questioning Contemporary Key Debates.* London: Routledge, 2005. Print.

Fraser, Nancy. "The Uses and Abuses of French Discourse Theories for Feminist Politics." *Revaluing French Feminism: Critical Essays on Difference, Agency, and Culture.* Ed. Nancy Fraser and Sandra Lee Bartky. Bloomington: Indiana UP, 1992. 177–94. Print.

Freaks and Geeks. Perf. Linda Cardellini, John Francis Daley, James Franco, Samm Levine, Seth Rogen, and Jason Segel. Apatow Productions and Dreamworks Television, 1999–2000. Television.

Gill, Rosalind, and Christina Scharff. *New Femininities: Postfeminism, Neoliberalism and Subjectivity*. New York: Palgrave Macmillan, 2011. Print.

Glee. Perf. Jane Lynch, Lea Michele, Matthew Morrison, Cory Monteith, and Chris Colfer. 20th Century Fox Television, 2009–present. Television.

Gonick, Marnina. *Between Femininities: Ambivalence, Identity, and the Education of Girls*. Albany: State U of New York P, 2003. Print.

———. "Between 'Girl Power' and 'Reviving Ophelia': Constituting the Neoliberal Girl Subject." *NWSA Journal* 18.2 (2006): 1–23. Print.

Hall, Stuart. *Representation: Cultural Representations and Signifying Practices*. Thousand Oaks: Sage and Open University, 1997. Print.

"Hammers and Veils." *Gilmore Girls*. Dir. Michael Katleman. Warner, 2007. DVD.

Harris, Anita. *Future Girl: Young Women in the Twenty-First Century*. New York: Routledge, 2004. Print.

High School Musical. Dir. Kenny Ortega. Perf. Zac Efron, Vanessa Hudgens, and Ashley Tisdale. Buena Vista Home Entertainment, 2006. DVD.

"The Incredible Shrinking Loreleis." *Gilmore Girls*. Dir. Stephen Clancy. Warner, 2007. DVD.

Inness, Sherrie A. *Geek Chic: Smart Women in Popular Culture*. New York: Palgrave Macmillan, 2007. Print.

Juno. Dir. Jason Reitman. Perf. Ellen Page, Michael Cera, and Jennifer Garner. 20th Century Fox, 2007. DVD.

Kelly, Deirdre M., and Shauna Pomerantz. "Mean, Wild, and Alienated: Girls and the State of Feminism in Popular Culture." *Girlhood Studies: An Interdisciplinary Journal* 2.1 (2009): 1–17. Print.

Kindlon, Daniel J. *Alpha Girls: Understanding the New American Girl and How She Is Changing the World*. New York: Rodale, 2006. Print.

Lareau, Annette. *Unequal Childhoods: Class, Race, and Family Life*. Berkeley: U of California P, 2003. Print.

"Like Mother, Like Daughter." *Gilmore Girls*. Dir. Dennis Erdman. Warner, 2007. DVD.

McRobbie, Angela. *The Aftermath of Feminism: Gender, Culture and Social Change*. London: Sage, 2009. Print.

———. "Notes on Postfeminism and Popular Culture: Bridget Jones and the New Gender Regime." *All About the Girl: Culture, Power, and Identity*. Ed. Anita Harris. New York, London: Routledge, 2004. 3–14. Print.

"Meet John Smith." *Veronica Mars*. Dir. Harry Winer. Warner Home Video, 2005. DVD.

Modern Family. Perf. Ed O'Neill, Sofia Vergara, Julie Bowen, and Ty Burrell. 20th Century Fox Television, 2009–present. Television.

Morris, Wesley. "'Juno' Lets Smart Girls Identify with Its Glib but Sweet Spin on a Teen's Life-Altering Decision." *Boston Globe* 24 Feb. 2008. Print.

Nash, Ilana. *American Sweethearts: Teenage Girls in Twentieth-Century Popular Culture.* Bloomington: Indiana UP, 2006. Print.

Never Been Kissed. Dir. Raja Gosnell. Perf. Drew Barrymore, David Arquette, and Michael Vartan. 20th Century Fox, 1999. DVD.

Niemi, Nancy S. "The Emperor Has No Clothes: Examining the Impossible Relationship Between Gendered and Academic Identities in Middle School Students." *Gender and Education* 17.5 (2005): 483–97. Print.

Pascoe, C. J. *Dude, You're a Fag: Masculinity and Sexuality in High School.* Berkeley: U of California P, 2007. Print.

"Pilot." *Gilmore Girls.* Dir. Lesli Linka Glatter. Warner, 2007. DVD.

"Pilot." *Square Pegs.* Dir. Kim Friedman. Sony Pictures Home Entertainment, 2008. DVD.

"Pilot." *Veronica Mars.* Dir. Mark Piznarski. Warner, 2005. DVD.

Pomerantz, Shauna, and Rebecca Raby. "Smart Girls: Negotiating Academic Identities in a 'Post-Feminist' Era." *Gender and Education* 23.5 (2011): 549–64. Print.

Radford, Marie L., and Gary P. Radford. "Librarians and Party Girls: Cultural Studies and the Meaning of the Librarian." *Library Quarterly* 73.1 (2003): 54–69. Print.

Renold, Emma. "'Square-Girls': Femininity and the Negotiation of Academic Success in the Primary School." *British Educational Research Journal* 27.5 (2001): 577–88. Print.

Renold, Emma, and Alexandra Allan. "Bright and Beautiful: High Achieving Girls, Ambivalent Femininities, and the Feminization of Success in the Primary School." *Discourse: Studies in the Cultural Politics of Education* 27.4 (2006): 457–73. Print.

Revenge of the Nerds. Dir. Bob Clark. 1984. Fox Home Entertainment, 2007. DVD.

Rimer, Sara. "For Girls, It's Be Yourself, and Be Perfect, Too." *New York Times* 28 June 2009. Web. 17 Sept. 2012.

Ringrose, Jessica. "Successful Girls? Complicating Post-Feminist, Neoliberal Discourses of Educational Achievement and Gender Equality." *Gender and Education* 19.4 (2007): 471–89. Print.

Ringrose, Jessica, and Valerie Walkerdine. "What Does It Mean to Be a Girl in the Twenty-First Century? Exploring Some Contemporary Dilemmas of

Femininity and Girlhood in the West." *Girl Culture: An Encyclopedia.* Ed. Claudia A. Mitchell and Jacqueline Reid-Walsh. Westport: Greenwood P, 2008. Print.

Sensoy, Öslem, and Elizabeth Marshall. "Missionary Girl Power: Saving the 'Third World' One Girl at a Time." *Gender and Education* 22.3 (2010): 295–311. Print.

She's All That. Dir. Robert Iscove. Perf. Freddie Prince, Jr., and Rachel Leigh Cook. Miramax Films, 1999. DVD.

Storey, John. *Cultural Studies and the Study of Popular Culture: Theories and Methods.* Athens: U of Georgia P, 1996. Print.

Walkerdine, Valerie, Helen Lucey, and June Melody. *Growing Up Girl: Psychosocial Explorations of Gender and Class.* Houndmills: Palgrave, 2001. Print.

Weedon, Chris. *Feminist Practice and Poststructuralist Theory.* New York: B. Blackwell, 1987. Print.

Westman, Karin E. "Beauty and the Geek: Changing Gender Stereotypes in the *Gilmore Girls.*" *Geek Chic: Smart Women in Popular Culture.* Ed. Sherrie A. Inness. New York: Palgrave Macmillan, 2007. Print.

Willis, Jessica L. "Sexual Subjectivity: A Semiotic Analysis of Girlhood, Sex, and Sexuality in the Film *Juno.*" *Sexuality and Culture* 12 (2008): 240–56. Print.

Wolf, Naomi. *The Beauty Myth: How Images of Beauty Are Used against Women.* New York: Anchor Books, 1992. Print.

"You Think You Know Somebody." *Veronica Mars.* Dir. Nick Gomez. Warner Home Video, 2005. DVD.

CONTRIBUTORS

CLARE BRADFORD is Alfred Deakin Professor of Literary Studies at Deakin University in Melbourne, Australia. She began her scholarly career as a medievalist and developed an interest in children's literature when she took up a teaching position in this area. She has published more than seventy essays and book chapters on children's and other literature. Her books include *Reading Race: Aboriginality in Australian Children's Literature* (2001), which won both the Children's Literature Association Book Award and the International Research Society for Children's Literature Award; *Unsettling Narratives: Postcolonial Readings of Children's Literature* (2007); *New World Orders in Contemporary Children's Literature: Utopian Transformations* (2009) (with Mallan, Stephens, and McCallum); and *The Middle Ages in Children's Literature* (2015). In 2009 she was awarded the first International Trudeau Fellowship. She was president of the International Research Society for Children's Literature from 2007 to 2011. She is a fellow of the Australian Academy of Humanities.

ELIZABETH BULLEN is a senior lecturer in literary studies at Deakin University, Australia. She researches in the fields of children's literature, the sociology of education, and the cultural studies of education, with a focus on class, consumerism, and gender. Her research on female sexuality attends to the intersection of these forces in fiction. Since the publication of *Consuming Children: Education, Advertising, Entertainment* (2001), she has published over thirty journal articles, chapters, and books, including *Haunting the Knowledge Economy* (2006).

KABITA CHAKRABORTY is an assistant professor in the Children's Studies Program at York University. Her key areas of research and teaching are girlhoods in slum communities in South Asia; young people's experiences of migration in Asia-Pacific; young women's sexual and reproductive health in South and Southeast Asia; participatory methods with children and youth; and problematizing international children's rights discourses. She is committed to the development of majority-world scholarship, especially through her research partnerships in South and Southeast Asia. Her forthcoming book *Young Muslim Women in India: Bollywood, Identity and Changing Lives* will be published by Routledge.

DAWN H. CURRIE is professor of sociology at the University of British Columbia, Canada. She is also past chair of the undergraduate women's studies program and past graduate advisor for the Centre for Research in Women and Gender Studies. Her research interests include girl cultures and feminist media education. She is author of *Girl Talk: Adolescent Magazines and Their Readers* (1999) and co-author of *"Girl Power": Girls Reinventing Girlhood* (2009), as well as a number of journal articles and book chapters on girl cultures, feminist theory, and feminist methodology. As part of her interest in teaching for social justice, during the past few years she has become involved in designing curriculum and resource materials for students taking service placements in Uganda, Swaziland, and South Africa.

SUZANNE DE CASTELL is dean of the Faculty of Education at the University of Ontario Institute of Technology, Canada. She has published extensively, initially in educational history, philosophy, and theory; moving on to literacy studies and to gender, equity, and technology research; and currently focusing on new media and educational technologies, particularly digital game-based learning.

SANDRINA DE FINNEY is an associate professor in the School of Child and Youth Care at the University of Victoria, Canada. A youth worker by training, she brings a strong interdisciplinary focus drawn from transnational, anti-colonial, and Indigenous feminist studies to her work as a community-based researcher, educator, and practitioner. Dr. de Finney is co-founder of *antidote*, an award-winning grassroots network for racialized girls and women, and a principal investigator for the Siem Smun'eem Indigenous Child Welfare Research Network. Her recent publications include essays in the journals *Girlhood Studies*; *Pimatisiwin*; *International Journal of Child, Youth and Family Studies*; *First Peoples Child and Family Review*; and *Journal of Intercultural Studies*.

STEPHANIE FISHER is a doctoral student in York University's language, culture, and teaching program in Toronto, Canada. Since 2006, Stephanie has worked on a range of research projects on the use of technologies for education, including developing and designing educational games, reviewing the integration of information and communication technology in formal education systems globally, problem-based blended and online learning in higher education, the cultivation of new media literacies in K–12 school and informal contexts, and ethnographic research on women and gender in digital games cultures. Stephanie provides academic and institutional support for Dames Making Games Toronto, a feminist organization dedicated to supporting female game hobbyists and professionals.

JENNIFER JENSON is a professor of pedagogy and technology in the Faculty of Education, York University, Canada. Her research and publications include work on gender and technologies, gender and digital gameplay, players and identities in MMOGs (massively multiplayer online games), technology and education, and technology policies and policy practices in K–12 education in Canada. In addition, she has designed and developed several educationally focused digital games with a team of people from York, Simon Fraser University, and Seneca College.

PAMELA KNIGHTS began her career as a teacher of English literature in sixth-form colleges (for sixteen-to-nineteen-year-olds) before moving into higher education. On joining Durham University, she retained an interest in teacher education, alongside her main role as a Senior Lecturer in the Department of English Studies; she taught and researched in American fiction and in children's literature, which she introduced in the early 1990s as a special topic for academic study. She has been involved in various UK nationally funded projects for innovative approaches with students, including a National Teaching Fellowship, and activities with the Higher Education Academy English Subject Centre, and the MEDAL project consortium. She was a board member and secretary of the International Research Society in Children's Literature (IRSCL), from 2006 to 2009, serving as the founding executive editor for the new IRSCL journal, *International Research in Children's Literature* (Edinburgh University Press), from 2007. Recent publications include essays on child cultures in *The Cambridge Companion to Kate Chopin*; on "The Marriage Market" in *Edith Wharton in Context*; and on nineteenth-century young American women travellers' experience of Venice, in *Venice and the Cultural Imagination*. She has introduced and edited various nineteenth- and early-twentieth-century authors, including *The Awakening and Other Stories*, by pioneer feminist Kate Chopin, for Oxford World's Classics (2000); R. D. Blackmore's *Lorna Doone*; and selected novels by Edith Wharton. She is also the author of *Edith Wharton's* The House of Mirth, with Janet Beer and Elizabeth Nolan (2007), and *The Cambridge Introduction to Edith Wharton* (2009). Having taken early retirement in 2011, she is now an independent scholar, and is currently working on a book about ballet and performance for children, to be published by Palgrave in the series New Critical Approaches to Children's Literature.

KERRY MALLAN is a professor in the Faculty of Education and director of the Children and Youth Research Centre at Queensland University of Technology, Australia. During her undergraduate and postgraduate studies in education, Kerry undertook majors in sociology and literary studies. She was introduced to the study of children's literature when she did a postgraduate qualification in teacher-librarianship. Her interest in gender studies began during her master's degree and was a key domain of her doctoral thesis. Kerry has published widely in children's literature. Her most significant publications are *Secrets, Lies and Children's Fiction* (2013); *Gender Dilemmas in Children's Fiction* (2009); *New World Orders in Contemporary Children's Literature* with Clare Bradford, John Stephens, and Robyn McCallum (2008); *Contemporary Children's Literature and Film: Engaging with Theory* co-edited with Clare Bradford (2011); and *Youth Cultures: Texts, Images and Identities* co-edited with Sharyn Pearce (2003: IRSCL Honour Book).

CLAUDIA MITCHELL is a James McGill Professor in the Faculty of Education, McGill University, Canada, where she is the founder of the Participatory Cultures Lab, and where she is a research associate of the Institute of Studies in International Development and the Institute of Gender, Sexuality and Feminist Studies. She is also an honorary professor in the School of Education, University of KwaZulu-Natal, in Durban, South Africa, where she founded the Centre for Visual Methodologies for Social Change. Her research spans such areas as youth and media studies, young adult literature, girlhood studies, and memory work and self-study with pre-service and in-service teachers, through to participatory visual and other arts-based methodologies. In developing and applying such methods as photovoice, participatory video, drawing, object-study, and recent work with mobile phones in "cellphilm" production, she has explored the links between participation and policy work in the context of addressing HIV and AIDS and related issues of gender-based violence in rural sub-Saharan Africa. She has authored, co-authored, or co-edited twenty books in the areas of girlhood, teacher education, and participatory visual methodologies, including *Doing Visual Research, Researching Children's Popular Culture* (with Jacqueline Reid-Walsh), *Reinventing Ourselves as Teachers: Beyond Nostalgia* (with Sandra Weber), *Memory and Pedagogy* (with Teresa Strong-Wilson, Kathleen Pithouse, and Susann Allnutt), *Methodologies for Mapping a Southern African Girlhood in the Age of AIDS* (with Relebohile Moletsane, Ann Smith, and Linda Chisholm), and the *Handbook on Participatory Video* (with E. J. Milne and Naydene de Lange). She is the co-founder and co-editor of *Girlhood Studies: An Interdisciplinary Journal*.

KRISTINE MORUZI is a lecturer in the School of Communication and Creative Arts and a Discovery Early Career Researcher in the Centre for Memory, Imagination and Invention at Deakin University, Australia. Her monograph, *Constructing Girlhood through the Periodical Press, 1850–1915*, was published in 2012. Her current research is on representations of colonial girlhood in Canadian print culture between 1840 and 1940. With Michelle J. Smith, she co-edited

Girls' School Stories, 1749–1929 (2014), a six-volume anthology published in Routledge's History of Feminism series. She is also co-editor of *Colonial Girlhood in Literature, Culture and History, 1840–1950* (2014) and a special issue of the *Australasian Journal of Victorian Studies* on colonial girlhood in 2013.

SHAUNA POMERANTZ is associate professor at Brock University, Canada, in the Department of Child and Youth Studies. She has a Ph.D. in education from the University of British Columbia, where she studied sociology of education, women's and gender studies, and cultural studies. Her research focuses on qualitative explorations of girlhood and youth culture, particularly in relation to how young people negotiate and challenge the discursive-material context of schools. She is author of *Girls, Style, and School Identities: Dressing the Part* (Palgrave, 2008) and co-author (with Dawn H. Currie and Deirdre M. Kelly) of *Girl Power: Girls Reinventing Girlhood* (Peter Lang, 2009). Shauna has also published articles and book chapters on the topics of gender and academic success, post-feminism, girl skateboarders, computer girls, representations of girlhood in popular culture, and girls' identity construction in school. Her forthcoming book with Rebecca Raby is *Smart Girls: Negotiating Academic Success in the Post-Feminist Era* (University of California Press).

REBECCA RABY has a Ph.D. in sociology and is a professor in the Department of Child and Youth Studies at Brock University in Canada. Her research and teaching are informed by a commitment to theorizing the meanings we attribute to childhood, and to critically addressing dimensions of social inequality as they affect young people's lives. *School Rules: Obedience, Discipline and Elusive Democracy* (University of Toronto Press, 2012) was the culmination of an investigation of secondary school dress and discipline codes funded by the Social Sciences and Humanities Research Council (SSHRC). She has also co-edited the textbook *Power and Everyday Practices* (Nelson, 2012). Her most recent SSHRC-funded study (with Shauna Pomerantz) is entitled "Smart Girls: Negotiating Academic Success in a Post-Feminist Era."

JACQUELINE REID-WALSH has taught in several universities in Quebec and is presently working as an associate professor in the College of Education cross-appointed with the College of Liberal Arts at Pennsylvania State University in the United States. She teaches children's literature and girlhood studies and is fascinated by early children's books, especially movable books, digital media, and girl culture. Graduating from McGill University with a Ph.D. in English literature (1989), she specialized in children's literature, eighteenth- and nineteenth-century women writers, and Metaphysical poetry. These areas have proven to be building blocks that she has mined, combined, and enhanced in different ways throughout her research career. She has published numerous articles and book chapters in these areas in American, Australian, British, and Canadian venues. As well, Jacqueline has co-authored and co-edited several books, including *Researching Children's Popular Culture* (2002) and *Girl Culture: An Encyclopedia* (2008), and is co-editor of *Girlhood Studies: An Interdisciplinary Journal*. She is presently engaged in a digital humanities project called "Learning as Playing," an animated, interactive archive of seventeenth-to-nineteenth-century narrative media for and by children. With colleagues and partners in rare books libraries in the United States, Canada, and Britain, she is developing a scholarly and public education website devoted to little-known, early movable books that contains interactive, movable simulations that the viewer will be able to play with. The initial phase is devoted to flap books or "turn-up" books both commercially produced in England and America from the mid-seventeenth to the nineteenth centuries and also made by children as domestic activities.

MAVIS REIMER is Canada Research Chair in Young People's Texts and Cultures, founding director of the Centre for Research in Young People's Texts and Cultures, professor of English, and dean of graduate studies at the University of Winnipeg, Canada. She is lead editor of the scholarly journal *Jeunesse: Young People, Texts, Cultures*. She is co-author, with Perry Nodelman, of *The Pleasures of Children's Literature* (3rd ed., 2003); the editor of a collection of essays, *Home Words: Discourses of Children's Literature in Canada* (2008); the editor of a collection of essays about *Anne of Green Gables*, entitled *Such a Simple Little Tale* (1992, 2003); co-editor (with three of her graduate students, Nyala Ali, Deanna England, and Melanie Dennis Unrau) of a collection of essays, *Seriality and Young People's Texts: The Compulsion to Repeat* (2014); and the author of more than thirty essays and book chapters on a variety of topics, including Canadian children's literature, Victorian girls' books, school stories, and literary pedagogy. Her primary project at present is a study of the cultural functions of homelessness in texts about young people and directed to young people. She is the founding president of the Canadian Association for Research in Cultures of Young People and current president of the International Research Society in Children's Literature.

JOHANNE SARACENO is a Ph.D. student in the School of Child and Youth Care at the University of Victoria, Canada, where she gained a master of arts on the topic of Indigenous girls and sexual exploitation in a rural British Columbia town. Her main disciplinary field is feminist counselling, but she also teaches at Vancouver Island University in the Department of Child and Youth Care.

Prior to her M.A. studies. Johanne worked for ten years in the field of feminist anti-violence prevention and counselling intervention. Her recent publications include two essays in the *International Journal of Child, Youth, and Family Studies.*

MICHELLE J. SMITH is a research fellow in the Centre for Memory, Imagination and Invention at Deakin University, Australia. She recently completed an Australian Research Council Postdoctoral Fellowship on the project "From Colonial to Modern: Transnational Girlhood in Australian, New Zealand, and Canadian Print Cultures, 1840–1940." She is the author of *Empire in British Girls' Literature and Culture: Imperial Girls, 1880–1915* (Palgrave Macmillan, 2011), which won the 2012 European Society for the Study of English book prize for junior scholars (literatures in English). With Dr. Kristine Moruzi she is the co-editor of the anthology *Girls' School Stories, 1749–1929* (Routledge, 2013) and the collection *Colonial Girlhood in Literature, Culture and History, 1840–1950* (Palgrave, 2014). She maintains a blog at www.girlsliterature.com.au.

INDEX

Page references followed by *fig* indicate a figure.

domestic responsibilities of girls in, 173–75; heroism in, 183; market for, 166, 167; nationalism in, 184; origin of production of, 161–62, 164; patriotism in, 172, 175, 184; reviews of, 166–68; romantic love in, 174; studies on, 184n3, 185n4; theme of fundraising in, 175, 177; transnationalism and, 169–70; women's suffrage and, 179–80, 183

Watt, Fiona, 81

Wenger, Etienne, 262

Westman, Karin, 295

Whelan, Gloria, 95

Whitlock, Gillian, 42, 48

Wild Kitty (Meade), 243

Williams, Raymond, 5

Willson, Robina Beckles, 94

Wilson, Jacqueline, 40, 41–42, 78, 86

Wimsatt, W. K., 70

Winn, Jillian, 269

Winship, Janice, 32n3

Wither, George, 222

Wolf, Naomi, 303

Wollstonecraft, Mary, 6

Woman at Home (magazine), 170

women: international movement of, 168–69; issues of Aboriginal, 122, 128–29, 132–33; magazines for, 20; wartime experience, 169–70. *See also* girls

Women and War Work (Fraser), 169

women's magazines, criticism of, 32n3, 32n5

women's suffrage, 179–80, 183, 186n15, 241

Woollacott, Angela, 241

Yep, Laurence, 94

Ziegesar, Cecily von, 10, 55

Zipes, Jack, 228

Books in the Studies in Childhood and Family in Canada Series
Published by Wilfrid Laurier University Press

Making Do: Women, Family, and Home in Montreal during the Great Depression |
Denyse Baillargeon; Yvonne Klein, translator | 1999 | ISBN 978-0-88920-326-6

Children in English-Canadian Society: Framing the Twentieth-Century Consensus
| Neil Sutherland; with a new foreword by Cynthia Comacchio | 2000 |
ISBN 978-0-88920-351-8

The Challenge of Children's Rights for Canada | Katherine Covell and R. Brian
Howe | 2001 | ISBN 978-0-88920-380-8

Love Strong as Death: Lucy Peel's Canadian Journal, 1833–1836 | J.I. Little, editor |
2001 | ISBN 978-0-88920-389-230-X

*Something to Cry About: An Argument against Corporal Punishment of Children in
Canada* | Susan M. Turner | 2002 | ISBN 978-0-88920-382-2

*NFB Kids: Portrayals of Children by the National Film Board of Canada,
1939–1989* | Brian J. Low | 2002 | ISBN 978-0-88920-386-0

Freedom to Play: We Made Our Own Fun | Norah L. Lewis, editor | 2002 |
ISBN 978-0-88920-406-5

*Evangelical Balance Sheet: Character, Family, and Business in Mid-Victorian
Nova Scotia* | B. Anne Wood | 2006 | ISBN 978-0-88920-500-0

*The Social Origins of the Welfare State: Quebec Families, Compulsory Education, and
Family Allowances, 1940–1955* | Dominique Marshall; Nicola Doone Danby,
translator | 2006 | ISBN 978-088920-452-2

A Question of Commitment: Children's Rights in Canada | R. Brian Howe and
Katherine Covell, editors | 2007 | ISBN 978-1-55458-003-3

Taking Responsibility for Children | Samantha Brennan and Robert Noggle,
editors | 2007 | ISBN 978-1-55458-015-6

Home Words: Discourses of Children's Literature in Canada | Mavis Reimer, editor
| 2008 | ISBN 978-1-55458-016-3

The Dominion of Youth: Adolescence and the Making of Modern Canada, 1920–1950 |
Cynthia Comacchio | 2006 | ISBN 978-0-88920-488-1

Depicting Canada's Children | Loren Lerner, editor | 2009 | ISBN 978-1-55458-050-7

Babies for the Nation: The Medicalization of Motherhood in Quebec, 1910–1970 | Denyse Baillargeon; W. Donald Wilson, translator | 2009 | ISBN 978-1-5548-058-3

The One Best Way? Breastfeeding History, Politics, and Policy in Canada | Tasnim Nathoo and Aleck Ostry | 2009 | ISBN 978-1-55458-147-4

Fostering Nation? Canada Confronts Its History of Childhood Disadvantage | Veronica Strong-Boag | 2011 | ISBN 978-1-55458-337-9

Cold War Comforts: Maternalism, Child Safety, and Global Insecurity, 1945–1975 | Tarah Brookfield | 2012 | ISBN 978-1-55458-623-3

Ontario Boys: Masculinity and the Idea of Boyhood in Postwar Ontario, 1945–1960 | Christopher Greig | 2014 | ISBN 978-1-55458-900-5

A Brief History of Women in Quebec | Denyse Baillargeon; W. Donald Wilson, translator | 2014 | ISBN 978-1-55458-950-0

With Children and Youth: Emerging Theories and Practices in Child and Youth Care Work | Kiaras Gharabaghi, Hans A. Skott-Myhre, and Mark Krueger, editors | 2014 | ISBN 978-1-55458-966-1

Abuse or Punishment? Violence Towards Children in Quebec Families, 1850–1969 | Marie-Aimée Cliche; W. Donald Wilson, translator | 2014 | ISBN 978-1-77712-063-0

Engendering Transnational Voices: Studies in Families, Work and Identities | Guida Man and Rina Cohen, editors | 2015 | ISBN 978-1-77112-112-5

Girls, Texts, Cultures | Clare Bradford and Mavis Reimer, editors | 2015 | ISBN 978-1-77112-020-3